Ordinary
Lives

Ordinary Lives

Platoon 1005 and the Vietnam War

W. D. Ehrhart

Temple University Press
Philadelphia

Temple University Press, Philadelphia 19122
Copyright © 1999 by W. D. Ehrhart
All rights reserved
Published 1999
Printed in the United States of America

Text design by Eliz. Anne O'Donnell

Frontispiece: *Platoon 1005, Company D, 1st Recruit Training Battalion, Recruit Training Regiment, Marine Corps Recruit Depot, Parris Island, South Carolina, August 1966. Senior Drill Instructor J. J. Oliver, Assistant Drill Instructor T. W. Evans, and Drill Instructor D. S. Bosch* (left to right) *are the three men in "Smokey the Bear" hats standing in front of the platoon on the grass. W. D. Ehrhart is in the second row from the bottom, eighth man in from the left.*

Library of Congress Cataloging-in-Publication Data

Ehrhart, W. D. (William Daniel)
     Ordinary lives : Platoon 1005 and the Vietnam War / W. D. Ehrhart.
        p.   cm.
     ISBN 1-56639-674-3 (cloth : alk. paper)
     1. Marines—United States—Biography.   2. Vietnamese Conflict, 1961–1975—Veterans—United States—Biography.   I. United States. Marine Corps. Platoon 1005.   II. Title.
     VE24.E37   1999
     359.9'6'092273—dc21   98-39963
     [B]

For Senior Drill Instructor J. J. Oliver
and Drill Instructors T. W. Evans and D. S. Bosch,
who for eight crucial weeks were
God the Father,
God the Son,
and God the Holy Ghost.

And for Anne and Leela,
who for all my days
are a blessing
and a benediction.

Contents

After-Action Report   *313*

Preface

Most of the many people to whom I owe thanks are mentioned one place or another elsewhere in this book, but some are not: Jeff Hurwitz, in addition to providing an original photograph of George Osada, made negatives of all the photographs lent to me by the men I interviewed, and from these produced the prints included in the book. Bill Quesenbery, for the fourth time in my writing life, read the book in manuscript and offered useful suggestions for its improvement. Michael Ames understood and supported my approach to the book, persuading his colleagues at Temple University Press to publish it, and Paul Lyons and Cindy Fuchs helped him to be persuasive. To each of them, and to others you will come upon as you read, I am deeply grateful.

The excerpt from "Mostly Nothing Happens" is taken from *Mostly Nothing Happens,* a hand-set letterpressed chapbook published in 1996 by Gary Metras at Adastra Press in Easthampton, Massachusetts. The poem can also be found in *War, Literature and the Arts* 6, no. 2 (1994), and *American Poetry Review* 25, no. 2 (1996).

In a number of places in the text, I quote from letters that contain errors of spelling, grammar, and usage. I have retained those errors in order to give you a sense of the original letters, but I have not used the usual notation "[*sic*]" to indicate that the errors appear in the original letters because it would have been too disruptive. It should be reasonably obvious when I am deliberately reproducing an error from an original letter.

At other places in the text, you will find phrases such as "this year," "last month," and "next week," as well as references to people's ages. These are relative to the date on which an interview or telephone conversation took place. For instance, Jackie Denfip was president of the Heartbeat of America Service Managers Club in 1996, and Matthew McBirney was 17 and a high school junior in March 1996.

Marine ground units are often indicated in this fashion: 1/1 for 1st Battalion, 1st Marines; 2/3 for 2nd Battalion, 3rd Marines. In these examples and others you will encounter, "Marines" is short for "Marine Regiment," not "Marine Division"; 1st Marines is therefore 1st Marine Regiment, 3rd Marines is 3rd Marine Regiment, and so forth, a regiment being a smaller unit than a division.

Most of the photographs in the book were provided to me by the various platoon members (or in some cases their surviving relatives). A few of the photos originally appeared in the platoon's graduation book, published by Albert Love Enterprises, Inc., of Doraville, Georgia (a company that apparently no longer exists); these photos carry the notation PB (for platoon book).

You may want to familiarize yourself with the explanatory lists and appendixes that appear after the "After-Action Report" before you delve too deeply into the heart of the book, "The Members of Platoon 1005."

The Search for
Platoon 1005

I

We were all silent as the bus pulled up to the gate lit only by a few small spotlights. It was almost midnight, June 17, 1966. A dozen or so of us had started out that morning from Philadelphia. We'd picked up a few more when we'd changed planes in Washington, D.C. And a few more when we'd arrived in Charleston, South Carolina, and transferred to the bus. Along the way, there'd been new friends made, strained camaraderie, talk of home and girlfriends and ambitions. But as the last miles of the journey rolled away beneath a shadowy arch of Spanish moss, the bus had carried each man ever deeper into his own thoughts. There was no conversation now, no sound but the mechanical grate and whine of the bus itself. Nervous anticipation—fear of the unknown—turned tongues wooden. I could see gold letters on a red brick wall illuminated by a spotlight: "Marine Corps Recruit Depot, Parris Island, South Carolina."

A uniformed guard waved the bus through. Soon it rolled up to the only lighted building on the sleeping base and stopped. A lone figure in a khaki uniform and dark brown Smokey the Bear hat strode through the glare of a spotlight shining down from the side of the building. The bus driver opened the door, and the lone figure stepped onto the bus, causing the bus to list noticeably to the right. He was eight and a half feet tall. And he was ugly. He blocked the huge windshield of the bus completely. His chest strained at the buttons of his shirt, so that they seemed about to fly off at any moment like buckshot from a scattergun. Standing there with his hands on his hips, he looked like a cross between Paul Bunyan, Babe the Blue Ox, and Godzilla. Then he opened his mouth, and out came the Voice of God.

"There's four columns of yellow footprints painted on the deck in front of those steps over there," roared the DI, jerking a thumb the size of a fire hydrant in the general direction of the lighted barracks. "When I give the word, you filthy pigs have three seconds to get outta this bus and plant yourself on one of those sets of yellow footprints. I don't wanna see nothin' but assholes and elbows flyin'. You will not talk. You will not eye-fuck the area. You will keep your head and eyes front at all times. You will do everything you're told instantly, and you will do nothing else. I'll kill the first cocksucker that fucks it up. You scuzzy shitbirds are *mine,* ladies! And I don't like you. Now, MOVE! *Do it! Do it!"*

The walls of the bus collapsed inward. One moment I was sitting on the bus getting my eardrums pummeled. The next moment I was standing on a set of yellow footprints. I don't know how I got from one place to the other, but the footprints were painted so close together that my face and body were smashed up tight against the guy in front of me, the guy behind me was smashed up tight against me, and we were all rubbing shoulders with the columns on either side of us—a formation we would soon come to know as "asshole to belly button."

I'd volunteered for the Marine Corps, and I knew Marine boot camp was supposed to be tough, but this wasn't at all what I'd had in mind. Wedged into the midst of that lump of bodies congealing in the hot southern night, with the Voice of God still pounding in my ears and my heart banging away at double quick time, I suddenly wanted to be anywhere but here. An overpowering sense of panic welled up inside of me. I wanted to throw up. I wanted to cry. I remember thinking, "Mommy. Please take me home, Mommy. I won't be bad anymore."

It was the last clear thought I would have for days. Again the Voice roared, "Get in the building!" Three or four more identical copies of Godzilla the Blue Bunyan materialized out of nowhere, all of them shouting, "Get in the building! Get in the building! Line up in front of the tables! Double time! Get in the building!" We began to surge forward frantically in one roiling mass, bodies in back climbing over the ones in front of them like stampeding cattle, stumbling and falling and crawling on hands and knees and getting up and falling again.

Inside, naked lightbulbs glared bright white above two long rows of tables. "Face the tables! Eyes front! Stand at attention! Chin in! Chest out! Thumbs along the trouser seams! Don't move! Don't move!" Drill instructors were everywhere, shouting in recruits' faces at distances ranging from three to six inches: "Keep your head and eyes front, piggy! Don't even breathe, piggy! What're you lookin' at, sweetpea?! You eye-fuckin' me, sweetpea?! You wanna fuck me, scum?! 'Zat it, shitbag?! You queer, piggy?! Fuck the deck, piggy! Down, piggy, hit the deck! Push-ups! One! Two! Three! Four! Lemme hear you squeal, piggy! *Squeal,* goddamn you!!" They had steel forge bellows for lungs.

"Empty your pockets onto the tables, wormies! Empty your ditty-bags onto the tables, wormies! Empty your wallets onto the tables, piggies! Put your wallets into the green bag in front of you! Put your money, jewelry, legal identification, draft card, driver's license into the green bag in front of you! No photographs! Nothing else! Is this your sweetheart, piggy? *Answer me,* shithead!"

"Yes."

"*Yes, sir,* you filthy scumbag!"

"Yes, sir."

"I can't hear you!"

"Yessir!"

"Louder!"

"YES, SIR!"

"She looks like a whore, puke."

Nothing.

"I said she looks like a whore!"

"No, sir."

"You callin' me a liar?!"

"No, sir."

"I can't hear you, piggy!"

"NO, SIR!"

"She looks like a whore!"

"YES, SIR!"

"She's probably fucking your father right now."

"YES, SIR!"

"Who do you think your mother's fucking?"

Nothing.

"You better answer me, you ape! I'll break your black ass a dozen ways to Sunday!"

In the meantime, everything else on the tables got swept into huge trash barrels by several volunteers: "Anybody here drive a truck?"—and the truck drivers were given big push brooms and ordered to clear the tables: spare clothes, soap, toothbrushes, photographs, combs, electric razors, aftershave, shampoo, books, everything disappeared into the trash barrels.

Then a DI with stripes all up and down his arms got up on the table and started pacing. "You boys wanna be Marines," he began in something very like a normal voice. "We didn't ask you to be Marines; you came to us. It isn't easy to make a Marine because Marines are the best there is. You're going to hate it here. You're probably going to wish you were dead. But most of you won't die—unless you try to run. This is Parris Island. It's called an island because it is an island. It's surrounded by swamps, and the swamps are filled with poisonous snakes. The snakes work for the Marine Corps. The causeway you came in on is guarded day and night, so you can't get out that way. If you get through the swamps, you have to swim a two-mile channel against some of the strongest currents in the world. And if you don't drown, the MPs will be waiting to pick you up when you get to the mainland. And they'll bring you back, and you'll go to the brig for six months, and then you'll begin training all over again. Don't try to run. The easiest way to leave this island is to march out the front gate on graduation day. Do as you're told, do your best, and you might make it."

The moment he finished talking, the decibel level shot back up to 232: "All right, hoggies, time to shear the sheep! Bleat, bleat, little sheep. *I said bleat!*" We all began to bleat. "Louder!" We bleated louder. The DIs were everywhere, a flurry of motion you could just catch from the corners of your eyes—you didn't dare look right or left or up or down or anywhere but straight ahead. Anybody who did got nailed instantly, two or three DIs descending upon him like avenging angels, hounding him into jello.

"Double time! Double time! Through the hatchway—not *that* hatchway, you goddamned stupid gorilla! Column of twos! Asshole to belly button! Line up on the yellow footprints!" There were yellow footprints painted all over Parris Island. Several barber chairs and several sleepy barbers waited for us at the end of this particular set of yellow footprints. Each haircut took about twelve seconds: zip, zip, and your skull was as smooth as an eggshell. While we stood there packed in line, the DIs assaulted anybody who had hair longer than an inch or two: "Hey, Goldilocks! Hey, sweetheart! You like your hair, pretty girl?! We gonna cut it all off. How do ya like that? You like that, sweetpea? That make ya happy? *Answer me,* you dumb fuck! When I ask you a question, you better have an answer! I'll spread your pea-brain all over the wall!"

"Yessir!"

"I can't hear you!"

"YES, SIR!"

"You look like a pussy, sweetpea! Are you a pussy?"

"No, sir!"

"You callin' me a liar?!"

"NO, SIR!"

"You look like a pussy, puke."

"YESSIR!"

"Tell me what you are, puke."

"I'm a pussy, sir!"

"I can't hear you!"

"I AM A PUSSY, SIR!"

We were herded off to the showers, looking like a bunch of freshly peeled onions. Finally, well into the early hours of the morning, we were herded upstairs into a large open squad bay lined with two rows of double-deck steel bunk beds. "Get in the rack! Lie at attention!" a DI commanded. "Sleep!" The lights went out.

But I didn't sleep. I don't know if anyone else slept because I was too frightened to look anywhere but straight up at the ceiling. I was terrified that if I went to sleep, I wouldn't wake up fast enough, and then I'd be killed instantly. My stomach churned. Someone inside my head was banging away with a sledgehammer, frantically trying to break out. With all my heart and soul, I did not want to be here. I couldn't understand how any of this had happened. I lay there for what seemed like hours in a kind of trance, staring at the ceiling, my mind in neutral and somebody flooring the accelerator. Jesus, Jesus, sweet Jesus, save me.

The lights went on. A swarm of DIs charged into the squad bay banging the metal lids of garbage cans against the metal bed frames. "Get up! Get up! Get up! Get in front of your racks! Stand at attention! Eyes front! Get up! Get up! Move, move, move! Time to slop the hogs, ladies! Everybody nice and hungry?! I asked you a question, goddamn it!"

"Yessir!" we all shouted in unison.

"Louder!"

"YESSIR!"

Still in civilian clothing, we were herded off, asshole to belly button, to our first breakfast in the Marine Corps.

The last thing I wanted to see was food. My stomach was the size of a walnut. But I had this voice inside of me, the guy with the sledge-hammer, that kept saying if I didn't take everything that was given to me and eat everything I had taken, I would be killed instantly. So I went through the chow line with my metal tray outstretched, shoulder to shoulder with everyone else, eyes staring straight ahead and stomach scream-ing, "Please don't do this to me!" as the messmen heaped on eggs, grits, sausage, French toast, butter, syrup, hot cereal, cold cereal, sugar, milk, juice, and a banana. I ate every bit of it, and every mouthful went down like rock salt. I had to swallow two and three times because it kept com-ing up again. The banana was an unholy nightmare. It was three feet long and weighed thirty-eight pounds. I saved the banana for last, hoping it would go away, but it wouldn't.

After breakfast the pace quickened into a kaleidoscope of shouting, screaming, lifting, toting, sweating, running, waiting asshole to belly but-ton, push-ups, squat thrusts, medical exams, dental checks, shot lines, written tests, forms, obscenities, screaming, and shouting:

- Packing up the clothes we were wearing and addressing the pack-ages to some place called home, casting off the last traces of another life and donning oversized green utilities designed to make you feel puny and lost and awkward and identical to everyone around you.
- Trying to march and failing miserably and being informed vocifer-ously of the failure, watching with envy and humiliation while ad-vanced platoons stepped by in perfect cadence and our own DIs roared, "You'll never march like that, you helpless, worthless shit-bags!"
- Receiving our issues of field gear, linens and blankets, seabags and extra clothing, and trying to drag it all across the sweltering parade deck without dropping any of it, and dropping it all over the place as DIs perforated your eardrums with their eyeteeth.
- Drawing our rifles, when a DI announced: "This is your life, ladies. The Marine Corps doesn't give a damn about you, but it loves its

rifles. And if anything ever happens to your rifle, if it so much as gets a tiny little scratch on it, the Marine Corps will hate you forever and ever. And then you'll be in the hurt locker, ladies, and you won't like that at all." I had no idea what the hurt locker was, but I was certain I wouldn't like it.

Another DI told us: "The Marine Corps is your father and your mother. The DI is your priest and your doctor and your lover. The Marine Corps will give you everything you'll ever need. If the Marine Corps doesn't give it to you, you don't need it. The Marine Corps will teach you everything you'll ever need to know. If the Marine Corps wants you to think, you'll be issued a brain. Until you're issued a brain, don't think, ladies. Don't even try to think. Jump when you're told to jump, and don't come down until the Marine Corps tells you to."

The sequence of individual events was without order or logic or foundation. The raging DIs in Smokey the Bear hats never relaxed and never slept and never let up, and they would kill you instantly if you did anything wrong. And you were always, always, doing something wrong. And they never missed a thing.

After a few days—looking back at the records I can tell you now that it was three, though at the time I didn't know if it was two or six or ten—three new DIs appeared in our barracks one morning. They were obviously in a foul mood. All DIs were always in foul moods. They said it was our fault. The three new DIs, we were unceremoniously informed, were our permanent drill instructors and we were about to begin our training cycle.

Jesus, Joseph, and Mary! Begin our training cycle?! I thought we'd begun days ago. What in God's name were they going to do to us now?

II

One beautiful warm June day twenty-seven years later, I was out walking in my neighborhood in Philadelphia when I noticed a group of eight or ten young black men farther up the block in the direction I was heading. They appeared to be just hanging around, going nowhere, and doing nothing in particular. My heart rate jumped abruptly, and I began immediately and involuntarily to consider my options: Do I keep walking? Do I turn around and go another way? If trouble starts, have I any chance at all against so many? Is there anything portable I can use as a weapon? What if one or more of them is armed? What if—

In the midst of this machine-gun series of uninvited questions, I suddenly found myself possessed of an overwhelming sense of shame because it suddenly came to me that were this another time and another city, one of these men I immediately perceived as a potential threat might have been John Harris.

Then another thought came quickly on the heels of that one: would Harris, too, find this situation threatening? What would he do, were he here on this sidewalk instead of me? What would he tell me I should do?

John Harris, you see, was the first black friend I ever had. Both of us had been members of Platoon 1005, Company D, 1st Recruit Training Battalion, Recruit Training Regiment, there at Parris Island that summer of 1966. He and I slept next to each other in the long open squad bay that housed the eighty recruits of Platoon 1005 in two long rows of double bunk beds.

There was no privacy for Marine recruits at Parris Island, and precious few opportunities to speak to another human being except your drill instructors, and then only when they spoke to you first, and always at the top of your lungs. But at night, after lights out, Harris and I eventually got bold enough to lean out over the space between us, drawing our heads together and talking quietly. After a while, we started reading each other the letters we received from our girlfriends. By placing the page flat on the linoleum floor, then putting a flashlight down on the page and turning it on, you could get just the faintest glow around the rim of the flashlight, and if you moved the light back and forth across the page, line by line, you could read.

This was risky business because if we got caught there would be god-awful hell to pay with the DIs, who were the meanest, toughest, nastiest men I'd ever encountered in my life and who, as nearly as we could determine, had absolute power and authority over us with no appeal, no recourse, and no mercy. I never would have dared such a thing in the first four or five weeks of boot camp, but in the last few weeks Harris and I began taking our chances because we were very lonely and very young and not quite so frightened as we'd been earlier.

Harris was especially fascinating to me because, as I said, I'd never before had a black person for a friend. Growing up in a very white small town in rural Bucks County, Pennsylvania, I'd had limited and fleeting and invariably superficial contacts with blacks. Beyond the racial aspect, however, lay another dimension to my fascination with Harris: he had a pregnant girlfriend. In the community in which I grew up, if you got a girl pregnant, you married her. End of discussion. Period. We called them "shotgun weddings," and it didn't matter if the bride was only fourteen years old and the groom just sixteen and the marriage doomed from the start: get pregnant, get married.

Yet here was Harris with a pregnant girlfriend he'd neither married nor abandoned. He wrote to her faithfully, and she wrote to him, and the two of them were trying to sort out what would be the best course for them to take; marriage was a possibility, but by no means a certainty, and as nearly as I could tell, the decision was not up to some father figuratively or literally wielding a shotgun, but rather, it lay entirely in the hands of Harris and his girlfriend.

Adding yet another dimension to my fascination with Harris was the fact that, while he was only a year older than me, he was quite obviously sexually experienced, while the one and only opportunity I'd ever had to get a girl pregnant had passed me by because I was too startled, too scared, and too inept to avail myself of it.

So Harris was a wonder, a revelation, and an education for me on multiple levels, though what I remember most about him to this day is how gently he'd rest his fingers on the back of my wrist as we moved the flashlight together, back and forth across the pages of our girlfriends' letters, and how sweet was his deep, rich voice whispering against the lonely weight of those hot southern nights far from all that was familiar to either of us.

And as I thought about John Harris that afternoon on Upsal Street in Philadelphia twenty-seven years later, realizing that for all I knew the young men up ahead of me might be just as kind, just as thoughtful, just as fascinating, if only I had the opportunity to get to know them, I decided to keep walking. By this time, you can bet my heart was pounding furiously, as if it would leap out of my chest in the next instant, but nothing at all happened. As I passed in front of them, I nodded and said an offhand hello, and got an equally offhand acknowledgment in return. And then I was by them. It had all been a tempest in a teapot inside my own head, lasting but the space of a few minutes from start to finish.

But as I continued on toward home, I couldn't stop thinking about John Harris. What *would* he have thought of this situation? Would *he* have felt threatened by a group of young black men half his age? What would he think of me and my instantly defensive reflex?

And that led to a larger set of questions: What had become of John Harris? Where was he now? Who was he now? I hadn't seen or heard from or of him in all these years. Life's like that when you're young and in the military. You spend some time together and you get to be buddies, and then you both move on in different directions and you mean to write but you never do. Instead you meet new people and you make new friendships. And then you move on again, and you meet still newer people. I changed duty stations nine times in three years in the Marines, and the attrition from rotations and casualties during my thirteen months in Vietnam produced additional dislocation. You carry your memories with you along with your seabag, but you fill the time at hand with whoever happens to be at hand.

And then another thought arose: Harris was my best boot camp buddy, my confidant and partner in crime—yet all I could tell you about him was his name, he came from Baltimore, and his girlfriend was pregnant. That was it. The sum total of my knowledge. And with one exception, I knew more about John Harris than I knew about any other member of Platoon 1005.

Eighty of us had gone through certainly the most intense experience I had ever encountered to that point in my life, living cheek to jowl day in and day out for eight grueling weeks (and here "grueling" is not a cliché), eating together, sleeping together, shaving together, showering together, shitting together (no such thing as private stalls in the heads at Parris Island, just a long row of toilet bowls one right after the other), marching together, exercising together, running together, cleaning the squad bay together, sweating together, polishing boots together, rubbing linseed oil into the stocks of our rifles together, memorizing the entire chain of command from our DIs up to the Commander in Chief together—you can hardly name an activity that we did not do together—and yet I knew next to nothing about any of them, in most cases not even their first names.

That's the way the Marine Corps wanted it. The purpose of boot camp was—and I suppose still is—not to bond the members of any particular training platoon to each other in an individual or personal way, but to bond each of us to the Marine Corps itself. You learn to respond to orders without hesitation or question; you learn to work cooperatively with whoever happens to be next to you; you learn to care about the other men in your unit not because they are Joe and Bob and Jack or even because they are likeable guys, which they may or may not be, but because you are a Marine and they are your brother Marines and they are depending on you to do your job and to do it right and you are depending on them.

I didn't understand this at the time, of course. No one sits you down and explains any of it. They just do things like if you screw up in close-order drill, the DI might haul you out of formation and have you count cadence while the other seventy-nine members of the platoon do fifty push-ups on their knuckles on the macadam parade deck in honor of your blunder. Or if one man fails to finish a three-mile run with full pack and rifle in ninety-degree heat, the whole platoon catches hell, so you do what you have to do to make sure the whole platoon finishes, and finishes together, even if it means that one guy carries two packs and another guy carries two rifles and two other guys get the flagging man's arms over their own shoulders like Jesus on the cross and drag him for the last mile and a half.

And it doesn't matter if that flagging man is the same guy who crapped out yesterday and the day before and the day before that. You can hate his guts and wish him dead a thousand times over again, but if he starts falling behind, you are going to move to his side and tell him, "Come on, man, you can do it. Keep moving. You can do it." And you're going to take his rifle out of his hands, easing his burden by eleven pounds—back then when we trained with M-14s—and carry it for him because he is a Marine and you are a Marine and he needs help.

That's what the Marine Corps wants you to learn in boot camp. The Marine Corps doesn't care if you know that Joe Blow has a '58 Chevy Impala or Ralph Doe's mother has muscular dystrophy or George Shmoe was the fastest high school sprinter in Tennessee. The Marine Corps doesn't want you to know. Not while you're at Parris Island, at least. And the Marine Corps doesn't give you the slightest chance to find out. You do what you are told to do. You speak when you are spoken to. And your latitude for activity or speech beyond those boundaries is almost entirely limited to late night tête-à-têtes with the guy sleeping next to you.

Even the one guy I actually knew before I got to Parris Island I virtually never talked to the entire time we were there. Harry Nelson and I both graduated from Pennridge High School in June of 1966, just nine days before we left for Parris Island. I didn't know Harry all that well because he'd been in parochial school until ninth grade, and we mostly traveled in different social circles, but we'd been in the senior class play together. So later in the year, when we discovered we were both joining the Marines, we figured we might as well join on what the Marine Corps called the Buddy Plan, which guaranteed that we'd be assigned to the same training platoon at Parris Island. What our recruiter didn't tell us is that we wouldn't ever get to talk to each other anyway, so we might as well be on different planets for all the comfort we got out of having a familiar face in the platoon. Ah, those recruiters, they're a helmet full of laughs.

In any case, what I knew about Harry Nelson I didn't learn in boot camp, and as little as I knew about John Harris, I knew even less about anyone else. We came together out of the night—really and truly out of the night—and we spent those eight weeks together, and after we graduated on August 12, 1966, we all went up to Camp Lejeune, North Carolina, for three more weeks of basic infantry training. But at Lejeune we were broken up and mixed in with the 240 Marines from the other three platoons in our boot camp training series who had graduated the same day we had. We were no longer Platoon 1005. And when we left the Infantry Training Regiment, we scattered out into the Corps to receive whatever specialized training each of us had been assigned and to meet whatever our individual futures held.

I saw Harry Nelson at home in Perkasie in the spring of 1968, and again in 1983, and at our twentieth and twenty-fifth high school reunions in 1986 and 1991. Terry J. Bowles ended up in my battalion in Vietnam in 1967, and I shared a beer with him and his twin brother Jerry once or twice that summer at our battalion's command post near Hoi An. But with these few and fleeting exceptions, I never saw any of the other members of Platoon 1005 again.

Who were these men who'd joined the Marines in the summer of 1966 just as the Vietnam War was rising toward a terrible and sustained crescendo of savagery? Where had they come from? Why had they joined? Where had they gone after we finished basic training? How many of them had gone to Vietnam? How many had come back? What had they done with their lives in the years since? What did they think now? By the time I got home from my walk that afternoon in June 1993, I had decided to find out.

III

But how to go about tracking them down? From a platoon book that was sort of like a lean, mean version of a high school yearbook, I had each man's name. I also knew that each of us had come from somewhere east of the Mississippi River because anyone living west of the Mississippi was sent to the other Marine Corps Recruit Depot in San Diego, California. That's all the information I had with which to start my search, and the trail twenty-seven years old.

The first thing I did that evening was to write a letter to George C. Wilson, the former Pentagon reporter for the *Washington Post* and the author of a number of books on the military, including *Mud Soldiers* and *Supercarrier*. Wilson and I had traveled together in postwar Vietnam in 1990 with a group of writers sponsored by the William Joiner Center of the University of Massachusetts at Boston, and he was the best print journalist I've ever met. He seemed to have no agenda of his own, no axes to grind, no point to make. He wanted to know what *you* had to say. He wanted to hear *your* story. And when he picked up his pen, that's what he wrote. When I began to interview and write about the members of Platoon 1005, it was George Wilson's example I tried to emulate.

But I was far from interviewing anyone in June 1993. Except for Harry Nelson, whom I could locate through high school alumni records, I had no one to interview. I figured if anyone knew how to track people who'd been in the military, it would be Wilson, and indeed he had several good suggestions, one of which was to check the platoon roster against the *Vietnam Veterans Memorial Directory of Names*. "I found the directory invaluable when I was writing *Mud Soldiers*," he replied. Then he added, because I'd told him how the idea to track these men down had come to me, "I hate to tell you this in such a cold way, but in my copy of the directory, a Marine lance corporal John Lee Harris, Jr., of Baltimore, was killed on 21 September 1967. He was born on 12 September 1947, so I fear he is your friend."

For a long time I stared at Wilson's letter. All these years, I thought, and that goddamned war is still taking friends away from me. I hadn't seen Harris in over a quarter of a century, but he had always been a touchstone for me, as he was that day on Upsal Street, a way to help me keep the world in perspective. I had always assumed a world with John Harris in it, but he was not and had not been for a long time. It was eerie, and it made me very sad.

When my own copy of the *Directory* arrived from the Friends of the Vietnam Veterans Memorial, it looked and felt like a telephone book. But instead of telephone numbers and addresses, it contained the names of the American dead in Vietnam—fifty-eight thousand of them—their rank, branch of service, hometown, dates of birth and death, and the panel and line numbers for locating each name on the Vietnam Veterans Memorial in Washington, D.C.

In it, in addition to John Harris, I found three other members of Platoon 1005: William C. Blades III, Billy Blades of Massachusetts, who'd been a road guard with me on our platoon's endurance hike to Elliott's Beach, the two of us in bright orange vests far enough out in front of the rest of the platoon to be able to hold a rare conversation; Roosevelt Tharrington, Jr., of North Carolina, who was terrified of shots (the medical kind); and Francis L. Langley of Alabama, about whom I could recall nothing at all.

One lost life is one too many, and I would soon come to know just how devastating each loss was to the people who knew and loved these men. But these four were, in truth, far fewer than I had expected to find on that cold, black stone slab. We'd finished boot camp at a time when General William C. Westmoreland was calling for ever larger numbers of troops, and Lyndon Baines Johnson was still giving him what he asked for, and Marine casualties were mounting. I had been fully prepared to find ten, twelve, fifteen platoon members among the dead.

So I'd accounted for four members of the platoon, but what about the others? I began by placing notices in military and veterans' publications. Over the course of the summer, these turned up only one more man, Gary S. Davis, a *Leatherneck* reader. But a retired Army enlisted man from Florida named Ben Myers saw my notice in the CAP Unit Veterans Association newsletter and offered to share his computerized national directory of listed telephone numbers and addresses.

Talk about the kindness of strangers. He said, "Send me the names and home states of the men you're looking for." I said, "I don't know their home states." He said, "Okay, then just send me their names." I said, "We're talking seventy-five guys here." There was only a moment's hesitation in his voice before he said, "That's okay, send them anyway."

A couple of weeks later Myers sent me a stack of computer printouts. Some names, such as Harold E. Feighley and Gaetan L. Pelletier and Richard Quashne, Jr., weren't listed at all. Others, such as Thomas M. Brown and John E. Green and Kenneth E. Smith turned up by the hundreds—far too many to be usable. But there was only one Michael C. Albon, and he was the guy I was looking for. Other names turned up by the half-dozen or the dozen or the score, and I wrote letters to all of them.

I wrote to thirty-nine Joseph B. Taylors and got no reply, but I wrote to twenty-one Jeffery S. Browns and received a phone call from the one who'd been in Platoon 1005. Stephen T. Summerscales wasn't on the list, but a Ruth Summerscales was listed in a town not far from Philadelphia, so I picked up the telephone and called; she turned out to be his mother. George D. Osada wasn't on the list, but a George H. Osada was listed in Philadelphia, so I called. I got a woman who had just bought the house from the son of the previous owner, who had recently died. She said the son lived in Philly too, and the son turned out to be our Platoon Guide (the guy who marches at the front of the platoon with a little pennant on a pole that says "1005"). All told, I eventually located twenty-nine platoon members through Myers's list, and another half-dozen from my own computerized directory once I acquired a CD-ROM drive for my own computer in December 1994.

Meanwhile, in December 1993 at a conference on the Vietnam War at Notre Dame University, I met Constance Menefee of Ohio, who put me in touch with retired Army lieutenant colonel Richard S. Johnson of Military Information Enterprises, Inc., San Antonio, Texas. From Johnson's book *How to Locate Anyone Who Is or Has Been in the Military,* I learned additional methods for finding platoon members.

Under the Freedom of Information Act (FOIA), for instance, anyone can request the military records of anyone else who's ever been in the service. You need only to provide enough information for the civil servants at the National Personnel Records Center in Saint Louis to identify the files of the person you want. The federal Privacy Act forbids release of such information as current address, medical records, or social security number, but NPRC is supposed to make available a service person's record of promotions, military occupational specialty (MOS), education level, duty assignments, awards and decorations, records of court-martials if applicable, and other basic information pertaining to that person's military service.

From the Commandant of the Marine Corps, I had already obtained the company reports from Company D, 1st Recruit Training Battalion, for June and July 1966, and from these I was able to get the men's service numbers (most of them, at least; a few were not legible, since what I received were poor photocopies of fourth or fifth carbon copies done on a manual typewriter, which is how copies got made before there were photocopy machines). I could therefore give NPRC a name, service number, beginning month and year of active service, and branch of service. I began sending one request each week, and continued this process for more than a year and a half, until I had requested the records of every member of the platoon.

The turnaround time on a request varied from a few months to a year, and what I got back was equally inconsistent. Sometimes I received six or seven or eight pages of material photocopied directly from a man's service record book (SRB). Other times I got as little as a hastily hand-written and incompletely filled out FOIA cover sheet. As nearly as I can tell, it depended on which clerk handled your request, how diligently that clerk wanted to do his or her job, and what sort of a mood he or she was in on the day the request was filled. Eventually, I received at least something from NPRC on all but three men, whose files, NPRC told me, could not be located on the basis of the limited information I could provide.

Initially I wanted these records so that, in the event I could not lo-cate a man, I could still learn what his military job had been, whether or not he had served in Vietnam, and whatever else the records might tell me. But I realized as soon as I began receiving records that sometimes I would get an unexpected bonus.

The hometown of Terry J. Bowles at the time of his enlistment, for instance, was Glasgow, Kentucky. There was no Terry J. Bowles listed in Glasgow, Kentucky, in my telephone directory, but there were thirty-two other people named Bowles. I wrote to all of them, and got a phone call back from his niece by marriage, who gave me his parents' address and telephone number. By the same method, I found Gaetan Pelletier, who no longer lives in his hometown of Madawaska, Maine, but who has a sister who does, and she got one of my letters.

Sometimes the bonus didn't cost so many postage stamps. I haven't been able to figure out why, but some SRBs had a man's social security num-ber at the bottom of each page, while others did not. For those that did, the clerks at NPRC were supposed to black it out before sending the records along, and usually they did, but every once in a while I'd receive four pages of material and the social security number would be blacked out on the first three pages, but when you turned to page four, there it was. Once you have a social security number, you can take it to any number of tracing services, and for a fee they'll run a check and usually come up with a fairly current address. Military Information Enterprises ran a number of traces for me.

Another way to track veterans is through the Department of Veter-ans Affairs (VA). If a veteran has ever placed a claim with the VA, there will be a file on him or her. What you do is send a list of names and ser-vice numbers to the VA, and they'll send you back a list of VA claim num-bers. Then you can write letters to the people you're trying to locate and send the letters to the VA, and the VA will forward them to the last known addresses they have. I found four more members of Platoon 1005 using that route.

And that route, too, sometimes yields bonuses. Since the early to mid-1970s, depending on the branch of service, a service person's social security number is also his or her service number and VA claim number. It wasn't that way when I was in the Marines. Your service number meant something only within the Marine Corps. Likewise, your VA claim number pertained only to the VA system.

Most of the men in Platoon 1005 would probably have the older VA claim numbers, but if a platoon member didn't apply for VA benefits until as late as 1974, his VA claim number would be his social security number. In December 1993, I requested VA claim numbers for forty-five members of Platoon 1005. I got back a list of thirty-six men who had made claims with the VA. Twenty-nine of them were the old eight-digit numbers, but seven were nine-digit social security numbers I could then have traced. By this route, I was able to get in touch with four more members of the platoon.

A few more men I located through leads given to me by other platoon members. Rey Waters remembered that Stephen Sofian came from Atlantic City, New Jersey. George Osada recalled that Tom Tucci was from South Philly. Gaetan Pelletier was able to get a telephone number for Gerard Sirois's sister. Over the course of three years between the summer of 1993 and the spring of 1996, I eventually located or at least accounted for nearly three-quarters of the eighty members of Platoon 1005.

IV

For a dozen years after I left Vietnam, I had nightmares about the war. At first realistic and factual in nature, as the years passed the dreams became ever more surreal and fantastic. In the last dream I had, in the early spring of 1980, Viet Cong rats were jumping into the bedroom of my third-floor apartment in Chicago through a broken window, and I kept trying to get my girlfriend to realize that we were in danger, but she wouldn't listen.

When I started courting the woman I would marry, the nightmares about the war stopped. Perhaps they'd been occasioned as much by loneliness as by the trauma of war. Perhaps Anne's presence beside me gave me back something of what the war had taken away. Perhaps her love redeemed me. I don't know. I only know that for years I dreamed about the war, but when Anne began to sleep beside me, the dreams stopped.

What didn't stop were and are the anxiety dreams I have always had about being back in boot camp. To this day, three or four times a year, I'll dream that I'm back at Parris Island. The details vary from dream to dream, but the basic dream is always the same: everyone else is exactly who and what they were in the summer of 1966, but I'm who I am now; I've got my usual longish hair and I'm wearing maybe blue jeans and sneakers and a La Salle sweatshirt or whatever. We're all standing at attention in front of our racks in the squad bay, and I'm screaming with terror inside my head because I know any moment Drill Instructor Evans is going to notice me standing there completely out of uniform, shaggy-haired and soft around the middle, and then I'm going to be in the hurt locker. And I always wake up sweating like a stuck pig, my heart running riot until the fog of half-awake gives way to wakefulness and fear gives way to amused wonder.

It's amazing to me that even the most unpleasant memories of war can be held at bay by the love of my wife, yet nothing can save me from Parris Island and my drill instructors, even after thirty-two years. And even though a part of me knows, even as the dream unfolds behind my closed eyes, that this isn't real and the DIS won't really kill me and never really intended to, still the dreams come, and the heart races, and it is always a relief to wake up. Parris Island was a tough place for a 17-year-old kid who'd never before encountered an adult more threatening than a teacher wielding a detention slip. Still, that dreams about boot camp should persist years after dreams about the ultimately much more terrible war have ceased is something to contemplate.

In his documentary film, *War: A Commentary,* when Canadian journalist Gwynne Dyer wanted to explain how ordinary young men are transformed into soldiers—that is to say, people whose job it is, finally, to kill other people—he chose Marine boot camp to make his point, and he filmed that segment at Parris Island, because Marine boot camp is among the toughest and most effective military basic training programs in the world. A lot of people have a lot of misconceptions about what goes on in Marine boot camp, however (or at least what went on when I was there; you might want to look at Ron Schirmer's story for a more contemporary look at Parris Island). Yes, you are stripped of your individuality and trained to respond without hesitation or question. Yes, you are dehumanized and desensitized and taught to fight with your bayonet and even your bare hands. Yes, they swear at you a lot and shout at you a lot and make you do a lot of things that seem to be utterly pointless and gratuitously stupid.

But you need to understand that the popular image of the sadistic

DI force-marching frightened recruits through deadly swamps in the middle of the night is derived from one single such incident that happened in the 1950s. You need to understand that the U.S. Government was going to send large numbers of young men to fight in Vietnam whether they had been trained well or poorly, whether the war was a good idea or not, whether you approved of the war or didn't. You need to understand that within five to twelve months three-quarters of the men of Platoon 1005 would find ourselves fighting in Vietnam, and when you have to think clearly and act bravely even when you are taking incoming mortar and small-arms fire and two of your buddies are down and screaming for their mothers and all you want to do is crawl up into your own mother's womb and never come out again, you begin to realize that the things we were made to do in boot camp no longer seem either pointless or stupid. You need to understand that we were not training for a garden party.

If you are going to send young men to war (and women, too, these days), you had damned well better train them, and though I came to hate the American War in Vietnam, I have never hated the Marine Corps, and I will always be grateful to Staff Sergeant J. J. Oliver, Sergeant T. W. Evans, and Sergeant D. S. Bosch, and to the training program for which they served as point men, for preparing me as well as anyone could have prepared me to bear up under the awful obscenity of war. The Marine Corps had not come looking for me; I had gone looking for trouble. I was young and headstrong and naive, and I believed President Johnson when he said that if we did not fight the Communists in Vietnam, we would one day have to fight them on the sands of Waikiki, and when I got to Vietnam and it all began to come unraveled, the only thing that kept me functioning from day to day was the knowledge that I was a Marine, that other Marines were depending on me for their lives, that if I gave in to despair and exhaustion and fear, they would die. The Marine Corps called it esprit de corps. I've heard others call it brainwashing. Call it what you like, I'm convinced I would never have left Vietnam alive had it not been for the training I received at Parris Island.

V

In 1961 I'd scrawled onto the cover of my school notebook, "Ask not what your country can do for you; ask what you can do for your country." In 1963 I'd stood for eight hours, all through a cold late November night, just to get a glimpse of John F. Kennedy's casket lying in state beneath the Capitol rotunda. In the winter of 1966, only months before I'd enlisted, I'd written in a journalism class, "What more noble a cause can a man die for than to die in defense of freedom?" I turned down four colleges to join the Marines.

And when I didn't initially receive orders to Vietnam, I badgered my boss at Marine Corps Air Facility, New River, North Carolina, Master Gunnery Sergeant Bergman, day after day, week after week, for two months, until one morning he finally said, "You wanna go to Vietnam, Ehrhart?" I said, "Have you been listening, Top?" Which was a pretty smart-ass answer for a young private first class, but Top Bergman let it pass. "I got a message here says they're looking for Oh-Twos in the infantry in Vietnam," he said. I'd been assigned to the field of combat intelligence, which is designated in the Marine Corps as 02. "Sign me up," I said.

I arrived in Vietnam in early February 1967. I left in late February 1968. I have spent much of my adult life dealing with the personal consequences of my decision to join the Marines and fight in Vietnam. Anyone familiar with the body of my writing—and even more so those who know me personally—already knows this. What those people may be shocked and amazed to hear is that I have finally tired of writing about myself. What more can I say that I haven't already said?

If you want to know what happened to me in Vietnam and how it has affected my life, you need only consider the titles of some of my books: *Vietnam-Perkasie: A Combat Marine Memoir; Passing Time: Memoir of a Vietnam Veteran Against the War; Busted: A Vietnam Veteran in Nixon's America; Going Back: An Ex-Marine Returns to Vietnam; In the Shadow of Vietnam: Essays 1977–1991; Carrying the Darkness: The Poetry of the Vietnam War.* If you want to know more than that about me, read one or two of those books. My personal favorite is *Passing Time,* but *Vietnam-Perkasie* seems to be more appealing to most people.

Ordinary Lives is not a book about me. It's a book about the other seventy-nine men of Platoon 1005. And it's a book I could not have written even ten years ago, let alone fifteen or twenty. None of these men, at least among those I've had the opportunity to sit down and visit with, shares my perspective on the war or the depth and breadth of my knowledge about its origins and causes and history. And for a very long time I was so angry about the war, and so impatient with anyone who didn't see things my way, that it would not have been possible for me to sit for three or four or five hours in the same room with someone who thinks we could have won if only the politicians wouldn't have interfered, or if only we had invaded North Vietnam, or if only any of the other myriad ideas and beliefs Americans hold about the war. Yet in the course of doing these interviews, I spent a lot of time with people who didn't see things my way, and rather than arguing, as I would have done without hesitation a decade ago, I just kept my mouth shut and listened.

Why now when not before? What has changed over the years? Certainly not the world we live in, which has only traded Vietnam and Biafra for Bosnia and Rwanda. Certainly not our government, which has gone from Watergate to Iran-Contra to renting out the Lincoln Bedroom with hardly more than a fare-thee-well. Certainly not my feelings about American involvement in Vietnam, which in my opinion was doomed from the moment our government chose not to recognize Ho Chi Minh's September 2, 1945, declaration of Vietnamese independence.

What's changed, I think, as I write in a poem called "Sleeping with General Chi," is that "I'm tired of fighting." I'm nearly 50 years old. I'm having to recognize that for better or worse, what I think doesn't make much difference to the world, certainly not the kind of dramatic and visible difference I had once hoped it would make. My opinions are just my opinions, however passionately I may hold them. Some people will agree with me and some people won't, but the fate of the world doesn't hinge on my successfully persuading everyone else to see things my way.

You might wonder why it's taken me so long to figure this out. I wonder, too. Whatever the reason, it's made it possible for me to look at other perspectives and other points of view without feeling that anyone who thinks differently from me is either foolish, evil, or idiotic. Call it mellowing, call it maturity, call it wisdom, I don't know. But I do know that when in June 1993 my thoughts first went to John Harris and then to the rest of the platoon, it allowed me to wonder for the first time and with genuine and simple curiosity: who were those guys anyway, and what happened to them? It has allowed me to listen to the stories the men of Platoon 1005 have had to tell me.

VI

While this is not a story about me, I am its chief beneficiary because I have been blessed and enlightened and enriched by the lives that have touched mine over the past five years. Three sisters, a nephew, a niece, and a couple of brothers-in-law of Billy Blades's gathered at his parents' house to spend a day with me, including me in a family-style lunch that offered a glimpse of what Billy's life might have been like had he lived. Lessie Langley sent me away with handmade gifts for my wife and daughter, though she has never met them and probably never will. Charles Mahone sent a money order with a note saying that it was to help defray the costs of tracking down platoon members. Gerry Sirois woke me up one morning at 4:25 to see the yearling moose that was standing in his driveway not twenty feet from the window of the bedroom in which I was sleeping. Jerry Bowles and I passed as fine a warm spring afternoon as you could ever imagine fishin' the pond out behind his house hardly a stone's throw from the Ohio River. And I fed a two-gallon baby bottle of milk to a two-day-old calf one evening in Bob Fink's barn while the hungry little gal stomped all over my shoes and slobbered all over my trousers.

When I'd first called Fink to ask if I could interview him, he didn't say no, but he didn't sound too eager either, so I was feeling a bit anxious the morning I arrived at his farm. He was unloading feed bags from the back of a truck when I got there, lifting them with his massive arms and tossing them as if they were feather pillows. I struggled as well as I could to help out, though the value of my effort was clearly in the gesture, not in the result.

For the next nine hours, Fink moved from one task to the next, never working hastily, but always working steadily, me tagging along, trying to help when I could, asking questions when I could, writing down the answers in a small pocket notebook. When he finally took a break for an 8:00 P.M. supper, after what had turned out for me to be a wonderfully fascinating day, I felt confident enough to say, "You know, Bob, when I got here today, I wasn't sure what to expect from you. You hadn't sounded too keen on having me come." He laughed and said, "When you called me and said you wanted to interview me, I thought you wanted me to sit down and talk for a few hours or something like that. You can see I don't have a few hours just to sit and talk. I didn't know what I was going to do with you. But you followed me around pretty good out there today. You can come and visit me any time."

Not everyone was willing to have me come and visit. Steven E. Dudley flatly refused my request for an interview, writing that there were too many hurts, memories, and bad times he didn't want to talk about or have people read about. Stephen Sofian wavered back and forth for several years, putting me off, then calling me up and saying he had lots of stories to tell me, then putting me off again when I'd try to follow up, though never refusing me outright. The last time I called, however, his wife told me, "He has nothing to say to you." I haven't heard from him since.

I scheduled an interview with Paul Robison in Maryland only to have him cancel it a few days before it was to take place with no explanation beyond "I just don't feel comfortable." I scheduled an interview with Roosevelt Tharrington's sister in North Carolina only to have her cancel it a few days before it was to take place, saying only that she'd made other plans. Leonard Hibbler did not return my telephone calls, though I spoke to his mother, and to others I think were his wife and his son. My wife talked to a woman who said she was Jerome Carter's wife and who called one day while I was out, and I subsequently talked to a boy who might have been Carter's son, but Carter himself never called or wrote. Lonnie Milligan did not answer any of my four letters, nor did Gregory Hawryschuk ever respond to the letters I sent him.

Who knows why? Not me, and it's a fair bet I never will, but I can well understand that people might be more than a little suspicious of someone who writes or calls up out of the blue and says, "Hi! You don't remember me, but I was in your boot camp training platoon a million years ago." And most of the men didn't remember me because Parris Island was the one place in my entire life where I tried fervently to be as inconspicuous as possible—the last thing I wanted was to draw attention to myself—and I had mostly succeeded. It's not hard to imagine them thinking, "What the hell is this guy after?" There are a lot of strange people in the world.

I was far less surprised by the wariness of some than I was by the openness and warmth of so many others: John Ramsell wishing my family well in a voice near breaking; Guy Haas telling me how he'd gotten tears in his eyes watching his 15-year-old son dress up in his old winter green uniform; Rey Waters and Larry Maxey offering tips on where I might start looking for other platoon members; William Summerscales making copies for me of all the letters his son had written to him from Vietnam; Tim Jenkins taking me to the wedding banquet of a young family friend because I happened to be there and, what the heck, the more the merrier.

Even more to my surprise, a few of the men really did remember me. Steven W. Dudley and George Osada had both read *Vietnam-Perkasie*, and Dave Hewitt had read *Passing Time*. Mahone said he'd seen me in the public television documentary *Vietnam: A Television History* ten years earlier and had read about me in Stanley Karnow's companion book, *Vietnam: A History*. Mahone told me that I was "like a brother" to him because of our shared experiences in boot camp.

Those shared experiences were often enough to overcome whatever initial reluctance I encountered—not always, but often. Whoever I was and whatever I wanted, even if they didn't remember me, they knew I had to have been in Platoon 1005 once I started talking about Sergeant Bosch's voice suddenly jumping an octave in the middle of a harangue, or Staff Sergeant Oliver's penchant for the phrase "every swingin' dick and poppin' pussy," or Sergeant Evans' nightly order: "Pray for war!" Men who seemed stiff and wooden when a conversation first began would often become downright voluble as the hours wore on.

Two men, unfortunately, told me stores about their military service so divergent from the records sent by the National Personnel Records Center that I could not reconcile the two versions. I asked each man—in writing—if he could explain the discrepancy, but got no reply from either. I have therefore chosen to use their Marine Corps Service Record Book entries to tell their stories. These men, too, served their country.

So also did the two men I can't trace after we left Parris Island, John Green and Harold Feighley, and the men I can't trace beyond their service in the Marine Corps. There are a lot of success stories, large and small, among the men I've found, but there are some sad stories, too. I stumbled upon the fates of Steve Summerscales and George Schrenker only by accident; my guess is that most of the wreckage of the platoon—the homeless, the incarcerated, the incapacitated, the dead—lies among those for whom the record stops after the Marine Corps. I can only hope that most of the men I cannot find are alive and well and doing fine.

VII

Given that all eighty members of the platoon volunteered for the Marine Corps in the summer of 1966 on the rising tide of American involvement in the war, one might reasonably expect us to be a fairly homogeneous group. Within certain broad limits, however, we turned out to be surprisingly diverse. Some men were well aware of the war when they enlisted; others were almost oblivious to it. Though we had no college graduates among us, a number of the men had had some college. Most of the others, though not all, were high school graduates. We came from both the working class and the middle class, from farms and small towns and big cities, from broken homes and close-knit families. Our ages ranged from 17 to 23, though only one man was over 21 and most were 18 or 19. Two were married, one with a child, the other with a child on the way—and Harris, of course, was also a father-to-be. There were sixty-three whites and seventeen blacks. As far as I know, we were all Protestant or Catholic—everyone had to be something; you weren't allowed to be an atheist or an agnostic, and anyway everyone always wanted to go to chapel on Sunday morning because that was the only hour of each week when someone wasn't yelling at you. That notwithstanding, not everyone found Parris Island and our DIS as intimidating as I did; whether you were 17 or 20 seemed to make a lot of difference in that regard.

Platoon 1005 was highly unusual, if not unique, for several reasons. First, though the Marine Corps did draft some recruits in the mid-Sixties to accommodate manpower demands created by the Vietnam War, we had no draftees in Platoon 1005. Second, though one military option was to enlist as a reserve, serving six months on active duty followed by five and a half years of monthly meetings and summer camps (thus precluding service in Vietnam—the option former Vice President Dan Quayle chose, though not with the Marines), we also had no six-month reservists in Platoon 1005. Finally, we graduated the same eighty men on August 12, 1966, as we'd started with on June 20, a rare accomplishment. Usually some recruit will break an arm and have to drop out to recuperate, while another will develop severe allergies and have to be discharged entirely, while still another gets sent to the brig for gross insubordination and yet another will have to go home for a father's funeral. There are any number of reasons a recruit might be bumped from his original platoon, and if he's not released from the Corps entirely, he'll be added to a later platoon that has already lost members, picking up the training cycle where he left off. But Platoon 1005 started together and ended together, leaving no one behind.

After boot camp, almost one third of the platoon was assigned to the infantry, a few as riflemen, a few others as recoilless riflemen, most as machine gunners or mortarmen. A smaller group ended up in ground combat support fields such as shore party, artillery, engineering, and amphibious tractors. Another group, about a dozen men, enlisted for four years under a program that guaranteed you an MOS somewhere in the Marine Air Wing, provided you could pass whatever schooling to which you were assigned. Two men failed to finish their aviation schooling and ended up in the infantry; the rest became mechanics, air traffic controllers, or navigators. Six men became either administrative or disbursing clerks, another a legal clerk. The rest of the platoon, in ones and twos, received an assortment of MOSs, including intelligence, embarkation, food service, warehousing, communications, nuclear demolitions, motor transport, and bulk fuel handling.

In one capacity or another, at least sixty-one members of Platoon 1005 served in Vietnam. Though I seem to have been the only one who became actively involved in the antiwar movement after I got out, the range of opinions about the war, as you will see, is broader than one might expect from such a self-selective group. Likewise, what has become of us is also remarkably diverse.

When I set out in search of the other men from Platoon 1005, I had no idea what I might find. It was a journey driven not by any desire to make this point or that point, but by the simple curiosity to know who were and are these men whose lives intersected mine at so crucial a point in my life and the life of the nation. Certainly, the Vietnam War was the most turbulent and wrenching experience of the post–World War II era, framing and shaping the second half of the twentieth century, affecting the lives of people not even born when it finally ended in April 1975 along with all of us who lived through it, both those who fought and those who didn't.

It was, in short, history, and each of these men was and is a part of that history, and I believe their stories are important. For if history is shaped and moved by huge forces like capitalism and communism and powerful men like presidents and secretaries of state, the nameless millions who suffer the consequences of those huge forces and powerful men do in fact have names and lives and stories to tell. What you will find on the pages that follow are some of those stories.

What might they tell you about the United States of America either in the midst of the Vietnam War or at the end of the twentieth century? Or about the 26.8 million draft-eligible males of the so-called Vietnam Generation? Or even about the 260,000 men in the Marine Corps in 1966? I am either too timid or too wise—take your pick—to try to offer any sweeping conclusions from what I've learned about the eighty men of Platoon 1005. I'm not much inclined even to attempt to generalize broadly about the platoon itself, given the many gaps in the story I've been able to reconstruct.

Don't misunderstand me, however. I do think what I've learned and what I've written does offer significant information about and insight into each of these things—the platoon, the Corps, the Vietnam Generation, and the United States both then and now—but I also think you are just as capable as I am of drawing your own conclusions. That may be less satisfying and more work than you had hoped for, but life's like that sometimes. A lot of the time. As we used to say in Vietnam, "There it is."

Moreover, if I go much beyond what I have actually written in the pages that follow, I run the risk of entering territory into which I do not wish to go. What can I say about a person who has a personal relationship with Jesus but thinks we should have blown North Vietnam off the face of the earth? What can I say about a person who is convinced the United States could have won the war if only the military had been allowed to fight to win, but who has never read a book about the American war in Vietnam, or the French war in Vietnam, or the long history of Vietnam and China? About a person who believes someone's a hero just because he's dead? About a person who wishes he'd served in Vietnam from the comfortable position of never having done so?

This is America. Everyone's entitled to his or her opinion. As I've already said, I've put my opinion in every other book I've ever written. But not this one. This is a book about other people's opinions and other people's lives, and these particular people have trusted me to tell their stories fairly and honestly and evenhandedly. That's what I've tried to do.

There are, no doubt, scoundrels and liars and losers among these men, but as a group they have mostly impressed me with their decency and their loyalty and their hard work and their perseverance in the face of the hardships and hurdles, the everyday obstacles and challenges that make even ordinary lives extraordinary. Far more often than not, these are men who did their duty to their country as they understood it, and who have continued throughout their lives to do their duty to their families and their communities, and I have found much to admire and respect and appreciate in each of them. Indeed, over the past five years I have developed a deep affection for the members of Platoon 1005, and above all else, I hope that I have served them well and done their stories justice.

The Members of
Platoon 1005

Michael C. Albon

Albon was the platoon's high shooter—that is to say, he had the highest qualifying score on the rifle range—which earned him upon graduation from boot camp one of the platoon's eight meritorious promotions to private first class.

Only one Michael C. Albon appeared on the list retired Army master sergeant Ben Myers so graciously provided me in August 1993. When I got no answer to a letter I sent, I called on September 24, and he turned out to be the Albon I was looking for. He didn't remember me—no surprise there—and said he had virtually no memory of anyone from Platoon 1005. He was very reserved, answering questions briefly and volunteering little additional information, but based on our conversation and records subsequently received from the National Personnel Records Center, I learned that Albon was born on December 4, 1945, graduated from high school, and started college, but enlisted in the Marine Corps at Buffalo, New York, before completing his first year.

After boot camp and special weapons training as a mortarman (0341), Albon was assigned to Headquarters & Support Company, 2nd Battalion, 3rd Marine Regiment in Vietnam from November 1966 to December 1967. For nine months of that time, his battalion was deployed aboard ship as Battalion Landing Team 2/3, going ashore every few days wherever reinforcements were needed. For his service in Vietnam, he received the Purple Heart Medal and a Presidential Unit Citation, in addition to the National Defense Service, Vietnam Service, and Vietnam Campaign Medals.

From January until June 1968, when he was released from active duty with the rank of corporal, Albon was assigned to Company E, 2nd Battalion, 8th Marines, based first at Camp Lejeune, North Carolina, then at Guantanamo Naval Base in Cuba.

Albon has worked for the U.S. Border Patrol since shortly after his release from the Marines, first in El Paso, Texas, then in Tucson, Arizona.

"Two more years and I can retire," he says. Married with two children (ages 17 and 11 at the time we spoke), he belongs to the Veterans of Foreign Wars and Disabled American Veterans.

Richard A. Beauvais

If you had told Richard Beauvais back in the early 1960s that he would end up as a certified public accountant with a master's degree in taxation and his own business, it is not likely he would have believed you. He might well have asked what planet you came from. "I was one of those students who didn't know what was up in high school," he says. "I was an average student. I just floated through. I didn't care."

Eight Richard A. Beauvaises had shown up on the Myers list, so I had written them all. On September 10, 1993, I received a brief letter beginning, "It appears you have found one of the members of Platoon 1005." Almost three years later, on July 28, 1996, as we sat in his office at Beauvais & Company, he told me his story. It was a Sunday morning, and he was dressed in a coat and tie.

Private Richard A. Beauvais, August 1966. (PB)

Growing up in Worcester, Massachusetts, Beauvais played a lot of baseball and basketball. He even made the varsity basketball team as a ninth grader at Saint Peter's Catholic High School. But he didn't like Saint Peter's, and even though the school offered him a basketball scholarship to stay, he transferred

Richard Beauvais (far right) *with wife Patricia* (left) *at oldest daughter Kerry's graduation from Nichols College, 1996. Beauvais's younger brother is at far left. "That's what I looked like ten years ago," Beauvais says of his brother.*

at the beginning of tenth grade to South High School, the public school across the street. "I promptly quit basketball," he says, instead taking a part-time job at one of New England's first McDonald's hamburger stands (you could hardly call them restaurants thirty years ago), "just to have pocket change. Get a car."

He worked at McDonald's until he graduated from South High in 1965, then took a full-time position at the huge Worcester warehouse of Thom McAn, a shoe manufacturer. "Pulling shoes," he says, by way of describing his job. "Stores would send in their orders, and we'd pull the shoes off the shelves, box them, and ship them to the store. So many size nines, this style or that style. We'd send the order to the shipping department on a big conveyor belt."

Late that fall of 1965, Beauvais was called for a preinduction physical examination, but he wasn't worried. "I never thought I'd pass it," he explains. "I'd had medical problems as a kid. It had been corrected with surgery, but there was lots of scar tissue." Two months later, in February 1966, he got a letter from the Army. "'Greetings! You've passed your physical!' They actually send you a letter like that, congratulating you," he says, the tone of his voice a perfect blend of contempt and wonder. When he asked a woman at his local draft board what the letter meant, she told him it meant he'd be drafted by June.

The very next day he received a letter from a local Marine Corps recruiter. "We know you got a letter from the Army," Beauvais recalls that letter saying. "Why don't you come and talk with us?" So Beauvais did: "'You don't want to be in the infantry,' the recruiter told me. 'Sign up with me and I'll guarantee you aviation. You won't have to be a grunt.'"

Taking advantage of a 120-day delayed enlistment option, Beauvais signed on the spot. That afternoon, he told his friend Donald Bowles what he'd done, whereupon Bowles went down to the recruiting station and signed up, too. Four months later, the two young men took the train from Boston to Charleston. "It must have stopped at every station along the way," Beauvais says. "It took forever."

As for Parris Island, he says, "Who doesn't remember arriving at the training depot at two o'clock in the morning? Remember those long tables where you had to dump everything you'd brought with you? The guy standing across from me passed out. He just fell right over." As the days turned into weeks, Beauvais tried to keep in mind the advice he'd received from a friend's father, himself a Marine veteran of World War II: keep your mouth shut and do what they tell you. "It was good advice," Beauvais says. "I never got into trouble. The DIS never bothered me except once."

The single exception came one morning while the platoon was preparing for a big inspection. Senior DI J. J. Oliver found an unbuttoned pocket on Beauvais's uniform. "He cut the button off with my bayonet," Beauvais recalls. "Then he told me to put the button in my mouth and keep it there all day. And he checked on me all through the day."

Among Beauvais's most vivid memories of boot camp, however, is not what he did there, but rather what he didn't do. "I never ever saw the obstacle course," he says. "Not once." Because he had an uncanny ability to disassemble and reassemble an M-14 rifle, he was chosen to be a member of the platoon's rifle assembly relay team for the battalion field meet. "Anytime the platoon went to the obstacle course," he says, "the DIS would send us to practice stripping our rifles."

He also remembers "The Skyscraper." A particularly nasty component of the final Confidence Course recruits had to complete to graduate from boot camp, it consisted of three platforms, one on top of the other and each about eight feet higher than the one below it. Recruits had to chin themselves up from one platform to the next, then come back down. "I only went up to the first platform," he says. "Then I ducked across and came back down. I didn't get caught."

After boot camp and basic infantry training, Beauvais was sent to the Naval Air Technical Training Center, Naval Air Station, Millington, Tennessee (which everyone always referred to simply as Memphis). "The first phase of training," he says, "was kind of like basic training. You learned drown proofing, jumping out of airplanes, how to jump in the river without ruining your family jewels—stuff you'll never use, but they teach you anyway."

Next came a battery of aptitude tests, as a result of which Beauvais qualified for training as either a metalsmith or an aviation clerk. Not liking either of these options, he persuaded his career counselor—"like a high school guidance counselor," he says—to let him go to electronics school. The counselor agreed, provided that Beauvais bring him his weekly tests every Friday. When Beauvais got forty-nine points out of fifty on the first test, the counselor quietly dropped that requirement, and when electronics school concluded, Beauvais had done so well that he was sent on to radar school.

After nine months of aviation training, Beauvais was assigned a military occupational specialty of 6236, acquisition radar technician, and sent to Headquarters & Maintenance Squadron 32 at Marine Corps Air Station, Beaufort, South Carolina. "It was nothing fancy," he says of duty there. "We just basically worked our day-to-day shift." As for the looming war in Vietnam, he says, "My attitude was, 'If they want me in Vietnam, they'll let me know.' I'm the only person in the squadron who didn't volunteer for Vietnam. And guess who got his orders first?"

He arrived in Vietnam in May 1968 and was sent to Marine Fighter Attack Squadron 115, flying F-4 Phantoms out of Chu Lai. The day he arrived, he says, all the new guys were issued M-16s and live ammunition, then taken to a firing range to test their weapons. Only after this were the men delivered to their various units for duty. "That was pretty scary," he says. "I thought, 'Jesus, this is for real. We're not playing games anymore.'"

The "old timers," of course, immediately began to tell the new guys about rocket attacks. "I thought they were just telling sea stories," Beauvais says. "It can't be that bad. But when my first attack came, it was pretty scary. Then about a month after I got there, a hooch across the road from mine took a direct hit and I realized, 'People are gonna get hurt over here.'" The base was rocketed often, he remembers. "Sometimes it seemed like once a day."

Occasionally Beauvais was assigned to base-perimeter guard duty, he says, "but nothing happened out there on guard. We'd get reports of a possible Viet Cong attack, but that was probably just to keep us on our toes. The scariest thing was the bamboo vipers. They're the most poisonous snakes in the world. I saw one once, but it didn't bother me and I didn't bother it."

Beauvais never shot at the Viet Cong, he says. "But I fired a rocket one night, right off the ground." One of his jobs, he explains, was to test the electrical firing circuits for the airplanes' Zuni rockets. One night, he was sitting in the cockpit of a plane testing the circuitry when one of the rockets fired. "It blew a hole in the hangar wall about this big," he says, stretching his arms wide apart, "but fortunately no one got hurt. After that, we weren't allowed to test with live ordnance on the planes."

Work shifts were twelve hours long at Chu Lai, six to six, either days or nights. "I spent most of my time on night crew," says Beauvais. Because the airplanes flew mostly in the daytime, the day shift had little to do except menial tasks like filling sandbags. The night crew did most of the actual aircraft maintenance, he says, and because they'd usually be able to finish their work by midnight or so, "you'd have from midnight to 6:00 A.M. to do what you wanted. Play cards. They'd let guys go early."

After Vietnam, Beauvais returned to H&MS-32 at Beaufort. By this time a sergeant, he was able to live off base in a rented house in downtown Beaufort. "It was a pretty easy year," he says. He and another sergeant were in charge of the radar shop night crew. "Night crew was the best place to be because there was never any brass around. Nobody messed with you. There was rarely enough work to keep everyone busy. We'd let guys off. We'd take turns every other night." On nights he wasn't working, Beauvais moonlighted as a waiter at a nearby resort restaurant.

He also took an English literature course through a University of South Carolina extension program, he says, "just to see if I could handle school again." Sometime during his four years in the Corps, Beauvais began to ask himself, "What am I gonna do with my life? Pack shoes in a warehouse?" In the spring of 1970, while he was still in the Corps, he applied for admission and was accepted at Nichols College in Dudley, Massachusetts.

He spent the summer of 1970 once again "pulling shoes" at the Thom McAn warehouse, and when September arrived, he started college full time, though he worked for McAn part time all through college, first in the warehouse, then in the accounting department. He gravitated toward accounting, he says, because "accounting courses were easy, so I just stuck with it. I was a straight A student in accounting."

By the time he graduated in 1974 with a bachelor of science degree in accounting, he'd already been married two years. He'd known Patricia Jones when they'd been classmates at Saint Peter's, but she'd stayed at Saint Peter's when he switched to South High, and their lives had moved in different directions. Only when he made her reacquaintance—at the Speedway Club after he'd gotten out of the Marines—did they begin to date.

The couple's first daughter, Kerry, was born the year Beauvais graduated and took his first job with the public accounting firm of Laventhol & Horwath, where he stayed for three years. In 1977 he was courted by one of Laventhol's clients, Walco Electric Company of Providence, Rhode Island, for whom he became controller. He spent three years with Walco, including perhaps the most stressful three days of his life.

Patricia was nine months' pregnant with their second child that Monday morning of February 6, 1978. It was Beauvais's birthday and also the baby's due date, but Beauvais went to work, figuring he could get home easily enough if the baby arrived. By noon, snow was falling. By mid-afternoon, Beauvais decided he'd better get home while he still could, but it was already too late. Roads were impassable.

So there he was, stuck in Providence while his wife was stuck in Woonsocket with a 3½-year-old and another child due any moment. He called home every hour for the next two days. Finally, on Wednesday, a friend in the Rhode Island National Guard drove his military police jeep from the Pawtucket armory to Providence, picked up the anxious father, and delivered him to Woonsocket—in plenty of time, it turned out, for Julie's belated arrival on February 19.

Two years later, Beauvais left Walco and returned to Laventhol & Horwath, then went on to Kelly & Picerne, a real estate firm, and two additional public accounting firms in succession: Rooney, Plotkin & Wiley; and Fiore & Assmusan. Going to school part time, by 1985 he'd also earned a master's degree in taxation from Bryant College in Smithfield, Rhode Island.

While with Fiore & Assmusan, Beauvais made the acquaintance of

Roland Senecal, the last surviving member of Ratcliff & Company, an accounting firm Senecal had helped to found. Up in years, Senecal wanted to retire and offered to sell Beauvais his practice. "I said to my wife," Beauvais explains, "'If I don't do this, I'm gonna be looking back all my life thinking I shoulda, woulda, coulda.' And the rest is history."

Beauvais & Company, two accountants and a secretary, operates out of an office suite in North Smithfield, Rhode Island. "Most people think we just sit here and play with numbers all day long, but we also do a lot of business consulting. The CPA today is a complete financial advisor. We don't just crunch numbers. We've got machines to do that for us. You don't need to be a great mathematician to be a good accountant. You do need to be able to add, subtract, multiply, and divide, but most of it is fairly simple."

Most of Beauvais's clients are small businesses with annual revenues ranging from $100,000 to $10 million. "We offer advice on computer systems," he says, "legal issues, tax issues, business problems. Sometimes it's as simple as what direction to go in. We identify business problems and find solutions."

As for the pressures of self-employment, Beauvais says, "I don't have any trouble with overwork because I'm not a workaholic." Though he regularly puts in ten-hour days, he never works on Sundays, doesn't work Saturdays in the summer, and gets away for a week at a time several times a year. An avid golfer, he and three friends spent a week this past spring at "Golf Heaven"—Pinehurst, North Carolina—sans wives, and in July he and Patricia spent a week in Waterville Valley, New Hampshire (where you can also play golf).

Of their trip to New Hampshire, Beauvais says, "It was the first year we've been away without the kids since Kerry was born, and that's only because they were both working. It was kind of nice, actually. Sort of like getting reacquainted." After a pause, he adds, "My wife and I spend a lot of time with our daughters. Even to this day. That's probably why I'm not a workaholic." (Kerry earned a 1996 degree in public administration from Nichols College; Julie started at Merrimack College in the fall of 1996.)

On top of a bookshelf in his office, Beauvais keeps an old coffee cup. The handle is gone, and the mug itself has been broken and glued back together again. On one side is the squadron emblem of the Silver Eagles, VMFA-115. "I dropped it against a porcelain sink one time," he explains, "but I couldn't just throw it away." He pauses, then continues. "I don't think now that [Vietnam] was the correct war for our country to be involved in, but what could you do at the time? I didn't have any idea what the politics of the war were. I just knew I'd joined the Marines and I was doing my job. I went because I thought I was doing something for my country. I never really thought about it. I did my time. I did my work." He picks up the mug and turns it in his hands, slowly, lovingly. It holds a lot of memories.

William C. Blades III

The last time Buddy Blades saw his son before Billy left for Vietnam, Buddy was in the hospital, where he'd just had surgery for a stomach ulcer. Billy was in uniform, and as he was leaving, he paused on the stairwell landing and turned to look back at his father, who was standing at the railing above him.

"'Take care of yourself,' I told him," says Buddy. "He saluted me and said, 'Take care of the family for me. I'll be away for a while.' As soon as he was out of sight, everything went black in front of me, and I saw Billy lying on a hill with his chest torn open."

Buddy collapsed to the floor, and when a nurse hurried over to help him up, he told her, "I'll never see my son again," but he couldn't bring himself to tell his wife Barbara about his vision. Even after twenty-three years of marriage, some things were never meant to be shared. Instead, he carried it alone through the winter of 1967 and into the spring.

Buddy knew about war. As a crewman aboard the USS *Stewart*, DE238, he had shot down a German airplane in Naples harbor.

High school senior William C. Blades III, 1965.

Headstone of Billy Blades, Billerica, Massachusetts.

He had married Barbara in 1944, and when World War II ended, he had come back to Massachusetts and started his own business as a plasterer. Buddy and Barbara had four children: Judy, Billy, Edie, and Sue. Soon after Billy arrived, the family moved from Medford to Billerica, where Buddy and Barbara still live, and where I interviewed them on June 24, 1995.

Also present that Saturday were Billy's three sisters; two brothers-in-law; and Kirk and Erin, Edie's kids. It was Edie who had finally called me on September 17, 1994, more than a year after I'd written to the only William C. Blades on the Myers list. "He's not much of a letter writer," she had said of her father, "but he's a great talker." And so he proved to be, though the rest of the family contributed to Billy's story as well.

No parent could ask for a better kid than Billy. He was active in Boy Scouts and the Catholic Youth Organization. He was a lineman on the Billerica Memorial High School football team for four years, and team captain his senior year. He was elected class president four years in a row—something no one else has ever done at BMHS, before or since. He was Chief Squire of the Columbian Squires, Knights of Columbus, and was named the Squires' Man of the Year in both 1964 and 1965.

Says Buddy, "The parents of the girls he used to date would tell me, 'Your son can go out with my daughter anytime.' Everyone liked him. He wouldn't fight with anyone. He wouldn't speak bad of anyone."

"It was just his way," says Barbara. "He was very helpful. He was always willing to do anything for anyone." Under his senior photograph in the 1965 BMHS yearbook is a quote that Billy himself wrote:

> and then end life
> when I end loyalty

After graduation, Billy went to work framing houses while taking night courses at a nearby college. Within a year, however, he announced that he was joining the Marines because, says Buddy, "he wanted to let the government pay for his college education." Buddy tried to talk him into joining the Navy because, as Buddy says, "you got three meals a day and you slept between clean sheets, but Billy said he wanted the best, and he figured the Marines were the best."

"He wanted to be where the action was," adds Judy.

After boot camp, Billy was designated an 0341, mortarman, and went to infantry training in North Carolina, then came home on leave with orders to Vietnam. Buddy arranged to get Billy a ten-day extension on his leave because of the upcoming ulcer operation. "I wanted to be sure I'd survive the operation before Billy left for Vietnam," says Buddy. Then came that final farewell on the hospital landing, and the long days and nights of waiting.

In mid-April, a Marine sergeant came to tell the family that Billy had been wounded. Buddy happened to be in Boston that afternoon, so the sergeant reached him by telephone and said they had to talk before the telegram arrived. "I dropped right to the floor," says Buddy. "I thought he was a goner." But the wound was not serious. When the telegram did arrive, it said that Billy had been hit in the left chest by mortar fragments on April 18, but that his condition and prognosis were good.

A few weeks later, a letter arrived from Billy dated May 1. "The wound wasn't that bad at all," he wrote. "I never left the field. I didn't get it in the chest. I got it in the back. I would have left the field, but I didn't feel it was necessary, and it wasn't. The doc's out here fixed me up and it is all healed now and you can't even see it.

"Oh, guess what I found out yesterday," he continued. "I have a month in grade as L/Cpl [lance corporal]. I now have my crossed rifles, and am almost sure that I'll get another stripe before I get home. I'm working on it. Now I'll be making a little more money, which will come in handy when I get home."

On May 6, Billy wrote again: "We have been getting hit up here [at Con Thien] just about every day now and they seem to be getting closer and closer every day. We had one guy leave us today. He went nuts. The rounds have been coming in close and then the guy just had mortar fatigue. He was so scared and shook up that he just cracked. He was a Cpl [corporal] at that. Things up here in the DMZ are pretty hot. . . . If possible, could you send me a jar of relish and a small jar of sweet pickles. You know the kind that I like."

By the time this letter arrived, Billy was dead. A Marine lieutenant and the parish priest broke the news. Most of the family was home, but Edie was working at Pinehurst Market (where Barbara also worked, and where Billy had worked when he was in high school). At one point when the store manager was on the telephone, Edie heard him say, "Oh, my God!" Later, when her shift ended, he gave her a ride home. "There were all these cars there," she says. And then she learned what the manager hadn't had the heart to tell her.

A few days later, when Buddy went to the bank, he noticed that all the flags in town were at half-mast, so he asked the teller, "What politician died?"

"Don't you know?" the teller replied. "Your son came home." Local police had been monitoring the progress of Billy's casket, and when the hearse in which it was traveling crossed the town line, all the flags in town had been lowered.

"He was the first one [from Billerica to die in Vietnam]," says Edie. "Talk about apple pie. That was Billerica."

Billy's was the biggest funeral the town had ever seen. The high school closed for the day. One friend of Billy's, then in the Air Force, went AWOL from Alaska to attend, though he was busted for it. Another friend left a Central Intelligence Agency training program to attend, though he was cashiered for it. Because Billy had always worn a crew cut, six long-haired friends all got haircuts, telling Buddy, "We can't go to Billy's funeral with long hair." Two Brothers [Catholic monks] who had taught Billy in catechism came from Norway to attend.

"When we waked him," says Buddy, "my hand was sore from shaking so many hands."

On the day of the funeral, it was raining hard. Someone told Buddy to bring an umbrella or raincoat, but Buddy said he wouldn't need one. The rain stopped when the limousine got to the church. It rained hard again during the service, but it stopped when Mass ended. It rained again on the way to the cemetery, but it stopped for the graveside interment. At the very end, when the casket had been lowered into the ground, the clouds parted and a ray of sunlight came through the canopy covering the grave and lit up the casket. Buddy had left by this time, but when he heard about the sunbeam, he turned to the two monks and said, "Well, I think he made it."

"We never had any doubts about that," one of them replied.

The family still did not know the circumstances of Billy's death, beyond what the official telegram had said: that he had "died 8 May 1967 in the vicinity of Quang Tri. . . . He sustained fragmentation wounds to the body from a satchel charge while on an operation against hostile forces." Subsequently, a letter arrived from Captain Melvin D. Trimble, acting company commander of H&S Company, 1st Battalion, 4th Marines:

> Bill was assigned as an ammunition carrier in our 81MM mortar platoon [wrote Capt. Trimble]. In the early morning of 8 May 1967 his platoon was assigned security watch for the company command post. Approximately 3:00 AM his position received enemy mortar fire. Realizing that a friend of his had been seriously wounded, he rushed to his aid but was seriously wounded while helping his buddy to safety. Bill was treated by a corpsman and administered morphine but failed to respond to treatment and died of multiple wounds at 4:30 AM. Bill received the last rites by Lieutenant Commander Ryan, Catholic Chaplain, U.S. Navy Chaplain Corps.

A month later, Buddy and Barbara received a letter from Great Lakes Naval Hospital written by Lance Corporal Angel Torres Campos: "If it would'nt of been for [Billy] I would be in some other world. He saved not only [my life] but others. He was my friend and that night I found out for the first time that men can cry." When they wrote back and asked if he could give them more information about how their son had died, Campos replied:

> Yes, I'll tell you every thing that happen'ed. . . . [At] 2:40 in the morning they start'ed to hit us with all they had as soon as about the first five mortar round's hit I was wound'ed and the only one around was Bill so I said Bill I'v been hit, he came up to me and said "Well lets get you to a corpman" so he did the corpman was in a bunker, Bill laid me down and sat by me and kept saying "Man Campos you're going to be fine" I said sure I

will" and then we hurt someone call for help and the corpman was busy with me so he told Bill to go and see who it was and about 30 min. later, the morphine the corpman gave me was still strong but I could hear someone else calling for help but this person I knew who it was I was badly wound'ed in the legs so I could'nt walk but he was'nt very far so I work'ed my way out and when I got to Bill I saw him and said whats the matter Bill? he said Man I'v been hit bad." I did'nt know what to do or what to say but I did say Bill if I'm going to make it so are you. he did'nt say nothing for awhile then he said get me some water. I said Bill you can't drink water you've got a chest wound.

Again he didn't say much but then he said Angel please get me some water! I started to cry because he want'ed water so much and I could'nt give it to him. then he said go and get a canteen come on? I looked around and saw a canteen laying on the deck so I reach'ed for it at this time enemy started to hit us with ground troops like mad but we still had enough men to hold them back, I could'nt get the canteen because it was to far, I had to get out of the trench so I got out and grab'ed the canteen and while getting back I was shot in my left arm I did'nt want to move because someone was ready to shoot me if I did move I laid there for about five min. then I got back to were Bill was he was still alive but did'nt answer me when I said I'm back I took out my handkerchief and got it wet and put it on his lips and stay'ed with him until the corpman came he ask'ed me how Bill was doing I said I did'nt know, he check'ed him and said to me, "don't do anything foolish Campos," he left us. . . . I'm sorry it had to be me who had to tell you how it all happen. . . . Bill was all ways happy.

So it had been a chest wound, after all, the wound that killed Billy Blades. And on a hill, too.

For his service in Vietnam, the U.S. government gave Billy two Purple Hearts, a Presidential Unit Citation, the Good Conduct Medal, and the Vietnam Service Medal, and the government of the Republic of Vietnam gave him the Military Merit Medal, the Cross of Gallantry, a Meritorious Unit Citation, and the Vietnam Campaign Medal. All but three of these were earned posthumously.

After Billy died, someone in town asked Buddy, "Doesn't it make you mad, these kids going to Canada?"

"Am I supposed to feel better if somebody else's son goes to Vietnam and gets killed?" Buddy replied. "If somebody else's family has to go through what we're going through? I don't want any more kids to die in Vietnam."

Listening to her father tell this anecdote more than a quarter of a century later, Edie says, "Billy would never [go to Canada]. He would never even think of that."

"I used to resent the draft dodgers," says Judy. "I thought, 'Why should they get out of it when Billy was killed?'"

"But Billy enlisted," Buddy says. "Those kids were going to be drafted."

Back when Billy died, the family felt they understood why the U.S. had to be in Vietnam, but now feelings and opinions differ. "I've never encouraged my sons to go into the military," says Judy, who now thinks the U.S. shouldn't have been in Vietnam. Edie, however, still thinks it was the right thing to do, while Sue isn't sure how she feels.

"I don't mind any war where they take you and me and everyone else fairly," says Buddy. "But when the people who send you stay home and make a good living, I don't support that. I just hope my grandchildren don't have to go to war."

Less than a month after Billy died, the people of Billerica dedicated a square in his honor. Soon thereafter came the William C. Blades III Scholarship Fund. A Little League team was named for him, as well as a Veterans of Foreign Wars post. In 1971 the CYO of Saint Mary's parish erected a flagpole in front of the rectory dedicated to Billy and the four other parish boys killed in Vietnam. In 1981 the people of Billerica dedicated Vietnam Veterans Park. The plaque by the flagpole reads, "In Honor of All Vietnam Veterans," but the six crosses in front of the pole carry the names of those who died in Vietnam (or of complications from wounds), and the first cross is Billy's.

"Billy is still on people's minds," says Buddy, "still in their hearts. Every time someone we know goes to the Wall [the Vietnam Veterans Memorial in Washington, D.C.], they come home with a rubbing of Billy's name. I can't count the number of rubbings we have."

When Billy's niece, Erin, was in junior high school back in 1989, she wrote an essay that began, "My uncle William C. Blades III is a great hero in my eyes, though I have never met him." His nephew Kirk, a Marine reservist, joined the Corps at least in part because he'd heard stories about "Uncle Billy" from his mother and grandfather. When he graduated from Parris Island on April 10, 1992—which would have been his uncle's forty-fifth birthday—he invited Buddy and Barbara to attend the ceremony, which they did.

For a while after Billy was killed, Buddy felt as if he'd lost everything, he says, but people reminded him that he still had three daughters, and they have since given him and Barbara nine grandchildren. "One or another of the grandchildren is always calling up and asking to spend the weekend with us," he says. "That's a great feeling."

Still, as Buddy talks about Billy more than twenty-eight years after his death, his eyes fill with tears easily and often. Barbara says almost nothing at all. Life goes on, but the loss is as keen today as it was nearly three decades ago. When the lieutenant and the priest came with the terrible news, Barbara, who had recently had a hysterectomy, said to the priest, "I can't give my husband another son."

"You could never give me another son like this one," Buddy replied. On Billy's gravestone, beneath the line that reads, "Killed in Action in Vietnam," are these words:

> And then end life
> when I end loyalty

Donald E. Bowles

It's a Monday afternoon, and Don Bowles is drinking a Guinness Stout in Tweed's, a restaurant and bar in Worcester, Massachusetts. As he drinks, he carries on a running conversation with a middle-aged waitress behind the bar, while keeping one eye on the television screen that gives the results of the latest keno game, on which Bowles has bet a dollar. Another woman, this one half Bowles's age, comes in, spots Bowles, and immediately comes over and begins to catch him up on her latest comings and goings. Though her smile is friendly, her voice is hard-edged and her vocabulary spicy. A short-order cook by trade, she could easily play a moll in a 1940s gangster movie.

One begins to get the impression that Bowles knows everyone in town. This is not quite true, but there are few people in the food and beverage service industry around Worcester that Bowles doesn't know because he's been a bartender for a quarter of a century, working in nearly a dozen local bars, lounges and restaurants over the years, and when you do that kind of work for that long, sooner or later you meet just about everybody else who's doing that kind of work, too.

Bowles is a native of Worcester, where I spent the better part of a day with him on June 26, 1995. One of eight men with the same name on the Myers list, he had received my initial search letter and had called me that same day, September 10, 1993. I stopped to see him almost two years later, during a swing through Massachusetts that also included visits with Guy Haas and the Blades family. As we sat in Tweed's drinking Guinness and eating really good greasy cheeseburgers—big fat burgers in thick heavy rolls, the kind you don't get in fast-food joints—he told me about his life.

Except for three years in the Marine Corps, Bowles has spent his entire life in Worcester. The second of seven children (three boys and four girls) born to a trucking company terminal manager and a housewife, he grew up playing sports. At Worcester's South High School, he lettered in football, baseball, golf, and hockey. A defenseman in hockey, he played on a team that was undefeated

Private Donald F. Bowles, August 1966. (PB)

in four years of Interhigh Hockey League competition, and he captained the team his senior year.

After graduating in 1964, Bowles took a job as a management trainee with Friendly's, the ice cream and restaurant company. "I thought the Friendly's was going to be a career," he says, "but it turned out not to be. I didn't fit their mold. I was a little too outgoing."

During this same period, the war in Vietnam was increasingly moving from the back pages to the front pages, and the draft was beginning to take more and more young men. One day, Bowles and his friend Richard Beauvais decided they were going to get drafted anyway, so they might as well join the Marines. "It was a spur-of-the-moment thing," says Bowles. "I never really gave it much thought until the draft started becoming so prominent."

At the induction center in Boston, Bowles and Beauvais found themselves in a room with a lot of other young men. "Maybe four hundred," says Bowles, "maybe six hundred. Then someone said, 'Everyone for the Navy, this way,' and half the room emptied. 'Everyone for the Army, that way,' and the room emptied completely. There were only five or six of us left who were going into the Marines."

Don Bowles with former racing dog and now family pet G's Sam Flake, 1995.

The oldest man in this small group was put in charge of getting them to the train. "This guy says, 'We're gonna be good Marines,'" Bowles recalls. "'We're gonna be tough Marines.' And I'm thinking, 'Oh, boy, what a jerk this guy is.' Then he says, 'But first we're gonna buy a half a gallon of orange juice and a bottle of Smirnoff.'" Bowles survived the train trip, which took over twenty-four hours, but he recalls eating only a bologna sandwich and some potato chips between Massachusetts and South Carolina.

Of his time on Parris Island, Bowles says, "My recruiter told me, 'Just keep your mouth shut and do what you're told,' and that's exactly what I tried to do." A major turning point came one day during pugil stick training (mock-bayonet fighting with padded poles). Bowles explains that he had already taken his turn, but another platoon member was afraid to take his own turn because his opponent was particularly large and intimidating, so Bowles took the frightened man's turn.

"I knocked the guy down," he says, "but he hit me under the chin while he was still down on his knees and knocked me silly." When Bowles came to, he found himself sitting under a tree being attended to by several drill instructors. "When I asked Mommy for another hot dog," says Bowles, "[Senior DI J. J.] Oliver put me in his car—it was a '57 Chevy—and took me to the aid station." After that, he says, "the DIs never messed with me." He thinks it was because they'd seen him taking the frightened man's turn.

Toward the end of boot camp, when platoon members were told what military occupational specialties they'd been assigned, Bowles found out he was to become a 3421. "I didn't know what that was," he says, "but I was smiling from ear to ear. I knew what a grunt was [an infantryman], and I knew that 3421 wasn't a grunt, so I was tickled pink."

His MOS turned out to be disbursing clerk, and after attending disbursing school at Montford Point, Camp Lejeune, North Carolina, he was assigned to the Marine Corps Supply Activity in Philadelphia, Pennsylvania. He remained there for the rest of his three-year enlistment, handling the pay for the members of the Marine Barracks at the Philadelphia Navy Yard and the various transient Marines who passed through.

"It was a really great job," he says. "I was in a position to really help people out. Guys would be coming back from Vietnam, and their pay records would be lost or all screwed up. I'd ask, 'How much do you need?' and they'd say, 'a thousand dollars' or whatever, and I'd say, 'You got it.'"

The job also afforded wonderful opportunities for payback on people who earned the disbursing clerks' wrath. "We'd send people's pay records to Greenland, Spain, wherever," he says. "When we were feeling particularly nasty, we'd overpay someone. No one ever complains about being overpaid," but eventually the error would be discovered, and the money would have to be repaid.

One night, Bowles recalls, he returned to the Navy Yard drunk and out of uniform, so the gate guard, a sergeant, arrested him and handcuffed him to a radiator. "'Do you know who I am?' I told the guy. 'I'm your pay clerk. Call my lieutenant.'" The guard was unimpressed, but did call the lieutenant, who came to the gate. "Do you know who this man is?" Bowles says the lieutenant asked the guard. "You take him to the barracks and put him to bed."

Bowles has fond memories of Philadelphia. The supply facility had a lot of female civilian employees, so he was often invited to someone's home for dinner. When he had money in his pocket, he would go to Smokey Joe's, a bar near the campus of the University of Pennsylvania. In uniform, he could get into Phillies games at Connie Mack Stadium, or Flyers games at the Spectrum, for just one dollar. "I used to go to a lot of hockey games," he says. "I was a big fan of hockey." An uncle who lived near Philadelphia would often take Bowles to his country club. "They didn't serve Heineken," Bowles says of the club, "so every time I went there, my uncle would make them go buy a case for me." When all else failed, he could take the bus home for the weekend for just thirteen dollars round-trip.

Bowles did have his difficulties, though. Thanks to several "office hours" (nonjudicial punishment under Article 15 of the Uniform Code of Military Justice), including one for remarks likening a certain captain of disbursing to a certain feature of human anatomy, Bowles spent two and a half years as a private first class. He also says he didn't much enjoy "cleaning floors for some [person] with half my intelligence just because he's got the time in."

Still, he was good at his job, and was frequently recognized for the quality of his work. "They tried to get me to reenlist by promoting me to lance corporal two months before I was supposed to get out," he says, but he chose to get out anyway. As he was checking out, Bowles says, his sergeant major asked him, "What would it take to keep you in?"

"I'd like to be a brigadier general," Bowles replied.

"Good luck and good-bye," said the sergeant major.

On his last night in the Corps, he says, he purposely left his locker door open so that anyone who wanted to could "steal" whatever they wanted or needed. The next morning—this was in June 1969—he put on his winter dress green uniform and a pair of wing-tip shoes—all he had left in his locker—collected a Good Conduct Medal, and went home to Worcester. "I didn't enjoy the military lifestyle," he says, "but it was a growing experience. I certainly matured. I wouldn't trade it."

Bowles has no regrets about not serving in Vietnam. "They were shipping people out to Vietnam left and right," he says. "They tabbed me for Vietnam a couple of times, but every time another guy who was sick of working in an office would volunteer to take my place. We did work eleven- and twelve-hour days in Philly, and some men thought Vietnam would be better, but not me. It was just obvious that it was better for me in Philadelphia than in Vietnam.

"A lot of guys felt like they weren't real Marines unless they went to Vietnam," he continues, "but I never felt like that. Politically, I had no opinion on the war. Not then. Now I just think it was a bad idea, like everybody else does. It's pretty universally accepted that it was a ridiculous idea. Why were we there? I don't pretend to understand it. It's like Grenada or Saudi Arabia. But I don't question the government. What difference does it make? There are things that we're not privy to."

Back in Worcester, Bowles got a job through the unemployment office selling tickets for a bus company. The pay was good, he says, but he got bad hours, mostly at night, because he had no seniority. Meanwhile, he was spending a lot of time in a bar called Tammany Hall, so he asked the owner about learning to become a bartender. The owner said he couldn't pay Bowles, but if he wanted to come in and work with the day bartender, that would be okay. He took the offer, and when the night bartender left, Bowles was hired to replace him. He's been tending bar ever since.

He even met his wife, the former Marie Spugnardi, in a bar. As Bowles tells the story, he was having a few drinks in Tammany Hall on his night off. He was supposed to go to a christening the next afternoon, so he asked Marie—who was a complete stranger at the time—if she wanted to go with him. "What are you, crazy?" she replied. So he took out his money clip, which had "fifty or sixty dollars in it," he says. "'Hold this,' I told her. 'I'll pick you up tomorrow.' She wasn't even ready on time because she never expected me to show up." They were married six months later in September 1972. Their daughter Cheryl, a high school sophomore, was born in 1980.

Bowles and his wife have both gone through some changes in the past few years. Marie worked for Filene's, a New England department store chain, for twenty-two years, but when the Worcester store closed two years ago, the best deal the company would offer her was a position at another store sixty miles away. Rather than make so long a commute, she left Filene's and took a job as the manager of a Michael's craft store.

At about the same time all of this was transpiring, Bowles decided to give up full-time bartending. By way of explanation, he says, "One [unpleasant] customer can ruin your whole day. I just got tired of it." So he quit and went to work as a receiving clerk at his wife's store, though he still tends bar three nights a week at Andrea's Ristorante.

What Bowles enjoys almost more than anything, however, is greyhound dog racing. "My father and I were track rats. I go to the track every opportunity I get," he says. "I consider myself an expert handicapper, even though I don't win. I think I'm going to win." When his father died, he decided to take his small inheritance and really begin to learn about dog racing.

Over a five-year period in the late 1980s and early 1990s, Bowles bought nineteen dogs, sometimes owning and running six or seven dogs at one time. "I've never read anything good about dog racing in the press," he says, but he insists that dog racing is honest and the dogs are well treated. "You can't fix races," he says. "The dogs have no jockeys. You can't make them slow down like horses. And they're treated much better than people think. There's so much negative press about dogs being euthanized, but it isn't true. Dogs are still destroyed, there's no way around that," he says of dogs who have been injured or become too old to race. But, he says, with the help of an organization called Greyhound Pets of America, the number of adoptions is growing every year.

Hinsdale Greyhound Park in New Hampshire, where most of his dogs have raced, has a retired greyhound kennel with thirty to forty dogs awaiting adoption, he says. His own trainer, Norm Dupont, has driven as far as Maryland to deliver a dog for adoption, with the track picking up the cost. Eighteen of his own nineteen dogs have found adoptive homes, Bowles says.

Once, when one of his dogs broke a leg during a race, track officials called to say they were going to put the dog down. "'Fix him up,' I told them. 'I'll pay for it.' The dog found a home with a family in Hamburg, New York. I was always more interested in the dogs than in the money. I don't care about the money. I just enjoyed the dogs."

His favorite dog, G's Sam Flake, a red-and-brindle male born in 1985, is now the family's pet. "He never had a bad race," says Bowles, who bought him from a man in Alaska. "He tried every time. He was the only dog I owned who ever paid for himself." In his prime racing years, 1987 and 1988, G's Sam Flake won twenty-six races and finished "in the money" (third or better) in 84 of 141 starts.

When Bowles began buying and racing dogs, he figured he could afford to lose the money he'd inherited, so he never got upset about losing, but as the dogs got older he couldn't afford to replace them. He's been out of racing for about two years now, but hopes to get back into it eventually. During the years he raced, Bowles invested and lost about $25,000, he says. "But I've had $20 million worth of fun. As soon as I get some more money, I'm going to buy some more dogs."

Terry J. Bowles

Terry and Jerry Bowles looked so much alike that even their older sister Dorothy couldn't tell them apart. That's why she was so happy when their mother got the twins different-color coats; now she could tell who was who by the color. What Dorothy didn't count on was her brothers' mischievousness: the boys used to switch coats just to trick their sister.

Growing up on the family farm outside of Glasgow, Kentucky, the

Twin brothers Terry and Jerry Bowles (left to right), *1st Battalion, 1st Marine Regiment, Vietnam, December 1967.*

twins turned mischief into an art form. Early one morning when they were six years old, they climbed out their bedroom window, shinnied down the television aerial, and went fishing. Their mother thought they were still in bed until they marched into the kitchen and presented her with a seven-and-a-half-pound catfish they wanted her to cook for their breakfast.

When they got a little older, their father would set them to hoeing in the tobacco fields on summer mornings, but as soon as he left for work at a local cheese-processing plant, the boys would hitch a ride into Glasgow on the milk delivery truck and spend the day at the swimming pool. In the afternoon, they'd race home, and by the time dad arrived, they'd be hard at work hoeing.

Jewel and Edna Bowles had bought the eighty-one-acre farm as newlyweds back in 1940, raising ten kids on it, five boys and five girls. The first six were born right there in the farmhouse, but Edna gave up home birthing after Jerry and Terry were born in 1947. With Jewel out looking for the doctor, Edna delivered Jerry with the help of a neighbor

Terry Bowles, sister Debbie Bowles Jeffries, and twin brother Jerry Bowles (left to right), *Glasgow, Kentucky, December 1994.*

only to discover that she'd been carrying twins. The doctor never did arrive, but Terry arrived thirty minutes later.

Of his father, Jerry says, "He was kind of like an old horse trader. He bought, sold, and traded almost anything. Watches, guns, whatever." For a while, Jewel worked for Swift Premium. And of course, there was the farm, where the family raised tobacco, corn, milk cows, pigs, and vegetables. "We never had much money," says Jerry. "We had to grow our own food. Almost everything we ate, we canned ourselves. We made our own butter and buttermilk."

The house had no running water until the late 1960s, and no indoor toilet or water heater until long after the children were grown. Drinking water came from a hand pump on the back porch, and on washing days they would have to lug water from a natural spring 150 yards away. "Mom and Dad did own their own farm, but we were just dirt farmers," says Jerry. "We pretty well lived back in the sticks, but I didn't know. We thought everybody lived like that."

Most of their neighbors did. All but the youngest Bowles children attended Lick Branch Elementary School, one of the last one-room schoolhouses in Kentucky, walking five miles to and from school each day. There were six grades in one room with an outhouse out back, and the student body ranged from thirty-three when the twins were in first grade to sixteen by the time they were in sixth.

After sixth grade, the twins went on to Temple Hill High School, but as they got older, they lost interest in school. It was more fun to catch and ride the neighbors' horses, or go fishing in the farm's pond and creek. "We ran around like a bunch of Indians when we were kids," says Jerry. "I wouldn't trade anything for our childhood."

When the twins were fifteen, they went up to Marysville, Indiana, to spend the summer with Dorothy, who was by this time married. They got jobs in a canning factory, and at the end of the summer, they pooled their savings, bought a 1952 Chevy coupe from a dealer in Louisville, and drove it home. "Dad didn't approve," Jerry says, "but we were pretty independent by the time we were fifteen."

As soon as they turned sixteen, they quit school. For the next few years, they mostly had fun. "Old T. J., he'd do anything for kicks, just for the hell of it," says Jerry, who always refers to his brother as T. J. Indeed, on more than one occasion they were caught drinking under age, drinking in a dry county, and drinking while driving. Finally, a judge gave them a choice: military service or reform school.

None too keen on school of any kind, the twins decided to enlist in the Marines under the four-year guaranteed aviation program. They joined on the Buddy Plan, and they were supposed to begin active duty in November 1965, but the night before they were to leave, Terry got into a car accident and broke his foot, so Jerry went while Terry waited for his foot to heal. It was the first time in the twins' lives that they'd been separated for any significant period.

Even then, however, their lives continued in parallel. After basic training, Jerry went to Memphis, Tennessee, for aviation mechanics school, but flunked out and ended up in the infantry in Vietnam. Meanwhile, in June 1966, Terry joined Platoon 1005; he too went to Memphis after basic training, but flunked out and ended up in the infantry, and after a brief stay with 2nd Battalion, 6th Marines at Camp Lejeune, received orders to Vietnam.

The day Terry arrived at the Marine transit facility in Da Nang in July 1967, Jerry—who didn't even know Terry had orders for Vietnam—was just returning from R&R in Taipei. Without orders or authorization, Terry accompanied Jerry back to 1st Battalion, 1st Marines, near Hoi An, where Jerry was assigned to Headquarters & Support Company, and the brothers persuaded Jerry's commanding officer to get Terry assigned to 1/1.

Though Terry was in Delta Company, he would visit Jerry every time he came in from the field to the battalion command post. During one such visit, the brothers were riding on a "mule"—a small four-wheel-drive vehicle with a 106mm recoilless rifle mounted on its flat bed—when Jerry, who was driving, flipped the vehicle over. Terry was unhurt, but Jerry got a severe cut on the head that required thirty-five stitches to close. It was an accident that would end up saving Jerry's life.

Only a few weeks later, in October, the battalion moved north to Quang Tri and almost immediately took part in Operation Medina. Early on, Terry got bitten by a poisonous snake and had to be evacuated to a hospital in Da Nang. A week or so later, by then nearly recovered, he was helping to unload wounded Marines from medevac helicopters when he realized that one of the wounded was Jerry.

Earlier that day, still on Operation Medina, Jerry's squad had been ambushed by North Vietnamese Army regulars, and Jerry had been hit in the chest with AK-47 rifle fire. The fighting had been so fierce that he had lain out in the open for four hours before anyone could get to him. By the time he arrived at the hospital, he was so swollen and bloody and dirty that Terry at first didn't recognize him. Only when Terry noticed the thirty-five stitch scar on Jerry's head did he realize he was looking at his brother.

Medical personnel quickly determined that Jerry was too far gone to be saved, but Terry refused to leave Jerry, staying by the litter and insisting that the doctors work on his brother until they finally did. Jerry learned all this from a hospital corpsman when he came out of a coma three weeks later on the hospital ship *Repose,* where he remained until December. The brothers had a brief reunion at Con Thien before Jerry rotated back to the U.S. in January 1968. Terry remained with 1/1 until August, participating in the relief of Khe Sanh and earning his own Purple Heart for wounds that didn't require evacuation.

Back in the States, however, life began to go bad for Terry. Before he'd left for Vietnam, Terry had married a woman he'd met in Marysville, but he came home after thirteen months to find her seven months pregnant. During his last ten months in the Marines, he served as a group guard (8151) at Marine Corps Air Station, Beaufort, South Carolina, but he was clearly struggling. Jerry doesn't know the circumstances, but Terry spent three weeks under confinement in the Beaufort brig, and had at least one subsequent unauthorized absence. He was also reduced in rank from corporal to private or private first class at some point prior to his early release from active duty in July 1969.

When he got out, Terry went back to Marysville, where his wife was living, and tried to make a go of it. He got a job driving a locomotive at the Indiana Army Ammunition Plant, but as Jerry explains, "They were real young when they got married. A situation like that [the wife pregnant by another man], somebody's got to move on." It wasn't long before she left, taking her son and filing for divorce.

Not long afterwards, Terry lost his job for carrying matches in his pocket, which was strictly forbidden at the ammunition plant, and Jerry thinks possibly for drinking on the job as well. He found another job driving a forklift for International Harvester in Louisville, but when a judge ordered Terry to pay child support for a child that wasn't his, he was so embittered by the decision that he simply disappeared.

Three years later, he showed up at Jerry's front door wearing bib overalls and flip-flops. He told his brother he'd been in Florida working various construction jobs. By this time, Jerry's first marriage had also come and gone (he has since remarried), so the brothers decided to go west together, spending six months in southern California and Mexico. "I got a job at a marina after a while," says Jerry, "but T. J. never did work. We just messed around mostly."

Tired of being broke all the time, and not much enamored of southern California, the brothers started east, intending to return to Kentucky, but Jerry met a woman in Denver and ended up staying in Colorado for the next two and a half years. Terry would come and go, disappearing for weeks and even months at a time. He told Jerry he was working construction jobs in Montana, Alaska, and Canada, but Jerry doesn't think so. "T. J. got involved with some pretty shady people," he says. "Maybe they were drug dealers. Maybe they were undercover cops. I have no idea."

One day, Terry showed up at Jerry's with a car and a wad of cash and said he was going to Chicago. "That's the last I saw of him," Jerry says. Not long afterwards, however, a man Jerry recognized as an acquaintance of his brother's came looking for Terry. The man was very aggressive and very threatening, so Jerry pulled a .357 pistol on the man, called the cops, and told them to come get him: "'He's either a cop or a drug dealer,' I told them, and then I left Denver and never went back. I don't know what was going on, but it was getting scary."

This was in 1974. Ten years later, Jerry tried to find Terry through a police officer who was a friend of his second wife, Jan. The police officer could find out only that Terry had a "presidential clearance," says Jerry, which barred the officer from finding out any other information.

Next Jerry tried to get an address for Terry by using Terry's name to buy a gun. In response to a routine background check by the gun dealer, the Federal Bureau of Investigation contacted the gun dealer, told him Terry Bowles didn't need a gun, and if the dealer wanted to keep his license, he'd better not be running any more background checks on Terry Bowles. "I think it's time we stop looking for him," Jerry told his wife. "We're gonna get in trouble if we don't."

The twins' youngest sister, Debbie, however, who was only twelve when her brothers had left for California, picked up the search in the early 1990s. Years earlier, both Jerry and Edna had sent letters to Terry by way of the Veterans Administration (federal agencies will forward letters to a last-known address, though they are forbidden by law to divulge that address), but he had not responded. In February 1994, however, in response to a letter Debbie sent through the Social Security Administration, Terry called home. It was his first contact with anyone in the family in two decades.

Terry was then living in Houston, Texas. "The whole family wanted to go there," says Jerry, "but T. J. didn't want a whole lot of people. It was all kind of new for him," so Jerry flew down alone. He found Terry living in a rough neighborhood, where he managed a boardinghouse for transients, apparently in return for his own room and utilities. He told Jerry he also worked construction and did barbeque catering.

"It was pretty neat," says Jerry. Both men had put on a lot of weight, but were still within five pounds of each other. Both men sported beards. "We even wore the same brand of underwear," Jerry says. "We were gonna go to the greyhound track. We never did get there. We were gonna go fishing. We never did get there. We just sat and talked for three days. We hardly left his place. He had an ugly old '72 Olds Delta 88. A big four-door sled. He called it the Green Hornet. He had a Chicana girlfriend. He seemed to have a lot of friends. People really liked him. He was always likeable."

Finally, Terry agreed to come home, though he warned his mother that if people started asking what he'd been up to all those years, he'd leave again. He returned to Glasgow in April 1994 and went to work for Debbie and her husband at an auto salvage yard. He lived with Edna and and Jewel at first, then rented a trailer near the salvage yard.

That fall, however, he began to get terrible headaches. He also began keeping more and more to himself, becoming quarrelsome and difficult to be with. By Christmas, he had quit the job, and, as Jerry explains, "He was just sitting there watching TV. He wouldn't cook. He wouldn't clean. Everybody thought he was just depressed, quitting his job and all, but I could tell he was in terrible shape."

Jerry persuaded Terry to come up to Marysville to live with him and his wife, which he did, but Terry's behavior became increasingly uncharacteristic. Usually fastidious about personal hygiene, Terry would no longer wash himself or his clothes. He spent a lot of time in bed. Finally, Jerry insisted that he go to the VA hospital in Louisville. Terry left the house that day, though Jerry doesn't think he ever went to the hospital.

In any case, that night Terry blacked out in Jerry's kitchen. After several more episodes of blacking out over the next few days, Jerry drove his brother to the VA hospital himself and got him admitted. By the time Jerry returned the next morning, Terry had been transferred to the University of Louisville Hospital, where doctors removed a brain tumor the size of a softball.

Over the next eight weeks, Terry received radiation treatments five days a week. Finally, able to walk only with difficulty and with the aid of a cane, Terry was discharged to Jerry's care. He stayed with Jerry for a while, then went to stay with his older brother Donald. "He wanted to go fishing on Don's pontoon boat," says Jerry, but a few days later he was back in the VA hospital, where doctors found that the tumor had grown back larger than before. There was no point in operating. Terry was transferred to a hospice in Bowling Green, Kentucky, where he died on May 25, 1995. Jerry had just fed Terry breakfast, and was at his side when he died.

Two weeks shy of a year later, I spent two days with Jerry and Jan Bowles, who took me into their home as if I, too, were family. Maybe I was, in a small way, having gone through boot camp with Terry and served in the same battalion in Vietnam with both Terry and Jerry. On my second day in Marysville, May 10, Jerry drove me into Louisville and we ate lunch with Jan at the Colonades Cafeteria, where Jan is the manager. Then we drove back to Marysville and went fishing at a neighbor's pond. Jan joined us there when she got home from work, the afternoon sun slowly dropping down below the tops of the trees, sending soft shadows across the surface of the water.

The first time I ever saw Jerry, in the summer of 1967, I thought he was Terry and hailed him by name, recognizing a familiar face I hadn't seen since boot camp. When he told me he was Terry's twin brother, I thought he was pulling my leg until I finally saw the two of them together. "See," Jerry said, grinning. "I wasn't kidding." Then the three of us went off to the plywood shack that masqueraded as our battalion's enlisted men's club and drank warm beers.

"[Terry's death] hit me harder than anything," Jerry says toward the end of that lazy afternoon of fishing so many years later. "Life goes on, but you never get over it. He didn't have much, but everything he had meant something to him. If he had five hundred dollars, he thought he was a rich man. Mother gave him a quilt she made. He just cherished that. He wrote his name on everything too. Maybe that came from the Marines. You remember those name stamps we had? When the VA gave him a wheelchair after his operation, the first thing he did was put his name on it."

As for all those missing years of his twin brother's life, Jerry can only speculate. "I asked T. J. about that presidential clearance once," he says. "He said it was just a screw-up. Maybe he got turned by the Drug Enforcement Administration. Maybe he became an informant. He could have been in jail for all I know. We'll probably never know."

Langston D. Branch

When I found Langston Branch, he was hoping for a new heart. There were four Langston Branches on the Myers list, but none of them responded to my initial search letter, so on January 4, 1995, I decided to call all four of them. With the first call, I got Branch's mother, who gave me her son's number (he was not among the four on the list), and within moments I was talking to Branch himself.

The first thing he told me was that he was awaiting a heart transplant. He would have had one by then, he said, but he also had a bleeding ulcer and needed to wait for that to heal before he could get the transplant. He was high on the heart recipient list, however, and hoped to get a new heart within a few months. When I said that it must be very scary, he replied, "Yes."

He also told me that after his time in the Marines, which included service in Vietnam, he had been a plant supervisor and the manager of several car dealerships before his heart disease left him unable to work. He was married to "a beautiful wife" of eighteen years, and had three sons, the oldest of whom was about to join the Air Force. He still lived in the Richmond-Petersburg area, where he'd grown up. Records I received from NPRC in May 1995 provided this additional information:

Branch was born October 9, 1945, and finished eleventh grade before enlisting in the Marines. After boot camp, he was trained as a rifleman (0311), but on arrival in Vietnam in November 1966, was assigned as a military policeman and guard with the Military Police Company, Headquarters Battalion, 3rd Marine Division.

In June 1967, he was reassigned as a rifleman with Company G, 2nd Battalion, 26th Marine Regiment, where he served as a fire team leader and then as a squad leader before leaving Vietnam in December 1967. His decorations include a Presidential Unit Citation and the National Defense Service, Vietnam Service, and Vietnam Campaign Medals.

Back in the U.S., Branch was assigned to Headquarters Battalion, Marine Corps Supply Center, Albany, Georgia, first as a guard (8151), then as a recreational assistant (8921) with Fields & Courts. In August 1968, he was apparently sentenced by summary court-martial to a week's confinement in the brig and reduction in rank. Branch was a private first class at the time of his release from active duty in July 1969.

In March 1996, I made arrangements to see Branch, who had not yet received his new heart, during a trip that would also include visits with Alvin Jordan and David McBirney, but when I called to confirm a few days before setting out, his wife told me he was in the hospital with an infection and wouldn't be able to see me.

On June 13, 1997, I made one more attempt to arrange a visit with Branch. His oldest son (who did indeed join the Air Force and was then stationed in Washington, D.C.) answered the telephone and told me that his father was now staying in a hospital permanently, but was still hoping for a new heart.

Jeffery S. Brown

"The Lord's been good to us," says Jeffery Brown. He and his wife have two grown sons, born in 1970 and 1977, the oldest a veteran of Operation Desert Storm. Then in 1993, they discovered that she was pregnant again. They decided to go ahead with the pregnancy, and a healthy and welcome Hannah Jo Brown arrived in the world on April 4, 1994.

Brown first called me on October 16, 1993, after receiving one of the letters I'd sent to the twenty-one Jeffery S. Browns on the Myers list.

He had only recently learned that he was about to become a father again at a time in life when most men are at least beginning to think about becoming grandfathers. We talked again on August 18, 1995, and I received additional information from NPRC in July 1996.

Brown was born May 24, 1948. A high school graduate, he was sworn into the Marine Corps at Montgomery, Alabama. After boot camp and basic infantry training, he spent October 1966 to May 1967 at the Naval Air Station in Memphis, Tennessee, training as an aircraft jet engine mechanic (6311) specializing in helicopters. He then spent the next ten months at Marine Corps Air Facility, Santa Ana, California, first with Marine Medium Helicopter Training Squadron 302, then with Marine Medium Helicopter Squadron 263.

In April 1968 he received orders to HMM-265 in Vietnam, where he served as a helicopter crew chief and door gunner until May 1969. During his tour in Vietnam, he participated in thirty-two combat operations, earning fifteen Air Medals and the rank of sergeant. He spent his last year in the Marines with HMM-261 at MCAF New River, North Carolina, including a four-month deployment aboard the USS *Guadalcanal*. In addition to his Air Medals, his decorations include the Combat Action Ribbon and the Good Conduct, National Defense Service, Vietnam Service, and Vietnam Campaign Medals.

After his release from active duty in June 1970, Brown began college. While in college, he decided he wanted to join the Army as either a chaplain or a helicopter pilot. To become a chaplain, he needed two years of active ministry, so upon graduation he took a position as a pastor and began seminary, but after nine months coping with the stress of working full time and attending school, he decided being a minister "was not my cup of tea" and gave up the idea of becoming a chaplain.

In 1976, however, Brown did enlist in the Army, working his way up to staff sergeant before attending Officer Candidate School and becoming a second lieutenant. By then, he says, his eyes were not good enough for flight school, so he spent his Army career in ordnance, finally retiring as a major. "I wanted to be a chaplain or a pilot," he says, "and I didn't get to do either of them, but that's the way the Lord calls it sometimes."

After his retirement from the military, Brown worked for a number of years for a manufacturing company in Huntsville, Alabama, engaged primarily in defense contracting. In 1994 he took a position as Director of Human Resources for the city of Tuscaloosa.

Of the eighteen years between Brown's youngest son and his daughter, he says, "We didn't plan it that way, but the Lord had other plans."

Thomas M. Brown

The Myers list produced 183 Thomas M. Browns—more than I had the stamina to try contacting—but I subsequently learned that the VA did have a record of the man I was looking for, so I sent him a letter through the VA in February 1994. On March 13, Brown called me. He said that he had stayed with fellow platoon member Warren Hills all the way from boot camp through Vietnam. He also said that he was not injured in Vietnam and had little trouble adjusting when he returned home. He now lives in Nashville, Tennessee, and works in dialysis. He has three children, including a set of twins, and his oldest son had just finished college not long before our conversation. "I'm twenty pounds overweight," he said, "but otherwise I'm doing just fine." NPRC was unable to locate his service records based on the limited information I was able to provide.

Jerome E. Carter

Jerome Carter is one of the men whose VA claim number turns out to be his social security number as well, and based on that I was able to get an address for him in West Virginia through Military Information Enterprises, Inc. In response to a letter I wrote him in February 1994, his wife called in early March. I was not home the day she called, but she told my wife that Carter was a truck driver who was only home on weekends.

On March 12, a Saturday, I called the number she had left. The young man who answered told me that Carter had been home the day before but was back on the road again and suggested I call the following weekend. I called several more times over the next few weeks, but never found him at home, nor did he return my calls or answer any of several follow-up letters.

In July 1995, I learned from NPRC that Carter was born on May 19,

1947. After boot camp and basic infantry training, he received additional infantry weapons training before being sent to Vietnam in December 1966. In Vietnam, Carter served with Company L, 3rd Battalion, 3rd Marines, first as an ammunition man, then as a gunner, until his return to the U.S. in December 1967. While in Vietnam he participated in thirteen major combat operations.

From January to March 1968, Carter served as a gunner with Company E, 2nd Battalion, 8th Marines, at Camp Lejeune, North Carolina. From March to May, he served with Company G of the same battalion at Guantanamo Bay, Cuba. He then returned to Camp Lejeune and Company E briefly before being released from active duty in June 1968 with the rank of corporal.

Carter's decorations include a Presidential Unit Citation and the National Defense Service, Vietnam Service, and Vietnam Campaign Medals. His home of record at the time of his release was Bluefield, West Virginia.

Larry J. Collier

Collier was another whose VA claim number turned out to be his social security number as well, but when Lieutenant Colonel Johnson at MIE, Inc., ran a trace, it turned up the address of a woman who was not named Collier. She did, however, live in Philadelphia, the same city in which Collier had been living at the time he'd enlisted, so I wrote to her but never received a reply to either of my two letters. I also checked the Philadelphia telephone book, but there is no listing for anyone with either her name or Collier's at that address.

Collier, I did learn from NPRC, was a high school graduate. After boot camp, where he earned a Marksman's Badge on the rifle range, and basic infantry training, he received additional training at the Food Service School, Camp Lejeune, North Carolina, before being assigned as a cook (3371). From February 1967 until February 1969, Collier served in Vietnam with Headquarters & Maintenance Squadron 17, Marine Wing Support Group 17. Upon his return to the U.S., he was released from active duty with the rank of lance corporal. His decorations include a Presidential Unit Citation; the National Defense Service, Vietnam Service, and Vietnam Campaign Medals; and a Certificate of Commendation.

James W. Cork

Two James W. Corks showed up on the Myers list. One replied that he was not the man I was looking for, the letter to the other came back stamped "Forwarding Order Expired." Cork had made a claim with the VA, so I sent a letter to be forwarded to him. I never received any indication from the VA that the letter had been returned to them (if it comes back undeliverable, the VA is supposed to send you a form indicating this, and did so in a number of other cases), but if Cork received it, he never replied.

According to records received from NPRC, Cork was born on January 8, 1948. After boot camp and basic infantry training, he attended Motor Transport School at Camp Lejeune, North Carolina, before being assigned a military occupational specialty of motor vehicle operator (3531).

After an additional month with Headquarters & Support Company, 2nd Shore Party Battalion, also at Camp Lejeune, Cork served in Vietnam with Marine Air Base Squadron 36, Marine Air Group 36, from December 1966 until April 1969. In May 1967, Cork was temporarily assigned to Marine Medium Helicopter Squadron 36 for four weeks as an aerial gunner, earning four Air Medals.

Returning to the United States, Cork was briefly assigned to Service Company, Service Battalion, at Quantico, Virginia, before being released from active duty with the rank of sergeant in June 1969. In addition to his four Air Medals, Cork's decorations include a Combat Action Ribbon, a Presidential Unit Citation, and the Good Conduct, National Defense Service, Vietnam Service and Vietnam Campaign Medals.

Gary S. Davis

Early one morning in November 1966, just a few weeks before he left for Vietnam, Gary Davis went into Oceanside, California, hoping to see a movie at a twenty-four-hour theater. To his surprise, he found the theater chained and padlocked. Then he noticed that everything else on the usually bustling street was closed too, and there was no one around.

"It was like 'The Outer Limits' or something," Davis says thirty years later. A United Service Organizations lounge was all he could find open, so he figured he might as well get a cup of coffee and a donut. No one was

Private Gary S. Davis, September 1966.

in the USO except the counterman, but as Davis sat with his coffee and donut, a man dressed like a priest or a chaplain sat down on the stool beside him and asked if Davis believed Christ had died for his sins.

"I'd be a fool if I didn't believe that," Davis replied. Then the chaplain asked if Davis had ever accepted Jesus as his Lord and Savior. When Davis replied, "Not in so many words," the priest asked if Davis thought that might be a good idea. "I guess it would," Davis replied. "Can I finish my coffee and donut first?"

The two men went into the chaplain's office, which was well-appointed with a large desk, several comfortable chairs, and book-lined walls. As the chaplain prayed, Davis recalls that he seemed to be lifted bodily out of his chair, as if he were floating, and when he left the USO that day, he says, "My feet never touched the ground."

The next day he went back to the USO to thank the chaplain, but when he asked where the priest was, the counterman replied, "There ain't no priest and no office, and there never was. You came in here yesterday and started talking to yourself, then you went over there and talked to yourself some more, then you blew out of here!"

"I knew then I'd been brought to Jesus by an angel of the Lord," says Davis, who would serve two full tours in Vietnam: the first with 1st Battalion, 3rd Marines, and 2nd Battalion, 9th Marines; the second with 1st Battalion, 9th Marines—all of it up along the Demilitarized Zone (which Davis calls the "Dead Marine Zone") or along the Laotian border. He would have his helmet shot off, his rucksack shredded, his canteens riddled, "all sorts of stuff," he says, but he was never wounded, though he would participate in some twenty-eight major operations.

Until this chance encounter at the Vietnam Veterans Memorial in Washington, D.C., in November 1984, Gary Davis (right) and fellow Platoon 1005er Dave Hewitt had not seen each other in eighteen years. (Photo provided by Gary Davis.)

"If I hadn't accepted Christ before I went to Vietnam," he says, "I wouldn't be here today." "Here" is where I interviewed Davis on June 22, 1996, a neatly kept mobile home in a trailer park fifteen miles west of Harpers Ferry, West Virginia— not all that far from his childhood home in Rockville, Maryland, and even closer to Frederick, where he graduated from high school in 1966. A regular reader of *Leatherneck,* he had seen one of my earliest locator notices in the magazine and had called me on September 1, 1993. Three years later, I drove to West Virginia to spend the day with him.

The second of four children, Davis was "into sports big time," he says. "If you had a bat or a glove or a ball, you just went down to the park in the morning and started playing. When another kid showed up, you had teams. I remember days we had thirty or forty guys on the ball field. It didn't matter. Everybody played." In junior high, he played basketball for his school and church teams simultaneously, and in high school he played football.

Though he graduated fifty-ninth in a class of five hundred, he didn't want to go to college. Davis's uncles and his father, an Army veteran of the third wave at Normandy, discouraged him from joining the Army, saying the Army wouldn't properly train him. "I ruled out the Air Force because there's nothing to hide behind up there," he says, "and I ruled out the Navy because I couldn't see bobbing around on the ocean like a cork. So that's why I joined the Marines."

His most vivid memory of Parris Island is of getting sent by Drill Instructor Evans to Motivation Platoon, a short-term disciplinary unit. Ordered to move a large pile of sand with only a teaspoon and a child's plastic beach bucket, Davis says he just started laughing and couldn't stop. When the officer in charge arrived, Davis says he told the major, "You gotta admit, that is awfully stupid." According to Davis, the man replied, "Anyone who can laugh like that in a major's face is definitely Marine material," and sent him back to Platoon 1005 before lunchtime.

Subsequently trained as a mortarman (0341), Davis arrived in Vietnam in December 1966. After five weeks with 1/3, he was transferred to 2/9, first with the 81mm mortar platoon, then as a rifleman with Hotel Company, and finally with the mortar platoon again. Of all the operations he participated in during his first tour, Operation Buffalo, which took place near Con Thien in July 1967, is the one he remembers most vividly.

As Hotel 2/9 was waiting to enter the battle, Davis wrote in a February 1986 letter to the Marine Corps Historical Center, "a small group of Marines [came by]—seven to be exact—and they identified themselves as the only walking combatant Marines left of Bravo 1/9. I said to Sealer, a buddy of mine in the same fire team, 'They look like they're dead, too.' He said, 'Yeh, but they're walking.' Then Reno, another friend and member of our fire team who was great at putting words in my mouth, passed the word down the column, 'Davis said here comes the walkin' dead.' Needless to say, that name stuck."

The next day, Davis says, Hotel 2/9 and Charlie Company, 3rd Tank Battalion, repeatedly engaged enemy forces, losing fifty-four infantrymen and seventeen tanks and ontos, but killing twelve thousand Chinese soldiers. He is adamant about both the number and the nationality of the enemy, adding that the Marines were told to deny the presence of Chinese troops, "even though there were twelve thousand of them lying there dead, and anyone with any brain can tell the difference between a North Vietnamese and a Chinese." The facts of the battle were suppressed for fear of an international incident, he says. "That's why it's not publicized."

Davis holds the dubious distinction of going through his entire first tour as a private first class. When he's asked why he never got promoted, a broad grin spreads beneath his neatly trimmed blond moustache, and he explains, "When they wanted someone to walk point, they came to me. When they wanted someone to do the hard jobs, they came to me. But when it came time to burn the 'shitters' [fifty-five gallon drums sawed in half and used for toilets], I was nowhere to be found."

From Vietnam, Davis went to the weapons training battalion at Quantico, Virginia, where he retrained as a marksmanship instructor (8531), then began teaching officers at the basic school. One day a general showed up to requalify with the pistol. The general kept firing low, and finally asked Davis what he was doing wrong.

"Have you ever lived on a farm?" Davis says he asked the general.

"No," the general replied.

"You could have fooled me," Davis said. "You're shooting that gun like you're milking a cow."

Most of the men Davis worked with, however, were brand-new second lieutenants right out of officer candidate school. After just six months at Quantico, Davis requested orders back to Vietnam because "there was too much petty bull at Quantico," he explains, "too many junior officers who didn't know what they were doing."

Davis wanted to be a sniper for his second tour, but he found himself assigned to the mortar platoon of "The Walking Dead." "As it turned out, 1/9 was pretty good," he says. The battalion had a high percentage of two-tour and even three-tour Marines who were experienced and savvy, which turned out to be a good thing indeed, given the general deterioration of the situation in Vietnam in Davis's absence.

"In 1967," he says, "you were down there to help out another country. You're an American in a foreign country to help those poor slobs. Patriotism was high. By 1969, you didn't have anything to fight for. Dissension at home, antiwar stuff—there was no more patriotism. In '67, you had a cause. In '69, you didn't have a cause. We would look out for each other before anything. We were gonna do whatever it took to stay alive. That was the whole purpose: stay alive."

Just as Buffalo seems to be the most significant operation of Davis's first tour, Operation Dewey Canyon, in February and March 1969, is the most significant of his second. An April 1986 article in *Leatherneck* magazine quotes former Sgt. Leslie Keown of the 1/9 mortar platoon:

"Rounds were coming in from everywhere. Then a corporal (Gary

Davis) who had been to sniper school spread the word to check the leaves on the trees. Leaves grow outward. He told us, if we see a clump of leaves near the top of the trees and the leaves are 'growing' inward, spray the tree. We began doing that, and snipers were beginning to fall. That corporal shot down a bunch by himself."

Davis says he shot twelve snipers that day. "The last one was the best," he says. Davis knew the general direction of the sniper, but couldn't pinpoint him. "Then the Lord said to me, 'And David threw one stone.' So I fired a shot, and the sniper fell out of a tree with a bullet hole in his forehead. I fell down laughing. It was either laugh or cry."

The next day, he says, he was operating as a rifleman with Charlie Company because the foliage was too dense to use the mortars when the Marines came under artillery fire from close range. Assisted by four men from Charlie Company, Davis says he advanced up a hill until he could see the Russian-made 122mm field gun, then captured it by firing between the gun shield and the tires until he hit the gunner. (The same gun, he says, is now on display at the Air-Ground Museum at Quantico.)

During his second tour, Davis was awarded the Vietnamese Cross of Gallantry and a meritorious promotion to sergeant, both of which, he says, came as a result of his actions during Dewey Canyon. As part of Richard Nixon's Vietnamization program, 1/9 was withdrawn from Vietnam to Okinawa, where Davis spent his last few weeks in the Corps before being given an early out in August 1969.

That fall, Davis enrolled at the University of Maryland, but found college an unpleasant experience. "The professors, and I use the term loosely," he says, "went out of their way to make me feel out of place. The sentiment at the time was antiwar. There were sticks and poster paper in all the girls' dorms. They were ready to demonstrate at the drop of a hat. They didn't even know what they were demonstrating for. I had to work to make sure they didn't know I was a Vietnam vet or they'd have gone after me."

Davis lasted one year before leaving to take a job at the Baltimore Livestock Exchange, where he weighed cattle for auction, cleaned stalls, and fed the cows. It was noisy, smelly work, and after six months he took a better job as a production planner for a company called Defense Electronics in Rockville. Unfortunately, the company went bankrupt six months later, so he moved to Scranton, Pennsylvania, in mid-1971 and found work doing collections, repossessions, and dealer audits for General Electric Credit Corporation.

By the following January, however, he decided to enlist in the Navy. Reporting to the Philadelphia Navy Yard as a seaman (E3), he took a battery of aptitude tests and was told that he'd qualified for any job the Navy offered.

"Make me an officer," Davis told the career counselor.

"We can't do that," the counselor replied, so Davis settled for fire control technician. Since that school didn't start for nearly a year, he was sent to Guantanamo Bay, Cuba, where he was assigned to the commanding admiral's VIP boat pool. He spent nine months in Cuba before receiving a transfer to Great Lakes Naval Base.

Almost immediately upon his arrival in Illinois, Davis caught pneumonia and landed in the hospital, coughing so hard that he tore open the incision made at Guantanamo during an operation to repair a hiatal hernia. One complication led to another, and the upshot was that Davis spent most of the next eighteen months in the hospital. When doctors finally recommended that Davis be returned to full duty, he appealed the decision, and a medical board ruled that he was eligible for a medical discharge, which he accepted.

(Davis still receives partial disability compensation for a bad knee, a faulty lower esophageal sphincter, and, since 1984, post-traumatic stress disorder. During his PTSD interview, Davis says the psychiatrist asked him what he would do if he got lost in New York City. Davis replied that he wouldn't get lost in New York City, but the doctor persisted with *what if,* so Davis replied that he'd watch which way the sun was traveling, then go west until he got out of the city. The doctor said that the correct answer was to ask a police officer for directions. "The guy reported that I have antisocial tendencies," Davis says, chuckling. "I call it self-reliance.")

After his discharge from the Navy, Davis spent the 1974–75 school year attending the Thompson School of Business and Technology in York, Pennsylvania, but the school went bankrupt that spring, so he took a job in a Grumman Aerospace machine shop in Sterling, Virginia. After several years, tired of the night shift at Grumman, he went to work for the Internal Revenue Service—which he calls the Infernal Residue Service—as an audit and revenue officer.

"I was a hatchet man for the IRS," he explains, "chasing deadbeats all over northern Virginia, but I up and quit [after two and a half years]. I walked out one day—February 2nd, 1980—because I'd had it with the bullshit. You get flack from everyone: taxpayers, congressmen, supervisors. By the end of the day, you can't stand up straight. Enough is enough."

Davis tried to start his own tax consulting business, but it didn't go well, so when he got an offer later in 1980 from the Department of Energy—courtesy of a recommendation from a friend in the personnel department—he took it. He's been there ever since, working as a lead account technician on accounts payable. "I do the spending," he says.

As Davis talks, one notices a number of photographs on the television set. Several are of his parents when they were young, his father in Army uniform. Three are of his children—Jennifer, 18, Chad, 16, and Steven, 13—who live with his ex-wife. Davis married in 1976, but divorced in 1987. "The kids have mostly closed me out," he says with obvious sadness. "All I can hope for is maybe someday they'll wake up."

Davis's spirits revive when he begins to describe his favorite pastime: relic hunting with a metal detector. Currently he has access to six farms totaling four thousand acres of land, mostly in Jefferson County, West Virginia, where a lot of Civil War activity took place. Over the years, he's found bullets and buttons, coins, watches, belt buckles, silver and pewter spoons, sleigh bells, suspender fittings, even a gunner's gimlet. "I'm an amateur archeologist," he says. "You can learn a lot about history. I've always been kind of a history buff."

Another activity Davis enjoys is writing and arranging country & western songs. Some of his songs, like "Faith Unseen," are based on his religious convictions; others are secular. "Misty Mountain" is based on Davis's recollections of one incongruously beautiful early morning on Hill 881 in Vietnam.

Speaking again of Vietnam, Davis says, "The war should have been over before I got out of high school. We should have invaded North Vietnam." As for his own part in the war, he adds, "[A lot of people] tried to make us feel ashamed for what we did. I didn't do anything to be ashamed of. And when I left, we were winning."

Jackie L. Denfip

Jackie Denfip never was all that eager to go to Vietnam. While working as a truck driver in Mississippi in the spring of 1966, he heard they were looking for truck drivers in Vietnam, but he didn't bother to pursue the lead. "Vietnam didn't mean anything to me then," he says, and in any

Private First Class Jackie L. Denfip with his bride, the former Norma Jean Henson, December 1966.

case he liked the job he had. Gulf Oil Company was building a new re-finery in Pascagoula, on the Gulf of Mexico, and Denfip drove a dump truck, hauling sand and fill to and from the construction site. On the weekends, he could go home to Calvert City, Kentucky, to be with his girlfriend, Norma Jean Henson.

"I had a good job before I joined the Marine Corps," he says. "I shoulda stayed with that." The two-truck company he worked for back then, he observes ruefully, now has five hundred trucks. His regrets notwithstanding, however, the choice wasn't his to make. One weekend a neighbor who sat on the local draft board told Denfip, then 19, that his name was at the top of the list and he could expect to receive a draft no-tice any day.

Faced with the inevitable, he decided to enlist in the Marines for two years. "That wasn't really smart reasoning," he says with a self-deprecating laugh. "I've never had a real good answer for why I [chose the Marines]. I always remember my older brother Don—a picture of him in his dress blue uniform. Maybe that was it."

Jackie Denfip with his granddaughter,
Ashley Lynnette, December 1994.

Denfip describes boot camp as "one long nightmare you woke up from on graduation day. But I never thought I wasn't going to make it. I wasn't afraid. I knew I could do anything. I just didn't know what was going on. And I didn't like having that little DI in my face." That little DI was Sgt. D. S. Bosch, the youngest and most junior of Platoon 1005's three drill instructors. "I could have taken him," Denfip says. "I would have loved to."

Other memories of Parris Island are more pleasant. "I loved the obstacle courses and the Confidence Course [a kind of super obstacle course,]" he says. "That was play to me." And graduation day was one of the proudest days of his life. His only real disappointment at Parris Island came on the day the platoon lost the company drill competition. "We should have won it. We were the best," he says, remembering that Staff Sergeant Oliver later told the platoon that the judges awarded first prize to another platoon only because their senior DI was about to retire.

After boot camp and basic infantry training, Denfip was given a military occupational specialty of 1371, combat engineer, and sent to demolition school at Camp Lejeune, North Carolina. "I was one of those idiots who was supposed to disarm mines," he says. In November 1966, he was assigned to C Company, 13th Engineer Battalion, 5th Marine Division, at Camp Pendleton, California. The company was just being formed; the day he arrived, there were only two other men in his barracks, both of whom had been to demolition school with Denfip.

For the next sixteen months, the men of Denfip's company alternated training themselves with training others. They practiced amphibious landings on the beaches of southern California, and built a floating

bridge across the Colorado River. They put newer Marines from the infantry training regiment through the infamous gas chambers (where you
had to take off your gas mask in a room filled with military-strength tear
gas, called cs gas, and sing the Marine Corps Hymn). They built a Viet
Cong village with nearly a hundred hooches, complete with simulated
mines and booby traps, that Vietnam-bound Marines used for training.
"We 'killed' a million Marines before they got to 'Nam," he says of the
vc village, but then adds that maybe the training saved a few lives, too.

Meanwhile, back in December 1966, he and Norma Jean, then just
17, had been married, and six months later she joined him in California.
By this time, other men in C Company had begun receiving orders to
Vietnam, but Denfip did not because he had less than a year to go on
his enlistment. Soon, however, the Corps began to whittle away at the
minimum requirement for overseas assignment, Denfip says, but his luck
held.

When the requirement was dropped to nine months, he had eight
months and three weeks remaining. When it was dropped to six months,
he had five months and twenty-eight days. "I was scared to death," he
says, admitting frankly that he wanted to go to Vietnam even less by 1968
then he had when he'd been driving a dump truck in Pascagoula.

His luck ran out when the requirement was dropped to three months
and his entire unit got orders for Vietnam. On the day they were to leave,
the men received all their inoculations, and had their gear packed up and
ready to embark, but Norma Jean's airplane, taking her home to Kentucky, had hardly gotten off the ground when Denfip's commanding officer announced that the ship would not be ready to sail until the next day.

With Norma Jean already gone, Denfip had nowhere in particular
to go, but he did have a car, and two buddies talked him into driving them
up to Los Angeles to see their girlfriends one last time. By the time the three
men started back to Pendleton that night, it was very late and Denfip was
very tired, so he let one of the other men drive while he climbed into the
back seat and went to sleep. Waking from that sleep would turn out to be
a small miracle, something like being born again.

Denfip was born the first time in Paducah, Kentucky, but that was
only because his hometown of Calvert City didn't have a hospital. His father installed—and at the time of Denfip's birth, owned and operated—
the first telephone company in Calvert City. The family—a sister and six
brothers, of whom Denfip is the next to youngest—shared their house
with the phone company office and switchboard, which Denfip's mother

operated, but eventually his father sold out to "Ma Bell" because he wasn't making any money.

"My dad was a man of all trades," says Denfip. "He was good at everything. He was a carpenter. A professional hunting guide." Most of what Denfip knows about his father, however, he learned secondhand from his mother and siblings because his father died of a stroke in his fifties when Denfip was just six years old. "I can't remember much about my father," he says. "The older I get, the more that bothers me."

After her husband died, Denfip's mother got by on social security, odd jobs, and the chickens and vegetables she raised. Meanwhile, Denfip grew up playing baseball—Pony League, Little League, pickup games, whatever was available—at least until he was fifteen. Then he bought a 1949 Ford for fifteen dollars. Thereafter, he says, his leisure pursuits consisted of "chasing women and getting drunk—that and drag racing on some side street somewhere."

At sixteen, Denfip quit school and went to Florida with one of his brothers. It was supposed to be a sort of vacation. But Denfip liked it there, so when his brother came home, he stayed, getting a job on a tropical fish farm in Gibsonton, near Tampa. He came home months later only because his mother had become sick with cancer. She never recovered, but his sister and brothers persuaded Denfip to stay home and go back to high school. "I still didn't like it," he says of school, and quit again within the year—but not before he met and began dating Norma Jean.

After leaving school the second time, Denfip took a job with one of his brothers hauling used cars from Detroit to Murray, Kentucky, which he calls "the used car capital of the United States." The cars would be refurbished in Murray, and then Denfip would haul them to auto auctions in Saint Louis, Indianapolis, and other midwestern cities. In Murray he met a truck owner who offered him the job driving a dump truck in Pascagoula, and from there he went to Parris Island and finally to Camp Pendleton, where he was headed on the night he let a buddy drive his car while he climbed into the back seat to sleep.

Denfip woke up two weeks later in the intensive care unit of Santa Ana Community Hospital. He would not be going to Vietnam after all, though chance had picked a tough way to allow him to avoid it. He had sustained a broken hip, broken ribs, and a broken shoulder. His liver had been lacerated, he had a punctured lung, and his spleen had been so badly damaged that the doctors had had to remove it. And while he was in the coma, he had caught pneumonia.

"There was about one tree between L.A. and Pendleton," Denfip says, "and we hit it. We couldn't have hit it more solidly if we'd aimed for it." He assumes the driver must have fallen asleep at the wheel, but he doesn't really know because his two buddies were both killed. He wasn't expected to live either, but he did. He spent the next two months in the hospital—first at Santa Ana, then at Pendleton—and was assigned only to light duty for his remaining weeks in the Corps. He was still on crutches when he was released from active duty.

Denfip came home to Kentucky and went back to work with his brother Bert hauling used cars. Unfortunately, he says, "I got cocky. I threw away my crutches too soon," and his hip began to bow out badly. When it got too painful, he finally went to the Veterans Administration hospital in Marion, Illinois. "All I saw was one-legged people," he says, "and it scared the hell out of me." When a doctor told him they might have to amputate his leg, he left the hospital so hastily that he was still wearing his pajamas. Next he tried the military hospital at Fort Campbell, Kentucky, where he had better luck. This time, however, he was put in a full body cast, just to make sure he didn't throw his crutches away too soon.

When the cast finally came off, he went back to hauling used cars for a while, then spent a year hauling steel out of Calvert City. But in 1971 he decided to become an independent trucker. He bought his own rig, a Ford cab-over, and began hauling produce over the road. "You followed the seasons," he explains of produce hauling. "You started in Florida and worked your way north." Mostly he hauled potatoes and onions "to Detroit, Chicago, and all points in between." All the potatoes, he says, went to various Frito-Lay processing plants to become potato chips.

"It was not a life for a married man," he says. He would be gone for a week at a time, stop by home to get clean cloths, and then be gone again. Often he'd be home as little as three days in a month. Then one day in 1976, he pulled up to his house—by this time he was living in Benton, Kentucky, where he has been ever since—and started throwing all of his things out of the truck. "'What are you doing?' Bert said to me. 'I quit,' I told him. 'I ain't doing this anymore.' I had ulcers and everything else," he says. "And that old truck was about wore out. It was just time to get out."

By this time, he and Norma Jean had two boys, Ricky, born in 1970, and Randy, born in 1973. "That's one of the reasons I quit," he says. "Ricky was getting old enough to play baseball. I started mechanicking and coaching baseball at the same time."

Denfip coached Little League baseball for thirteen years, right up until Ricky graduated from high school. He also got a job as a mechanic at a local Dodge-Chrysler dealership, though he'd never had any formal training as a mechanic. If you buy a fifteen-year-old car for fifteen dollars when you're fifteen years old, he explains, you learn to be your own mechanic. During this time, Denfip also began auto racing on the dirt track circuit, but he never won a race and quit after a year. "It's not a poor man's hobby," he says, succinctly summing up his brief racing career.

After two years with the Dodge dealership and a year with a General Motors dealer, Denfip decided once again to go into business for himself and bought a service station. "I thought I was going to make a million dollars running it," he says, "but I was there about a year and went bankrupt." The main problem was that Denfip hadn't outgrown his love of baseball, and coaching Little League just didn't give him enough of a "baseball fix," so he'd organized and become the president of the Benton Men's Softball League of Marshall County, Kentucky. There were eight teams, and they played doubleheaders every Sunday starting at 1:00 P.M.

Everything was going fine with both the gas station and the softball league until one Sunday afternoon when Denfip tried to slide into base, got stepped on by the baseman, and ended up with twenty-seven bone fragments where his ankle used to be. He spent the next nine months in a hip cast. Try fixing somebody's carburetor or changing a set of shock absorbers while you're hobbling around in a hip cast. "I tried to," he says, "but I just couldn't do anything." By the time the cast came off, he was in dire financial straits. "It put me so far behind," he says, "I just sold out."

Fortunately, it didn't take long to find a position with another local dealership, Phillips Chevrolet. Indeed, they called him as soon as they heard he was available. "I had a good reputation as a mechanic," he explains, "and a good mechanic can get a job just about anywhere. As a matter of fact, I'm looking for one right here." ("Here" is Country Chevrolet in Benton.) In 1985, Phillips sold out to Pete Gunn General Motors. In 1992, Denfip was promoted from mechanic ("They call them service technicians these days," he says) to service manager. And in 1994, Gunn became Country Chevrolet, where I interviewed Denfip on May 11, 1996.

Only one Jackie L. Denfip had appeared on the Myers list, and he'd replied to my initial search letter with a polite but brief letter of his own dated September 14, 1993. He acknowledged having been in Platoon 1005 and added, "We appreciate receiving your letter and look forward to hearing from you." In May 1996 I flew to Louisville, where I rented a car, crossed the Ohio River to visit Jerry Bowles, then drove down to southwestern Kentucky to see Denfip and Steven W. Dudley. I interviewed Denfip in his office at Country Chevrolet. Though I never did think to ask him why he'd used the plural "we" rather than the singular "I" throughout his four-sentence letter back in 1993, I asked him a lot of other questions, which he patiently answered.

As service manager, Denfip oversees an assistant manager, five mechanics, and a department that handles on average about thirty cars each working day. He still gets his hands dirty, though, helping his less-experienced mechanics troubleshoot problems. "I still get under the hood every day," he says. "Every day. I show these guys what to do." He is also president this year of the Heartbeat of America Service Managers Club, a trade organization that encompasses twenty dealerships in Kentucky, Missouri, Illinois, and Tennessee.

Also this year, Denfip earned inclusion in Chevrolet's "Only the Best Club" for exemplary service management based on customer satisfaction and other criteria. Along with the "Only the Best" plaque that hangs on the wall of his office, the award earned Denfip a trip for two to Florida and a set of golf clubs, though he's quick to say, "I'm not a golfer. I just play. I'm lucky to get out once a month."

He can't even say that much about baseball these days. His shattered ankle didn't keep him off the diamond longer than it took to get the cast off, but age finally caught up to him three years ago. He was playing in a church league softball game when he almost got hit in the face by a line drive before he could get his glove up. "My reflexes were gone," he says. "I realized it was time to quit."

Ricky had long since outgrown Little League, and Randy never did take to it, so Denfip's coaching days were already over. He's even given up the umpiring he used to do for the American Softball Association. "I was an old man trying to act like a young man," he says of umpiring. "It was supposed to be for enjoyment, but you're always arguing with someone." These days, his major recreational activities take the form of watching dirt track auto racing, riding his Honda motorcycle, and playing with 3-year-old granddaughter Ashley Lynnette, Ricky's child.

Had it not been for luck or the grace of God some twenty-eight years ago, there would be no Ashley Lynnette, nor any Ricky or Randy. That terrible accident, of course, had the ironic effect of keeping Denfip out of Vietnam, an outcome he had wanted all along. "I didn't want to go," he says of the war, "but that was then. Now I feel like I got cheated. There's something that happened that I didn't get to share."

Kelly W. Dilday

"I'm still wearing green and polishing my boots," Kelly Dilday told me on September 9, 1993, "but nobody yells at me. I'm as happy as a lark."

The letter I sent to the only Kelly W. Dilday on the Myers list came back marked "Forwarding Order Expired," and the telephone number on the list didn't work either, but I thought that if he hadn't moved too far, maybe he would have a new telephone listing, so I called directory assistance for Windsor, North Carolina, his last address. A new number was indeed listed, and when I called, it turned out to belong to the right Kelly Dilday.

In the course of this conversation and two others on March 18, 1996, and June 13, 1997, supplemented by records received from NPRC, I learned that Dilday was born in Suffolk, Virginia, on November 30, 1947, but grew up in Windsor. He joined the Marines on the Buddy Plan with Jessie F. Waters, and qualified as a Rifle Marksman in boot camp.

Achieving the rank of sergeant, he served four years on active duty, including thirteen months in 1967–68 with Company C, 1st Engineer Battalion, in Vietnam. While in Vietnam, he performed highway minesweeping duties and participated in five major combat operations. His decorations include the Navy Achievement Medal with Combat V for Valor, the Combat Action Ribbon, a Meritorious Unit Citation, and the Good Conduct, National Defense Service, Vietnam Service, and Vietnam Campaign Medals.

After his release from active duty, he became a wildlife officer for the state of North Carolina—thus the comment about wearing green and polishing his boots. He spent his entire career around Windsor, turning down promotions in order to stay in the area because he owns a farm there with his brother and doesn't want to leave. Dilday's son graduated from the University of North Carolina at Wilmington in 1993 with a degree in marine biology. Divorced in the early 1990s, Dilday remarried in August 1995 and retired as a state wildlife officer in January 1997. He still enjoys the outdoors and keeps a boat and weekend retreat on the sound side of the Outer Banks.

Steven E. Dudley

In a brief handwritten letter dated September 16, 1994, Dudley asked my forgiveness if he sounded rude, but said that he did not want to remember the past or be interviewed. A previous letter, received May 2, 1994, confirmed that Dudley had been a member of Platoon 1005 and gave the general outlines of his subsequent military service, but also said that his private life was his and nobody else's.

Both letters carried the return address of a National Oceanographic and Atmospheric Administration research vessel, an address I'd gotten from MIE, Inc., via the VA claim number route. Because I, too, had worked on ships—an Irish freighter in 1969 and a U.S. tanker in 1973 and 1974— I was curious to know how Dudley had ended up on a ship and what his duties were (the style and substance of the letters does not suggest that Dudley is a research scientist), but he never replied to my third letter.

From NPRC, I learned that he was born April 16, 1948, did not finish high school, and was living in Kentucky at the time of his enlistment. After boot camp and basic infantry training, he received further training at the motor transport school, Camp Lejeune, North Carolina, before being assigned to the Motor Transport Company, Service Battalion, Marine Corps Station, Quantico, Virginia, as an auto mechanic (3516) from November 1966 to March 1967.

Dudley served in Vietnam from May 1967 to May 1968, from May to October with Company C, 3rd Motor Transport Battalion, first as an auto mechanic, then as a motor vehicle operator (3531), and from October to May with Service Company, 11th Engineering Battalion, again as an auto mechanic. He was released from active duty in May 1968 with the rank of lance corporal; his decorations include a Presidential Unit Citation and the National Defense Service, Vietnam Service, and Vietnam Campaign Medals.

Dudley is the first cousin of Steven W. Dudley.

Steven W. Dudley

Anyone anywhere near Dong Ha on the morning of September 3, 1967, is not likely to forget it. North Vietnamese and Viet Cong rocket, mortar, and artillery attacks against the Marine base and airfield were almost routine by then, of course. The rounds would come in, frantic shouts of "Incoming!" would be raised, the warning sirens would go off, and everyone would scramble for cover and hope for the best. Sometimes there would be casualties, sometimes not; sometimes the damage would be extensive, sometimes not.

But on the morning of September 3, some nameless, faceless Vietnamese gunner hit the jackpot of jackpots—three cherries all in a row and out come the silver dollars—igniting what must have been the biggest conflagration of the Vietnam War. The entire bulk fuel farm of Force Logistics Support Unit One went up in flames. Guard towers were blown down. Seventeen helicopters were destroyed or damaged. As the fires raged,

Private First Class Steven W. Dudley arriving home in Paducah, Kentucky, after thirteen months in Vietnam, December 1967.

Steven W. Dudley with grandson Steven Michael Hulsey, 1995.

secondary explosions continued through much of the day, cooking off fifteen thousand tons of stockpiled ammunition. The column of smoke could be seen in Phu Bai, forty miles to the south.

One of the Marines who was there that day was Private First Class Steven W. Dudley of 3rd Shore Party Battalion. Dudley had been on perimeter guard all night, and had not yet been relieved. "We heard the rocket come in," he says. When the secondary explosions began, he thought at first that it was more rockets, but he soon came to believe that the entire chain of events began when a single rocket hit a fuel cell. (According to the 1967 volume of *U.S. Marines in Vietnam,* the incident began when enemy artillery hit Dong Ha combat base.)

Perimeter guards were ordered to hold their posts and be on the alert for a possible VC ground attack attempting to exploit the chaos of the situation, but Dudley says, "We knew the VC wouldn't be coming because we couldn't get out of our holes." Shrapnel and debris from the continuing secondary explosions "kept us in our holes all day," he says. "We didn't stick our heads up very much," he adds, though he could see enough to realize that exploding fuel cells had burned down his entire company area.

Dudley remembers thinking that no one in the company area could have survived, and was much relieved to learn subsequently that no one from his company was killed or even wounded seriously. That was the good news. The bad news was that Dudley would have to spend not just the rest of the day on the perimeter, but the entire next two weeks because there was nowhere to go until a new company area could be built.

Back home in Paducah, Kentucky, Dudley's wife had no idea any of this had happened to her husband. "His letters never said anything," she says, sitting across from him twenty-nine years later in the living room of their ranch-style home on the outskirts of Paducah. "He never told me what he was really doing or what was going on. He still doesn't talk much about Vietnam. That's why I've been listening so carefully. That's why Jeremy [the younger of the Dudley's two children] has been sitting here."

Lifelong natives of Paducah, where I spent a Sunday afternoon with the Dudleys on May 12, 1996, Steve and Pat have been together for a long time. They had their first date when they were 16 and she was still Patricia Ann Jackson. Dudley proposed on their second date (they were at the South Twin Drive-In Theater, though neither of them can now remember what movie they were supposed to be watching). They got married in November 1966. "Right before he went to Vietnam," says Pat. "What a honeymoon."

Dudley grew up playing baseball and basketball, fishing, swimming, and hunting rabbits and squirrels. In high school, he parked cars at the Midtown Parking Lot next to J. C. Penney's and collected tickets at the same drive-in where his marriage proposal was offered and accepted. Though he and Pat were already engaged when he graduated from Lone Oak High School in June 1966, he joined the Marines, he says, "because of John Kennedy. Do something for your country."

As to which branch of service to join, he adds, there was never any choice: "Go with the best. That's the way I thought about it." He enlisted for two years, he says, instead of three or four, "because I wanted to do what I could for the country, but I didn't want to stay in forever." He also enlisted on the Buddy Plan with his first cousin, Steven E. Dudley of Frankfort, Kentucky.

Dudley had heard a lot about what to expect on Parris Island before he arrived there. "My recruiter was thoroughly honest with me," he says, adding that he'd also gotten straight talk from his brother, who was ten years older and had also been in the Corps. Still, he says of boot camp, "I was really surprised that it was as bad as people had said. I thought they were exaggerating."

Being one of two Steven Dudleys in Platoon 1005 didn't make life any easier, either. "We used to get in trouble just because we had the same last name," he says. "At mail call, the DI would call out, 'Dudley,' and we'd have to shout, 'Sir, which one, sir?' So the DI would say, 'Steven,' and we'd still have to shout, 'Sir, which one, sir?'"

From his first day in the platoon, Dudley was assigned to the so-called Fat Body Platoon, those recruits the DIs considered overweight, who were allowed to eat only meat, dry cereal, lettuce, and skim milk. One day during supper at the rifle range, five or six weeks into boot camp, Drill Instructor Evans caught Dudley taking extra food. Dudley thought he was in for it, but Evans began by asking what score Dudley had fired that day. When Dudley told him—fortunately, he'd fired a good score—Evans just walked away. Though nothing got said explicitly, it was the de facto end of Dudley's inclusion in the Fat Body Platoon.

"I enjoyed the rifle range," says Dudley. "I was the one Evans said, 'Don't use Kentucky windage [an improvisational technique for sighting with a rifle].' After we got our shooting badges, Evans asked me how I did [so well]. I told him 'Kentucky windage.' He said, 'Don't ever tell another soul.'"

Out of boot camp, Dudley was assigned a military occupational specialty of 1381, shore party man. "They're actually the police of the beach," he explains, taking charge of virtually everything that arrives at a landing beach or an aerial landing zone. While still in shore party school, most of the members of Dudley's class—including Francis Langley of Platoon 1005—received orders to Vietnam, but Dudley got orders for 2nd Shore Party Battalion at Camp Lejeune, North Carolina. When Dudley, eager to go to Vietnam, complained about his assignment, his first sergeant was able to get the orders changed, but the delay ultimately resulted in Dudley's going to 3rd SP Battalion while everyone else in his class went to 1st SP Battalion.

Upon completion of shore party school, Dudley came home and got married, then left for staging at Camp Pendleton, California, arriving in Vietnam just in time to eat Christmas dinner in Dong Ha. A month later, however, his whole company was sent to an island off the coast, in the vicinity of Hue and Phu Bai, where jet and helicopter fuel was stored. "It was sort of like being on R&R," he says of the island. Base special services regularly organized beer parties on the beach, and Dudley even learned to surf there, courtesy of the surfboards provided by special services.

There were several villages on the island, and the Marines used to patrol both on foot and by amphibious tractor, but they never made contact with the vc, receiving exactly one round of sniper fire the entire time Dudley was on the island. After several months, however, Dudley's company rotated back to Dong Ha. He spent the rest of his tour there, except for occasional two-week trips to places like Hill 881 and Con Thien as a member of various helicopter support teams, and a truck convoy to Khe Sanh to deliver supplies.

Only near the end of his tour in December 1967 did Dudley learn that Francis Langley, with whom he'd become close friends through infantry training, shore party school, and staging battalion, had been killed in a helicopter crash nearly a year earlier. Dudley believes now that the foul-up of his original orders, which finally resulted in his going to 3rd sp Battalion instead of 1st sp Battalion, "probably saved my life." He reasons that he, too, might have been on the helicopter that killed Langley. Pat adds that it took her husband a long time to accept Langley's death. "He used to get depressed about it," she says.

Dudley served out the remainder of his enlistment with 2nd sp Battalion at Camp Lejeune, where every Friday afternoon, he says, his company would have to go on a twenty-mile forced march before being dismissed for the weekend. They also washed trucks and practiced beach landings. "It seemed like he did a lot of guard duty, too," says Pat, to which her husband replies, "That was just routine."

The Dudleys had a small apartment just outside the front gate of Camp Gieger, one of Lejeune's satellite camps. Pat remembers a fancy restaurant near the apartment, but then adds, "Everything to us was fancy back then. We didn't have any money." Once, in an effort to save money, Pat washed and starched Dudley's utility uniforms instead of sending them out to a professional laundry, but the spray starch she used left spots on the uniforms, and whatever money she had saved was more than cancelled by the grief Dudley got at the next inspection.

That spring Dudley, then a lance corporal, was offered a Caribbean cruise if he would extend his enlistment by three months, but he declined, and in June 1968 he and Pat went back to Paducah. He spent the next ten months as an ironworker, a builder of radiators, and a gas pump jockey before finally being hired as a patrol officer by the Paducah Police Department.

"It took a long time for the hiring to get approved because the city commissioners had to vote on it," he explains. While he was awaiting approval, the Dudleys' daughter Debra Lee was born. Had she been born one day later, medical insurance from his new job would have covered all the costs of delivery, but as it was, Dudley had to give the hospital his entire first paycheck as a police officer before they would release Pat and the baby.

Dudley spent three and a half years as a police officer, but he found the job too political for his liking. When he begins to elaborate on what he means, his wife quietly but firmly cautions him to consider his words carefully. "A lot of things were interesting," he says enigmatically, and lets it go at that.

Over the next seven years, Dudley worked a variety of jobs, trying to find the right niche for himself. He spent two years as a concrete inspector for Dravo-Groves-Newburg, a construction company building the Smithland Lock and Dam on the Ohio River under contract to the U.S. Army Corps of Engineers. When the locks were almost completed, he left Dravo to become a machinist apprentice with the Illinois Central Railroad, but was laid off after only eight months. "That was a real shocker," he says. "The railroad was supposed to be building up."

He next sold insurance for National Life for fourteen months, and did well at it, but discovered that he could never take time off. "You worked six days a week," he says, "and if you took vacation, the work backed up too much." Still looking for the right job, he spent four months as an assistant manager of a convenience store before taking a higher-paying job with Union Carbide as a maintenance mechanic, welder, and pipe fitter at a uranium enrichment plant, a job he held for the next three years.

During those three years, 1976 through 1979, Dudley went on Army active reserve duty with the 100th Division. His outfit was a unit of drill sergeants. At weekend meetings, the men would take turns being drill sergeants while everyone else would play the part of recruits. During summer camp, he says, "We went to Fort Knox and played with tanks." Entering as an E3, the same rank at which he'd left the Corps, Dudley worked his way up to E5 before the pressures and demands of yet another new job made it impossible to continue in the reserves.

That new job was with the federal Tennessee Valley Authority, where he's been ever since. TVA put Dudley through a two-year program, including eighteen months in the classroom and six months of on-the-job training, after which he was assigned as an assistant unit operator at

TVA's 150-megawatt Shawnee Steam Plant on the Ohio River in West Paducah. (The irony, he says, is that while he works for TVA and lives only miles from the Shawnee plant, his own home is powered by Kentucky Utilities.)

Dudley and I hop into his pickup truck and drive over to the plant for a quick tour. It's an impressive facility. To begin with, it is huge, containing ten units, each unit consisting of a coal-fired boiler and steam turbine. Above the building housing the boilers and turbines stand ten smokestacks, each several hundred feet tall. These are flanked—and dwarfed—by two additional stacks, each of these nine hundred feet tall, which have made the ten shorter stacks obsolete. Coal for the boilers arrives at the plant by rail and by river barge, and the electricity produced is entered onto a power grid through a vast array of transformers and high-tension wires. Once onto the grid, this power can be transferred to almost any place in the United States where it's needed.

As an assistant unit operator, Dudley's main job is to sit in a monitoring station (there is one monitoring station for every two units) and keep watch over a solid wall of instruments and dials and gauges—and a desktop full of computers—that make the room look like Mission Control at the Johnson Space Center. If and when problems arise, he must begin the process of initiating repairs, which usually means preparing a work order. "The operator runs the plant," he says. "The assistant operator does the leg work."

When he's not working, Dudley will sometimes accompany Pat on her visits to the two community dialysis clinics she has set up in southwestern Kentucky. (A registered nurse, Pat is the head of the dialysis unit at Paducah's Lourdes Hospital.) He still occasionally does a little hunting, too. But mostly, he says, "I take care of my grandbaby. My grandchild is my hobby."

His grandchild is Steven Michael Hulsey, born in 1995 to daughter Debra, who's a Murray State University graduate and a social worker at a nursing home in nearby Mayfield, and son-in-law Tommy, a high school and junior high history teacher. Dudley's son Jeremy, officially Steven Jeremy Dudley, is a high school student, class of 1997. "He's our firecracker," Pat says of Jeremy, who was born on July 4.

As for the war in Vietnam, Dudley thinks the United States lost because of "a failure of political will," he says. "I didn't think we were going to lose until way after I got back [to the U.S.]. I never would have dreamed we'd lose that war. Not then. When I was there, I thought we were winning the war. Anything we wanted to take, we took. We were definitely superior to their armed forces. We just didn't have the right people making decisions—take ground and hold it. We should have invaded North Vietnam."

Wayne A. Duffey

According to records received from NPRC, Duffey was born November 14, 1948. He was living in Camden, New Jersey, at the time of his enlistment, and had completed only tenth grade, though he later earned a General Equivalency Diploma. After boot camp, basic infantry training, and special weapons training, he was assigned to Headquarters & Support Company, 3rd Battalion, 8th Marines, at Camp Lejeune, North Carolina, as a 106mm recoilless rifleman (0351). From November 1966 until May 1967, Duffey's unit participated in a Mediterranean cruise aboard the USS *Fremont,* including stops in Spain, Italy, France, Corsica, Sardinia, Malta, Greece, and Crete.

Duffey then served in Vietnam from July 1967 to July 1968, first with K Company, 3rd Battalion, 9th Marines, as a gunner, ammunition man, and fire team leader, then with C Company, 3rd Recon Battalion, as a rifleman and squad leader, and finally with Headquarters & Support Company of 3rd Recon as assistant police NCO and then mail clerk. Duffey participated in ten major combat operations. He was wounded by shrapnel on two successive days in February 1968 near the Demilitarized Zone, but apparently neither injury required evacuation. In addition to his two Purple Hearts, his other decorations include the Combat Action Ribbon, a Presidential Unit Citation, a Meritorious Unit Citation, and the National Defense Service, Vietnam Service, and Vietnam Campaign Medals.

In August 1968, Duffey was assigned to the Naval Amphibious School, Little Creek, Norfolk, Virginia, as an instructor, apparently returning to his original MOS of 0351, 106mm recoilless rifles. He was released from active duty in July 1969 with the rank of sergeant.

I found no further trace of Duffey after his service in the Marine Corps, nor can the VA find any record of his ever having applied for veterans' benefits.

William D. Ehrhart

Ehrhart was born in Roaring Spring, Pennsylvania, on September 30, 1948, and graduated from Pennridge High School in Perkasie, Pennsylvania, in June 1966. Under the delayed enlistment program, he joined the Marines on April 11, 1966, and began active duty on June 17. While at Parris Island, he qualified as a Rifle Sharpshooter. Upon graduation, he received a meritorious promotion to private first class.

Ehrhart's first duty assignment after boot camp and basic infantry training was with Marine Aircraft Group 26 at MCAF New River, North Carolina, where he received on-the-job training in combat intelligence from October to December 1966. During this time, he also received temporary assignments to Montford Point, Camp Lejeune, where he completed a clerk-typist course in November, and to the Enlisted Basic Am-

Corporal William D. Ehrhart, 1st Battalion, 1st Marines, Con Thien, Vietnam, November 1967.

The Ehrhart family, 1995: Bill, wife Anne, and daughter Leela.

phibious Intelligence School at Naval Amphibious Base, Little Creek, Norfolk, Virginia, where he graduated first in his class in December.

After additional combat training with the 3rd Replacement Company, Staging Battalion, Camp Pendleton, California, Ehrhart left for Vietnam on February 9, 1967, and spent thirteen months with 1st Battalion, 1st Marine Regiment, first as an intelligence assistant, then as assistant intelligence chief. In March 1967 he was temporarily assigned to the Sukiran Army Education Center on Okinawa, where he graduated first in his class in basic Vietnamese terminology. While in Vietnam, Ehrhart participated in more than a dozen combat operations including the siege of Con Thien and the battle for Hue, where he was wounded by shrapnel from a B-40 rocket, though not evacuated. He received promotions to lance corporal in April 1967 and corporal in July 1967, and left Vietnam on February 28, 1968.

His next assignment was with the Headquarters Group of 2nd Marine Air Wing at MCAS Cherry Point, North Carolina, where he served from March to June 1968, receiving a promotion to sergeant in April. After a brief assignment with Headquarters Squadron of MAG-15 at MCAS Iwakuni, Japan, he was reassigned to Marine Aerial Refueler Transport

Squadron 152 at MCAF Futema, Okinawa, from July through October 1968. He completed his active duty with Marine Fighter Attack Squadron 122, based alternately at Iwakuni and Naval Air Station, Cubi Point, the Philippines, receiving his release from active duty on June 10, 1969.

Ehrhart's awards and decorations include the Purple Heart, Good Conduct, National Defense Service, Vietnam Service, and Vietnam Campaign Medals, the Combat Action Ribbon, two Presidential Unit Citations, a commendation from the commanding general of the 1st Marine Division, a Meritorious Mast from the commanding officer of VMGR-152, a Cross of Gallantry Meritorious Unit Citation, and a Civil Actions Meritorious Unit Citation. He was honorably discharged on April 10, 1972, with the rank of staff sergeant.

Ehrhart subsequently earned a BA from Swarthmore College in 1973 and an MA from the University of Illinois at Chicago in 1978. Over the years, he has worked as a construction laborer, merchant seaman aboard Irish and American vessels, warehouseman and forklift operator, legal aide for the Pennsylvania Department of Justice, roofer, reporter, political writer, health writer, and teacher at both the high school and college levels, but in recent years has mostly made his living as a freelance writer, poet, and lecturer.

He has held appointments as Visiting Professor of War and Social Consequences at the William Joiner Center, University of Massachusetts at Boston, Poet-in-Residence at the Downtown Detroit YMCA, and Artist-in-Residence at Unit One/Allen Hall, University of Illinois at Champaign-Urbana, and has received a Mary Roberts Rinehart Foundation grant, two Pennsylvania Arts Council fellowships, and a Pew Fellowship in the Arts. Currently, he is a research fellow of the American Studies Department, University of Wales at Swansea, United Kingdom.

After his release from active duty, Ehrhart became active with Vietnam Veterans Against the War, contributing poems to *Winning Hearts and Minds: War Poems by Vietnam Veterans,* edited by Larry Rottmann, Jan Barry, and Basil T. Paquet. Since then, he has published hundreds of poems, stories, essays, and articles, along with over a dozen books of prose and poetry. His books have been taught in high schools and colleges including the U.S. Military Academy, the U.S. Naval Academy, and the U.S. Air Force Academy. He has been a participant in the annual National Security Seminar at the U.S. Army War College, Carlisle Barracks, and he served as a reviewer for *1968: The Defining Year,* a 1997 volume of the U.S. Marine Corps series *The U.S. Marines in Vietnam.*

Ehrhart has been married since 1981 to the former Anne Senter Gulick. They live in Philadelphia, Pennsylvania, with their daughter, Leela, born in 1986.

Thomas O. Erickson

The first time Tom Erickson encountered the obstacle course at Parris Island, South Carolina, it nearly killed him. One of the obstacles was an eight-foot wooden wall with a smooth face. You had to jump up and hook your fingers over the top, then haul yourself up, roll over the top, and drop to the other side. Erickson had played center and linebacker on the varsity football team back at Washington Irving High School in Clarksburg, West Virginia, so he was no couch potato, but his massive bulk was much better suited to pushing tackling sleds and blocking for nimble halfbacks than to climbing and rolling over eight-foot walls.

After several game attempts to go over the wall, Erickson started to go around it. Suddenly drill instructors materialized out of nowhere, bellowing as if they had bullhorns in their throats instead of vocal chords. "Where do you think you're going, puke?! Get over that wall!!" The other seventy-nine members of Platoon 1005 were called off the course and ordered to stand at attention, watching in platoon formation as Erickson hurled himself against the wall over and over again, a circle of animated DIS surrounding him like a gaggle of angry hornets, buzzing, stinging, shouting.

It was an object lesson in what would happen to each of us if ever we failed to do what the DIS ordered us to do—even if we were physically incapable of doing it. But it also became, by the time it was over, a powerful testament to what a human being can do when driven by fear and adrenalin. After what seemed like forever, and with Senior Drill Instructor Oliver sitting on top of the wall, shouting, "You gonna get over or I'm gonna kick you over," Erickson reached down deep inside to a place he'd never even known existed, and found the strength and the will to get himself over that wall.

Boot camp was a harrowing and largely solitary experience. Each man lived within his own thoughts and fears and dreams. There was little opportunity to make friends, and the only people you remember are maybe

*Corporal Thomas O. Erickson, 3rd Engineer Battalion,
Vietnam, 1968*

your "bunkie" and a handful of others who made some lasting impression
for one reason or another. One man remembers this person, another remembers that person. But the more men I spoke with, the more I came to
realize that virtually everyone remembers Tom Erickson. And they speak
about him respectfully, as often as not with a sense of awe edging their
voices.

Erickson arrived at Parris Island carrying 250 pounds on his five-
foot-nine-inch frame. By graduation day, he weighed 165 pounds. That's
85 pounds in eight weeks. If that isn't awesome, nothing ever was or ever
will be. "Lettuce and skim milk," Erickson says. "That's the only thing I
ate three times a day. They made me wear the same pair of trousers the
whole time. By the end I could put both fists down my trousers."

A 1966 high school graduate, he had joined the Marines because "a
buddy dared me to join, so I did. Morrison, too [football teammate and
fellow Platoon 1005er David Morrison]. He dared us both." It was Er-

ickson's first time away from home, and he can't remember now if they rode the bus all the way from West Virginia to South Carolina, or if they flew part of the way. [They flew, according to another West Virginian, Timothy Jenkins.] "I was too scared to remember," Erickson says. "I was scared of everything. I didn't know what to expect."

What he got was raging DIS, lettuce, and skim milk. There were times in the dead of night, he says, when he seriously considered taking his chances with the snake-infested swamp behind the barracks and the long swim beyond the swamp from Parris Island to the mainland, "but Morrison would always talk me out of it." And as the weeks passed and the pounds came off, he began to understand that the DIS were actually rooting for him, especially Staff Sergeant Oliver.

"He did everything he could to get me through boot camp," Erickson says. "That's why I respected Oliver. He didn't give up on me." To-

Tom Erickson in 1996 with his dog, Sugar. "She's my pride and joy," he says of Sugar.

ward the end, when Erickson was still struggling to climb the knotted rope, a requirement for graduation, Oliver even had another recruit surreptitiously climb in Erickson's place. "I never could do that," Erickson says of the rope, but after all he'd accomplished, few of his fellow platoon mates begrudged him Oliver's deception.

After boot camp, Erickson was assigned a military occupational specialty of 0141, administrative clerk. "I wanted to be a cook so bad," he says, "but I ended up in an office." He also wanted to go to Vietnam, but he ended up at the Marine Air Reserve Training Center at Naval Air Station, Glenview, Illinois, twenty miles north of Chicago. He saw his first major league baseball game at Wrigley Field in Chicago. He also bought his first car in Chicago, a 1952 Pontiac with a 1953 truck engine. "As far as I know," he says, "it's still sitting in the middle of the Kennedy Expressway." He'd repeatedly requested orders for Vietnam, and finally got them in July 1967. "The car broke down the day before I was supposed to leave for [Vietnam via Camp] Pendleton. I took the plates and registration, and left it where it sat. Heck, I only paid seventy-five dollars for it."

He took no leave before departing for Vietnam. "I was just so anxious to get to Vietnam," he explains. "Just for the fun of it. I just wanted to see some action." Instead of action, however, he got Headquarters Company of the 3rd Marine Division, where he spent his first two months on mess duty before being assigned to the staff section. "I wanted to get out where the action was," he says. Not satisfied with his assignment, and after still more requests for a transfer, he was finally assigned to the 3rd Engineer Battalion.

A month later, he finally got to see some action when the Tet Offensive of 1968 came to Dong Ha and he found himself in charge of a .50-caliber machine gun. A lieutenant told him that if the Viet Cong overran the perimeter, he was supposed to pick up the gun and run for it. "No way," Erickson thought to himself, contemplating the prospect of carrying so awkward and heavy an object while trying to outrun advancing enemy soldiers. "I'll drop a grenade under it." Fortunately, it never came to that.

By June 1968, Erickson was the administrative chief of the 3rd Engineers. By this time, he was having doubts about the war. "I thought it was a useless war," he explains. "We weren't getting anywhere because the politicians were fighting it instead of letting the generals fight it. We had to get permission to load our weapons. You can't fight a war like that." In spite of his doubts, he continued to discharge his duties well enough to earn a Navy Achievement Medal. "I knew it had to be done," he says of his job. "I was looking for the next stripe. At that time, I had all intentions of staying in."

Leaving Vietnam in August 1968, Erickson spent the next eighteen months clerking for the chief of staff of the 2nd Marine Air Wing at Marine Corps Air Station, Cherry Point, North Carolina. "Oh, I loved that," he says of Cherry Point. "If I could have stayed there, I'd have stayed in for sure." By February 1969 he had earned his third stripe, and he and two other sergeants were living in a rented house at the beach. "I'd get up every morning and take a swim in the ocean before going to work," he says.

In December, with six months remaining on his original four-year enlistment, he reenlisted for another six years. He requested recruiting duty, but didn't get it because he was too heavy. "Bad image, I guess," he says, explaining that he'd regained much—though not all—of the weight he'd lost three years earlier. Instead, he was sent to Headquarters Marine Corps in Arlington, Virginia. He didn't like it there at all. "Too much brass," he says. "Spit and polish. It seemed like we had an inspection every day." Already unhappy, he was none too pleased when his first sergeant told him in November 1970 that he had to lose fifty pounds or get out of the Corps. When a legal officer told him the discharge would be honorable—officially a medical discharge under honorable conditions—he decided to take it.

Back in Clarksburg, Erickson pumped Exxon gas for six months before landing a job as a road construction inspector with the West Virginia Department of Highways. He helped to build the massive interchange where I-79 and I-68 come together just south of Morgantown. "That was fascinating," he says. "They moved a lot of dirt there." He took a particular interest in dirt since his job was to test its compaction. "The harder it is, the better," he explains, "because you don't want it to wash away once you put the concrete on it."

The job wasn't unionized, however, so the pay wasn't very good. After two years, he took a better-paying job as a stockroom supervisor with J. C. Penney. At about this time, he met Shirley Kerns at the Evangelical Congregational Church of Clarksburg. "The preacher introduced us after services one Sunday," he says, and they began dating. "I proposed to her pretty quickly, but it took her a year to answer me." They were married in April 1974.

Meanwhile, after two years at Penney's without a pay raise, Erickson went to work for Chesapeake & Potomac Telephone in July 1975, spending the next two years as a clerk before becoming an outside plant technician. As a technician, he worked with both aerial and underground cables. One of his assignments was to help lay a new cable from Clarksburg to Palestine, West Virginia, a distance of sixty miles. "I had to walk every inch of it," he says. "I had to inspect every pole. I did it by myself. It took me six months."

In April 1985, C&P transferred Erickson from Clarksburg to Washington, D.C., where he became an inside plant engineer. His job was to assign AT&T cable pairs to the then newly founded long distance carriers, MCI and Sprint. Because housing was so expensive in and around the capital, however, the Ericksons (now including son Philip, born in 1979) had to live seventy-five miles south of Washington in Fredericksburg, Virginia. Erickson found himself getting up at 3:00 A.M. to be at work by 8:00 and often not getting home again until 10:00 or 11:00 P.M. "That's the reason the job wore thin after a while," he says.

In June 1986, Erickson's father, retired and living in Florida, had a stroke. Tired of the long commute, and anxious to help his mother care for his father, Erickson quit C&P and moved to Florida, where he took a job driving a school bus for the Lee County Department of Education. He stayed for a year and a half, but Shirley didn't like it there—"She said it was too hot," he explains—so when his father was fully recovered, Erickson returned to West Virginia with Shirley and Philip.

He had hoped to land a job as a C&P operator, but was turned down because he turned out to be 95 percent deaf in one ear (not service connected), so he went to work at a Shoney's restaurant in Clarksburg, finally fulfilling his wish to be a cook. After three months, he received a promotion to kitchen manager at another Shoney's, this time in Parkersburg, West Virginia, and a year later, he was promoted to relief manager and sent to Zanesville, Ohio. He stayed there two years before being offered a manager's position at a Shoney's in Maryland. "That's the reason I quit Shoney's," he says. "They kept moving me around."

He returned to Parkersburg, and from January to October 1992, went to computer school, "but it didn't do me a lot of good," he says. "I'm a janitor. You don't need a computer to be a janitor." After he left Shoney's, he had taken the civil service general aptitude test, and had gotten several calls for job interviews, but each of them involved relocating for only a temporary position, so he declined the interviews. Finally he was offered a position with the U.S. Treasury Department's Bureau of

Public Debt in Parkersburg. "I started out as a messenger," he says. "It was the very bottom, but you've got to start somewhere. After two years I got a promotion—believe it or not—to janitor."

As a janitor, his job is to clean carpets. He works with two other people on a 10:00 P.M. to 6:30 A.M. shift in a building with 250 rooms on five floors. The crew starts on the fifth floor and works its way down to the first floor. It takes six months to do the entire building. When they're finished, they go back up to the fifth floor and start again. He likes the night shift because there is little supervision. "They know if we do the job," he says. "If we don't, they'll let us know."

Things haven't been easy for Erickson, especially in recent years. He had to declare bankruptcy four years ago, making it hard to obtain credit. He sometimes struggles with depression. He also has serious back problems that cause his lower legs to hurt whenever he's standing, and he's currently taking seven different prescription medicines, but he keeps working anyway. "You gotta do it," he says. "There's people worse off than I am."

No doubt there are, but you wouldn't have known it on September 19, 1996, the day I came to visit and found Erickson coughing and wheezing with the flu and a fever. He could have canceled our appointment with a clear conscience, and for the sake of his own health certainly should have, but he insisted on going ahead with it, saying it was the least he could do after I'd driven all the way from Philadelphia to Parkersburg. Sitting in a recliner chair in his living room, he managed to field my questions for nearly five hours.

Recently, he and Shirley, who cares for shut-in senior citizens for the West Virginia Department of Human Services, were able to buy a small house with no money down through the trust department of a bank. If they make the payments, in four years they'll own the house outright. They are slowly recarpeting, repaneling, and reinsulating as time, energy, and money become available.

When he's not cleaning carpets at the Bureau of Public Debt, or fixing up his house, Erickson enjoys playing golf with Philip, 17, a senior at Parkersburg High School. They sometimes drive three hours to Pittsburgh to see the Steelers or the Pirates play. Someday they'd like to see the Penguins play hockey, but for now every game is a sellout and tickets are almost unobtainable. Meanwhile, this past autumn, father and son bought season tickets to West Virginia University football games in Morgantown, two hours' drive from Parkersburg. "My boy's a sports nut," he says. "That's all he eats and sleeps. Sports."

Erickson can't help thinking sometimes about where he might have ended up had the Marine Corps not given him that ultimatum back in 1970: lose fifty pounds or get out. He only weighed 225 pounds at the time, he says, well below what he weighed when he enlisted in 1966. But what the Corps allowed during the big buildup years of the Vietnam War had become unacceptable in the lean years that followed. At first he felt bitter about being forced out of the Corps, he says, but he eventually came to see their point.

Of his time in the Marines, he says, "I don't regret a day of it except the time I spent in D.C. I'm glad I went in. I don't have any regrets about going to Vietnam. The only thing that disgusted me was the way the people of the United States treated us, that's all." No one ever called him "baby killer" or spit on him, or anything like that, he adds, but he feels there was "just a general lack of respect, a lack of gratitude for having fought for your country."

As for boot camp, he remembers lying in bed his first night at Parris Island counting holes in the ceiling, too afraid to sleep—and this was *before* he encountered the obstacle course. Things got a lot worse before they got better, but now he says, "I wouldn't change any of it. I think it was a learning experience. I think that's what made a man out of me."

Harold E. Feighley

I can find no record of Feighley after we left Parris Island. No one with his name appears on any of the computerized telephone directories to which I've had access over the past five years. The National Personnel Records Center reported that they were "unable to identify a military service record from the information given." Feighley did apply for benefits to the Department of Veterans Affairs, but did so prior to July 1, 1972, the date the VA switched to using social security numbers as claim numbers. In early 1994, the VA forwarded to his last known address a letter I had written, but whether he ever received it or not, he never replied.

Robert M. Fink, Jr.

The Fink farm sprawls across two hundred acres of rolling hills on the western edge of the Allegheny Mountains some thirty miles southeast of Pittsburgh, Pennsylvania. "Suburban creep" from the once-sleepy town of Greensburg has reached to within a few miles of the farm, but none of it is yet visible from the farm itself. A narrow, winding country road divides the barn and silos from the houses of Robert M. Fink, Sr., and Robert M. Fink, Jr. The pastures on either side of the road are dotted with black-and-white Holstein dairy cows lazily grazing on a sunny but chilly autumn afternoon, October 5, 1994.

That morning I had set out from Philipsburg, a small town in central Pennsylvania where I'd spent the previous day with my old high school classmate and Platoon 1005er Harry Nelson. Vast stretches of the interior of Pennsylvania are covered with forests, especially up in the mountains through which I traveled for most of the three-hour drive, and the leaves were just beginning to turn with the onset of autumn. Along the way, I passed within a few miles of the tiny town in which I was born, though I have no memory of Roaring Spring, since we moved when I was less than a year old. I thought about driving through the town, just to have a look, but decided I'd rather spend the time with Fink.

He had been one of thirteen Robert M. Finks who showed up on the Myers list (often these computerized phone lists can be hit-or-miss affairs; Fink was on the Myers list, but his father—also Robert M. Fink—was not), and he had responded to my initial search letter with a telephone call. When I came to visit a year later, I found him in his barn, unloading sacks of cattle feed from the back of an old truck with wooden sides.

"That's what I did this summer," says Fink, nodding in the direction of a solid wall of hay bales and straw bales piled all the way to the roof of the barn. He turns back to the feed bags on the truck, pulling off another and tossing it down a wooden chute that leads to the feeders above the milking parlor on the ground floor of the barn. He handles the sacks easily, his huge biceps bulging. "I usually grow everything the cows need," he says, "but this year the corn didn't come up right away, so I'm a little short."

Fink moves the big truck to a nearby shed, climbs into a pickup truck, and heads down the road to check on his father, who is clearing a cornfield, cutting and chopping the old stalks into fodder for the cows. Bob, Sr., is

Lance Corporal Robert M. Fink, Jr., loading a
106mm recoilless rifle in Vietnam, 1967.

supposed to be retired, but "I don't like walls," he says, climbing down
from the tractor and taking a moment to chat while his son grabs a wrench
from under the tractor's seat and starts fiddling with a leaking hydraulic
line.

Bob, Sr., who is still wiry tough at 75, has been working this farm
since 1944. His father was a deep-shaft coal miner, and farming seemed
like a better life than coal mining, so he got a government loan and has
been here ever since. But if dairy farming is a better life than coal mining,
it is anything but an easy life.

"I tried to talk him out of farming," says Bob, Sr., nodding toward
his son, "but he wanted to do it. 'Where am I going to find a bigger challenge than this?' he told me."

Fink gets the leak more or less fixed, then father and son climb into
the pickup and head back to the barn to get another tractor and wagon.
The wagon was new when Fink was in junior high school. The tractor,

one of four on the farm, starts up reluctantly, its spark plugs in need of replacement. Fink uses the tractor's engine to power a blower that empties fodder from the wagon and lifts it to the top of the silo. When the wagon is empty, Bob, Sr., pulls it away from the silo and starts off for the field he's just been working in, then stops, climbs down, wrench in hand, and begins to tinker with an errant spark plug.

"Our newest tractor is twenty years old," Fink says. "All of our equipment is worn out, but we can't afford to replace it." He says that the last good years for farmers were during Jimmy Carter's presidency; the economy was better then, and Carter's policies were more favorable to farmers than those of subsequent presidents.

"We got more money per gallon of milk," he explains, "and the things we needed were cheaper to buy. The cost of everything has gone up, but we earn even less than we did then. Five or ten cents more per gallon, and I could afford new equipment. It's not much, but it adds up over a year. The retailer in the store makes more money on every gallon of milk

Bob Fink (center) *with sons Daniel* (left) *and David at Daniel's high school graduation, 1993.*

he sells than I do." The tone of voice is matter-of-fact, a simple statement of the way things are.

After Fink graduated from Greensburg-Salem High School in 1964, he enrolled at Potomac State College, but a year and a half into his studies he contracted mononucleosis and had to leave school to recuperate. Even before he was fully recovered, he got a draft notice. "I figured if I was going to go," he says, "I might as well go first class," so he enlisted in the Marines for two years.

By the time he returned to civilian life in 1968, college tuition had doubled. "I knew I was going into farming," he says, "and I didn't see that I'd get my money back if I went to college. The GI Bill had nothing for me. It just wasn't enough." So Fink settled down on the farm where he'd grown up, marrying his high school sweetheart and building a house right next door to his parents.

"It's all I ever wanted to do," Fink says of dairy farming, "but now I wish I'd thought of something else. The cows are still young, but I'm not. Those last eight or nine years are going to be tough. My dad can still help out for another year or two, but then I'll be on my own." Fink hasn't encouraged his two sons to follow him into farming, and neither has done so. "They're better off with eight-hour jobs," he says. "There's no money in farming.

"I don't know what's going to happen in ten years," he continues. "I don't know where the food's going to come from. There's no young people going into farming. I can't blame them." Fink explains that the average age of farmers is fifty-six. One fifth of all farmers quit farming every five years. Moreover, 90 percent of the food is produced by just 25 percent of those classified as farmers; the other 75 percent produce almost nothing, using farms as secondary activities, hobbies, or tax write-offs.

On foot, Fink crosses the road, walks out into the pasture, and begins to herd the cows toward the barn for their evening milking. "Come on, Number Sixteen, get on up there," he calls in a loudly affectionate voice. "Let's go, Number Thirty-seven." Extensive computerized records are kept on each cow by both Fink and agricultural researchers at Pennsylvania State University, and for these purposes the cows are numbered. Fink used to give them names as well, but that got too cumbersome, so now the cows have only numbers.

Fink has forty-six milk cows and thirty-eight heifers ranging in age from two days to two years. When things work as they should, each cow has a calf every year, most by artificial insemination, though he keeps two bulls for cows who prefer the old-fashioned method of impregnation. Fe-

male calves he keeps for milking; male calves he sells within days to pro-
ducers who will turn them into veal. If a cow doesn't get pregnant within
a year and a half or so, she ceases to be any use as a milk cow and is con-
signed to the butcher.

When Fink first got out of the Marines, he and his father had seventy-
six milk cows and worked over three hundred acres of land, but over the
years they've had to cut back on both cows and acreage. For a while,
Fink's two sons were able to help out, but now David, 23, is working for
Union Carbide through a work-study program administered by the University of Pittsburgh, and Daniel, 20, is attending the Erie campus of Penn
State. Hiring help is just too expensive, Fink explains, so the only choice
has been to reduce the size of the farm.

Fink doesn't remember a lot about Platoon 1005 or boot camp, he
explains as the cows slowly make their way toward the barn. "After the
first few days," he says, "I wasn't bothered by the DIS yelling all the time.
I thought they were kind of silly sometimes." He chuckles softly, as if to
himself.

Out of boot camp, Fink was given an MOS of 0351 and sent for
training with 106mm recoilless rifles, flame throwers and 3.5-inch rockets. He was assigned to 3rd Battalion, 8th Marines, at Camp Lejeune,
North Carolina, but two weeks after he got there, the battalion embarked
on a six-month Mediterranean cruise. Two weeks after the battalion returned to Lejeune, he says, "they gave everybody another stripe and orders for Vietnam."

As the cows head for the barn, a school bus has to stop and wait for
them to amble across the road. "Every day I see that guy," Fink says. "He
doesn't like my cows too much."

Fink spent ten months in Vietnam, instead of the standard Marine
tour of thirteen months, because he had less than a year of his enlistment
remaining when he got his orders. He was assigned to 106s with 1st Battalion, 7th Marines, on Hill 10 near Da Nang, but was frequently detached to other units, including a long stretch with a Combined Action
Platoon. "One time we held a bridge with one tank and a squad of
Marines for a couple of weeks. We got replaced by an entire company [of
the U.S. Army], and the very next night the VC overran the position and
blew up the bridge."

In the milk house, which houses a one thousand–gallon steel holding tank that gets emptied every other day by a truck from the Carl
Colteryahn Dairy in Pittsburgh, Fink washes and prepares the automatic
milking system. He steps into the milking parlor and connects the six

milkers to the overhead vacuum tubes that suck the milk out of the cows and deposit it in the holding tank next door.

There are four stalls on one side of the milking parlor and seven on the other, each with a feed trough so the cows can eat while they're getting milked. One of the cows has managed to get into the parlor prematurely, and is in backwards to boot. "Come on, Number Forty-five, turn around," Fink says. The cow responds by defecating. "You're insisting on making a mess, aren't you, girl?" says Fink, shooing the cow out.

Once Number Forty-five is back where she belongs, Fink opens a door and lets in the first four cows. Each gets a bucket of "chop," a mixture of grains and grasses, as Fink sprays each cow's teats with disinfectant, then hooks up the automatic milkers, one cow at a time, one teat at a time. Then he lets in six cows on the other side of the parlor and begins to ready them.

"You think they know what they're doing," Fink says of the generals and politicians responsible for the war in Vietnam, "and then you get there and look around: 'What kind of a way is this to fight a war?' I knew two months after I got there we weren't going to win. Westmoreland had to know his strategy wouldn't work. He should have had the courage to say, 'Do it right or I quit.' He let the politicians fight the war."

As he talks and works, Imogene, his wife of twenty-five years, enters the milking parlor, picks up the bottle of disinfectant, and slips immediately into the same routine Fink is following. She has just gotten home from her job as a program administrator with the U.S. Department of Agriculture in Greensburg, a job she took seven years ago to help put the boys through college. "I go to work before I go to work in the morning," she says. "Then I go to work again when I come home from work in the evening."

Fink and his wife methodically go about the milking, unhooking cows that are finished and moving them out, letting more in, feeding, spraying, and hooking them up, back and forth, from one side of the milking parlor to the other, then back again. One of the cows is sick. Fink can tell because she has stopped eating. "Put food in front of a cow," he explains, "and she won't stop eating unless she's sick." He takes the cow's temperature with a rectal thermometer, and sure enough, she has a fever. He heads for the medicine cabinet in the milk house.

Fink believes the only way to have won in Vietnam would have been to line up at the very southern tip of the country and move slowly north in a line. "But you'd have to decide if you were willing to risk a war with China," he says. "If you weren't, then get out."

Would even that strategy have worked? "I don't know," he says, thinking back to his time with the CAP unit. "You'd be talking with some young woman one day, and the next day you don't see her, so you ask where she is and you find out she's gone off to join the Viet Cong. And you were just talking to her the day before."

Government regulations require Fink to keep medicines for lactating and nonlactating cows in separate cabinets. The cabinets must be kept unlocked. Previously they were required to be locked. Before that, medicines weren't allowed to be kept in the milk house at all. His entire operation, in fact, is subject to frequent unannounced visits by federal, state, county, and Colteryahn inspectors. All of this he explains with a kind of stoic wonder.

Or perhaps it is bemused irritation. In either case, Fink returns to the milking parlor and gives the sick cow a shot of antibiotic. Then he sprays her udder and flank with blue ink so that he'll remember at a glance not to allow her milk to get mixed in with the rest until she's well again and off medication.

"The problem with dairy farming is that you never get away," he says. He and Imogene have never had a vacation. "The cows have to be milked twice a day every day," he explains. "It costs too much to hire someone, and then you have to worry about that person screwing up and costing you a holding tank full of milk. Or worse."

A few weeks earlier, Fink and his wife began milking an hour earlier than their usual 4:00 A.M. starting time, then drove four hours to West Virginia, another four hours back, and did the evening milking an hour later than usual—all of this to spend two hours with David on his twenty-third birthday.

"When I get to be sixty-three," Fink says, "I'm gonna sell the cows and go see something of the world besides these few acres."

"Can I get that in writing?" says Imogene, laughing. She pauses, then adds, "In blood." A few minutes later, while Fink is in the milk house, Imogene says, almost apologetically, "Bob loves farming. And he's good at it."

Once the cows are milked, all of the equipment must be cleaned again, and the milking parlor, its floor now covered with cow droppings and spilled feed, must be cleaned and hosed down. The cows have given a total of 1,385 pounds of milk this evening, which translates into 161 gallons. "The more you can get them to eat, the more milk they're going to give," Fink explains, but more feeding means more work. "It depends on how much you want to mess around."

Nearly three hours after Fink first began to herd the cows in for milking, Imogene heads for the house to start supper while her husband goes to the upper barn to feed more hay and straw to the cows, dropping it down through holes in the floor to the cows below. "It takes a lot to keep these girls happy," he says, throwing bale after bale down from a wagon.

Part of the last load of straw he brought in from the fields this year got damp. The cows won't eat as much if it's damp, he explains, and if they eat less, they'll produce less milk. Fink has to decide if it costs him more to discard the straw or to settle for a smaller yield. "I'm at the mercy of Mother Nature," he says. "Whatever she wants to throw at me, I've got to live with."

Next he feeds the heifers, which are kept in four separate enclosures according to size and age. If you put different-sized heifers together, he explains, the bigger ones will push the smaller ones aside and not let them get enough to eat. The two smallest heifers are kept in the barn. The two-week-old can drink milk from a bucket, but the two-day-old must be bottle-fed by hand. "That takes a lot of time if you've got five or six little ones," Fink says.

At last all eighty-six cows and the two bulls are fed, and Fink heads for the house to feed himself. It's 8:45 P.M., and the Finks have been up since 4:00 A.M., but the day isn't over yet. After supper, while Imogene cleans up the kitchen, Fink will go back out to the barn and turn the milk cows out to pasture for the night. Only then will the day be done. In less than seven hours, another one will begin.

Charles P. Fraley

Twelve Charles Fraleys appeared on the Myers list, but none of them responded to my initial search letter. Fraley apparently did apply for veterans' benefits, but never replied to the letter I sent via the VA. Records received from NPRC in May 1995 indicate that he was born March 10, 1949, worked as a busboy for a year and a half before graduating from high school, and enlisted in the Marines at Jackson, Mississippi. After boot camp and basic infantry training, he spent five weeks with the Supply School Company at Camp Lejeune, North Carolina, before being assigned as a disbursing clerk (3421) with Headquarters Company, Headquarters & Support Battalion, Marine Corps Recruit Depot, San Diego, California.

Fraley remained at San Diego for his entire two years of active duty. He reached the rank of lance corporal in July 1967, but was absent without leave from 23 to 26 December 1967, and was subsequently reduced in rank to private first class two weeks later. In May 1968, he was reduced in rank again, this time to private. He was released from active duty in July 1968.

Curtis R. Friday III

Larry Maxey found Curt Friday for me. Though they had not known each other previously, they'd both grown up around Columbus, Mississippi, where both still live, and had met the day they set out for Parris Island along with Leonard Hibbler. When Maxey and I first spoke on September 9, 1993, he said he hadn't seen Friday in about five years, but thought he could track him down. He called again on September 17 to tell me he'd just talked to Friday's wife and to give me their telephone number. Two days later, I reached Friday.

From that conversation and records received from NPRC in May 1996, I learned that Friday was born in West Point, Mississippi, on February 20, 1948, and graduated from West Point High School in 1966. After boot camp and basic infantry training, he was sent to Naval Air Station, Millington, Tennessee, for training as an aircraft jet engine mechanic (6318) before being assigned to Marine Fighter Attack Squadron 531, Marine Air Group 24, Marine Corps Air Station, Cherry Point, North Carolina, from March 1967 until October 1967.

From November 1967 until December 1968, Friday served with Headquarters & Maintenance Squadron 13, Marine Air Group 13, at Chu Lai, Vietnam. While serving in Vietnam, Friday earned a Navy Commendation Medal with Combat "V" device. His citation reads in part:

> Assigned the duties of coordinating, planning and scheduling intermediate maintenance, responsibilities normally assigned to a more experienced Marine of higher rank, he skillfully accomplished all assigned tasks and consistently provided his command with outstanding support. On 23 August 1968, when his unit came under an intense enemy rocket attack which ig-

nited several fires in the Ground Support Equipment area, Lance Corporal Friday rushed to the area with a fire extinguisher and began spraying the burning equipment. With complete disregard for his own safety, he ignored the enemy rounds impacting nearby and continued his efforts to extinguish the fire until crash trucks arrived.

Returning to the United States, Friday was next assigned to H&MS-20 back at MCAS Cherry Point in January 1969. In October he was transferred to Headquarters Squadron, Fleet Marine Force Pacific, Honolulu, Hawaii, where he remained until being transferred to Marine Corps Air Station, Beaufort, South Carolina, in February 1970. He was released from active duty in June 1970 with the rank of lance corporal (E3). In addition to the Navy Commendation Medal, his decorations include a Presidential Unit Citation, the Combat Action Ribbon, and the Good Conduct, National Defense Service, Vietnam Service, and Vietnam Campaign Medals.

After he got out of the Marines, Friday went back to Mississippi and "dawdled around doing this, that, and the other thing for a while. I found one hell of a terrific gal," he told me, and married her in 1971. He also went to college, then became a control systems engineer for the Cargill Corporation. Since 1981, he has worked as a project engineer for the Weyerhaeuser Company at its pulp and paper complex in Columbus, Mississippi. He has one daughter and one grandchild.

Coulbourn H. Godfrey, Jr.

One afternoon well into the training cycle of Platoon 1005, Drill Instructor Evans was teaching us how to twirl our M-14 rifles around our wrists, a maneuver somewhat like a majorette twirling a baton. It was scary at first because an M-14 weighs considerably more than a baton, and the worst offense you could commit in boot camp was to drop your rifle, but once you got the balance right, it wasn't so hard: you just let the rifle rest in your left palm, then smacked the stock with your right hand and the rifle would spin like a baton or a propeller.

After a little practice, we were all feeling pleased with ourselves and our new trick, which we could add to our small repertoire of flourishes during close-order drill, when Sergeant Evans called us to attention in the

*Platoon 1005's "Outstanding Man," Coulbourn H. Godfrey,
Jr., receiving congratulations from the commanding officer of
the 1st Recruit Training Battalion, August 12, 1966.* (PB)

squad bay. "Think that's neat?" he said with his usual sneer. "Watch this.
Godfrey, show 'em Queen Anne's Salute."

No recruit had ever before been singled out for anything but punishment, which in itself made the moment memorable. But as the other
seventy-nine recruits stood in front of our bunks watching, Private Godfrey
slowly marched up and down the long aisle between the two rows of forty
double bunk beds while twirling, tossing, hurling, spinning, tapping, and
sliding his rifle in a display of precision drill beyond anything any of us had
ever seen or even imagined. In a matter of only a few moments, Godfrey
acquired almost mythical status that afternoon—just as everyone remembers Tom Erickson, though for different reasons, they all remember Coulbourn Godfrey—and it surprised none of us when a few weeks later at our
graduation he was named the platoon's "Outstanding Man."

Coulbourn Godfrey with his daughter, Christine, 1996.

Though few of us knew it because we didn't know anything about each other, Godfrey had spent three years in Junior Reserve Officers Training Corps at Thomas Jefferson High School in Richmond, Virginia, where he'd learned the Queen Anne's Salute as a member of the school's honor guard, and another two years in regular ROTC at the University of Richmond. "My father got me interested in it," he explains. "Plus the friends I was with, they were in it."

The senior Godfrey had been a Marine officer in World War II, participating in three of the four Pacific Island campaigns fought by the 1st Marine Division, and the younger Godfrey was well aware of his father's service. Godfrey's mother died when he was only eight, leaving his father, a salesman, to raise his son "Cogie" and his daughter Corina by himself. "It was part of his way of teaching me stuff," Godfrey says of his father's reminders of and references to his military service. As for Godfrey's participation in ROTC, he says, "This is what Dad expected of me." He mostly didn't enjoy ROTC all that much, he says, though the experience certainly would come in handy at Parris Island.

While still in high school, Godfrey began dating a girl who was a year older than him. Accepted as a premedical student at Hampton-Sydney College, he chose to attend the University of Richmond to remain close to his girlfriend. But her parents didn't approve of her "going steady," so they sent her off to a women's college in the Tennessee mountains. There she got pregnant, he says, "and I wasn't the father."

Godfrey did not take the news well. By the spring of his sophomore year, he was studying very little and drinking heavily. He decided to enlist, choosing the Marines without any hesitation because his father had been a Marine. "I was drunk when I went to the recruiting office," he says, "but that didn't stop the recruiter. He signed me up anyway."

Because of his ROTC experience, boot camp didn't bother Godfrey. "I was used to the hazing and harassment," he explains, "so it didn't really phase me all that much. I knew what to expect. I'd already done almost everything they did there. I was used to military psychology."

When he enlisted, Godfrey had requested to be an infantry rifleman, he says, "but I never made it to a rifle company." After boot camp, basic infantry training, and staging, he arrived in Vietnam in late November 1966 and found himself assigned to the Military Police Company of Headquarters Battalion, 3rd Marine Division, at Phu Bai. The company's main duty was to help the line companies hold the perimeter of the big base—performing guard duty, maintaining listening posts, and running local night patrols.

Two months after his arrival, during a rocket and mortar attack on Phu Bai, Godfrey was hit by shrapnel in his right side, face, and right eye. He was evacuated to a hospital ship in the South China Sea, but when it became clear that the ship didn't have the resources necessary to save his eye, he was transferred to better facilities on Guam. He spent three months recuperating from his injuries, not returning to his outfit until April 1967. "I was glad to get back," he says, "The friendships there meant a lot. That was the big thing."

The war itself was a different matter. "The less you tried to figure it out," he says, "the better off you were mentally. It took me years to forget a lot of it." One of the most disturbing incidents occurred not long after Godfrey first arrived in Vietnam. The base was once again under rocket and mortar attack, and Godfrey was in his fighting hole trying to stay out of the way of the incoming fire. "The next thing I know," he says, "there's a Viet Cong right on top of me. He came right into the hole on top of me." Godfrey killed him. He was armed with an AK-47 assault rifle, says Godfrey, but he couldn't have been more than fourteen or fifteen years old.

During another mortar attack in September 1967, while assisting an inexperienced civilian photographer to cover, Godfrey was wounded a second time, though much less severely. In spite of all this, he extended his original tour by another six months, not leaving Vietnam until July 1968. By then a sergeant, he returned to the U.S. through Norton Air Force Base in California.

There, he says, he and the other returning veterans were greeted at the front gate by antiwar protesters. "Oh, they cussed us out," he says. "They threw cans at us. Called us baby killers." The men changed into civilian clothing in a bathroom before leaving the base.

After four months at Camp Lejeune, North Carolina, Godfrey was given a choice between Officer Candidate School and Marine Security Guard School. "The life expectancy of second lieutenants wasn't very good at that time," he says. "I figured I had a better chance of living if I took security guard school." There, he explains, he learned "how to handle classified materials, how to work safes, how to be a diplomat, how to eat properly. We did hand-to-hand combat. You had to be a bodyguard when needed. You had to be seen and yet not seen."

Godfrey hoped to be assigned to an embassy in Europe, but a week before he graduated he received orders to the American Embassy in Saigon. He arrived back in Vietnam in March 1969. After the debacle of the Tet Offensive a year earlier, when VC sappers had gotten onto the grounds of the embassy, the thirty-member security detachment worked in full combat gear rather than the traditional dress blue uniform usually worn by Marine embassy guards, but Godfrey's year in Saigon was mostly quiet. "Snipers would occasionally take shots at the embassy," he says. "They tried to blow up the gate a few times. That was about it."

The detachment lived in a hotel downtown, working eight-hour days on swing shifts. "It was one big party really," he says. "We had a bar there. We were allowed to go downtown in civilian clothes. Each of us had our personal weapons." Godfrey's was a 9mm Baretta.

What he remembers most about being on duty is going through all the offices each night after working hours and locking up classified documents left on embassy staff members' desks. "You wouldn't believe what people left lying around," he says, "even the ambassador."

Another vivid memory is of people who would show up at the embassy gate in combat uniforms but with no rank or branch of service insignia and oddly nondescript identification cards with no governmental department affiliation indicated. The guards would call for clearance and it was always granted with no explanation, just orders to admit whoever these people were. Godfrey assumes they were involved in covert operations. "There was a lot of that stuff going on," he says.

He also says that most of the men in the security detachment knew by 1969 and 1970 that the war was a lost cause. Godfrey got to know a number of Vietnamese people employed by the embassy, and others through volunteer work he did with Vietnamese orphans. "Once you got away from the tourist areas of Saigon, and the people who were making money off the war and the Americans," he says, "you realized that the Vietnamese didn't want us there. We were just in the way. We were a nuisance."

Godfrey extended his original four-year active duty commitment by an additional two years, and in March 1970 he went directly from Vietnam to the American Embassy in Tokyo, Japan. His most memorable experience there, he recalls, was a conference attended by fifty ambassadors, "a lot of generals," and U.S. Secretary of State William Rogers, during which he was assigned to the Secret Service agent responsible for Rogers. "I had to look pretty and be quiet," he says. His final year in the Corps Godfrey spent with 1st Battalion, 2nd Marines, first at Camp Lejeune, then on a six-month Mediterranean cruise that included joint U.S.-British exercises in Turkey as well as more sociable stopovers in Greece, Italy, France, and Spain. "So I got to Europe after all," he says.

But when he got out of the Corps in June 1972, he adds, "I had nowhere to go, nothing to do, and no ideas." His father had remarried and moved from Richmond to Chicago, but he didn't want to go there. "Too cold," he says. While he was trying to decide where to go, he was asked to come to Kinston, North Carolina, to be best man in a friend's wedding. He woke up the morning after the wedding in his friend's empty apartment. The newlyweds had gone on their honeymoon, but "I just stayed," he says. "I got a job and hung around. Kinston was a pretty quiet town. Small. Everybody kind of knew everybody."

He also got into drugs and alcohol. "It was like you were reliving the sixties," he explains. "And it was a way to cope." It was also a way into trouble: that same year, 1972, he got busted for possession of a pound of marijuana. "Believe it or not," he says, "I bought it for myself." Sentenced to three to five years in prison, he was instead given five years' probation because of his good service record. "Then I had to stay in Kinston," he says, adding, after a pause, "for years."

He has stayed for twenty-five years, but they have not been easy, many of those years. Through most of the 1970s, he worked a succession of jobs at places like Hardee's and Kentucky Fried Chicken, or in construction, or with home remodeling companies installing aluminum siding. And he partied. "You go up and down a lot," he says. "It depends on who you're with, whatever social group. Once you got into a drug-oriented crowd, it was hard to get out of it. Unless you become a Baptist, it's hard to break in around here."

He even tried religion for a while, but that didn't do it for him either. He joined a motorcycle club. "I just went from one extreme to another," he says. "I think it was the idea that when I got back [from Vietnam and the service] you were shunned and looked down upon. I guess I was trying to reestablish some sort of self-respect."

But none of his attempts worked. "You wake up one morning and you realize you've got nothing," he says. "Starting over isn't easy. You're in your thirties, you've got no goals, no children, no savings, no education. Where do you start?"

By then, the late 1970s, Godfrey felt he was too old to go back to a four-year college. "I thought it best to get a trade," he says, so he enrolled at Lenoir Community College in 1978, earning an associate's degree in electronics in 1980. "I've been in that field ever since," he says. This finally brought a measure of stability into his life. He spent six years with Buehler Products as a production calibration technician, and since 1987 has been an electronics technician repairing office equipment for Kinston Office Supply.

But he still found himself in and out of trouble. Not big problems like the 1972 drug bust, he explains, but "little stuff. Traffic accidents. Drunk driving. I traded shots with a neighbor one time—he had a .45; I had a shotgun—until I realized, 'Geez, this is nuts.' I smacked a cop once." One bit of trouble, however, led to the best thing in his life.

In 1989, Godfrey lost his driver's license for driving while under the influence of alcohol, and he needed someone to get him around. Friends told him about a young woman named Kathy Perry who was having a rough time herself, and he offered to take care of her and her two young children if she would drive for him. "It began as a business relationship," he explains, but resulted in the birth of his daughter Christine in 1991.

"When Christine was born," he says, "that was a Godsend. It kind of straightened me out." The relationship with Perry didn't last, but the two are on reasonable terms and Godfrey spends a great deal of time with Christine. "I don't want to miss these years," he says. He got a late start at being a parent, he adds, but he's more patient because of his age, and more able to "stop and appreciate the trees."

I got to meet Christine when I interviewed Godfrey on August 10, 1997, though she wasn't much interested in hanging around listening to a couple of grown-ups talk about boring stuff and soon went outside to play with a friend. I happened to be vacationing that week with my wife, daughter, and niece on Bogue Bank on the North Carolina coast, and since Kinston was only seventy miles away, I drove over that Sunday afternoon to visit.

Godfrey lives in a large mobile home fourteen feet wide and eighty feet long with an interior that he designed himself. "You can watch TV while you work in the kitchen," he points out. He's traded his Harley-Davidson Sportster for a moped. And he likes to go fishing, something he's enjoyed all his life. "I used to fish ponds and creeks when I was younger," he says, "but now I mostly go ocean fishing. A group of guys'll rent a boat and go out thirty or forty miles, fish for game fish." He belongs to the American Legion and the Disabled American Veterans (he has a 30 percent disability from his eye injury).

Godfrey doesn't regret his decision to join the Marines. "I was flunking out of school," he explains. "I had to have a change. It was the easiest thing to do." About the war, however, he feels differently. His military records indicate that he was awarded the Vietnamese Cross of Gallantry. The date suggests that it was given for his service with the embassy security detachment, but he does not remember when or why he received it. "A lot of guys had a tough time after Vietnam," he says. "Should we have been there? No. We never could understand those people." Then he quotes from the movie *Apocalypse Now*. "The horror," he says. "The horror."

John E. Green

As with Harold Feighley, I can find no record of Green after we left Parris Island, but unlike Feighley, whose name appears nowhere, I can't find Green because there are just too many of them. Ben Myers's computer search turned up 514 John E. Greens with listed telephone numbers in the eastern U.S. alone; he didn't even bother to check west of the Mississippi. As a practical matter, I could not have contacted them all in any case, and didn't try. To make matters more difficult, Green's service number from those old 1966 company reports was not readable, so I couldn't provide the VA or NPRC with even that minimal identifier, and thus could receive no help from either of those sources.

Because I at least have Feighley's service number and VA claim number, and don't even know that much about Green, Green has the distinction, such as it is, of being the member of Platoon 1005 about whom I know the least.

Guy D. Haas

When Guy Haas first arrived in Vietnam in December 1967, he was assigned to Headquarters & Maintenance Squadron 36 at Phu Bai. He had already been in the Marine Corps for eighteen months, most of that time learning and practicing the skills necessary to be an airborne navigator—math, celestial navigation, loran navigation, and meterology—first at navigators' school, then with Marine Aerial Refueler Transport Squadron 252 out of Marine Corps Air Station, Cherry Point, North Carolina. He was ready to do what the Corps had trained him to do.

Thus, he was both surprised and dismayed to discover that H&MS-36 had no C-130 Hercules, the four-engine aircraft on which he had trained. Instead, Haas found himself assigned as a navigator on the squadron's one C-47, a twin-engine relic of the Second World War. This might have been okay, except that the plane was not even equipped with a navigator's station. He spent very little time flying and a whole lot of time burning fifty-five-gallon drums full of human excrement while contemplating the idiocy of his assignment. This was not what he'd had in mind when he'd enlisted.

Airborne Navigator Guy D. Haas beneath the wing of a C-130 Hercules aircraft from Marine Aerial Refueler Transport Squadron 152, 1968.

The older of two brothers, Haas was born in California, but moved to Florida with his mother after his parents divorced when he was four. He grew up in North Miami Beach and West Hollywood, Florida, but by age sixteen, he found his mother too restrictive and went to live with his father in Bethesda, Maryland. Graduating from Walter Johnson High School in 1964, he enrolled

The Haas family, 1995. Left to right: son Jason, daughter Erica, wife Roberta, and Guy.

at the University of Maryland as an engineering student, but after two years of college, he concluded that he'd never finish. "I was too into partying," he says. "I figured I'd flunk out and get drafted, so I decided to enlist."

Two factors led Haas to choose the Marine Corps over the other services. One was his stepfather. His mother had remarried in Florida, and Master Sergeant Grayson D. Williams, a veteran of both World War II and the Korean War, was still on active duty when Haas was growing up. "I really admired my stepfather," says Haas. "He was a big influence on my decision to join the Corps."

The second was his lifelong fascination with aviation. As a kid, he explains, he was always shooting up rockets and flying model airplanes. "Build 'em and crash 'em, build 'em and crash 'em," he says, laughing. But when Haas learned about the Marines' guaranteed aviation program—a four-year enlistment in return for the guarantee of a job somewhere in the field of aviation—that settled the matter: Marine aviation it would be.

"I was psyched about going [to boot camp], but when I got off that bus at Parris Island," he says, "all my thoughts of having a pleasant time dissolved. It was totally another world." Haas was surprised by the vulgarity of the drill instructors, their strictness, and the verbal and physical violence. "The intensity of the experience shocked me, and there was nothing you could do about it. I still don't understand why they have to use such terror tactics."

Haas feels that Drill Instructor Evans, in particular, had it in for him. "I struggled with the physical stuff," he says, "those long runs in the heat with all our gear. Maybe Evans saw I was struggling and wanted to see if I would break." One time, he says, Evans strangled Haas with Haas's own web belt during a buckle inspection. Another time, Evans came up behind him and whacked the back of his "chrome dome" (helmet liner) for no reason that Haas could discern.

Haas has few good memories of Parris Island. "Chowing down was pleasurable," he says, "and taking showers at the end of the day. That's about it. Mostly I remember coming and going. Everything in between was just a blur. I'm glad I went through it because I think I'm a stronger person, but I wouldn't want to go through it again." Still, he adds, "I was proud to graduate. I never thought I'd survive this, but I had. I felt like I was sitting on top of the world. I came out of boot camp really proud to be a Marine."

Such fierce pride was not always an asset, however. He tells of coming home on leave after boot camp and roaming the bars in the Georgetown section of Washington, D.C., looking for fights. "I was one ready killing machine," he says. "My friends thought I was nuts. I thought I was invincible when I got out of boot camp." Luckily for all concerned, he found no takers.

After that first home leave, Haas was sent to Memphis, Tennessee, for testing. Though it was his first choice, he was surprised when he received an assignment to navigator school because there were few positions available and the competition for them was stiff. "I wanted to be a pilot," he says, but that required a college degree. Flight navigator was the next best thing. "That was the best job you could get in the air wing for an enlisted man," he says.

He graduated second in his class of thirty from the twenty-six week course, then went to VMGR-252 at Cherry Point. "It was cushy," he says. He flew lots of training missions, always in the company of a senior navigator, and sometimes got to go to Europe on NATO flights. He remembers sightseeing in Italy. "But everyone knew it was just a matter of time before we all got orders to Vietnam," he says. "We all knew we'd go sooner or later."

What Haas had not anticipated was ending up as the navigator for an airplane that didn't carry one. It took several months to unscrew the error, but finally he was transferred to VMGR-152, a squadron flying C-130s out of MCAF Futema, Okinawa, with a substation at Da Nang. The squadron's air crews spent about half their time in Vietnam and the other half split between squadron headquarters on Okinawa and missions to Japan, the Philippines, and Thailand.

Haas arrived at VMGR-152 just in time to participate in the squadron's efforts to support the besieged defenders of Khe Sanh. "You had to keep the planes rolling to avoid fire," he says of landing at Khe Sanh. "You'd stop just long enough to let people get on and off. The time you have to sit there and wait for another plane or something, you're just praying that the mortars won't hit you."

Several times the pilot of his plane had to take evasive action to escape North Vietnamese surface-to-air missiles fired from within the Demilitarized Zone, and once a bullet penetrated the fuselage, missing Haas by three feet. "I still have the bullet," he says, explaining that after they got back on the ground, he found the external bullet hole, traced the trajectory, and found the bullet embedded in the fuselage near the pilot.

The worst part of these missions was carrying out the wounded and the dead. "I still remember the smell of charred flesh," he says of a group of South Vietnamese soldiers who had been badly burned. "Some of them died on the flight from Khe Sanh to Da Nang. And we carried a lot of body bags, too. Some of the bags would only be half full. Some would be dripping blood."

Haas's first of twenty-eight Air Medals came during the siege of Khe Sanh. It reads in part: "Despite adverse weather conditions and intense North Vietnamese rocket and mortar fire, . . . Lance Corporal Haas skillfully monitored his radar system, . . . ably assisted the aircraft commander with technical information, . . . and undaunted by accurate fire impacting near the aircraft, assisted in unloading the cargo and embarking the casualties."

In addition to flying into Khe Sanh, the squadron flew air-to-air refueling missions, day logistics (food and supplies, medevacs, personnel transport), and night augmentation missions (magnesium flares). For night flare drops, the crew would load an airplane with flares, take off at sunset, and fly until sunrise. Because he was in radio contact with units on the ground, Haas could often hear firefights going on. And from seven thousand feet, he could see small-arms tracer fire and napalm from jets. "It was eerie," he says. "You could see the tragedy of war without being directly in it."

When his thirteen-month tour of duty was up, Haas extended for another six months. "I had no reason to go back," he explains, "and I was making good money—base pay, combat pay, flight pay, overseas pay." Then he adds that he was also "ranching" on Okinawa—living with an Okinawan woman. Of his eventual return to the U.S. in June 1969, he says, "It was just time for me to come back. I was really sad when I left [the woman he'd been living with]. It was sad because I really liked her, but I couldn't marry her."

Haas, by now a sergeant, was assigned once again to VMGR-252 out of Cherry Point. Over the following year, he flew missions to the Azores, Cyprus, England, Greece, Iceland, Lebanon, Spain, and Turkey, eventually earning membership in Lockheed's C-130 2000-Hour Club. He also married a woman he'd met in Maryland after his tour in Vietnam. When his enlistment was up in June 1970, he reenrolled at the University of Maryland, this time as a business major.

Haas graduated with a bachelor of science degree in 1973, then went to Cleveland to attend graduate school. Though his marriage had produced a daughter in 1971 (Jeanne, now a graduate of George Mason University), it was on shaky ground by 1973, and his wife chose not to go to Cleveland with him. The couple was divorced the following year.

In Cleveland, Haas began studying part time toward a master's degree in business administration while working full time for Cleveland Trust as a buyer and seller of securities for trust funds. Roberta Arcuri also worked in the trust operations department. "I got bored with banking," says Haas. "I worked there just long enough to start dating Robbie."

Haas left the bank after six months and took a job in computer sales with Sperry Remington. In 1974 he accepted a transfer from Cleveland to Boston to become a branch sales manager, and in 1975 he and Robbie were married. He never did finish his MBA, though he eventually took courses at four different schools, and he has changed jobs many times over the years. But he's still in the high-tech computer industry, he still has the same wife, and they still live in the greater Boston area.

Since Haas first began working in the computer industry, in fact, he has had only one job not related to computer marketing and management.

In 1993, he decided to try to combine his enjoyment of beer with his business acumen by starting his own microbrewery. He quit his job as eastern regional sales representative for Data I/O, raised half a million dollars, and started the Lowell Brewing Company. By the summer of 1993, the company was ready to begin brewing beer under its brand name label of Mill City.

Unfortunately, in order to raise the necessary capital, Haas had to give up 51 percent interest in the brewery. "I was the founder," he says. "I came up with the plan, I raised the capital, and I did all the work for that first year, but I didn't have controlling interest. And I was making no money." The following year, when PADS Software, Inc., an engineering and electronics software company, offered him the position of director for North American sales and service, he took it.

The brewery is now producing classic lager, German pilsner, amber ale, oatmeal stout, blond ale, and a nonalcoholic root beer, and the operation is finally nearing the break-even point, but Haas, who still owns a 30 percent interest, is not involved in day-to-day operations. "I have a full-time job now," he explains, "so I don't do much with the brewery. I look at it as an investment."

Meanwhile, Haas's love of flying didn't end with his discharge from the Marines. While still on active duty, he earned his private pilot's license, and in 1974 he bought his first airplane, a single-engine Piper Cherokee with fixed landing gear. After he earned his instrument rating, he traded in the Cherokee for a retractable-gear Piper Comanche. Then came a Piper Arrow, and finally a Beech Baron.

Haas was able to afford to fly only because he could legitimately write off much of the cost as a business expense. But in 1989, the company he was then working for, concerned about company liability should Haas be involved in any kind of mishap or accident, told him he could no longer use his plane for company business. Unable to afford to fly solely for pleasure, he sold his airplane and hasn't flown since. With his current job, he says, he could once again use a plane for business, but with two kids nearing college, he can't afford to fly now even with the business write-offs.

But if Haas is without wings these days, he can still soar with his voice. Along with aviation, Haas's other lifelong interest has been music. He played viola in elementary school and saxophone in high school, and he and Robbie have a one hundred-year-old, nine-foot concert grand piano in their living room. So in 1987, when Haas discovered the Lowell

Barbershop Chorus, also known as the Gentlemen Songsters, he joined right away.

Haas describes the fifty-member chorus as "sort of a men's singing fraternity." Various members of the chorus also mix and match to form barbershop quartets. At the moment, Haas is in a quartet called the Harmonistix, three of whose four members are also in the chorus. The quartet placed fourth out of twenty-eight entrants in a recent local competition, which qualified them for a regional competition in Lake Placid, New York.

As for the rest of the family, Robbie works as a sexual assault counselor for the Rape Crisis Center of Greater Lowell, son Jason is a senior in high school, and daughter Erica is in ninth grade. Both of the children are serious competitive swimmers. The family lives in a sprawling Victorian house built in 1896 by James B. Francis, the man who built the canal system that powered the once ubiquitous and still (in some quarters, at least) infamous textile mills of Lowell, Massachusetts. It is an elegant home with high ceilings, three full floors, and a large screen-porch. Of much more recent vintage is the gazebo with swing seat that stands in the side yard. One next-door neighbor is another member of the Harmonistix; until his death, the other was Paul Tsongas, the former senator and presidential candidate.

Haas was the only Guy D. Haas on the Myers list. In response to my initial search letter, he had replied on September 4, 1993, with a letter of his own. "Your letter," he wrote, "inspired me to dig out my USMC trunk, which I haven't opened in probably 20 years. . . . My son was with me as I rummaged through the trunk. He put on my USMC winter greens. It brought tears to my eyes."

On June 25, 1995, during a swing through Massachusetts that included visits with Don Bowles and the Blades family, I stopped to see Haas. That evening Haas set up a projector and screen and showed me, Robbie, and Jason several hundred slides from his Marine Corps days while I sampled various Mill City beers. The blond ale and the oatmeal stout were particularly fine. Several times Jason asked, "Don't you have any battle pictures, Dad? Where's the war?" Eventually he wandered off in search of more interesting activities.

Haas has few regrets about the way his life has unfolded, but one of them is the Vietnam War. When the fact of his being a veteran comes up in conversation, he explains, he always brushes it off, not wanting to talk about it. "We left in shame," he says. "We got beaten. What did all those men die for?"

Still, he hastens to add, "I have nothing to be ashamed of at all. I'm sad for America. I'm sorry the country didn't pull together to support the politicians, right or wrong. I'm sad I can't display my medals proudly—I can't even find them! I think we could have won if we had pulled together on it," he concludes. "If we'd have thrown enough into it, we could have beaten them. The U.S. has the resources and the technology to win just about any war on this planet."

John L. Harris, Jr.

"John didn't write about what he was doing in Vietnam," Melva Harris told me on February 25, 1995. "He didn't talk about the war. He'd say things like, 'We didn't get too much sleep last night,' but he wouldn't say why. Was he up reading a book or what? Well, I knew it wasn't that, but I didn't know what it was. Mostly he asked about the baby and I answered his questions. I used to say that I would have to have a maid and a butler. I kind of got away from thinking about the worst. Then when he was killed, it just blew me away. At the funeral, they kept having to give me smelling salts. I kept passing out."

As I've already explained, former *Washington Post* Pentagon reporter George Wilson first told me that Harris had died twenty-six years earlier, but I still had questions for which I wanted answers. Had he married? Had he had a son named John, or a daughter like mine? What had become of the child? Perhaps I could find surviving family members. The address list that retired master sergeant Ben Myers had sent me included three John L. Harrises in the Baltimore area, and since Harris had been a "junior," perhaps one of these was his father. In September 1993, I wrote to all three. No luck. Dead end.

More than a year went by. Meanwhile, Connie Menefee had put me in touch with Richard Johnson. Colonel Johnson had a friend who had access to death records of American soldiers housed at the Lyndon Johnson Library in Austin. In late December 1994, Colonel Johnson was able to provide me with the following information:

At the time of his death, Harris was married to Melva J. Harris of Baltimore and had a son named John L. Harris III. His father, John L. Harris, and mother, listed as Mrs. Betty L. Johnson, were both dead, but an aunt named Mrs. Ethel Muise was also listed as surviving him.

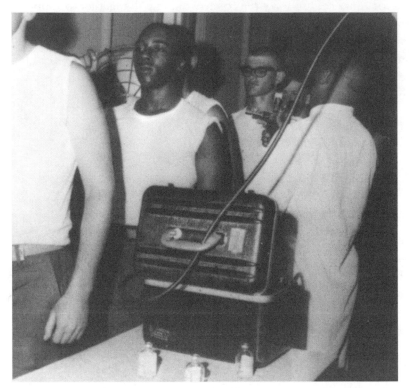

Marine recruit John Harris receiving inoculations at Parris Island, South Carolina, June 1966. (PB)

By this time, I had acquired my own computerized directory. It didn't seem likely that Harris's widow would never have remarried, but I checked Melva Harrises anyway. I found six east of the Mississippi River, but only one in Maryland and none in Baltimore. I then tried directory assistance and learned that there were two Melva J. Harrises in Baltimore, but both had unlisted numbers.

I then called Arnold Isaacs, a friend and a former Baltimore *Sun* reporter, to see if he had any ideas on how to proceed. He called back a few hours later to say that he'd checked property tax rolls at the public library and found an address for one of the two Melva J. Harrises. I wrote a letter, stuck it in the mail, and crossed my fingers. On January 10, 1995, I received a telephone call from Harris's widow.

Melva Harris told me that John III, now a lieutenant in the Marine Corps, was born on January 4, 1967, and that Harris had never gotten to see his son before he was killed. John III knew of his father only through pictures, and through the stories of his mother and Uncle Bobby, Harris's younger brother. She had never remarried. We made arrangements to meet the following month at her home, which turned out to be a small two-story row house in a hilly neighborhood on the north end of Baltimore.

Melva J. Smallwood, known then as Peggy, first met Harris when she moved onto his street in her early teens. "We lived on the same street," she said. "We were just in the 'hood' together. Back then, we called it the neighborhood. He would wave on his way to get a soda, or we would walk to the store together, or just sit and talk. I don't know why I was attracted to him. I don't have a clue. We just started talking. He wasn't a fighter. He wasn't a bully.

"We did things together," she continued, "but we didn't look at it as dating. We were just hanging out. We'd go see Gladys Knight and the Pips, or the Temptations. John wasn't the only one there. There was Bobby, Tracy—a group of boys and a group of girls. We were a gang, but it wasn't like things are today. We didn't harm anybody. We weren't violent. It was nothing for fifteen of us to go to the movies. We'd take the bus or walk. We were like brothers and sisters. We would help each other out with money. If somebody didn't have enough money for the movies, we'd come up with a nickel here, a dime there, whatever extra anybody had."

Melva knows very little about Harris's childhood or family life. She seldom went into his house, but thinks his mother was sick and his father was in a wheelchair by the time she moved onto his street. "I don't know anything about them," she said, and she can't explain why those

Private John L. Harris, Jr., August 1966. (PB)

death records give his mother's name as Johnson rather than Harris. She remembers watching Harris play football, so she thinks he must have been on the team at Carver High School. She thinks he graduated in 1965, though records I subsequently obtained from the National Personnel Records Center indicate that he only finished the eleventh grade.

Harris was good at working with his hands, she recalls. After high school, he didn't have a regular job, but he sometimes did home remodeling and renovating. She remembers him installing a window, taking out a wall and putting in a new one, and building a table and chair.

Melva was working as a waitress in a Chinese restaurant and waiting to hear about a job with the Social Security Administration when Harris enlisted in June 1966. "He always wanted to be in the service," she said. "I don't know why he chose the Marines. He never talked about that." Melva didn't know she was pregnant until after Harris had enlisted. "He thought I was pregnant when he left [for Parris Island]," she said, "but I didn't think so. We'd had sex before and nothing had happened, so there was no reason to think anything would happen. Then I had to write and tell him he was right. I never figured out how he knew."

Harris wrote to say he would marry her, but she wrote back saying he didn't have to. "I did love him," she explained. "It wasn't that. It's just a woman thing. I wanted him to marry me for me, not just because I was pregnant. And he was going off to war. I heard stores about people getting married, and then the man goes off to war and gets killed. I didn't know if I wanted to deal with that. And then my worst nightmare came true after all."

When Harris came home after basic training, it took him three weeks to persuade Melva to marry him. They were married on October 24, 1966. Just six days later, he reported for staging at Camp Pendleton, California, with orders for Vietnam. Melva planned to meet Harris in Hawaii during his rest and recreation leave, but his Aunt Ethel, who apparently had been his legal guardian after his parents died, wouldn't give Melva the money to go because she said the young couple should be saving what little they had for the baby. Because Melva couldn't join him, Harris decided not to go either. Had he gone on R&R, he would have been in Hawaii on the day he stepped on a mine and died.

"I have to believe she regretted her decision," Melva said, "but she never said anything. Back then, adults didn't admit mistakes. She made the best decision she could. She was thinking about the baby. She thought it was the right decision when she made it."

At the time, Melva was living with her parents. When she called home one day to tell her mother where she was, she was told two officers were waiting to see her. "John is hurt and they need to take me where he is," she recalled thinking. "I didn't even prepare myself for what they told me. They said, 'Sit down.' I wanted to know what I needed to get together to go with them."

With Harris's government insurance, Melva moved into an apartment, paid the rent for six months, and bought furniture, clothes, and a car. "Things were very depressing for me at a young age, but I couldn't stay there because I would have died too, emotionally if not physically." After six months, she went back to waitressing, and in 1968 she got the job with Social Security, where she still works. She acknowledges that her husband's death has shaped her attitude about work: "I think that's why I have a rebel attitude. When I was younger, I used to feel like, 'Hey, my husband died for these people, and they're treating me like dirt.' I'm better than I used to be, but it's still there."

Though she never remarried, she did have two additional children, Edward, now a high school art teacher, and Yolanda, currently in banking. Both are college graduates, as is John III, who earned a degree in architecture from the University of Maryland in 1990 before joining the Marines. He wanted to join out of high school; Melva didn't want him to join at all, but she knew she'd have to compromise, so she asked him to go to college first, then go in as an officer.

Of her husband's death, she said, "I don't think about it because I can't. Life goes on. If I dwell in the past, I won't get done what I need to do. I had a son to raise, and my other children. But memory never dies. I can bring John forth any time I want to."

Earlier, she had said that she never remarried because she felt she couldn't balance children and a husband, but toward the end of the afternoon she volunteered that she hadn't remarried because "I haven't let go of John. And it's been twenty-seven years. I know there's things I have to do, but I can't do them yet. I haven't been to the [Vietnam Veterans] Memorial yet. I hated that war. It destroyed by husband. When you go off to war, you're supposed to be fighting for something. You're supposed to be defending something. What were we defending? Why were we in Vietnam? What were we doing there?"

The day I came to visit, Melva explained that she still had all of her husband's things in her basement, but she didn't feel up to going through them that day. Perhaps I could go through those things, she said, and also meet Harris's brother, at another time. It was clear that the afternoon was over, that Melva Harris needed a break from my endless questions.

In July 1995, NPRC sent me Harris's military records. From these I learned that after boot camp, Harris received training as an 81mm mortarman (0341) before going home on leave on September 29, 1966. He reported for duty with the 4th Replacement Company, Staging Battalion, on October 30. On February 6, 1967, he was transferred to the 3rd Replacement Company, then detached on February 9.

He must have traveled to Vietnam by ship because his next assignment, 0341 ammo man with F Company, 2nd Battalion, 4th Marines, 3rd Marine Division in Vietnam, is dated March 9. After just six days, he was reassigned as an 0141 admin man with Headquarters & Support Company, first with S-5 civil affairs for ten days, then with S-3 operations from March 25 to June 2. From June 2 until June 8, he was assigned to E Company as an ammo man. On June 9, he was reassigned back to H&S Company, this time as an 0311 rifleman and S-2 scout.

Harris was killed in action on September 20, 1967, in the vicinity of Quang Tri. He was awarded the Purple Heart, the National Defense Service Medal, the Vietnam Service Medal, the Military Merit Medal, the Cross of Gallantry, and the Vietnam Campaign Medal. At the time of his death, he was twenty years and eight days old.

In the meantime, two subsequent telephone calls and two letters to Melva Harris went unanswered, so I finally got the address of John III from the Commandant of the Marine Corps and wrote to him in October 1995, hoping that he might be able to help me gain access to his uncle and to the things in his mother's basement. A month later, I received his reply, dated November 14, 1995:

> I have presented your requested audience to both mother and my uncle. They refused to assist your efforts at this time. In your letter you asked for advice and assistance. The death of my father was devastating for the both of them. To ask their support to draft an article is too painful of a task. One might think that 28 years is enough time to recover from any misfortune. I would agree if they were Marines. However, reality dictates my father's resurrected memory causes an enormous hurt. I suggest you discontinue efforts to accumulate dad's biography. . . . I realize this news disappoints you, but I wish to be completely honest.
>
> Sincerely, J. L. Harris III, 1STLT USMC.

John III, his mother told me, wears a Marine Corps ring that used to be his father's. She still has the matching ring his father gave to her nearly thirty years ago. The hinges and clasp of the box in which it came and in which she still keeps it are badly rusted, but the ring itself looks as if it had been bought only yesterday.

Daniel R. Hawryschuk

Only one Daniel R. Hawryschuk appeared on the Myers list, but the letter I sent to the Rochester, New York, address was returned undelivered, so on September 20, 1993, I called directory assistance for the Rochester area and got two numbers, one for a Daniel and another for a Daniel, Jr. Initially, this led me only to two answering machines, but I left a message on each and later that day received a call from one more member of Platoon 1005.

Hawryschuk told me that Daniel, Jr., is his oldest son, who was then a recent college graduate. He has another son, Jason, then a college junior. He also mentioned that his younger brother, Gregory, who was also in Platoon 1005, was living on the other side of Rochester. He said nothing else about his brother, but described himself as "upper middle class" and said that he was "still married" and held a master's degree in business administration. He added that he was at the moment involuntarily between jobs, though otherwise "doing okay," but a 1995 Christmas card from his wife, Marcia, said that she was writing because her husband was always so busy with his work, which suggests that he'd found another job since we'd spoken.

In February 1996, I learned from NPRC that Hawryschuk was born on March 7, 1946, in Kreglingen, Germany, but was living in Rochester, New York, at the time of his enlistment. He graduated from high school in 1963 and completed two and half years of college before enlisting. He qualified as a Sharpshooter on the rifle range at Parris Island, requalifying in 1967 with a lower score as Marksman, and again in 1968 at the highest category of Expert.

After boot camp and basic infantry training, Hawryschuk received nine months' training at Marine Corps Recruit Depot, San Diego, California, as an aviation radar repairman (5944). He was then assigned to Headquarters & Headquarters Squadron, Marine Corps Air Station, Beaufort, South Carolina, in July 1967. From October until December, he received additional training at the Naval Training Center, Great Lakes, Illinois, before returning to MCAS Beaufort, where he remained for the rest of his enlistment. He earned the Good Conduct and National Defense Service Medals and was released from active duty in June 1970 with the rank of sergeant.

Gregory Hawryschuk

Daniel Hawryschuk said in September 1993 that he would forward a letter to his younger brother, and Marcia Hawryschuk included her brother-in-law's address in her 1995 Christmas card, but Gregory Hawryschuk has never responded to any of my several letters. Records received from NPRC in February 1996 indicate that he was born on February 16, 1948, graduated from high school, and was living in Rochester, New York, at the time of his enlistment. After boot camp and basic infantry training, he received on-the-job training as an embarkation assistant (0431) with Headquarters Company, Headquarters & Support Battalion, Camp Lejeune, North Carolina.

From December 1966 until December 1967, Hawryschuk served in Vietnam with Force Logistics Service Group A, 3rd Service Battalion (later redesignated Support Battalion, 1st Force Service Regiment), Force Logistics Command, including a month's temporary duty aboard the USS *Washburn.*

For the remainder of his enlistment, Hawryschuk was assigned to Amphibious Group #2, first at U.S. Naval Base Little Creek, Norfolk, Virginia, then aboard the USS *Taconic,* followed by the USS *Pocono,* and finally back at Little Creek. He was released from active duty in April 1970 with the rank of sergeant. His decorations include the Combat Action Ribbon, a Navy Unit Commendation, and the Good Conduct, National Defense Service, Vietnam Service, and Vietnam Campaign Medals.

David A. Hewitt

If you want to understand just how deeply the Vietnam War etched itself into David Hewitt's life, ask him about the Welcome Home parade New York City gave for Vietnam veterans on May 7, 1985. "We didn't know how people were going to react to us," he says. "At first we were all really quiet, but people along the route shouted, 'Lift your heads up! Be proud!' It was incredible. We were wading through ticker tape ankle deep, knee deep."

As Hewitt talks, the tears well up in his eyes, then spill down his cheeks. They don't embarrass him. He has earned them. "That was real emotional," he says of the parade. "I'm proud of what I did [in Vietnam],

Private First Class David A. Hewitt dropping a round into an 81mm mortar, Vietnam, April 1967. "This photo is posed," says Hewitt, a mortarman for the first half of his tour in Vietnam. "I wouldn't really be loading a mortar in my shower shoes."

The Hewitt family, 1994. Left to right: *David A., son David M., wife Sandy, and daughter Carol-Beth.*

and if anybody wants to thank me for it, I'm ready. Okay, it's fifteen years later, but people along the parade route were really sincere. It was a good experience."

If Hewitt had had his way, he never would have been a combat Marine in Vietnam. After graduating from Southern Regional High School in 1965, the Tuckerton, New Jersey, man went to work for Pacemaker Boats, but got a draft notice in the early winter of 1966. "I missed a 2-S student deferment from Ocean County Community College by only a few days," he says. "I didn't want to get involved in any of that [Vietnam] stuff. I didn't want to go into combat. If I could have gotten into the National Guard, I would have done that."

He tried to join the Navy, but failed the general aptitude test. "I don't know how that happened," he says, his voice still full of wonder after all these years. "I'm not *that* stupid. Then I tried to get into the Coast Guard, but the waiting list was as long as your arm. The Army wanted me right away, but I joined the Marines because I could delay my enlistment for four months. I guess it was pride, too. If I was going to go into combat, I wanted to be in the Marines. They were better trained. I had a better chance of surviving, or at least that's what I thought. I was eighteen, what the heck."

By December 6, 1966, after boot camp, infantry training, mortar school (Hewitt had been designated 0341, an 81mm mortarman) and staging, he found himself in Vietnam, assigned to 2nd Battalion, 26th Marine Regiment. "When I went over," he says, "I didn't think I would come back. I thought I was going to die there." It didn't help his spirits, he says, that he arrived just as the monsoon season hit, or that he found himself not just a new guy but an outsider in a battalion that had come to Vietnam the previous summer as a coherent unit.

Hewitt battled depression along with the Viet Cong through most of his first four months in Vietnam. One source of support and comfort he could draw upon was periodic visits with his hometown friend, Walt Horner, a 1964 Southern Regional graduate assigned to 2nd Battalion, 9th Marines. The two battalions often seemed to be based in close proximity, and Horner and Hewitt visited whenever they could.

Hewitt's spirits worsened, however, when an old nemesis reappeared. While working at Pacemaker Boats, Hewitt had developed neurodermatitis, a painful skin disease, probably caused by contact with the strong chemicals used in boat manufacturing. The neurodermatitis had recurred at Parris Island, but in the spring of 1967 it recurred with a vengeance. His hands and arms swelled up, his fingers became gnarled, and he could hardly eat or dress, let alone perform his duties with the mortar crew. He was placed on light duty for thirty days.

(Many years later, when Hewitt obtained his medical records from the government, he discovered that there was no record of his ever having been treated for neurodermatitis, either at Parris Island or in Vietnam. "I've never thought my neurodermatitis was related to Agent Orange poisoning," he says. "I've always blamed it on the boatbuilding, but I guess they weren't going to take any chances.")

In May 1967, the rest of his battalion took part in Operation Hickory, but Hewitt stayed in the rear because of his light duty status. "I took a lot of crap from the guys around me because I couldn't do anything," he says. "People thought I was a skate, a shirker." Indeed, Hewitt's squad leader, a corporal, never forgave him for what he perceived to be malingering. A buddy of the squad leader died on Operation Hickory, and when the squad leader came back in from the field, he told Hewitt, "You should have died instead of him."

"It was very hurtful personally," says Hewitt, who was already feeling rotten enough because only a few days earlier he'd learned that Walt Horner had been killed in action. Two other corporals tried to defend Hewitt, then a private first class, reminding the squad leader that while he had lost a Vietnam buddy, Hewitt had lost a home buddy. "But it didn't matter," says Hewitt. "Right up until he rotated home two months later, my squad leader used to say to me, 'I hope you die today.' Things like that."

Finally in July, since Hewitt's skin rash continued to hamper his ability to perform his duties with the mortar crew, and because there was a shortage of forward observers, he volunteered to become a forward observer. "Then I became like a grunt," he says. "I spent more time in the bush than anybody. I got some respect back when I became an FO. The depression and the feeling that I was going to die began to lift. I became more confident. I finally found a job I could do in spite of my skin problems.

"I liked being an FO," he continues. "I got to use my head. And I knew what was going on because I was part of the 'inner circle' [company commander or platoon leader, senior noncommissioned officers, and radiomen]. Out in the Ashau Valley, I had access to naval gunfire, air support, and Army 175mm 'Long Tom' cannons in addition to Marine artillery. I trained my radioman to know everything I knew, and he trained me in everything he knew. That way, if one of us got injured or killed, the other could still get the job done."

From July until he rotated home in late December 1967, Hewitt divided his time among convoy duty, battalion sweeps, and combined action operations. "I was lucky the combined action units I was assigned to didn't get attacked," he says. "I don't know what would have happened. The PFs [Popular Forces: Vietnamese local militia] weren't very dependable. They were as likely to run as to fight."

It bothered Hewitt that Saigon's forces, both militia and regular army, seldom held up their end of the fight, but he was equally bothered by Marines who threw C-rations at beggar children, trying to hurt them. "The kids were irritating," he says, "but I didn't hate them. I didn't hate the Vietnamese."

Hewitt believes American soldiers initially went to Vietnam to win the war but also believes that attitude changed with the infusion of large numbers of draftees. "We used to debate the merits of the war," he says, "but I never felt as if I was doing something that wasn't right. I was never antiwar while I was in Vietnam."

After he left Vietnam, Hewitt was assigned to 3rd Battalion, 6th Marines, spending the first several months of 1968 at Camp Lejeune and several more months on a Caribbean cruise. "During the cruise, we were sent through jungle training in Panama," he says. "This is after Vietnam. Eighty-four percent of the battalion has already been to Vietnam, and then they send us to jungle school."

At the end of the cruise, in July 1968, Hewitt was reassigned to Pearl Harbor, Hawaii, where he served out his three-year enlistment as a military policeman with a security battalion guarding gates, secure areas, and headquarters installations. "It was a spit-and-polish job," he says. "On Sundays we wore dress blue trousers with khaki tropical shirts, white hats, white gloves, and whistles."

But the new assignment was less than ideal. Much of what Hawaii offered turned out to be too expensive for a junior enlisted man, a paradise that was largely beyond reach. Moreover, for six months straight, Hewitt's unit had to stand what he calls "running guard" (four hours on, eight hours off, around the clock, seven days a week) because the unit was understaffed. There was a lot of drug use in Hawaii, he says, at least partly in response to the stress of running guard. Hewitt himself nearly got into trouble when another man borrowed his shirt, then got busted with several joints in the shirt pocket. "He tried to claim the joints were mine," says Hewitt.

Though Hewitt avoided drug troubles while in Hawaii, he did receive an Article 15, resulting in a loss of rank from lance corporal to private first class, for "falsifying a document. About ten of us went to the club one night," he explains. "Two guys got into a fight with some sailors. All the rest of us did was lie about who started the fight. We all said the sailors started it, but our guys started it." By the time he was separated in June 1969, however, he had earned back his stripe, and was honorably discharged as a lance corporal.

Hewitt returned to Tuckerton, where I interviewed him on January 8, 1995. I'd first spoken to him by telephone in March 1994 after Gary Davis gave me his number. The two men had met by chance at the Vietnam Veterans Memorial in Washington, D.C., on Veterans Day 1984, recognizing each other though they hadn't been together since boot camp, and have stayed in touch since.

Hewitt's family has very deep roots in Tuckerton. Both sides of the family hail from Lincolnshire, England, his mother's family arriving in the Tuckerton area in 1675, followed not long thereafter by his father's side of the family. Hewitt's father, now deceased, was chief of police in Tuckerton for twenty-two years. Hewitt himself took a succession of jobs over the next few years, none of which caught fire.

What did catch fire was his relationship with Sandy Kann. Hewitt had been engaged twice already, but neither engagement had ended in marriage. "I was anxious to get married," he says. "I was ready to settle down. I just couldn't find the right woman." Until he met Sandy, that is. The two were introduced by a mutual friend, had their first date on the day Hewitt was to have been married the second time, and were married in January 1971, seven months after that first date.

Both Sandy and her mother worked for Acme at the time, and in 1972 Hewitt got a job there, too, working on the night crew stocking shelves and ordering new inventory. Though he stayed for eight years, Hewitt says it wasn't always the easiest place to work. "I had two coworkers who were very antiwar *and* antivet," he says. "One of them was even a Stateside Vietnam-era veteran, but it didn't matter. I always felt like I had to be on the defensive. There were only five people on the night crew, and there was lots of time to talk, but I couldn't ever get those two guys to change their minds about anything. I finally stopped talking and avoided the subject altogether."

When that particular Acme closed down, Hewitt left rather than make the long commute to the store in which he was offered a replacement position. After another brief succession of forgettable jobs, he ended up on a night crew at Shop Rite, where he spent six more years until taking his current position eight years ago in retail lumber sales at Tuckerton Lumber Company (where Sandy also works in the hardware division).

"My Shop Rite experience helped me feel a lot better about being a vet," he says. "It was a much better working atmosphere than Acme. There were twenty-three people on the night crew, including five Vietnam veterans. The vets respected each other, and the rest of the crew respected them. It was also a different time. The Vietnam Veterans Memorial [the Wall] was dedicated in 1982. People began to listen to individual soldiers' experiences. And all the books that were getting published helped to change public perceptions. Before that, people just made assumptions about Vietnam veterans, like with drugs. I didn't do any drugs until Hawaii, but lots of people just assumed I must have been doing drugs in Vietnam."

Hewitt didn't make it to the dedication of the Wall, but he took his whole family (Sandy, son David M., born in 1978, and daughter Carol-Beth, born in 1982) to the dedication of the Frederick Hart statue the following year. The other vets at Shop Rite wouldn't go to see the Wall, he said, because they'd "bought into that black gash of shame theory, but I found it very moving. Seeing the names on the Wall makes them real people, not just numbers. I looked up Walt Horner's name," he adds.

As our afternoon together progresses, 13-year-old Carol-Beth (the namesake of one of Hewitt's sisters, who died in young adulthood) flits through the house like a fairy sprite, sometimes visible, mostly not, but 17-year-old David M. sits in the living room for several hours, quietly listening to his father. Hewitt doesn't suffer from "Silent Vietnam Veteran Syndrome," so both children are very much aware of the impact of the Vietnam War on their father's life. Though Carol-Beth was too young to remember anything but the fuzzy edges, she rode in a stroller the whole length of the parade route that day in 1985, and David M. remembers the parade vividly. The kids have been lucky, Sandy adds, to have several teachers in school who have also encouraged exploration and discussion of the war.

Children, both their own and others', are a main focus, perhaps *the* main focus, of the Hewitts' lives. From the time David M. was six, he began playing organized T-ball, and Carol-Beth soon followed. Hewitt coached both kids' teams for three years. When David M. went on to baseball, Hewitt coached his son's baseball team for four more years, and when Carol-Beth went from T-ball to softball, Sandy went with her. Carol-Beth is still playing after four years, with Sandy in her third year of coaching.

Meanwhile, Hewitt is in his second year as president of the local organization that oversees all of this, the Bay Shore Athletic Association (affiliated with Babe Ruth League baseball), while Sandy has been a board member for three years. "You've got to want to do it," says Hewitt of the league presidency. "You have to give up a lot of time. You have to be diplomatic. The league encompasses four municipalities, and there are Democrats and Republicans. You have to learn to beg because you always need money and sponsors."

As if these activities were not enough, father and son coach daughter's Junior Wildcats basketball team while Sandy helps out with the team's "girl-specific needs," all of this as part of a recreational basketball league sponsored by the local public school system.

The Hewitts are a tight-knit family, their lives revolving around

Tuckerton and surrounding Little Egg Harbor Township. "We've got access to everything we need right here," says Hewitt. "We went to Philadelphia once to see the Franklin Institute, but we couldn't figure out how to get off the Vine Street Expressway and we ended up at the zoo instead." Though their house is almost within sight of the neon glitter of Atlantic City, the Hewitts have never been to the casinos. And though the Atlantic Ocean is almost close enough to throw rocks into, the Hewitts haven't been to the beach in six years because, as Hewitt explains, "It's too crowded, and you have to pay. We have a backyard pool if we want to cool off."

David M. excuses himself and heads off to choir practice. Soon afterwards, Sandy leaves to take Carol-Beth to church. "When I first got to Vietnam," Hewitt says, "I didn't have any pictures of my family. Walt had a picture of my sister, so he gave it to me. I think the reason I can't completely say the war was wrong is because my friend was killed."

On the table in front of Hewitt lies an old yellowed copy of the *Tuckerton Chronicle* dated Wednesday, May 31, 1967. On the front page is a two-column article headlined "In Tribute to a Fellow Marine." Most of the article consists of a letter Hewitt wrote to his parents on May 18, 1967, soon after he learned that Walt Horner was dead. Near the end of that long ago letter, Hewitt had written: "I am deeply shocked and grieved at [Walt's] death. It will take some time for me to get over it." More time, it seems, a lot more time, than the twenty-eight years that have already passed.

Leonard T. Hibbler

Some men were easy to find, and some were not. Some men wanted to talk, and some did not. Hibbler is a case in point.

No one named Leonard Hibbler showed up on the Myers list in August 1993, but in February 1994 I got Hibbler's social security number through the VA claim system and MIE, Inc., ran a trace that turned up three different addresses in Long Beach, California. I sent letters to all three. Two came back undeliverable. I got no response from the third. Six months later, I wrote again to the third address; this time it, too, came back undeliverable.

In December 1994 I got a CD-ROM drive for my computer, enabling me to run my own newly acquired computerized telephone directory, which listed yet another address in Long Beach for Hibbler along with a telephone number (the social security traces came with addresses only, not phone numbers). But the letter I sent once again came back undeliverable, and the telephone number turned out to be no longer in service.

A couple of months later, in February 1995, I was going through my notes and rediscovered what Larry Maxey had told me back in September 1993: his recollection was that Hibbler had come from Hattiesburg, Mississippi. I checked Hibblers in Hattiesburg on my phone disk and found five of them. I wrote to all five, hoping at least one of them might be related to Leonard. Three weeks later, on March 17, 1995, I got a call from Hibbler's mother, Sarah Warren.

Mrs. Warren told me she'd been talking with a niece who happened to mention that her mother had gotten a letter asking about a Hibbler who had been in the Marines. Hibbler's cousin and aunt didn't know who the letter was talking about because all of his friends and relatives had always called him "L. T.," not Leonard, but Mrs. Warren realized the letter was about her son. She dug out her son's old platoon book, and there I was. Having satisfied herself that I really had been in Platoon 1005 with her son, she called me.

She told me that Leonard was indeed living in southern California, in or near Long Beach, that his fiftieth birthday was in two days, so that might be a good day to call, and that I should tell him she had given me his phone number. She said she thought he would be happy to hear from me.

Eager to connect with Hibbler after searching for him for more than a year and a half, I didn't wait for his birthday but called immediately. I could hear a young child or children crying in the background as the woman who answered told me that Hibbler had just stepped out. She expected him back shortly, and took my name and phone number. Over the next two days, Hibbler did not call back, so I called again on his birthday. The same woman answered. She said she was surprised that he hadn't called back because she had given him my message, and she would remind him again to call.

I did not receive a callback, however, so a week later, on March 26, 1995, I called again. Twice. Each time I got a recording that said, "We're sorry. You have reached a number that is not in service. Please check the number and dial again." The next day I called Hibbler's mother. She did not know why the telephone number no longer worked, but said she would forward a letter to him. I sent the letter to her that day, but I never received a reply.

Six months later, on September 5, 1995, I tried the last number I'd had for Hibbler once again. This time, the number was back in service. It was answered by a young man who said that Hibbler was not there but that he would convey my message to him. Once again, I never got any reply. At this point, I concluded that Hibbler did not want to talk to me and stopped trying to reach him.

Records received from NPRC indicate that Hibbler was born on March 19, 1945, in Shuqualak, Mississippi. A high school graduate, he was living n Hattiesburg, Mississippi, at the time of his enlistment. After boot camp and basic infantry training, he spent four weeks at the Marine Corps Engineer School at Camp Lejeune, North Carolina, receiving training as a combat engineer (1371). Hibbler spent a total of two years on active duty, all of it in the continental United States, achieving the rank of lance corporal and receiving the National Defense Service Medal.

Warren Hills, Jr.

One of six Warren Hillses on the Myers list, Hills received my initial search letter and called me on September 18, 1993. From that conversation and records received from the Commandant of the Marine Corps in June 1996, I learned that Hills grew up in Philadelphia, but moved when he was in his mid-teens to Coatesville, Pennsylvania, where he completed his last year of high school before graduating in 1966. He received a draft notice even before he graduated, which was deferred when he told Selective Service that he was still in school, but he knew then that the draft was waiting. "I wasn't going into the Army," he says, "so I enlisted in the Marines."

Along with Jessie F. Waters, Hills was designated by Platoon 1005's drill instructors as platoon "house mouse" because of his diminutive size. The house mice served as "gofers" for the DIS, running errands, getting coffee, taking care of the duty room, and performing other tasks as required. Upon graduation from boot camp, he received a meritorious promotion to private first class.

Hills subsequently received on-the-job training as a general warehouseman (3051) with Headquarters & Support Company, Base Materials Battalion, Camp Lejeune, North Carolina, before being assigned to the Communications Company of H&S Battalion, 2nd Force Service Regiment, Force Troops, Fleet Marine Force Atlantic, at Camp Lejeune from November 1966 to March 1967.

In May, Hills joined H&S Company, Support Battalion, 3rd Force Service Regiment, stationed on Okinawa, where he served until June 1968. He then went directly from Okinawa to Vietnam, where he served with Marine Air Control Squadron 4, Marine Air Control Group 18, before being transferred in August 1968 to Headquarters & Maintenance Squadron 17, Marine Wing Support Group 17.

Hills's initial three-year enlistment was due to expire simultaneous to the completion of his tour of duty in Vietnam, but instead of going back to the States and getting out, he reenlisted in the Marines and extended his tour in Vietnam by an additional six months. "Home wasn't the same," he says. "My friends were still running the streets and going nowhere. Nobody changed but me." He talked to his father about reenlisting, and his father said that if that's what he wanted to do, then he should do it. "So I did," he says.

Hills remained in Vietnam with H&MS-17 until December 1969. Over the next nineteen years, he would serve at bases ranging from Camp Butler, Okinawa; Pearl Harbor, Hawaii; and Santa Ana, California; to Camp Lejeune, North Carolina; and Norfolk and Quantico, Virginia. His duty assignments ranged from general warehouseman to subsistence support man to fiscal clerk to marksmanship instructor.

As he rose through the ranks, however, and the Marine Corps changed over the years, Hills had an increasingly difficult time adjusting to what he calls "the new Marine Corps." It reached the point, he says, where you had to explain to junior enlisted men why it was necessary to swab a floor when it was dirty. Moreover, he adds, "Staff NCOs coming up now aren't worth the salt you put in your bread." At one point, his base sergeant major reprimanded him for not understanding "the new Corps," he says. "I was supposed to make E9 [the highest enlisted rank] within two years, but I knew if I stayed in, I'd get busted." Then he received orders once again for Okinawa. "I'd already been there five or six times," he says. "I didn't want to go overseas again. And I realized my son [born in 1972] was growing up fast and I was missing out on that experience."

It all added up to a decision to retire, which Hills did in 1988 with the rank of master sergeant after twenty-one years and seven months on active duty. His decorations and awards include the National Defense Service, Vietnam Service, and Vietnam Campaign Medals, seven Good Conduct Medals, the Combat Action and Sea Service Deployment Ribbons, and a Meritorious Mast.

Married since 1971, Hills now works as an ammunition handler for the U.S. Army in northern Virginia. And in spite of his difficulties with the changes in the Marine Corps over the years, he says, "Would I do it again? Yeh."

Timothy J. Jenkins

For a quarter of a century, Tim Jenkins didn't think much about what he'd seen and done in Vietnam. Within a few years of his release from active duty, he got a job in the coal mines of his native West Virginia, and when he wasn't down in the mines, he was driving a lumber delivery truck, or helping his wife build and run their mom-and-pop variety store, or serving as a volunteer firefighter, or leading a Boy Scout troop. Life was full, time for reflection short.

Then in October 1995, after twenty-two years in the mines, Jenkins was laid off, and he suddenly had more time than he ever wanted, more time than was good for him. He began to think about a lot of things he hadn't thought about before. He began to think about the war. One incident in particular kept coming back to him. His unit had come under Viet Cong attack. One of the attackers was only a boy, perhaps eleven or twelve.

"I think I killed him," Jenkins says. "He was armed, but that doesn't make me feel any better about it." As the months passed, Jenkins became more and more depressed until he began to think that living wasn't worth the effort. The long ago war in Vietnam was threatening to claim another casualty.

Jenkins had joined the Marines in the first place, he says, because "I wanted revenge." His boyhood friend James Sawyer had joined the Marines a year earlier and had died in Vietnam on August 18, 1965. All through his senior year at Clay-Battelle High School in Tentress, Jenkins

Lance Corporal Timothy J. Jenkins (left) *with two buddies from 1st Shore Party Battalion, Da Nang, Vietnam, 1967. The man at the far right is Private Wayne L. Kelly, another member of Platoon 1005.*

knew what he wanted to do when he graduated, and in June 1966 he left for Parris Island.

Like any former Marine, Jenkins has stories from boot camp. Once a fellow recruit accidentally bumped Jenkins's rifle, knocking it to the floor with a clatter. The drill instructors thought Jenkins had dropped it, a cardinal sin. "I really didn't drop it," he says, "but I never got a chance to explain, and they wouldn't have believed me anyway." That night, Jenkins's rifle spent the night in bed with him. Another time, he was ordered to do the manual of arms with his footlocker. "I tell that story to my friends and they don't believe me," he says. "'How can you do the manual of arms with a footlocker?' I tell 'em, 'When those DIS are screaming at you, you figure out real quick.'"

But Jenkins also remembers a time when Senior DI J. J. Oliver took the whole platoon out behind the barracks one day. "When I joined the Marines," Jenkins recalls Oliver saying, "I was told you had to go out and get the clap and get drunk and get into fights to be a Marine. But I'm here to tell you that you don't have to do any of that to be a Marine."

"I'd like to thank those guys," Jenkins says of the DIS. "They saved

Janet and Tim Jenkins, circa 1990.

my ass." He believes strongly that the training they gave him in South Carolina kept him alive in Vietnam. After additional training as a shore party man (1381), Jenkins arrived in Vietnam in mid-December 1966, assigned to C Company, 1st Shore Party Battalion.

His first assignment was as a messman. Every morning it was his duty to make coffee, a process that consisted of throwing loose coffee grounds into a huge vat. "I was supposed to dip out the officers' coffee first, then the NCOS', then give the dregs to the enlisted men," he explains with a mischievous twinkle in his voice, "but I always did it the other way around."

Jenkins's war got serious soon enough, however. During his first combat operation, Sierra, six members of C Company were killed when their helicopter crashed at sea. One of the dead was fellow Platoon 1005er Francis Langley, whom Jenkins had known since the first days of boot camp. When Jenkins asked a corpsman why he wasn't asked to identify Langley's body, the corpsman replied, "You wouldn't have recognized him."

Throughout 1967 Jenkins alternated between minesweeping duty and helicopter support team duty. While on a minesweeping patrol in early October, Jenkins sustained shrapnel wounds to both arms and both legs when a fellow shore party man triggered a booby trap. "If it had been a mine instead of a homemade booby trap," he says, "we'd have both been killed." As it was, he spent a week in a hospital in Da Nang, then returned to duty.

Six weeks later, during Operation Foster, while assigned to a helicopter support team attached to F Company, 2nd Battalion, 7th Marines, Jenkins earned a Navy Commendation Medal with Combat V. His citation reads in part:

Early in the evening [of November 26, 1967], the company came under heavy enemy mortar attack and sustained several casualties, including the support team leader. Displaying exceptional initiative, Corporal Jenkins assumed command of the helicopter support team, manned the radio and called for a medical evacuation mission. Fearlessly exposing himself to the intense hostile fire, he organized teams and directed the movement of casualties to the landing zone he had established. . . . When the helicopter arrived, Corporal Jenkins . . . repeatedly exposed himself to enemy small arms fire to guide [the helicopter] into the insecure zone.

The fighting continued for more than twenty-four hours. After his team leader was hit and evacuated, Jenkins's remaining team member said, "He was lucky. We're not getting out of here." When that man too was wounded, Jenkins says, "I began to wonder." But he survived Foster unscathed, served out the remainder of his tour, and returned to the U.S. in January 1968.

He spent the next year assigned to 2nd Shore Party Battalion at Camp Lejeune, North Carolina, but spent most of that year on a Caribbean cruise with Battalion Landing Team 3/6, followed immediately by a Mediterranean cruise with BLT 3/2. In February 1969, he was transferred to the Marine Barracks on Guam and received a promotion to sergeant and assignment to the detachment guarding the naval magazine.

While on Guam, Jenkins had his only brush with the Uniform Code of Military Justice, receiving an Article 15 (nonjudicial punishment), a story he relates with no little amusement. It seems that one day while he was on guard duty, two sailors in a pickup truck pulled up to his post and said, "Bang! Bang! You're dead." Realizing this was a training exercise, Jenkins did what he would do if it were the real thing: with his "dying breath," he closed the gate on the truck. During the Article 15 proceeding, his company commander, a lowly lieutenant, told Jenkins that under different circumstances he'd be giving Jenkins a medal—but a Navy captain (the equivalent of a full colonel in the other services) was demanding disciplinary action. Jenkins received a one-sentence reprimand in his service record book, duly noting that he had cost the U.S. Navy $138.90 in repairs to the truck.

After his release from active duty in June 1970, Jenkins enrolled in college, but before classes began he wrecked his knee in a motorcycle accident and spent the better part of a year immobilized. By the time he was healed, he had so many bills to pay off that he had no choice except to find a job. He spent six months filling and delivering gas bottles for Hagedorn Bottled Gas Company, but then got the opportunity to apply for a job in the mines, so he quit Hagedorn.

Unfortunately, he failed the eye test and didn't get the mining job after all, so he took a job with the West Virginia University physical plant, spending the next two and a half years raking leaves, shoveling snow, and cutting grass at the Morgantown campus. It was a job he enjoyed, but when he got a second opportunity to apply for the better-paying mine work, he took it. How did he get around the problem of his weak eyes? "I memorized the eye chart," he says, again with that twinkle in his voice.

Jenkins spent his entire mining career at Consolidated Coal Company's Arkwright #1 Mine, the same mine where his father worked. One of Jenkins's three brothers also worked there for a while, but didn't like mining and quit. Jenkins, on the other hand, loved it. "The coal mines I worked in," he says, "I didn't have to duck down, at least not that often. We had eight-foot coal seams. Big chambers. You could work standing up." It was hard work, eight hours a day, six days a week, but the pay was good and so were the benefits.

"I know I was making more money than some people with college degrees," he says. "And all the guys were safe, too. Consolidated ran a good mine. It never bothered me to go down in the mine. I never thought about it." Though immediate safety was never a concern, he says, he does admit that after the first ten years or so, he began to worry about black lung disease, especially after his father died in 1987 of lung cancer, probably induced, Jenkins thinks, by a combination of smoking and mining.

About the time he became a miner, Jenkins also got married, but the marriage, after producing a daughter, ended in divorce six years later. Meanwhile, the same year Jenkins got married, a twenty-year-old named Janet Lipscomb married her high school sweetheart, Kenneth "Spike" Lynch. Lynch was a supervisor at Consolidated, and when he was seriously injured in a car accident in 1983, Jenkins was among those who donated emergency blood. It was to no avail, however: six days later, Lynch died, leaving a widow and a boy of eight.

Jenkins had never met Lynch's wife, but a few months after the accident they were introduced by a mutual friend, and soon began to spend time together, though always in groups, never alone. "When my first husband died," says Janet, "I fell apart. Tim helped me through a really bad time. He would talk with me on the telephone for hours; then he'd hang up and go to work." Later that year, they went to Florida together—again as part of a group—but Janet's sister, unbeknownst to her, had bought a "sexy nightgown" and stashed it in Janet's luggage. One thing led to another, and the two were married in September 1983.

For the next twelve years, life was full and fast and generally good. Jenkins and Janet built a small store just down the road from their house, and Janet ran it for seven years before they got a buyout offer too good to refuse, whereupon Janet got her real estate license. She also continued the package-tour travel business she'd started during her first marriage, arranging charter bus trips to places like Atlantic City, Niagara Falls, Nashville, and Disneyworld. Jenkins became stepson Michael's Boy Scout troop leader. In 1986 he also joined the Cool Springs Volunteer Fire Department, and by 1993 had become fire chief, an elective post he's held ever since.

The only real unhappiness during those years was a falling out Jenkins had with his daughter, resulting in their estrangement from each other. She is now married and has a child of her own, but Jenkins says next to nothing about either his first marriage or his daughter.

Then came the mine closing in 1995. Though it came only after plenty of advance warning—officially, Consolidated gave sixty days' notice, but unofficially the miners had known almost a year earlier—no amount of advance warning could have prepared Jenkins for the powerful impact of so drastic a life change. As the months passed, his depression deepened into a black and paralyzing despair.

Fortunately, Janet's support never waivered, and by the summer of 1996, realizing that he'd better get help, he approached the Department of Veterans Affairs. He found it more than a little disconcerting that the first VA doctor he met turned out to be Cambodian, but he went back again and was eventually diagnosed with post-traumatic stress disorder and awarded a 30 percent disability. Since then, he's been participating in group counseling sessions at the Vet Center in Morgantown, and life is looking brighter again.

Jenkins, in fact, is looking forward to a whole new career. Since Arkwright #1 was closed because the coal remaining in the mine is too high in sulfur content to be burned without causing unacceptable levels of air pollution, the laid-off miners are eligible for federal funds for job retraining through the Clean Air Act. Taking advantage of these funds, in September 1996 Jenkins began a one-year nursing program at Fayette

County Vocational School in nearby Uniontown, Pennsylvania, at the end of which he'll earn certification as a licensed practical nurse. Nursing seemed like a logical career path to choose, Jenkins explains, given that he already has six years of training and experience as an emergency medical technician with the fire department.

After a few hours in the Jenkins house, where I spent the day on September 21, 1996, it's hard to imagine that Jenkins ever had too much unoccupied time on his hands. The house is full of people. It's hard to tell who's family and who's not because even the people who aren't in the family might as well be. Michael, now grown, lives in a trailer just down the road and is in and out constantly, often accompanied by the Jenkins's grandson Ashton Michael, born in 1993. Living at the house are Stephanie Tousel, 27, Tim Truman, 38, and Billy Wells, 20, all of whom have been placed with the Jenkinses through the West Virginia Adult Care Home Program. Though Janet is primarily responsible for them, Jenkins too plays an active role in their lives.

Over the years, beginning even before she married Jenkins, Janet has taken in nearly a dozen "kids" ranging in age from seventeen to seventy. They have ended up in the program because they come from abusive homes, or they're mildly retarded, or they have drug problems, or they're hyperactive, or—the range of problems is sweeping, but Janet's way of handling them is always the same: "If you can't get along," she says, "you wash walls. I don't care what time of the day or night it is." It works, too. When Billy came to the Jenkins house three years ago, he was too hyper to attend school; now he's a mainstream high school senior.

"The state pays her," says Jenkins of his wife, "but she always spends more than the state provides." Orphaned at six and raised by a grandmother who also took in two retarded kids, Janet can't close her door to those in need. Take Thornton, for instance. Now 28, Thornton lived with Janet when she was still Janet Lynch, but was later moved to another program. Unhappy there, he called Janet and asked if he could come back. Though she got no state funding for him, she took him back anyway. He's been part of the family ever since.

On this particular day, Thornton's brother is getting married, so the whole family troops off to the wedding, me included—I'm part of the family now, too, at least for today; that's the way things seem to work in the Jenkins household. Afterwards, there's a post-wedding dinner at the fire hall, but in the middle of dinner, Jenkins is called away to the scene of a hit-and-run accident, from which a helicopter medevacs the twenty-year-old victim. Supervising helicopter medical evacuations would seem to be an eerie echo of the Vietnam War, but Jenkins insists that it's never been a problem for him. Perhaps not surprisingly, he says he enjoys the adrenalin rush of firefighting and emergency rescue work.

As for the war itself, Jenkins says he never could understand why the Marines would sweep the same villages week after week, killing and maiming comrades, but making no progress. "They didn't want to win it," he says of the war managers. "The government didn't want to win because big business was getting rich and who runs the government? Big business. Somebody was getting rich off it. I could have won that war in a year. Take the ROKs [the South Korean military, units of which had fought in Vietnam], put 'em in the south and have 'em sweep north."

Looking back at the war from across the years, he concludes, "I don't think we should have been there." Even so, he adds, if he had it to do all over again, "I'd go back. I lost some patriotism for the government, but not for the flag or the country. It still burns me to a frazzle to see somebody standing with a hat on when they're playing the national anthem. I believe in the U.S. It's just the people running it . . ." His voice trails off, leaving the sentence unfinished.

Robert W. Johnson

There are not as many Robert W. Johnsons in America as there are John E. Greens, but there are a lot of them: 221 in the eastern U.S. alone, according to the Myers list. Fortunately, I did have an accurate service number for Johnson, so NPRC was able to locate his service records. I was never able to locate Johnson himself—even after I learned that he'd come from Alabama and was still living there as late as 1983, I was still left with too many Robert W. Johnsons and no way to narrow my search any further—but the records I received in May 1995 provided the following information:

Johnson was born on December 23, 1946. A high school graduate, he joined the Marine Corps in February 1966 at Montgomery, Alabama, under the delayed enlistment program, beginning his active duty in June.

After boot camp, basic infantry training, and special weapons training as a machine gunner (0331), Johnson arrived in Vietnam in November 1966 and was assigned to Company F, 2nd Battalion, 3rd Marine Regiment, first as an ammunition carrier, then as an assistant gunner.

In March 1967, Johnson's battalion sailed from Dong Ha, Vietnam, aboard the USS *Bayfield,* spending a month on Okinawa before returning to Dong Ha aboard the USS *Princeton.* On April 23, Johnson sustained a gunshot wound to the lower right arm and was evacuated to the *Princeton,* where he convalesced until returning to duty on June 11. On June 19 he was wounded again, this time by shrapnel, and spent three days convalescing aboard the USS *Tripoli.*

After sustaining his second Purple Heart, Johnson was transferred out of Vietnam to the Service Battalion at Camp Smedley D. Butler, Okinawa, where he served as a brig guard (8151) from late June until his return to the U.S. in November 1967.

In December, Johnson was assigned to Company B, 2nd Recon Battalion, Camp Lejeune, North Carolina, first as a rifleman (0311), then as a scout driver (still 0311). He was listed as absent without leave from January 14 to January 24, 1968, and again from April 15 to April 29, 1968, and was reduced in rank at least once during his time with 2nd Recon Battalion.

In July 1968, Johnson was transferred to Company F, 2nd Battalion, 8th Marines, based at Guantanamo Bay Naval Base, Cuba. After a month as an assistant machine gunner, he was assigned in August to mess duty, first as a messman, then as a cook striker. He remained on mess duty until December 1968, transferring from Company F to the battalion's Headquarters & Support Company in November.

Returning to Camp Lejeune in December, he was assigned as a rifleman to the security platoon of Headquarters Company, 8th Marines, 2nd Marine Division, where he remained until his release from active duty in April 1969.

In addition to his two Purple Heart Medals, Johnson also received the National Defense Service, Vietnam Service, and Vietnam Campaign Medals, as well as a Presidential Unit Citation.

As of January 1983, Johnson was married, with one daughter, and living in Alabama.

Alvin L. Jordan

Back in the fall of 1990, when Operation Desert Shield became Operation Desert Storm and the possibility of war in the Middle East became the probability of war, many of the junior members of E Company, 111th Field Artillery, Virginia Army National Guard, eagerly looked forward to being called up and deployed to the war zone. That prospect, however, was far less appealing to Platoon Sergeant Alvin Jordan. "You've shot at targets on a range that don't shoot back," he told his young charges. "What you see on television isn't the way it's going to be for real."

Jordan knows about "for real." Twenty-four years earlier, he had been a machine gunner and mortarman with A Company, 1st Battalion, 26th Marines in Vietnam. On his first day in-country, the truck in which he was riding with other replacements for 1/26 had been ambushed. None of the replacements had even been issued weapons yet; only the driver and "shotgun" had been able to return fire.

As it turned out, Jordan's National Guard unit (redesignated C Battery, 1st Battalion, 111th Field Artillery, in February 1996) was placed on standby during the war with Iraq, but it was not called up for active duty. "I was kind of relieved we didn't go," says Jordan, who has since been promoted to first sergeant. Though he doesn't say it in so many words, he seems not quite convinced that his men are ready for the rigors of battle.

When Jordan first joined the National Guard, he says, the pay wasn't very good. People joined mostly out of pride and the pleasure of being part of an organization; young soldiers today are too often just in it for the money. "You got to get on 'em for haircuts and stuff," he says; "they have no desire to make the organization better, no pride in the uniform, and they don't want to work.

"'What are you doing in the Guard?' I want to ask some of these kids," he says. "I tell them, 'Tomorrow you could be in another country fighting. Are you ready?'" At first sergeant school, he says, he was told he needs to treat young soldiers as if they were his sons. He's not supposed to swear at them or make them feel bad about themselves. Instead, he's supposed to take them aside and counsel them. It's an approach about which he clearly has some reservations.

Jordan joined the Guard in 1983, thirteen years after he left active duty with the Marines. "That was quite a difference," he says, comparing the Guard to the Corps. "Here [in his Guard unit] they say, 'Let's get in the trucks and go.' As an infantryman, you were used to walking every-

Corporal Alvin L. Jordan, Camp Lejeune, North Carolina, May 1968.

where you go. They even sleep in the trucks, but I still do the same thing I did when I was a Marine: we go into the woods, I sleep on the ground!"

All reservations and comparisons aside, however, Jordan readily volunteers; "I love being battery first sergeant. That's a great job." The battery, which had 105mm guns when he first started out as an assistant gunner, now consists of eight 198mm guns—each capable of hurling a ninety-five-pound projectile fifteen to thirty miles—and an authorized strength of 130 men. Jordan must make sergeant major within three years in order to remain in the Guard. "If I don't make it," he says, "I won't mind. I've enjoyed every minute of it." He's currently number two on the promotion list, so his prospects for making the cut seem good.

One of the reasons Jordan joined C Battery, rather than a Marine reserve unit or another Guard unit, was the sheer convenience of it: the battery is located in Emporia, Virginia, where Jordan lives, where he's a corporal in the town's police department, and where I spent an afternoon with him on March 23, 1996.

Jordan was born in Emporia, and except for his four years in the

Corps, he has lived there all his life. A 1966 graduate of Edward Wyatt High School, he played catcher for the school's baseball team and quarterbacked the football team. "I loved playing football," he says. "I liked being in charge. On many Saturday mornings I couldn't get out of bed, I was so sore." He was also the trainer for the basketball team. "I could shoot baskets," says the five-foot-eight-inch Jordan, "but I was too short to play on the team."

Along with school and sports, from the eighth grade on, Jordan also worked part time at the same plywood factory where his father worked, Interstate Veneering Company. "My parents didn't have a lot," he says, and with what they had, they were trying to raise five children (Jordan is the second child and oldest son). If Jordan wanted something, he had to earn the money to buy it—including his class ring and his graduation cap and gown.

On many a day, he would go to school, do sports in the afternoon, finish his homework, and then go off to work until midnight. "It was

Left to right: *Captain Pete Daughtry, Sergeant Thomas Pearson, and Corporal Alvin Jordan of the Emporia Police Department, Virginia, circa 1995.*

tough," he says. "I guess that's one of the reasons I went into the military. I had relations in the Army, but nobody around here that I knew of was ever in the Marine Corps. I saw that recruiter with that pretty uniform, standing so tall, and I said, 'That's what I'm going to join. That's what I want to be.'"

Of the war in Vietnam, he says, "it wasn't an issue to me at the time," and it didn't become a reality until he got orders for staging battalion. Parris Island, though, was a different matter. "Now that was a real shocker," he says. "I still see those footprints" (the infamous yellow footprints in front of the receiving barracks upon which every new recruit begins his life in boot camp).

"What have I gotten myself into?" he remembers thinking, but then adds, "I don't think I was really afraid. It was just the environment itself. It was really strange. Before I got there, other people told me, 'Just play the game. Do the best you can, and just do what they tell you to do, and you'll be okay.' So that's what I did."

After boot camp, he went on to infantry training. "Weapons training was very exciting," he says. "To know how things function. Tearing down an M-60 [machine gun]. These young soldiers at Charlie Battery struggle with the M-60. I can still take it all apart. I can take apart stuff these kids didn't even know came apart."

Soon after Jordan arrived in Vietnam, his unit went north to an area just below the Demilitarized Zone in the vicinity of Khe Sanh. Though this was well before the famous siege, fighting was nevertheless frequent and heavy. The North Vietnamese Army regularly assaulted U. S. positions, and though they never overran Jordan's outfit, mortar and artillery attacks were constant. "You could hear the rounds fire," he says. "That's how close they were when they fired."

Jordan recalls that for weeks on end his unit received sniper fire from a nearby village. Just about every day, a Marine would be killed or wounded. People in the village always told the Marines, "No VC! No VC!" But the sniping continued. Finally the Marines managed to kill the sniper—who turned out to be a woman. Even after this incident, the Marines were not permitted to clear the village because it had not been designated a free fire zone. They used to talk about leveling the village anyway, Jordan says, but nobody ever did.

"In the back of my mind," he says, "I'd wonder, 'Why are we doing this or that? Is this supposed to be a war or not?' I didn't realize at the time that it was the politicians. It was a political game. We had to play that political game. We had the firepower to end the thing, but we had to play by [the politicians'] rules."

Jordan was one of those unlucky Marines who got to spend not one, but two Christmases in Vietnam, arriving December 7, 1966, and leaving December 29, 1967. He was next assigned to K Company, 3rd Battalion, 8th Marines, at Camp Lejeune, an assignment that also included a Mediterranean cruise, but in September 1968 he was sent to sea school at Portsmouth, Virginia, in preparation for sea duty aboard the submarine tender USS *Holland*.

"I didn't even know there were Marines on ships," he says, until he received the assignment. When he finally joined the *Holland* and it put out to sea for the first time, he says, "I stayed sick for five days." He'd been on ships during sea school, he says, but "it didn't bother me until I couldn't see land anymore. Man, I was a miserable guy." He eventually found his sea legs, however, and thereafter was fine.

"Sea duty was the best duty I had," he says. "It was a lot of spit and polish. It was hard work, but you got the best of everything. We were more or less the police department." The Marine detachment of about twenty-five men did police duties on ship and ashore, ran the ship's brig, provided security for the ship's captain and a color guard for visiting dignitaries, guarded restricted areas, and raised and lowered the flag every day.

Once a month or so, the *Holland* would steam out of home port in Rota, Spain, to meet a submarine on the high seas. "In the middle of nowhere," Jordan says, "the sub would just surface. I didn't realize subs were so big. You see one of those three-story tall missiles disappear down a silo, you realize that's a big sub. A little while later, the sub would disappear. Just gone."

By now a sergeant, Jordan was released from active duty in June 1970 and returned to Emporia, where he spent a rough summer looking for work. "That was really a depressing time," he says. "Where's your next meal coming from? Filling out job applications, but nobody wanted you." He was considering going back in the Corps, but finally got hired by the Brown & Williamson Tobacco Company in Petersburg, just up the road from Emporia.

His job at Brown & Williamson was to load cases of cigarettes onto railroad boxcars. Each loading crew of four men had to load two boxcars a day. Though each case weighed only thirty-five pounds, he says, "after you lift them hour after hour, they get really heavy. In the summertime, it would get really hot inside those steel boxcars, but I loved the work. I loved working outside."

He worked at Brown & Williamson for thirteen years, and would be there still except that Brown & Williamson decided to relocate the plant to Macon, Georgia, after Petersburg refused to allow the company to move an historic church in order to expand its operations. For employees who didn't want to make the move—this included Jordan—Brown & Williamson offered job counseling and employment help, and when Jordan was asked what he wanted to do, he decided on police work.

"I'd just bought a house, and I had a family to support," he explains. (He'd married in 1970, and son Alvin L. Jordan, Jr., had arrived in 1972.) "At the time, all I wanted was a way to pay the bills." He wasn't especially interested in police work, but the Petersburg department was hiring, and he figured the chances of layoffs in police work would be less than with other jobs. "I was looking for longevity, job security, benefits, that type of stuff. You do what you have to do to make ends meet. I had bills and responsibilities."

Jordan served with the Petersburg department only from May to November 1983, then applied for and received a position with the Emporia department. Though he wasn't initially drawn to police work, he's come to enjoy it very much. "Every day you go in, it's something different," he explains. "In a small town, you know people by name, you know people by sight. 'I never saw that guy before.' It's interesting. You gotta like people, though."

With a small force (twenty-two officers) in a small community (twelve thousand), Jordan explains that all the officers pretty much do everything: "helping stranded motorists, helping the housewife who's locked herself out, shoplifters, speeding, shootings, bank robberies, everything. Basically, for a guy who wants to learn about police work, this is the place to be."

Perhaps surprisingly—considering that when Jordan was growing up in Emporia, segregation was open and institutionalized (Wyatt was an all-black school, for instance, and its teams competed only against other all-black schools)—race has seldom been a problem for Jordan in the discharge of his duties. Only once has it ever been an overt issue, when Jordan responded to a call from an older white woman. When he arrived at her house, he says, she refused to speak with him, saying she wanted to talk to a white officer. "It didn't bother me," he says. "I just thought, 'The sergeant can handle this. That's his job.'" So he had the woman call his sergeant, who told her, "We don't have white officers. We only have police officers." The woman talked to Jordan.

Jordan has seen a disturbing increase in drug-related crimes in the past decade. What used to be weekly occurrences now happen daily. Much of it, he says, originates with people who went north years ago, then came south again to save their children from urban problems. But along with the urban lifestyles the kids have brought with them to Virginia—"baggy pants, weird hairdos," he says—they've also brought urban problems.

Still, he says, major crimes are relatively rare: three or four murders a year, an occasional rape or bank robbery. Most of the felonies are things like driving on a suspended license, not major crimes. The most recent bank robbery, last year, failed because the would-be robber parked his car across from the bank and locked it, then with the loot in hand, ended up fumbling with the keys while trying to unlock his car again, delaying his getaway long enough for the cops to give chase. (He was killed in a shoot-out with police, but no one else was injured and all the money was recovered.)

But cop and soldier aren't the only hats Jordan wears. He also holds a Class B electrical contractor's license. Back in the early 1980s, even before Brown & Williamson announced its relocation, he began to wonder, "What happens if I lose this job?" So he began taking courses at South Side Virginia Community College, and earned certification in applied electricity. He has his own truck and tools, and, as Jordan's Electric, does wiring and electrical work on houses, churches, and industrial plants. "Some weeks I have a lot of work," he says. "Some weeks I don't. Most of it comes in warm weather. In the winter, it's mostly furnace repairs."

Since the early 1980s, Jordan has also put more than his share of time and energy into raising his son. When Jordan and his wife divorced in 1983, she took a job in Baltimore. Alvin, Jr., stayed in Emporia, however, to finish school, so Jordan was pretty much a single parent from the time his son was eleven. (Alvin, Jr. has since graduated from Hampton University, class of 1995, and is currently a second lieutenant in the U.S. Army.)

Looking back, Jordan says, "I was lucky I was never hit in Vietnam. I have no regrets about going into the Marine Corps. I think it helped me a lot. I have no problems dealing with adversity, stress, problem solving. The Corps taught me real life, how things really are. And it taught me how to be with people, different races and different kinds of people. It taught me discipline and how to take care of myself."

Wayne L. Kelly

None of the nineteen Wayne Kellys on the Myers list responded to my initial search letter, and the VA could find no record that Kelly ever filed a claim for benefits, but based on records I received from NPRC in July 1995 and the recollections of his fellow West Virginians in Platoon 1005, I was able to learn this much:

Kelly was born Jun 12, 1947, and graduated from high school in 1966. He enlisted at the same time as Tom Erickson, Tim Jenkins, David Morrison, and Clarence Potts, all of whom were sworn in together at Charleston, West Virginia, before leaving for Parris Island. After boot camp, where Kelly qualified as a Rifle Marksman, and basic infantry training, he received additional training as a shore party man (1381) before arriving in Vietnam in December 1966, where he was assigned to Company C, 1st Shore Party Battalion, with whom he served until his return to the U.S. in January 1968.

Kelly's tour in Vietnam was interrupted by an emergency leave that lasted from April 14 until May 31, 1967, and he was then assigned to temporary duty at the Marine Barracks, Naval Air Station, San Francisco, before returning to Vietnam on June 18 to finish out his tour. Military records do not indicate the reason for the emergency leave, but Potts and Jenkins, who were also in 1st Shore Party Battalion, both say it was occasioned by the death of Kelly's father. Jenkins recalls that there was some delay in notifying Kelly of his father's death, and consequently he did not get home until the day after his father was buried.

Kelly was next assigned to Company A, 2nd Shore Party Battalion, Camp Lejeune, North Carolina, in February 1968, with whom he remained until October 1968. During this time, however, he was twice assigned to temporary duty with Headquarters & Support Company, 3rd Battalion, 6th Marines, for shipborne amphibious training deployments to Puerto Rico aboard the USS *Fort Snelling*.

In November 1968, Kelly was reassigned to H&S Company, 1st Battalion, 27th Marines, 1st Marine Brigade, in Hawaii (in November 1969, 27th Marines was redesignated 3rd Marines), where he remained until his release from active duty in February 1970. He achieved the rank of corporal, and received the Good Conduct, National Defense Service, Vietnam Service, and Vietnam Campaign Medals.

Both Potts and Jenkins say that Kelly got married while he was stationed in Hawaii. Potts heard the woman was dark-skinned; Jenkins says she was Samoan. Jenkins recalls that Kelly came to see him in the hospital in 1970 after Jenkins injured his knee in a motorcycle accident; soon afterwards, Kelly's mother told Jenkins that Kelly had enlisted in the Army. Potts also heard Kelly had joined the Army after he got out of the Marines. In 1996 both Potts and Jenkins thought they might be able to track down Kelly's mother or sister, and through them find Kelly, but neither man had any better luck than I did.

Samuel A. Kendrick

None of the five Samuel Kendricks on the Myers list responded to my initial search letter, and the VA could find no record of Kendrick ever having applied for veterans' benefits. According to records received from NPRC in January 1996, Kendrick was born October 6, 1946, graduated from high school in 1966, and was sworn into the Marine Corps at Richmond, Virginia. After boot camp and basic infantry training, he received additional training as a shore fire control party man (0849). He was then assigned to the 2nd Air-Naval Gunfire Liaison Company, Force Troops, Fleet Marine Force Atlantic, Camp Lejeune, North Carolina, from early January to early February 1967, but spent most of that month on temporary duty with the Marine Barracks, U.S. Naval Base, Guantanamo Bay, Cuba.

In April 1967, he arrived in Vietnam. He served with Headquarters Battery, 1st Battalion, 11th Marines, an artillery regiment, for one month before being transferred to the Communications Company, Headquarters Battalion, 1st Marine Division. In January 1968, he was transferred again, this time to the battalion's Service Company Sub-unit #1, where he served until the completion of his tour in Vietnam in May 1968.

Kendrik was released from active duty with the rank of lance corporal upon his return to the U.S. in mid-May. His decorations include the National Defense Service, Vietnam Service, and Vietnam Campaign Medals. As of 1968, Kendrick was married and had one son. His residence at that time was Lynchburg, Virginia.

Michael C. Landauer

Landauer called me from Las Vegas, Nevada, on September 6, 1993, after receiving my initial search letter, and we spoke for about half an hour. On March 29, 1996, I received records from the National Personnel Records Center that did not square with what Landauer had told me about his military service. I wrote to Landauer on August 3, 1996, explaining the discrepancy and asking if he could offer any explanation for it, but I never received a reply.

According to his Service Record Book, Landauer was born on January 15, 1948. He was assigned successively to 1st Recruit Training Battalion, Recruit Training Regiment, Marine Corps Recruit Depot, Parris Island, South Carolina, June 17 to August 13, 1966; 2nd Infantry Training Battalion, 1st Infantry Training Regiment, Marine Corps Base, Camp Lejeune, North Carolina, August 25 to September 12, 1966; 1st Schools Company, Marine Corps Engineering School, Camp Lejeune, September 13 to October 17, 1966; U.S. Naval Hospital, Camp Lejeune, October 17 to November 8, 1966; 1st Schools Company, Marine Corps Engineering School, Camp Lejeune, November 8 to December 9, 1966. He achieved the rank of private first class and was awarded the National Defense Service Medal.

Francis L. Langley

When Francis Langley was in the third grade, says his mother Lessie, he came home from school one day very upset. When Lessie asked him what was wrong, he told her that another boy had ended an argument by shouting, "Your mother's not your mother anyway."

"But you already know you're adopted," Lessie told her son.

"Yes," Francis replied, "but I don't like to hear it from him."

Lessie remembers the incident because it was so uncharacteristic of her son. "He was such a happy boy," she says. "Always smiling." Indeed, the only apparent consequence of his being adopted was that the family celebrated two special days each year instead of one: his birthday and his adoption day.

Langley was born to a married woman and mother who'd gotten

pregnant once too often, this time while her husband was overseas. Unable to have children of their own, Coley Frank Langley and Lessie Lee Morris Langley adopted him when he was not yet five months old, and he grew up on their farm three miles outside of Waverly, Alabama, a one-street country town between Opelika and Dadeville.

When the farm was at its peak, Frank and Lessee kept twenty-five polled Herefords on 145 acres of land, tended five thousand chickens, and harvested nuts from a dozen huge pecan trees. "We were self-sufficient out here," Lessie says. "We had pigs. We did our own meat and lard."

Francis L. Langley on his graduation day from La Fayette High School, Chambers County, Alabama, 1964.

Though an only child, Langley was surrounded by family. Both Frank and Lessie had deep roots in the area. The farm had been started by Frank's parents in 1910, Lessie's family had moved to Waverly when she was a schoolgirl, and the two families provided Frank and Lessie's son with seven aunts and uncles. "Francis had thirteen first cousins," Lessie explains. "One or another of the boys was here every weekend."

Frank's retarded sister, Mary Alice, whom everyone called Mimi, also lived with Frank and Lessie. Though forty years old when Langley arrived, she was always just a child. "Mimi and Francis were kids together," says Lessie. "They loved each other so." At various times during Langley's childhood, each of his grandmothers lived with Frank and Lessie, too.

Langley attended elementary school in Waverly, then went on to La Fayette, the regional high school for Chambers County. He didn't participate in extracurricular activities, because the school was eighteen miles away and he had no way to get home if he missed his school bus. But he

Private First Class Francis Langley (left) *with a buddy from 1st Shore Party Battalion, Vietnam, December 1966.*

enjoyed pickup basketball, and he loved to fish and to hunt raccoons, squirrels, rabbits, and birds. When he got older, he went into business for himself, cutting pulpwood that grew on the farm and selling it to local paper mills.

In the 1964 *Le Marquis,* the school's yearbook editors chose this quote to place under Langley's senior portrait: "A good heart is better than all the heads in the world." Classmates and friends wrote handwritten messages in Langley's copy. "May you always have the best in life," wrote one girl. "You are a very *cute* and *sweet* fun-loving boy. I hope our friendship never ends. Love, Nancy." Johnny Boone wrote, "Remember the time we slept in the woods and went rabbit hunting with Jimmy Eiland? (Ha! Ha!) Francis, I wish you all the luck in the world and may you have everything life has to offer because you really deserve it."

After graduation, Langley went to work as a broker for Montgomery Cotton Company, learning to buy and sell cotton, but in February 1966, he joined the Marines under their delayed enlistment program. "I think he was brainwashed," says Lessie. "They have a way of making it look so fancy and nice. The recruiter's uniform looked so good." He was scheduled to begin active duty in June.

Then on a blind date arranged by a friend, Langley met Jeannie White from Jackson Gap. They fell in love. They wanted to get married. He was 19. She was 17. "I thought they were too young," says Lessie. "'It's going to be harder to leave a wife than a girlfriend,' I told him." But the couple was insistent. They were married a few weeks before he left for boot camp. Later that summer, while Francis was still at Parris Island, Jeannie wrote to say that she was pregnant.

After boot camp and infantry training, Langley received a month's training as a shore party man (1381), came home on leave, then departed for staging at Camp Pendleton with orders for Vietnam. He wrote to Lessie often, beginning each letter "Dear Mama," always asking about Mimi, and admonishing his father not to work too hard:

November 11, 1966 (from Camp Pendleton, California): "We leave to go to Viet Nam the 14th of Dec. That means I might be back in time for Christmas next year."

December 17 (from Vietnam, where Langley had been assigned to 2nd Platoon, C Company, 1st Shore Party Battalion): "I am alright. So far it isn't as bad as I expected. . . . It hasn't been anybody killed yet in the company I am in. I am glad of that. I am in Chu Lai, south of Da Nang. . . . I have heard shooting and mortar rounds go off. That is all."

December 30: "You ought to see the people here. They are unbelievable. They are dirty. . . . They live in grass shacks and use the bathroom in the rice paddies. That is how they fertilize the rice. . . . We haven't seen any action since I have been here. . . . If I see [a Viet Cong], though, he might as well hang it up. I am getting an itchy trigger finger."

January 3, 1967: "We had some action around here last night. The V.C. liked to have got some of our men that were out on ambush last night. But they didn't. It is hard to get a Marine. I hope so anyway. . . . If the Good Lord is willing, I will see ya'll in Dec. . . . Don't work too hard, grandmom. How do you like that name? It won't be long now." (Jeannie was due in March.)

January 8: "Martha Rae was here in person. She was real good. I laughed so much. It sure did wonders for the morale. . . . It is raining here tonight. Nothing unusual though. I am about use to it. The mud here is something else though. It is nearly ankle deep. . . . How [is Daddy] feeling about being a grand-daddy? I love him and I miss him. . . . I love you and miss you too."

Before Langley's letter of January 8 reached them, however, Frank and Lessie learned that their only child was dead. He had died on January 11 when the helicopter in which he'd been riding crashed into the South China Sea. A Marine major named Vreeland came in person to deliver the news. Then he drove Lessie to Alexander City, where Jeannie was living with her sister, and together they told her that she was now a widow. "He was so nice," Lessie says of Major Vreeland. "He couldn't have been more kind."

It took three days to recover Langley's remains from the ocean. "When they called to tell me that they'd found the body," Lessie says, "it was like somebody lifted a load off my heart." The casket, sealed because Langley's body had been in the water for so long, arrived in Alexander City on January 25.

The funeral service was held the next day at the Waverly Methodist church, followed by a military burial with a seven-man firing detail. A sergeant major, a first sergeant, two gunnery sergeants, a staff sergeant, and a sergeant served as pallbearers for PFC Langley. During lunch at the farm house after the funeral, the Marines joked that the service should have been held at Waverly's Baptist church, because they would only have had to carry the casket up and down four front steps instead of the twenty or so the Methodist church had. Lessie speaks highly of the Marines who attended to her family after her son was killed. They were, she says, professional, solicitous, and caring.

Even before the funeral, and long after it was over, letters of condolence arrived from the commanding general of the 1st Marine Division, the Commandant of the Marine Corps, the President of the United States, the Governor of Alabama, Jeannie's Congressman, Frank and Lessie's, too. These, at least, mentioned both the living and the dead by name, though only the Marines avoided platitudes.

The ones from the adjutant general of Alabama, the Alabama American Legion, the Alabama American Legion Auxiliary, and AMVETS, began with salutations like "My Dear Fellow Alabamians," "My Dear Friend," and "To the Family of the Deceased," and spoke about "your loved one" and "your loss," quoting variations of "Greater love hath no man" or paraphrasing the Gettysburg Address. "I got tired of them," Lessie says of these letters. "I thought, 'When is it going to stop?'"

The many letters from friends and relatives, however, spoke from and to the heart. Two letters from Vietnam were especially meaningful. The first, dated January 12, came from Captain G. R. Holiday, Langley's company commander, who wrote: "[Francis] was highly thought of in the brief period we came to know him. . . . It is particularly sad that he leaves an unborn child behind. In the years to come please inform the child that [Francis] was a fine man and a father to be proud of. He was courageous in combat and a good leader. His quiet likeable manner, his sincerity and his eagerness to help won him the respect and admiration of his fellow Marines." Included with Captain Holiday's letter was a copy of the memorial service program held on January 12 in honor of Langley and the other five members of 1st Shore Party Battalion who died in the crash.

The second letter, dated January 14, was addressed to Jeannie Langley, and came from PFC William Auble, who had served with Langley since the previous summer. "I'm sure I don't have to tell you what a wonderful guy [Francis] was," Auble wrote. "I know there's not much I can say that would be much comfort to you now. Except that I share some of your sorrow and I know your loss. . . . Please take care of that baby of yours. [Francis] wanted that kid almost as much as he wanted to get back home to you."

Because they still knew very little about the actual circumstances of their son's death, Frank and Lessie wrote to Captain Holiday asking for more information. On February 12, he sent them a copy of the accident report prepared by an investigating officer from Marine Air Group 36. According to the report, Langley and five other members of C Company were on their way from Ky Ha to Quang Ngai for medical evacuation standby duty as part of Operation Sierra when the pilot of the UH-34D in which they were riding radioed that he was experiencing engine trouble.

Thirty seconds later, the pilot reported complete engine failure and said that he was attempting to ditch the helicopter at sea about three hundred yards off the beach at Chu Lai. No one witnessed the crash. Another helicopter arrived on the scene only a few minutes later, but already only the downed helicopter's belly, landing gear, and tail pylon were visible. One crewman was observed in the water, but rescue efforts were unsuccessful due to very rough seas. The wrecked helicopter sank rapidly. By the time a more systematic search-and-rescue effort could be mounted, there was no trace of either the aircraft or its four crewman and six passengers.

All ten bodies were eventually recovered. The cause of death in each case was drowning. The helicopter itself was not recovered, but in the opinion of the investigating officer, the cause of the accident was due solely to "an engine failure of an undetermined origin. The sea conditions of waves 4–8 ft., heavy surf, and strong undertow which rolled the helicopter on its back after ditching caused disorientation and/or injury to the occupants to such a degree that they were unable to survive."

Captain Holiday added his own conclusion to that of the investigating officer: "In our duties here we place great reliance in our men and their equipment and necessarily we all do our utmost to take care of both. But there is a point beyond which we cannot foresee and avoid the coming of a tragedy such as the one which took the life of your son and the others in that aircraft. . . . From your letter I know you understand this."

When the news of Langley's death first arrived, Lessie feared that the shock would cause Jeannie to go into premature labor, but she carried the baby to full term, and Lee Langley came into the world on March 24, 1967, the twentieth anniversary of his father's adoption by Frank and Lessie. In July 1967, Jeannie married Devon Knowles, who raised Lee as his own son, though at Frank and Lessie's request, Lee kept the name of Langley.

Today, Jeannie is a correctional officer and Devon is a Baptist minister. They have no other children. Lee is a municipal police officer and the father of Lessie's great-granddaughter, Magan. He is divorced from Magan's mother, but recently remarried. Jeannie, Lee, and Magan all live in the Florida panhandle only a few hours' drive from Waverly.

Frank and Lessie worked the farm until 1980, when Frank was finally no longer able to keep the fences mended and the cattle out of the neighbors' yards and gardens. He died in 1986, and is buried in the family plot in the Waverly cemetery with his son. Lessie's headstone is already in place, and when she dies, she will lie between them. In the same plot are Lessie's parents and a headstone for a sister of hers who died in infancy and is buried in Montezuma, Georgia. Just up the hill are buried Frank's parents and his sister Mary Alice, beloved Mimi, who remained a child all her eighty-five years.

Lessie and I drove the few miles from the farm into Waverly on May 9, 1995, and we walked among the headstones in the graveyard as she pointed out who was buried where, before standing together for a few quiet moments by the graves of her husband and her son. I put my arm around her because it felt like the right thing to do, and she reached up and squeezed my hand as if to say that it was. Then she showed me the church where the funeral had been, and took me into the tiny post office, where she introduced me to the postmistress as "a friend of Francis's."

I knew from the *Vietnam Veterans Memorial Directory* that Langley had come from Waverly, Alabama, so I'd asked Ben Myers if he could find any Langleys listed there. He had come up with a Coley Langley, and I had written, receiving a reply from Lessie dated October 5, 1993. She had signed it, "Love," as she was to sign all the other letters I've received from her since.

I spent two gloriously beautiful days with Lessie, arriving early enough in the spring to avoid the oppressive heat and humidity that would soon descend on Alabama like a cloak. Not once in those two days did she let me feel as if she might be thinking, "Why did you live while my boy died?" She sent me away with gifts for my wife and daughter. Her warmth and kindness and generosity seemed completely impervious to the sadness of the circumstances that had brought our lives together. Her very being seemed to say, "Life takes good turns and bad turns, and the best you can do is to do the best you can."

And she has. The farm is pretty well overgrown now with pine trees and privet hedges and even bamboo that Frank planted years ago, but Lessie keeps the house up, and flowers still blossom in the yard. She and her sister Nell find the time and energy to volunteer two days each week at the nursing home in Opelika. Lessie's homemade fig preserves are the best you'll ever taste on this planet, and her butter beans and deep fried okra aren't far behind.

There are photographs of her son in just about every room in the house, but they mostly hang in the company of other photographs of Frank, Jeannie, Lee, and Magan, parents and brothers and sisters, uncles and aunts and nephews and nieces, grands and great-grands, a photographic family tree, a gallery of generations. Francis Langley was always surrounded by family, and still is.

"Francis loved this farm," Lessie says. "He loved every rock on it. If he had lived, he'd still be here." She pauses, then continues. "What were we fighting for over there? Can you tell me? It still seems like a nightmare. I never thought he would die over there. I was afraid he would come home with mental problems, emotional problems, maybe drug problems, but I didn't think he'd get killed. I guess I worried about the wrong things.

"I didn't want Francis and Jeannie to get married," she adds, "but the Lord knows best, doesn't he? Jeannie's been a real daughter to me. What would I do now if I didn't have her and Lee and Magan? And I have so many happy memories. I've always got those, you know. No one can take them from me."

Lonnie Leggett, Jr.

Ben Myers could find no listing for Leggett, and though I sent a letter to him through the VA, I never received a reply. According to records received from NPRC in July 1995, Leggett was born on June 9, 1946, and graduated from high school in 1966. He was sworn into the Marine Corps at Raleigh, North Carolina. After boot camp and basic infantry training, he received additional training at Camp Pendleton, California, as a bulk fuel man (1391) before being assigned in December 1966 to the 7th Separate Bulk Fuel Company at Pendleton. The entire unit was immediately deployed to Vietnam, aboard the USNS *General LeRoy Eltinge,* arriving at Chu Lai the day after Christmas.

Leggett spent the month of January 1967 receiving on-the-job training as a general warehouseman (3051) with the Supply Company of Force Logistics Support Group B, Force Logistics Command, but returned to his primary military occupational specialty, bulk fuel man, upon being transferred to Marine Air Base Squadron 36, Marine Air Group 36, in late January. In October, he was transferred to Marine Air Base Squadron 16, Marine Air Group 16, where he remained until he returned to the U.S. in January 1968.

In February 1968, he was assigned to the Bulk Fuel Company, Supply Battalion, 2nd Force Service Regiment, at Camp Lejeune, North Carolina. From July until December, he participated in a Mediterranean cruise while temporarily assigned to Headquarters & Support Company, 3rd Battalion, 2nd Marines aboard the USS *Yancey.*

Upon completion of the cruise in December 1968, Leggett returned to the Bulk Fuel Company of 2nd FSR. During the next fourteen months, he was absent without authorization four times for periods ranging from one day to three and a half months. He was confined as a prisoner on at least one occasion in February 1970, and was also reduced in rank.

Leggett was discharged in March 1970 with the rank of private. His decorations include the National Defense Service, Vietnam Service, and Vietnam Campaign Medals. As of 1978, he was living in Brooklyn, New York, and was married, with one son and one daughter.

Charles Mahone

Charles Mahone, a machine gunner with Company H, 2nd Battalion, 9th Marines, shouldn't have been in the field that day in December 1967. He was too short—had too little time left to serve in Vietnam—but because his orders had not yet arrived, he was told he had to go, so he went. What he found that day was a kind of trouble he had not foreseen. But then, when Mahone had enlisted in the Marines eighteen months earlier, he had not foreseen being in Vietnam at all. "I went into the Marines thinking I was going to avoid Vietnam," he says.

He'd grown up in Macon, Georgia, but after graduating from Ballard-Hudson High School in 1965, he moved to Philadelphia to live with an older brother. For most of Mahone's first eighteen years, Macon's neighborhoods were strictly segregated, as were the city's schools, its buses, and its opportunities. Like many southern blacks, he says, "I thought moving north was going to be the solution to all my problems. I was going to make it in the big city."

Philadelphia wasn't quite the paradise he'd expected, but he did get to see Hank Aaron knock one out of Connie Mack Stadium, and he did find work, first with the Quaker Maid Hat Company, and then for the Navy Exchange at the Philadelphia Naval Shipyard.

In the spring of 1966, however, he received a call-up letter from his draft board back in Macon. He was aware of the growing war in Vietnam, but he associated it exclusively with the Army. "I didn't know the Marines were over there too," he says. "That's how

Private Charles Mahone, August 1966.
(PB)

Charles Mahone with his granddaughter, Kierra, 1994.

naive I was. And I'll never forget that [sergeant in the dress blue uniform] in the recruiting office. He just bowled me over."

Five months later, Mahone found himself in Vietnam. In the midst of his first firefight, with the screaming and crying of the wounded and the din and confusion of battle all around him, he found himself thinking, "Hey, this ain't the way John Wayne did it." But he survived that fight and many more. From Phu Bai, where he first joined 2/9, he went to Dong Ha, then to Cam Lo. By July, though only a lance corporal, he was a weapons section leader in charge of six machine guns and as many as twenty-four men, a job usually held by a sergeant.

Mahone remembers when civilians still lived in the area between Dong Ha and the Demilitarized Zone. He remembers the stink of rotting corpses in the aftermath of the terrible ambush that nearly wiped out Company B, 1st Battalion, 9th Marines. And the North Vietnamese flags he could see from the battlements of Gia Linh, an outpost on the DMZ that he helped to build. And the body parts lying loose on the ground in the aftermath of B-52 raids. He remembers C-130s spraying defoliants. "We hated the jungle," he says. "We got ambushed in the jungle in June. We were glad for defoliants. We didn't know they were bad for you."

He remembers the month he spent at Con Thien, where he first encountered North Vietnamese heavy artillery firing from the other side of the DMZ. "It was the darkest time of my life," he says. "It was cold. It was wet. It was miserable. We were taking two hundred rounds of incoming a day. You could hear the rounds dropping in, sometimes followed by the screams of the wounded, and you'd be wondering who had been hit and at the same time you were thankful it wasn't you." He remembers lying in a foxhole under an artillery barrage, praying to Jesus, "If you just get me out of here, I'll try to do right."

In November 1967, 2/9 came down off Con Thien and went to Camp Carroll to provide security for the U.S. Army 175mm "Long Tom" cannons stationed there. It was from Camp Carroll that Mahone, by then a corporal, went out on that last patrol he shouldn't have been on because he was too short.

Company H ran into a bad firefight that day. Mahone wasn't hit, but other Marines were. One of the new guys lost his composure under fire when he, like Mahone a year earlier, discovered for the first time that wounded men look like nothing you've ever imagined and sound even worse. After the shooting died down, he says, the rest of Mahone's squad went ahead, but he stayed back with the new guy, providing cover and comfort, trying to settle the man down.

At this point, Mahone says, the company gunnery sergeant came upon the two men and ordered Mahone to move out, but Mahone wanted to give the new guy more time "to get his head together," so he did not immediately go forward. When the company gunny returned a few minutes later, he accused Mahone of refusing to advance.

This wasn't the first run-in Mahone had had with the gunny, who was a white man from Alabama, a detail Mahone thinks of no small importance. "Up at Con Thien, he thought I had too much influence with the men," Mahone says. "He was from the old school. He didn't like us young Marines thinking on our own."

Still, had Mahone let events run their course, he believes he would probably have been given only an Article 15, nonjudicial punishment in accordance with the Uniform Code of Military Justice. "But I was right," he says. "I felt I was just doing my job. I was trying to console the boy." Mahone demanded, and received, a summary court-martial.

"That gunny damaged my honor, my integrity," he says, clearly still smarting after all these years, "but I was naive to demand a court-martial. It was a gunnery sergeant's word against a corporal's. The outcome was a foregone conclusion." The major presiding found him guilty of disobeying a lawful order. It cost Mahone a stripe, an extra month in Vietnam, which he spent as "permanent NCOIC of the shit-burning detail," and ultimately a potential career.

It also cost the Marine Corps a good man. Mahone spent the next two and a half years with Charlie Company, 1st Battalion, 6th Marines at Camp Lejeune and on cruises to the Caribbean and Mediterranean Seas, eventually winning back his corporal's stripes, and earning sergeant's stripes and a Good Conduct Medal as well. He even extended his four-year enlistment by three months to finish out an assignment instructing Navy Seabees in Rhode Island.

But he declined to reenlist in the Corps, even when he was offered drill instructor's school. "It was tempting," he says. "I had two goals when I joined the Marines: to make staff sergeant, and to earn a Good Conduct Medal. I got the Good Conduct Medal, but that court-martial kept me from making E6. That soured me on the Corps. I was afraid I might run into another guy like that gunny."

Instead, in September 1970, Mahone became a civilian. He spent a year with Sunnyside Egg Company in Greenville, North Carolina, then went to work with the U.S. Post Office in Greenville. Over the next four years, he says, "I discovered that I'm not made to sit at a desk. The post office paid well, but I was bored."

Mahone had married in 1970, while still in the Marines, and though the marriage produced two children (Kimberly, born in 1972, and Marshall, born in 1978), it was never on solid ground. "My first wife is a wonderful person," he says, "but we were just too young. We had no business getting married. When my marriage went south, I did too." He returned to Macon and began working part time for Sears while taking courses at a local community college.

"I always wanted to work on the railroad or in the post office or in law enforcement," he says. "I tried the post office, and I decided it wasn't what I wanted, so I decided to try law enforcement." He took a position in 1977 as a correctional officer in the Georgia state prison system, hoping to parlay that into an appointment as a Georgia state trooper. But in only six years, he rose through the ranks to become a lieutenant, and at that point decided to stay in corrections.

"I'm best suited for law enforcement work," he says. "With the post office, I'd call in sick at the drop of a hat. Once I started working in corrections, I didn't take a sick day for eleven years." He made captain in 1986 and was promoted out of the uniformed ranks in 1989. Today, he is deputy warden of Central Correctional Institution (CCI) in Macon, where I interviewed him on May 10, 1995.

CCI is a close-security prison, he explains, one step down from a maximum-security facility, though most of the 750 inmates are only on medium-security status, doing time for burglary, bad checks, or other property crimes. There is no death row at CCI, but some of CCI's inmates initially received death sentences that were subsequently commuted. "Murderers," he says, "mass murderers. We got 'em all."

About 150 of the inmates work outside the prison during the day, doing sorting and baling for the Macon municipal recycling program, grounds and buildings maintenance for Macon College, or road work for the city, county, and state. Inmates who work outside the prison are first screened very carefully, he explains. Every once in a while, one tries to make a run for it, but not often. The rest of the inmates work inside the prison. "Everybody does something," says Mahone. Inmates receive no pay, but every good day of work goes toward parole consideration and early release.

Mahone believes that inmates who can afford to pay for their own care and upkeep ought to be required to do so. He explains that while inmates are allowed to spend only thirty dollars a month for cigarettes, candy, and other sundries, some inmates have as much as fifteen hundred dollars in their accounts. Many inmates aren't poor, he says; they have access to money.

"It costs fourteen thousand dollars a year to house an inmate," he explains. "Whatever medical problems they have—AIDS, diabetes—they get free treatment. Meanwhile, we've got veterans out there who have to jump hoops to get treatment. There's something wrong with society when you get ironies like that. If inmates have money, they should pay for their own medical treatment and other services, the same as me."

At the same time, he believes a lot of people in prison shouldn't be there. "The good Lord made some criminals," he says, "but a lot of the men in prison aren't really criminals." He explains that at least 200 of his 750 inmates have mental problems. Fifteen years ago, he says, these men would have been living in institutional settings for the mentally handicapped and probably wouldn't have gotten into trouble with the law.

In addition to being a deputy prison warden, Mahone is also a master sergeant in the Army Reserve. "I've always been a legal hustler," he says. "When I joined the reserves back in 1974, it was a way to make some extra money. I joined the Army Reserve instead of the National Guard because governors can activate the guard, but only the president or Congress can call up the reserves."

As a member of the Combat Services Support Forward Battalion of the 108th Training Division, Mahone's duties include providing instructional support for Army Reserve noncombat military occupational specialties. "Office pogues," he says with a laugh, using the Marine Corps term for rear eschelon personnel.

Unable to mask a still-fierce pride in the Corps, he admits that he would have joined the Marine Reserves in 1974, but for the fact that the nearest unit was two hundred miles away from where he was then living. "Everything they told us in boot camp about the Army is true," he says, laughing again. "I wouldn't want to go into combat with Army guys." Indeed, when the Persian Gulf War resulted in large-scale call-ups of reserve and guard units, Mahone was none too eager about the prospect of "going into combat with Army guys," but his reasons actually had little to do with interservice rivalries.

After his first marriage ended in divorce, Mahone married Nadine Boxton in 1979. Over the next ten years came five children: Lakeeta, Lakesa, Charles II, Corey, and Craig. Then in 1989, Nadine was diagnosed with breast cancer. Only 34 years old, she died in August 1990, just about the time George Bush was drawing a line in the sand. Mahone had no idea who would care for his children, the youngest of whom was then only sixteen months, if he was activated. "The bottom line was I didn't want to go," he says.

He didn't have to, as it turned out, but he still had his hands full. He had not realized his wife's illness would be fatal until very near the end. "I kept thinking, 'She's sick, but she's going to get better.' If I hadn't had my Marine Corps experience," he says, "I wouldn't have handled Nadine's death as well as I did." He recalls standing over the body of the first friend of his to die in Vietnam and thinking, "This morning we were cooking C-rations together, and now we'll never do that again. When Nadine died, I thought, 'Okay, this is the hand I've been dealt, and I'm going to have to play it.' I wasn't looking for another wife."

He found one anyway, and right under his own nose. Faye Rowland was a correctional officer at CCI. She was also willing to help raise five children who were not her own. Mahone and Rowland were married in 1993. Though she, too, has since been diagnosed with cancer, her prognosis is good and Mahone is optimistic about their future.

Mahone is a resilient man. He endured a court-martial and went on to earn sergeant's stripes, a Good Conduct Medal, and an honorable discharge from the Corps. He failed to qualify on the rifle range at Parris Island, but subsequently fired Expert with an M-60 machine gun, Expert with an M-14 rifle at Camp Lejeune, Expert with an M-16 rifle in the Army Reserve, and Expert with both a .38 revolver and a shotgun as a corrections officer. Rejected by the Air Force in 1965 for scoring too low on the intelligence test, he has achieved positions of great responsibility in not one profession, but two: corrections and the military reserves. And he continues to hold his family together in the face of sometimes daunting odds. "If I died this second," he says, "I'd have no regrets. God's been good to me."

Mahone credits his resilience to the Marines. "The Marine Corps was the best thing that ever happened to me," he says, the never-quite-forgotten pain of his court-martial notwithstanding. "The Corps was my initiation into manhood. It helped me get my feet planted firmly on the ground. I needed the discipline. If you go in with the basic elements of a man, the Marine Corps will bring that out.

"I was always proud that as much action as I was in, I didn't get any Purple Hearts. It's like our DIS said: 'The more you sweat in peace, the less you bleed in war.' I feel a debt of gratitude to our DIS. I didn't get any Purple Hearts, but it wasn't because I wasn't in it. It was the grace of God and our training.

"I saw children killed and women raped—though I didn't do any of that kind of stuff myself—but I still think [fighting against communism in Vietnam] was right. I was deeply disappointed when Saigon fell in 1975. I've always been proud of my service. I didn't regret it in 1975. I was just disappointed. I thought about all those guys that died, my friends. What did they die for? But when communism fell, I felt like we finally won in the end."

David P. Mauro

Rey Waters remembered that Mauro came from the area around Buffalo, New York, and one of the five David Mauros on the Myers list was in Niagara Falls, so I called on September 24, 1993. Mauro's wife told me he was working a double shift that night, so I called again the next day and reached him.

From our conversation, records received from NPRC in April 1996, and a questionnaire Mauro completed in July 1997, I learned that Mauro was born in Niagara Falls, New York, on February 2, 1947, and graduated from La Salle High School in 1965. After boot camp and basic infantry training, he received additional training in teletype communications (2501), before being sent to Okinawa in January 1967. Upon his return to the U.S., he was stationed first at Camp Lejeune, North Carolina, then at Quantico, Virginia. He was released from active duty in June 1969 with the rank of corporal; his decorations include the Good Conduct and National Defense Service Medals.

While he was stationed on Okinawa, Mauro says, he used to read the death notices as they came through on their way from Vietnam to the United States. One day, he happened to read the death notice for a close friend of his. "What a waste," he says, referring to his friend in particular and to the war in general. "What a waste of time and money and lives."

Mauro got married in 1968 while he was in the Marines and is still married to the same woman. He returned to Niagara Falls, where he still lives, and started college after getting out of the Corps, but didn't finish. He has been in and out of work since then, working "three years here, five years there." He has worked for General Motors, as a laborer for both the Nicet Corporation and Harrison Radiator, as a chemical operator for Hooker Chemical, and as a machinist for Union Carbide. Currently, he works the midnight shift for DuPont as a process technician at a caustic chlorine plant he helped to start from scratch. "You do what you have to do to get by," he says.

Mauro has two daughters, both of whom have been through college and are married. For fifteen years, Mauro played league softball, but now he plays golf instead of softball. Among his friends, he says, he is the only one who served in the military; all the others went to college. He remembers very little from boot camp or the Marine Corps. "I blocked a lot of it out," he says, "but I guess I lost a lot of the good memories, too." He doesn't remember Rey Waters.

Larry B. Maxey

Three Larry Maxeys showed up on the Myers list, and I wrote to all three of them. Two called to say that they were not who I was looking for. The third letter, to an address in Columbus, Mississippi, came back marked "Forwarding Order Expired," so I called directory assistance for Columbus on September 9th, 1993, and discovered that the telephone number accompanying the outdated address was still in service. When I called the number, I got the man I was looking for.

From our conversation, and records received from NPRC in April 1996, I learned that Maxey, a native of Mississippi, joined the Marine Corps after his junior year in high school. After boot camp and basic infantry training, he went to the Student Unit of Naval Air Station Memphis, Tennessee, where he received promotion to private first class and began training in aircraft mechanics and maintenance. He was reduced to private on February 15, 1967, however, and a week later was transferred to Company A, 1st Battalion, 2nd Marines, at Camp Lejeune, North Carolina, as a machine-gun ammunition carrier (0331).

On March 1, 1967, he was again promoted to PFC, and in April his military occupational specialty was changed to rifleman (0311) and he was transferred to the Marine Detachment at the Naval Detention Center, Portsmouth, New Hampshire, where he was assigned as a correctional services guard (8131). On June 6, by order of a summary court-martial, he was again reduced to private, and later that month he received orders to Vietnam.

Maxey arrived in Vietnam in August 1967 and was assigned to Company E, 2nd Battalion, 3rd Marines (operating until the end of November as Battalion Landing Team 2/3), where he ended up in the same platoon as fellow 1005er Ron Schirmer. He was once again promoted to PFC in October 1967. Between August and December he participated in nine major combat operations in the three most northern provinces of South Vietnam, but on December 4, 1967, during Operation Denver in Quang Nam Province, he sustained shrapnel wounds to the left upper arm, right leg, and lower left thigh, and was evacuated to a U.S. military hospital on Guam.

In January 1968 he was transferred to the U.S. Naval Hospital at Bethesda, Maryland, where he remained until April, when he was transferred to Henderson Hall, Headquarters Marine Corps, Arlington, Virginia, pending the results of a physical evaluation board. In August he was medically discharged with a physical disability due to permanent nerve damage in his right arm, for which he still receives a small monthly disability payment.

Maxey's decorations include the Purple Heart, National Defense Service, Vietnam Service, and Vietnam Campaign Medals. He still lives in Mississippi. After spending fourteen years working as a railroad mechanic fixing boxcars, he is currently a mechanic in a furniture factory.

David C. McBirney

"I pulled a Dan Quayle," says David McBirney of his decision to join the Tennessee Air National Guard. He shrugs his shoulders and grins, but the more he talks, the less he sounds like our former Vice President. Whatever motivated the former senator from Indiana to join the National Guard, what motivated McBirney was not the fear of ending up in Vietnam but only the desire to become an officer before he got there.

McBirney had just dropped out of Vanderbilt University. He was prime meat for the draft, but he didn't want to be an enlisted man, so he joined TNANG to stave off Selective Service while he figured out the best way to earn a commission. Though an enlisted man in TNANG, his plan

Second Lieutenant David C. McBirney (front center)
escorting Spanish and American dignitaries aboard the cruiser
USS Columbus, *Barcelona, Spain, 1968.*

David McBirney (right) *with his son, Matthew, March 1996.*

was to go to flight school, earn his wings and his commission at the same time, then transfer to the regular Air Force.

But McBirney had too much integrity to go through with it. TNANG received only three slots for flight school, and TNANG officers made it very clear that McBirney was expected to stay with TNANG after he got his wings. When push came to shove, he couldn't bring himself to say he'd stay with TNANG when he knew that's not what he wanted and not what he intended to do.

It wasn't the first time McBirney's plans to become an officer failed to work out, nor would it be the last time. When it came to becoming an officer in the United States military, hard luck seemed to be the only kind of luck McBirney had.

Born in Salt Lake City, Utah, in the midst of the Second World War, McBirney moved with his parents and older sister to Oak Ridge, Tennessee, where his father, an engineer, went to work on the Manhattan Project, helping to develop the atomic bomb. The project was so secret, McBirney's mother told him, that a shipping company at first returned the family's belongings to Utah, saying there was no such place as Oak Ridge.

McBirney was too young to remember either the move itself or the few years he spent at Oak Ridge before his parents divorced and he moved to Chattanooga with his mother and sister. (His mother still lives in the house in which he grew up. His father died of cancer when McBirney was ten or eleven; he thinks the cancer was quite possibly radiation-induced.) At Chattanooga High School, McBirney wrestled on the school team and participated in Junior Reserve Officers' Training Corps. JROTC was required his first year; thereafter it was an elective, he explains, but the only other choice was gym class, so he stuck with JROTC.

His greatest ambition since at least junior high, however, had been to attend the Air Force Academy, and he didn't think he'd get in if he stayed at Chattanooga, so he took his senior year of high school at Marian Institute, a military boarding school in Marian, Alabama. "I thrived on that type of discipline," he says. "I went from a C+ student to an A+ student." But one good year wasn't enough to get him into the Air Force Academy. So much for Plan #1.

Plan #2 was to attend Vanderbilt for a year, then reapply to the Academy. He fulfilled all the requirements for admission on this second try, but one other applicant for the same position did just a little better than McBirney, and so got the appointment. "If I had known how things worked," he says, "I could probably have gotten in on my third try," but he didn't know how things worked, and he didn't reapply.

"When I didn't get into the Academy," he says, "I felt like I'd lost something. I just kind of drifted." Without much academic desire or incentive, he stuck it out at Vanderbilt for two and a half years, but after that first year, his grades fell precipitously, and he knew he was on his way to flunking out, so he quit. That's when he came up with Plan #3 and joined the Tennessee Air National Guard.

Meanwhile, after leaving school, McBirney first drove a delivery truck, then took a job doing a time and motion study for a manufacturing company. When his third version of "How to Become an Officer" went belly up, McBirney began talking to recruiters from all the services, trying to determine which service offered him the best chance to earn a commission.

"Oh, man," the Marine recruiter told him, "two years of college, you'll get OCS no sweat," so he got himself discharged from TNANG, enlisted in the Marines, and wound up in Platoon 1005. He immediately told his drill instructors that he wanted to apply for OCS, but was told he couldn't apply until he got to the Infantry Training Regiment at Camp Geiger, North Carolina.

Meanwhile, McBirney didn't just want to be an officer; he wanted to be an infantry officer. "My feeling was," he explains, "if you're going to be in the Marine Corps, you gotta be a ground-pounder." During his initial aptitude tests at Parris Island, he had told his interviewer that he couldn't type but could navigate by the North Star. In each case, the truth was exactly the opposite, but he figured his responses were more likely to get him an infantry military occupational specialty. "I wanted infantry," he says. "I was scared to death they'd make me something else." A squad leader in Platoon 1005, he was meritoriously promoted to private first class, and he got the MOS he wanted: 0331 machine gunner. "I asked for it," he says. "I geared the tests for it."

Alas, it was time for Plan #4 to go bust: at ITR he was told that if he'd wanted OCS, he should have applied while he was at Parris Island. (As I've already said, Platoon 1005 was unusual in that all eighty original members of the platoon went through the complete training cycle together, neither adding nor dropping anyone. McBirney thinks the drill instructors' lack of forthrightness might have been connected to their wanting to achieve this rare accomplishment.)

But if the best laid plans of mice and men often go awry, sometimes good things happen when least expected, and McBirney was due for a little good luck. Nearing completion of machine-gun school and already with orders for Vietnam, he was befriended by an officer who took an interest in his still keen desire to earn a commission and helped him apply to OCS. McBirney's orders to Vietnam were cancelled, he was given temporary orders to serve as a clerk typist at Camp Geiger, and after six months on hold, he began OCS at Quantico, Virginia, in the spring of 1967.

"You think Parris Island was tough?" he says. "PI pales in comparison to OCS, at least physically." The main aim of OCS, he says, seemed to be to wash out anybody who was not absolutely fit physically and mentally. The wash-out rate for his group was very high, he recalls, perhaps as high as 40 percent.

"After ten weeks, you get commissioned," he says of those who didn't wash out, "but you don't know anything. They didn't want to loose all those dumb second lieutenants on the Marine Corps without teaching them something," so after OCS came six months of Basic School where, he says, "you learn how to be an officer in the Marine Corps. Treat the troops right—they really instill that in you." His new MOS was 0301, infantry officer.

His first assignment out of Basic School was as the executive officer of the Marine detachment aboard the guided missile cruiser USS *Columbus* out of Norfolk, Virginia. The detachment of about fifty men performed police duties, ran the ship's brig, guarded restricted areas and "nuclear capable" weapons ("They never told us if nuclear warheads were actually on board," he says, "but I assume they were"), and performed ceremonial duties. "It was an enjoyable job," he says, "but that's not why I joined the Marine Corps." He repeatedly requested, and finally received, orders to Vietnam.

Arriving in February 1969, he was assigned to 3rd Battalion, 26th Marines, where he was immediately made company commander of Company L in spite of the fact that he was only a lieutenant (company commanders are usually captains). Except for one brief stint as executive officer of Company L when a captain in the rear decided he wanted to command a rifle company (a desire that didn't last very long), McBirney spent his entire tour as a company commander, first with Company L (twice), then with Company M.

If it was unusual for a lieutenant to command a rifle company, it was even more unusual for an officer to spend more than six months in the field before being reassigned to a rear echelon job, but McBirney spent his entire tour with a line company. Succeeding battalion commanders kept asking him to remain in the field for the sake of continuity, and by the time his third battalion commander told him he could come in from the field, McBirney felt he had too little time left in-country to try to make the transition.

On his first day in the field, he got hit in the face with a piece of shrapnel from a mortar. "Oh, shit," he recalls thinking. "This is going to be a long war." It turned out to be the only time he was ever injured, but those around him were not so lucky. "I lost a lot of friends," he says, "and I don't like to think about it." The hardest part was having to write letters of condolence to the families of members of his company who had been killed. After one staff sergeant he was particularly close to got killed, he stopped forming close attachments, and he admits that he still sometimes suffers the pangs of survivor's guilt.

Racial tensions between black and white Marines sometimes surfaced, he says, but mostly only in the rear, and most incidents were drug- or alcohol-related. That notwithstanding, in his opinion drug problems were not so bad as what he reads now would make one think. Far more problematic, he says, were the large number of higher-ups who were just in Vietnam "punching cards" (enhancing their careers). Once, he says, some general wanted McBirney to cut a helicopter landing zone for him in the middle of an engagement. "We're too busy fighting the gooks," McBirney radioed back, and got away with it that time, but, he says, "we were always cutting LZs for those damned generals."

McBirney left Vietnam in February 1970 with a Bronze Star with Combat V for the performance of his duties while with 3/26, and, after a brief assignment with the Judge Advocate General's staff at Camp Lejeune, he was released from active duty in March 1970 (while on inactive reserve, he subsequently received a promotion to captain). After a few months of travel, including a sojourn to Africa, he returned to Vanderbilt that fall.

Much had changed in the years he'd been away from Vanderbilt. In the mid-1960s, he'd studied vacuum tubes in engineering, and beer drinking on campus was an offense for which one could be expelled. By the early 1970s, he was studying solid state electronics, and personal behavioral standards boiled down to a de facto, if not official, "anything goes."

"When I went back to school," he says, "I wasn't interested in academics. I was interested in that sheepskin. When you go looking for work, there's a big difference between three years of college and a college degree." After three semesters, he graduated in 1971 with a bachelor's degree in electrical engineering and took a job with Arnold M. Diamond, Inc., a construction company specializing in building fossil fuel power plants.

He spent fifteen years with Diamond, going "wherever the power plants were," he says: New York, Las Vegas, Norfolk, and various locations in the Midwest. Meanwhile, after courting her long-distance for nearly four years, McBirney married the daughter of the French ambassador to Malta, whom he'd first met while on sea duty aboard the Columbus, and their son Matthew was born in 1978. In his first few years of schooling, Matthew had already had to change schools several times because of his father's job-related moves, so to give Matthew some stability, McBirney left Diamond and settled in the Norfolk area.

After several jobs of short duration, McBirney went to work for Independence Construction, a builder of restaurants and shopping centers. He stayed with Independence for eight years, where he was a vice president, project manager, and estimator ("jack-of-all-trades," he says), building Olive Gardens, Taco Bells, and Wendy's, but in June 1994 he left Independence and founded his own company, MidCoast Builders, Inc.

The name of the company, he points out, derives from his own initials. It consists mostly of himself and the subcontractors he hires as needed, and specializes in building renovations. He has done work for the National

Aeronautics and Space Administration, and for the giant supermarket chain Food Lion. Recently, he renovated a locker room used by the Navy's SEALS.

"Anything I can do for a buck," he says. "I'm not a skilled craftsman. When I can do something and save a buck, I do, but I'm not too skilled, so I have to hire people. I ain't proud. I'll sweep the floor while some craftsman is doing the skill work." And if his new company doesn't make it? "I don't know," he says. "If it doesn't, I'll just go out and get another job.

"I don't have a lot of spare time," he continues. For the past three months he's been working from 5:00 A.M. to midnight almost every day. But he does belong to Kiwanis, a service organization that does volunteer work and fund-raising for such causes as the Salvation Army, the Young Men's Christian Association, and Children's Hospital of Norfolk. "We get so wrapped up in our own lives," he says. "We forget about the wider world. [In Kiwanis] we try to do for others—just make life better for everybody and anybody."

Most of his spare time, however, he spends with Matthew, now 17. McBirney and his wife separated in 1990 and divorced in 1994, but he stays in close contact with his son. Because he himself grew up in a broken home, McBirney explains, "I am determined to be here for him." They'll take Matthew's boat and go out fishing, or go to dinner and a movie together. Matthew, a high school junior, is active in Navy JROTC and wants to become a military pilot, explaining that he'll join whichever branch of the service will let him fly. Through much of the afternoon of March 24, 1996, Matthew sat quietly in his father's bachelor apartment, listening to McBirney tell me about his life. When Matthew finally had to leave, father and son embraced, then kissed each other unself-consciously.

McBirney is quietly but fiercely proud of his time in the military. When he first saw the newsreels of helicopters evacuating the last Americans from Saigon in April 1975, he says, he felt that the war in Vietnam had all been a waste, but as time has passed, he has come to believe that the U.S. did what it should have done. He believed in the U.S. commitment when he went to Vietnam, he says, and he still believes in it.

"I'm a great believer in the Domino Theory," he explains. He feels that the U.S. could have won the war outright if it had not been for Soviet and Chinese support of Ho Chi Minh and the Viet Cong, but also feels that "we did what we were supposed to do: stop communist expansion. Show a will to resist." Had we not stood up to the Communists in Vietnam, he believes, Thailand, Malayasia, and eventually many other countries would have fallen to the Communists.

"There are things that shouldn't have happened," he acknowledges, harking back to the "ticket punchers" and hovering generals demanding LZs. Though he never committed any atrocities, he says, nor saw any committed, he knows that they happened. But in spite of these things, he says, "the effort was worth it. I'm sad that people feel it was such a waste. Vietnam did more than [President Ronald] Reagan did to defeat communism."

Clifton McKnight, Jr.

I was unable to locate McKnight through telephone records, and though he had filed a claim for veterans benefits, the letter forwarded to the last address the VA had for him was returned undeliverable. Based on records received in November 1995 from NPRC, I know that McKnight was born March 1, 1948, graduated from high school, and was living in Nashville, Tennessee, at the time of his enlistment. After boot camp, where he earned a Rifle Marksman's Badge, and basic infantry training, he received additional training as a cook (3371) at the Food Service School, Camp Lejeune, North Carolina. McKnight then served in Vietnam with Headquarters & Maintenance Squadron 17, Marine Wing Support Group 17, from February 1967 until February 1968, subsequently serving with various companies of the 2nd Infantry Training Regiment at Camp Pendleton, California, from March 1968 until his release from active duty in June 1970. He achieved the rank of corporal, and received the Combat Action Ribbon, the National Defense Service, Vietnam Service, and Vietnam Campaign Medals, and a Certificate of Commendation.

After three years as a civilian, McKnight reenlisted in the Marine Corps in May 1973. He was assigned as a food service man, and then as a cook, at the Marine Corps Air Station, El Toro, California, from his reenlistment until February 1975, when he was admitted as a patient to the hospital at Naval Air Station, Miramar, California. Between February and May, while apparently undergoing treatment at the Naval Drug Rehabilitation Center at Miramar, he was absent without leave on two occasions, the first time for four days, the second for a week. He was subsequently discharged in May 1975.

McKnight married and had two daughters, but there is no indication of when this information was current.

Lonnie Milligan

I was able to get an address for Milligan from Lieutenant Colonel Johnson at MIE, Inc., who traced his social security number, which I'd gotten when I requested Milligan's VA claim number. Between February 1994 and September 1995, however, four letters to that address went unanswered, and directory assistance had no telephone number for Milligan, listed or unlisted. Since it's less than thirty miles from my house, I thought a number of times about just getting into my car and seeing what I might find at that address. Then I'd begin to imagine all of the things I might find and remember that looking for trouble is a good way to find it.

I did learn from records received from NPRC in February 1995 that Milligan is a 1966 high school graduate from southeastern Pennsylvania and joined the Marines on the Buddy Plan with Howard A. Purcell, Jr. After boot camp, basic infantry training, and special weapons training as a machine gunner (0331), he reported to Staging Battalion, Camp Pendleton, California, in late October 1966 in preparation for departure to Vietnam. From November 12 until December 9, he was a patient in the U.S. Naval Hospital at Pendleton, however, and did not complete staging until mid-December.

Milligan embarked aboard the USNS *General N. M. Walker* at San Diego on January 7, 1967, and arrived at Da Nang, Vietnam, on January 25, where he was assigned the following day as an ammunition carrier with Company F, 2nd Battalion, 26th Marines. Ten days later, he received a gunshot wound to the left leg, and was hospitalized for a month before being returned to duty.

In July his primary duty was changed from ammo carrier to gunner. In October, he was transferred to Headquarters Battalion, 3rd Marine Division, as a rifleman (0311), and from November 1967 until February 1968, he was assigned to the 3rd Combined Action Group, III Marine Amphibious Force, again as a rifleman.

Returning to the States, Milligan served as a guard (8151) with Headquarters & Support Company, Base Materials Battalion, at Camp Lejeune, North Carolina, from March 1968 until his release from active duty in June. He achieved the rank of corporal, and received the Purple Heart, National Defense Service, Vietnam Service, and Vietnam Campaign Medals.

Thomas J. Morgan

None of the forty-five Thomas J. Morgans on the Myers list responded to my initial search letter, and the VA has no record of his ever filing a claim for veterans' benefits. Records received from NPRC in June 1995 indicate that he was born January 7, 1947, in Cumberland, Maryland. He graduated from high school in 1966 and was living in Baltimore at the time of his enlistment.

After boot camp and basic infantry training, in October 1966 he was assigned to Battery A, 3rd Light Anti-Aircraft Missile Battalion, 2nd Marine Air Wing, Marine Corps Air Station, Cherry Point, North Carolina, as an anti-aircraft weapons battery man (6742). He served with 3rd LAAM Battalion until October 1967, including a month-long deployment to Vieques Island, Puerto Rico, in March 1967 aboard the USS *DeSoto County*.

From December 1967 until December 1968, Morgan served in Vietnam with Battery B, 1st LAAM Battalion, 1st Marine Air Wing.

In January 1969, he returned to Cherry Point, this time with Headquarters & Maintenance Squadron 27, where he served until his release from active duty in April 1969. A lance corporal, he was awarded the National Defense Service, Vietnam Service, and Vietnam Campaign Medals.

David L. Morrison

None of the twenty-three David L. Morrisons on the Myers list responded to my initial search letter, but I got Morrison's social security number through the VA claim system, and with that information, MIE, Inc., was able to get me an address. I wrote in February 1994, but got no reply. I wrote a second time in January 1995, and this time Morrison called me on January 15. He said he'd gotten my 1994 letter, but had been too busy with Little League umpiring to reply. When he got my second letter, however, his wife and several friends had urged him to reply.

From our conversation, and records received from NPRC in February 1995, I learned that Morrison was born on September 23, 1947, in Clarksburg, West Virginia. He played varsity football for Washington

Irving High School, and when he graduated in 1966, he and teammate Tom Erickson joined the Marines on the Buddy Plan. The two men were sworn in at South Charleston together with fellow West Virginians Tim Jenkins, Wayne Kelly, and Clarence Potts.

After boot camp and basic infantry training, Morrison went to Naval Air Station, Memphis, Tennessee, for training as a metalsmith and aircraft structural mechanic (6341) from October 1966 until March 1967. Then from April until October 1967, he served with Marine Composite Reconnaissance Squadron 2, Marine Aircraft Group 14, at MCAS Cherry Point, North Carolina.

Morrison next received orders to Vietnam, where he served with VMCJ-1, MAG-11, from November 1967 until December 1968. At the expiration of his standard thirteen-month tour, he voluntarily extended for an additional six months in Vietnam, which he served with Marine Observation Squadron 6, Provisional Marine Aircraft Group 39. He was released from active duty upon his return to the United States in July 1969. His decorations include the Navy Achievement Medal with Combat V, and the Good Conduct, National Defense Service, Vietnam Service, and Vietnam Campaign Medals.

Morrison says the group of Marines he left Vietnam with that July 1969 were part of President Richard Nixon's first troop withdrawals, but that none of the men were being withdrawn prior to their scheduled rotation dates; all were at the end of their tours anyway. He also says that their plane was greeted by hostile crowds when it landed at MCAS El Toro, California, but that he was not bothered again by antiwar demonstrators once he left California.

As a civilian, Morrison took a job with Pratt & Whitney in Connecticut. "But then the snow started falling," he says, so he headed for Florida in 1970 and has been there ever since. He left the aviation field behind when he moved south, and has been working in the uniform rental industry. He has a grown daughter and son by his first marriage, which ended in divorce, and a teenaged stepson and a toddler son by his second marriage. Morrison, who lives in the Tampa–Saint Petersburg area, says he has found a niche for himself as a Little League umpire, an activity he took up in 1989 and in which his wife is also involved. He calls about 130 games a year.

Barry L. Moyer

Most people may not think of Moyer as a name in the same league as Green, Johnson, or Smith, but where I grew up in southeastern Pennsylvania, Moyers abound. At Pennridge High School, we had seven different Moyers in my graduating class of 276. Of the fifteen Barry L. Moyers on the Myers list from all over the eastern United States, eight of them were from southeastern Pennsylvania, but none of them responded to my initial search letter, nor had the Barry L. Moyer with his service number ever applied for veterans' benefits. When I got Moyer's records from NPRC in August 1995, it turned out that he had indeed come from Linfield, a small town in southeastern Pennsylvania, so I called directory assistance for Linfield, but found nothing either listed or unlisted.

From NPRC, I did learn that Moyer was born on November 2, 1946, and graduated from high school before enlisting. After boot camp and basic infantry training, he received additional training as a machine gunner (0331) before being sent to Vietnam in December 1966, where he was assigned as an ammo carrier with Company M, 3rd Battalion, 9th Marine Regiment.

In January 1967, Moyer's entire battalion boarded the USS *Bexar* at Da Nang and sailed for Okinawa, returning to Dong Ha, Vietnam, six weeks later aboard the USS *Bayfield*. In June, Moyer was moved up to gunner. On July 1, 1967, during Operation Cimarron in the vicinity of Dong Ha, he was wounded in the left side by shrapnel, though the wound was not serious enough to require evacuation. From September until his departure from Vietnam in December, he served as a machine-gun team leader.

Moyer was next assigned to Company L, 3rd Battalion, 8th Marines, Camp Lejeune, North Carolina, in January 1968, but less than a month later, he was reassigned as a security guard (8151) at the Marine Barracks, U.S. Naval Station, Argentia, Newfoundland. He was reduced in rank on October 11, 1968. He remained in Newfoundland until June 1969, then spent a week as a guard at the Marine Barracks, Naval Air Station, Quonset Point, Rhode Island, before being released from active duty with the rank of private first class.

While in Vietnam, Moyer participated in thirteen combat operations. In addition to the Purple Heart Medal he received when he was wounded, he was also awarded the National Defense Service, Vietnam Service, and Vietnam Campaign Medals, along with a Presidential Unit Citation.

Harry V. Nelson, Jr.

"I've fulfilled the American dream," says Harry Nelson. He is sitting in the living room of his two-story frame house in Philipsburg, a town of three thousand nestled in central Pennsylvania's Moshannon Valley, where I visited him on October 4, 1994. I'd had no trouble locating him because we'd been classmates at Pennridge High School and had seen each other now and then over the years, most recently at both our twentieth and twenty-fifth class reunions.

"I've got a house and a wonderful wife, food in the refrigerator, two cars. I love my job and really enjoy going to work each day. The bills are paid, I belong to the country club, and if I scrape a bit, I can afford to send my boys to college." Then, as if he can't quite believe it, he adds, "And I'm happy. I'm thrilled with life."

Nelson is chief designer and pattern maker for Charles Navasky & Company, Inc., a century-old fourth-generation manufacturer of men's suits, sportswear, and topcoats. He is Navasky's only designer and pat-

Private First Class Harry V. Nelson, Jr. (right) *with one of his instructors at air traffic controllers' school, Keesler Air Force Base, Biloxi, Mississippi, 1967.*

tern maker. When he was first hired sixteen years ago, he was one of five, but as the others moved on or retired, they were never replaced. Navasky wanted someone "young and hungry who could grow with the company," Nelson says, and Nelson turned out to be that someone.

As Nelson talks, first one son, Ryan, 13, then the other, Harry III, 17, quietly comes into the room and sits down on the floor to listen to their father talk about his life before reluctantly turning to the night's homework. Kathy, Nelson's wife of twenty-one years, briefly interrupts to show off the altar cloth this year's catechism class is embroidering for Saints Peter and Paul Church. A registered nurse, she still finds time for church work between caring for her own father, who suffers from Alzheimer's disease, and serving as a private-duty nurse for a four-year-old child with a degenerative disease.

Corporal and basketball player Harry Nelson, Headquarters & Headquarters Squadron basketball team, Marine Corps Air Station, Beaufort, South Carolina, 1968.

Born in Philadelphia, Nelson grew up in Sellersville, a small town in southeastern Pennsylvania, and attended Saint Agnes Catholic School through eighth grade before moving on to the local public high school in nearby Perkasie. By the time he graduated in 1966, he had already joined the Marines on a delayed enlistment. "The Marine recruiter [who came to the school] looked so cool in those dress blues," Nelson says. "He was so fit, and I was this 148-pounder [on a six-foot-four-inch frame]. I went up to him and asked, 'Can you make me look like you?' and he says, 'Yes, we can.'"

There were other reasons for joining, too. "I wanted to prove I was a man," Nelson explains. "I knew I wasn't going to college. My parents

Harry Nelson, an avid fan and booster of the Pennsylvania State University ice hockey club, with Penn State's mascot, the Nittany Lion, 1994.

didn't have the money for that. And I was brought up to believe that for every right there's a responsibility. I bought into the Domino Theory on Vietnam, too."

About boot camp, Nelson says, "Very honestly, I was so concerned with just surviving those eight weeks, I really didn't develop any lasting friendships. The main thing I remember about Parris Island is the absolute fear I felt. I remember looking out into the swamp behind the barracks at night and thinking, 'Please, God, get me through this. Don't let me die here.' Everyone else seemed to be so much stronger than me. Robert Fink was my bunkie for awhile. He was this big strong farm boy. We'd be doing push-ups in the squad bay, and I'd be dying, and Fink would be going up and down, up and down, like it was nothing."

Nevertheless, Nelson was made a squad leader early on ("Because I was so tall," he says self-deprecatingly. "They wanted the tall guys up front"), and only once relinquished that responsibility. "I qualified poorly on the rifle range," he says, "so [Sergeant] Bosch demoted me. But the same night, [Staff Sergeant] Oliver came in and said, 'What are you doing back there, Nelson? Get up front where you belong.' That was my biggest lift in boot camp. I went from misery to ecstasy that day." He also received a meritorious promotion to private first class upon graduation.

Nelson had enlisted for four years under a program that guaranteed him an aviation MOS, so after boot camp and basic infantry training, he was tested at Memphis, Tennessee, and assigned an MOS of 6713, radar air traffic controller. Because the Marine Corps air traffic controllers' school in Glenco, Georgia, was full, Nelson and fifty-nine other Marines were sent to school at Keesler Air Force Base in Biloxi, Mississippi.

They were the first detachment of Marines to train at Keesler, says Nelson, "and most of us weren't that long out of boot camp. We were gung ho. We thought we were the baddest guys on the block. We were squared away, and we looked good when we marched along in formation, but the zoomies and doggies [airmen and soldiers] used to hang out of the barracks windows and call us jarheads and other taunts."

One evening, the ranking man, a corporal, called the detachment to a halt in front of a barracks from which Nelson says the insults were flying thick and fast. "We're Marines," the corporal told his charges. "We don't take that from anybody. Go in there and kick some ass."

The raid lasted just three minutes, but the repercussions traveled a long way. The commandant himself, General Wallace M. Greene, Jr., came to Keesler to remind the detachment that they represented the Marine Corps and henceforth ought to behave accordingly. He left a senior staff NCO behind to see that they did. Just the same, according to Nelson, no Marine ever trained at Keesler again.

Upon completion of his training, Nelson picked up another meritorious promotion to lance corporal, and was posted to MCAS Beaufort, South Carolina. Soon after he arrived, he got involved in a pickup game of basketball, someone suggested he try out for the base team, and he did. "I wasn't as good as I thought I was," he says, "but the team was outstanding. We just killed people. We'd spot other teams twenty points and still beat them. One team we spotted sixty points and still won."

Eventually, Nelson became a player/coach. He still has a set of orders to MCAS Cherry Point, North Carolina, dated February 4–11, 1968, authorizing him to play in the East Coast Regional Basketball Tournament. "It was only fifteen dollars a day," he says, "but I got paid to play basketball!"

Meanwhile, ever since his arrival at Beaufort, Nelson had watched others getting orders to Vietnam, first those who had arrived before him, but then even those who'd arrived later. "I always expected to go," he says. "When it became clear that I was either very, very lucky or someone was steering orders away from me, I started asking questions and was told I wouldn't be going. No one said as much, but it was implied that I played basketball too well.

"All I know for sure is my orders never came up," he continues. "I had ambivalent feelings about it. By that point, I'd seen enough people come back who weren't in the best of shape, and I wasn't so gung ho anymore. Plus I was pretty comfortable down there playing basketball and being an air traffic controller. We got treated pretty well."

Nelson left active duty in June 1970 as a sergeant, and returned to his hometown, bringing with him a wife and two small children. He got a job with Lehigh Valley Dairies delivering milk door-to-door in Philadelphia. Most of the drivers belonged to the Teamsters Union, but Nelson did not believe in unions and declined to join. "I've always been a believer that I can do it on my own," he says. "If I do my job well enough, they'll pay me. If I don't, then I ought to be fired."

Not everyone approved of Nelson's independence, however. As he was making his rounds early one morning on a dark and deserted street, he was approached by several strangers. "I got told that I really should join the Teamsters," he says. "They beat me up." When he still refused to join, he was approached a second time, again by strangers who rocked his truck severely, breaking a large portion of that day's deliveries.

Nelson told a sympathetic supervisor about the incidents, and was given a less isolated route in Lansdale, Pennsylvania. Meanwhile his troubled marriage had collapsed (to his regret, he has since had little contact with his children by that marriage), but a customer on the new route introduced him to her daughter, Kathy Zohil, and the relationship flourished. They were married in 1973.

Soon after the route change, however, the dairy announced that it was reducing home deliveries. Nelson could see the writing on the wall and took a job filling fire extinguishers for Dependable Fire Extinguisher Service of Telford, Pennsylvania. But the job was a career dead end, so after only a few months he took a job as a cutting-room trainee at Royal Pants Factory in nearby Perkasie. His father, who had been a driver for the dairy most of his life, had already gotten a job at Royal, and they would soon be joined by Nelson's mother as well.

But he was not getting paid enough to support his new wife and their infant son, so he had to take a second job six nights a week pumping gas. "After a year or two, I realized this wasn't what I aspired to be,"

Nelson says of the cutting room, "but I could see that the pattern maker got to work on his own, and he got a lot of respect from the owners, so I asked to be a pattern maker."

Royal sent him to the Cybics School of Apparel Design in New York City. "Every student had his own teacher," Nelson says, "so you could learn in six months what it took others four years to learn." Nevertheless, it was a long six months. Nelson took a two-hour bus ride to New York every Monday morning, stayed "in a really crummy hotel" all week, then took the bus home again Friday nights.

But when Nelson finished at Cybics, he was put back on the cutting floor and told he couldn't be a pattern maker until the current pattern maker retired. "The current pattern maker had no plans to retire anytime soon," says Nelson. "That's when I knew I wasn't going anywhere at Royal. So I wrote up a resume, contacted a headhunter, and went looking for a new job."

He got an offer from Navasky. "The job had everything I was looking for," he says. "It was a family business in a small town. I could call the owner by his first name. And he offered me more money than I was making at Royal and the gas station combined. When he offered to pay for my first year's membership at the country club, too, that clinched it. It was just a real sweetheart deal."

Nelson works on the top floor of a three-story brick building overlooking the Moshannon Creek, one of nine buildings housing Navasky & Company operations in Philipsburg and nearby Chester Hill. The pattern room contains a long table where he draws the initial patterns by hand, rack after rack of suits and topcoats, other racks with cardboard patterns hanging from them, and bolts of cloth stacked on shelves.

Several posters of scantily clad women grace the walls, along with posters advertising Falcone and Damiani suits, two of Navasky's upscale lines. One is a poster of heavyweight boxer Evander Holyfield in a Falcone suit, a gorgeous young woman in a tight pink gown clinging to his body. (Nelson has designed suits for Holyfield, ex-champ Larry Holmes, rock star Prince, and former president Jimmy Carter, among others.)

Next door is the computer room, containing five terminals, a digitizer for transferring the initial patterns into the computer system, and a plotter, which can draw anything in the system from a single piece of a pattern to an entire marker (a marker is the single large piece of cloth from which an entire suit is cut).

Before computers arrived at Navasky in the mid-1980s, Nelson explains, the company used to offer three or four suit models per season, perhaps as many as six. Now they can do thirty to forty models. "The computer does in seconds what it used to take up to six hours to do by hand," he says. "It can do a marker in four minutes, as opposed to twenty minutes by hand, and it can do it using less cloth. The computer may only save ten inches of cloth per marker, but when you're making twenty thousand suits a day, that adds up.

"We're always looking for ways to save money," Nelson continues. "It's the only way we can compete with offshore [foreign] companies. The Philippines, China, Singapore, Pakistan, you name it. Their labor costs are cheaper; they don't have the safety standards. In China, they use prison labor." Hanging from the ceiling of one of the cutting rooms in Nelson's building is a hand-lettered sign that says, "Fewer Restroom Breaks Means More Money."

Only once has Nelson had any reservations about Navasky & Co. When computers were first introduced, he says, he was given one week's training with a representative of Lectra Systemes, the company that provided the system, and provided with a stack of manuals. "I was doing my regular job during the day because we couldn't just stop working," he says. "Then I'd be up half the night trying to learn how to use the computer." When the situation persisted without any extra pay or apparent recognition of his efforts, Nelson got discouraged and went looking for another job.

He received a good offer from one of Navasky's competitors and gave Navasky thirty days notice, but when Navasky discovered that they would have to pay substantially more to hire another pattern maker with comparable experience, the company matched their competitor's offer, and Nelson stayed. "Things were a little tense for a while after that," he says. "But that's all in the past."

Indeed, Nelson has sunk deep roots in the Philipsburg community. He has been elected to the local school board ("I'm considered by my friends as an ultraconservative," he says, laughing. "To put it in perspective, let me say that I view Rush Limbaugh as a centrist"), and has served on the board of governors at the Philipsburg Country Club.

The entire Nelson family has also become avid fans of nearby Penn State University's hockey team. Nelson was president of the Icers, the team's booster club, for three years, and just recently took over the club's merchandising, an operation that generates forty thousand dollars annually in sales of hats, sticks, pucks, jerseys, and other team souvenirs. The money is used, Nelson explains with proprietary pride, to help support the team: buying ice time, hiring tutors for players who need academic help, providing scholarships, travel money and extra meal money. "Anything we can do within NCAA guidelines," he says.

As the hour grows late, Nelson returns once more to the subject of Vietnam. "I've always had mixed emotions about not going," he says. "Even back then, I remember thinking, 'What am I going to tell my kids about what I did in the war? Played basketball?' But I also know how lucky I am. I've got a good life here. I went to the Vietnam Memorial in Washington and looked up Kenny Worman's name. [Worman was another high school classmate of ours; he enlisted in the Army and was killed in action in the Central Highlands in May 1967.] I stood in front of it and cried like a baby, but I was thankful to be able to be there doing that."

George D. Osada

George's American Cafe sits on a street corner in a white working-class community of Southwest Philadelphia. The surrounding area has seen better days—open spaces attest to the many buildings that have been razed and not replaced, and serious urban decay is only blocks away—but the immediate neighborhood around George's stubbornly refuses to bow to the ravages of time. Prominently hanging from the front of George's are two large American flags. Inside, half a dozen smaller American flags hang at intervals above the bar.

Also inside is George Osada, owner and manager of George's American Cafe, which Osada describes as "a typical neighborhood taproom." It's a no-frills shot-and-beer tavern. There used to be a grill, but it had to be removed in order to comply with Pennsylvania Liquor Control Board regulations on minimum seating capacity, so now Osada makes do with a crockpot and hot plate, along with ready-made sandwiches from a local delicatessen. "People don't come here to eat anyway," he says. "They come to drink."

I didn't come to eat or drink, but I had a few beers anyway, along with a shot of Goldschlager, the stuff with the little flakes of gold floating around in it, compliments of Osada.

Only one George Osada had come up on the Myers list, and though

*Private First Class George D. Osada,
1967.*

the middle initial was wrong, since it was a local address I tried the telephone number that came with it on September 23, 1993. The woman who answered said the previous owner had just died and she had bought the house from his son, who also lived in Philadelphia, so I checked my telephone book and found a G. D. Osada. When I called that number, I got the dead man's grandson, who said I had the right Osada and gave me the number of the bar.

As soon as I said my name, Osada knew who I was, telling me that he owned a copy of *Vietnam-Perkasie* and had read my 1986 article in the Philadelphia *Inquirer Magazine* about going back to Vietnam in 1985. It seemed like a promising start—certainly better than I'd done with Michael Landauer, who'd said several times, "What did you say your name was? I don't remember you at all." Almost immediately afterwards, however, Osada added, "You got my stripe."

Eight members of Platoon 1005 received meritorious promotion to private first class. The promotions usually went to recruits who had had special duties or earned distinction in some way, such as squad leader, house mouse, or high shooter. I'd been none of those things, but had gotten promoted anyway. Osada had been our platoon guide, but had not gotten a stripe. "Hey, I wasn't the guy who made those decisions," I said, which was true, but I was thinking, "Not so promising a start after all." Nevertheless, we arranged to meet the next day—the first of two meetings, the second coming on October 15, 1994—and he never mentioned the offending stripe again.

When I arrived at the bar, he was wearing a red Marine Corps baseball-style cap he'd recently bought at a K-Mart. "I named it George's American Cafe for two reasons," he says of his bar. "The Koreans are hard workers, and I give them credit for that, but they're taking over every small store in Philly. And all the little restaurants are owned by Greeks. That bothers me a lot. I was also thinking of Rick's American Cafe in *Casablanca*. I like that movie." Only American beer is sold in George's American Cafe.

Osada was born in Philadelphia and has lived here all his life. The oldest son of an Abbott's Dairy maintenance worker and a housewife, he grew up in Northeast Philly and went to Father Judge Catholic High School, where he was student council president and a varsity football player. "We went both ways in those days," he says. "I played tight end and linebacker. We won the all-city championship. We beat Frankford High, the public league champions."

Upon graduation in 1965, Osada was recruited to play football for a new junior college called Delaware Valley Institute. Describing himself as only "an average student" academically, he availed himself of the opportunity. It seemed like a good deal until he discovered that the school was only a small row house on Baltimore Avenue with two classrooms on

Sergeant George Osada with a Vietnamese girl from the village in which his Combined Action Platoon was stationed, 1969.

George Osada behind the bar of George's American Cafe, Philadelphia, September 1994. (Photo by Jeff Hurwitz.)

the second floor, and the football practice field was a public park with no locker room facilities of any kind.

They did play a few games that fall, but the school abandoned the football program before the season was completed, and when Osada discovered that the school itself wasn't even accredited, there was little incentive to assert himself academically. "Mostly I fooled around for the rest of the school year," he says.

Meanwhile, the war in Vietnam was getting hotter and hotter, and the biggest musical hit of the year was "The Ballad of the Green Berets." "That's what inspired me to join the Marines," he says. "I was going to join the Green Berets, but the Army would only take three-year volunteer enlistments. I wanted to go in, get it over with, and come back."

In June 1966 he enlisted for two years. "The thing I remember most about boot camp," he recalls, "was having that first cigarette after two weeks—standing in that stupid smoking circle out behind the barracks—and then nearly falling over from being dizzy." After basic training, where he was platoon guide, and supply school, he was sent to the big Marine supply base near Barstow, California.

"I enlisted to go to Vietnam," he says. "I didn't want to sit in the desert for two years." So after less than three months at Barstow, Osada extended his enlistment for two additional years in order to get assigned to a year-long Vietnamese language school in Washington, D.C. "I figured if I learned Vietnamese, they'd have to send me to Vietnam." And eventually they did, but not before he'd been to Camp Pendleton, California, Army interrogation school at Fort Holabird, Maryland, and back to Pendleton again.

Finally, in October 1968, he got orders to Vietnam, where he was assigned to the naval hospital near Quang Tri as part of the 5th Interrogation and Translation Team. "I could see real early that there was a big mistake there," he says, referring to the war. To begin with, Osada says, the Vietnamese assigned to his ITT could speak English much better than any of the Americans could speak Vietnamese. Moreover, the language school had taught the Americans to speak what Osada describes as "city Vietnamese," but most of the people they came into contact with were peasants who spoke "rural Vietnamese." On his first interrogation, a Viet Cong defector from the Chieu Hoi center in Quang Tri, his Vietnamese counterpart had to do the entire interrogation because the VC couldn't understand Osada at all.

Osada was also troubled by the attitude of many Americans. "People with short-timers' calendars thought they were superior to the Vietnamese who'd been there all their lives," Osada says. "The Vietnamese could do the job better than we could, yet we're supposed to be telling them what to do. The whole arrangement was ludicrous."

After six months, Osada volunteered for a combined action platoon because "I still wanted that taste of doing something. Even in Quang Tri, I didn't feel like I was really in Vietnam. I didn't feel like I was doing anything worthwhile." Osada was the only bilingual person, American or Vietnamese, in the village where his CAP unit was stationed, so all communications between the Marines and the Popular Forces militia and village civilians had to come through him. Consequently, of necessity, his Vietnamese improved markedly.

He enjoyed living among the Vietnamese, but found the PFs mostly "uninterested in the war. They were farmers and peasants like the rest of the villagers, [and] all the villagers cared about was planting their rice. They didn't care if Ho Chi Minh lived next door, or Lyndon Johnson." In spite of this, he found himself comfortable with the PFs. It was Saigon's regular army, the Army of the Republic of Vietnam, that he distrusted.

"When the ARVN went on an operation," he says, "they always came driving trucks, making noise, giving the operation away. I don't want to say they sabotaged their own operations, but . . ." Osada shrugs and does not finish his sentence.

"I'll tell you why we lost the war," he says. "It was our short-timers' attitude. We should have gone for the duration. And giving up hills and all as soon as we'd take them. What kind of a way is that to fight a war?" Asked if we could have won the war had we done things differently, Osada pauses for nearly a minute, deep in thought. At last he says, "I don't know. It seems a lot like Korea. Did we win there? Vietnam was a no-win situation, a civil war. Maybe if we invaded North Vietnam, but probably not. We did that in Korea, and look what happened."

Osada finished his tour in Vietnam in November 1969. By this time a sergeant, he served out his enlistment at Montfort Point, North Carolina. "There wasn't a lot of interpreting or interrogating to do in North Carolina," he says. "I played a lot of basketball. I wanted to get out so I could grow sideburns. I even got a head start on them, but they made me get a haircut the day before I got out. Whitewalls."

"It was 1970," he says of his reentry into civilian life, "but I still had a 1966 mentality. The four years I was in are the four years everything changed. When I graduated from high school, I had a crew cut. Four years later, high school grads had hair down to their shoulders. I didn't get any grief [about being a Marine and a Vietnam veteran], but I found that it didn't mean anything either. You just stood in line like everybody else." Osada enrolled at Pennsylvania State University for one year, but left without receiving any academic credits.

"The antiwar movement didn't affect me one way or the other," he says. "I never got any of that baby killer routine. I was pretty much unaffected by any of that. It didn't bother me. I couldn't even tell you when Kent State happened. I think I was still in the Marines. Too much had changed, that's all. I just couldn't fit in."

A succession of jobs followed. He answered a Beneficial Finance ad for management trainees, but soon discovered that management training meant dunning people for bad debts. "I shudder to think of some of the places I went," he says. He lasted two years at that job before becoming a New York Life insurance agent, a position he kept for three years, but "I wasn't good at it. It required too much self-discipline. I was playing league softball and football. I sold most of my policies to barmaids after games."

Unhappy working for others, he decided to go into business for himself. With some help from his two younger brothers, both also Marine Corps veterans, he took over operation of a newsstand under the Frankford elevated railway, selling papers and magazines, sodas, hot dogs, soft pretzels, and water ice. After two years, however, the stand was mysteriously destroyed by fire in what Osada suspects was teenaged arson.

Undaunted, he tried again, this time securing a loan from the Small Business Administration to buy a delicatessen just across the street from where the newsstand had been located. Behind on his loan payments from the very beginning, however, he was not able to make good three years later when the SBA demanded that the entire debt be paid off in one lump sum. One afternoon at 3:30, he says, "two lawyers showed up, told me I was no longer the owner, threw me out, and changed the locks. I thought that was that."

Unfortunately, it was not. "I'd made the mistake of having my wife co-sign the loan," he explains. Two years later, a letter arrived stating that the government was suing them for the amount of the foreclosed loan. "It said, 'United States of America versus George and Barbara Osada,'" he says. "The whole country against the two of us? It seemed a bit out of proportion. We had to take out a second mortgage to pay off the loan. It left me feeling very bitter about the United States of America. I'd served my country. I was struggling to make it. It didn't seem fair, especially when you see so many others allowed to walk away from much larger debts."

After the bankruptcy, Osada spent a year as a househusband. He'd first gotten married in 1969, only weeks after he returned from Vietnam. "She wrote great letters," he says of his first wife, but he knew the marriage was in trouble from the very beginning. In 1972 it was annulled, but not before a daughter was born. "I bought my annullment for four hundred dollars," he says. "It was bullshit. That's when I stopped going to church." Osada met his current wife, Barbara, an operating-room nurse at Temple University Hospital, on Long Beach Island in New Jersey in 1973, and they were married two years later.

Osada next got a job in the cashier's office of Temple University Hospital. "My wife got me the job just to get me doing something," he says, "but it didn't sit right. It was like going back to Marine supply. It was a desk job, which I didn't like." He lasted a year before he concluded, "I was spending so much time in bars anyway that I decided to work in one."

For the next four years, he bartended and managed two different bars. Then, six years ago, he bought the second bar from his boss, renamed it George's American Cafe, and has been making a go of it ever since. "It's a nice little spot," he says. "It reminds me a lot of the neighborhood I grew up in. The mortgage isn't too high, and it'll be paid off in another five years. That is, if the city of Philadelphia doesn't tax me out of business first. That's a real possibility. It's a day-to-day operation."

He runs the place himself with only some part-time help, working long hours six days a week. "It's a lot of work, but I enjoy it. In the insurance business, you're trying to sell something," he says, addressing how he can be self-employed when he didn't have the self-discipline to sell insurance. "In the bar business, people want to buy something."

By this time our conversation has moved from the bar to Osada's home on the eastern bank of the Schuylkill River, still Philadelphia but almost in Montgomery County. Osada's wife has owned this property since before they were married, and they lived in two different trailers before putting a prefabricated home on the site in 1980. The house is covered in greenery, with a well-tended garden outside and potted plants in every nook and cranny of the interior. "Barbara's doing," he says of all the plants, "The house is hers. I look after this."

As he speaks, he walks across River Road—which runs between the house and the river—to a patio, several outbuildings, and a dock right by water's edge. "This is my domain." The patio has an outdoor grill, a picnic table, and assorted other lawn furniture. Osada rebuilt the dock himself after the old one was destroyed by severe ice and high water. Over the years, they've had a number of power boats, but all of them were used, and none lasted more than a season. "There's always something with a used boat," he says, "and you can't get anyone to work on them. You have to get a new one. It's a little embarrassing to live here and not have a ski boat." Then he adds, "Next year. Next year."

Meanwhile, though he's finally given up team sports, he and his wife both remain active outdoors people, enjoying snow skiing in winter and the beach in summer, along with golf and their canoe. When the weather permits, Osada swims in the river every day, plunging in right off the dock. "It's pretty shallow right here," he says, standing on the dock and pointing down, "You have to dive out a little."

Just then a tall long-haired lad with a couple of rings in one ear leans over the fence by the riverfront patio and asks Osada for the keys to his

pickup truck. It is David, the older of two sons from Osada's second marriage, who graduated from Kennedy-Kendrick High School last spring
and will begin at Temple University in January. Younger son Danny is
still a student at Kennedy-Kendrick, a parochial school in Norristown,
Pennsylvania. Kimberly, Osada's daughter from his first marriage, lived
with him for her last two years of high school before going off to American University as a Merit Scholar. Recently married, she plans to finish
her last year of college in New Orleans, where her husband is a graduate
student.

Flying from the dock beside the river is yet another American flag.
How does he reconcile his overt attachment to America with his bitter-
ness over the incident with the Small Business Administration? "I don't
know how to reconcile it," he says. "I guess I make a distinction between
my country and the government. This is the only place I'd want to live.
We were lucky to be born here. I don't even want to travel outside the
United States. I like it here."

Larry J. Payne

The older I get, the more aches and pains I discover, but I never found
the Payne I was looking for—though one of the fifteen Larry J. Paynes
on the Myers list called to say he'd gone through boot camp at the Marine Corps Recruit Depot in San Diego, California, in the summer of
1964. I teased him about going through "Disneyland" (which is what
Parris Island Marines used to call MCRD San Diego and maybe still do),
but had to admit that it might have been more difficult to endure the pressures of boot camp with the outside world only a chain-link fence away
and often in plain sight than it was with a dangerous swamp and a long
swim through treacherous waters between Parris Island and the illusion
of freedom. At Parris Island, most of us understood that there was no escape.

In any case, according to the records I received from NPRC in July
1995, Platoon 1005's Larry J. Payne graduated from high school in 1966
and was sworn into the Marine Corps at Baltimore, Maryland. After boot
camp and basic infantry training, he was assigned to Company B, Headquarters Battalion, Headquarters Marine Corps, in Arlington, Virginia,

while undergoing thirty-two weeks of Vietnamese language training at the Defense Language Institute in Washington, D.C.

Upon completion of training, he was assigned to Headquarters Company, Headquarters Battalion, 5th Marine Division, Camp Pendleton, California, as an intelligence linguistics interpreter (0251) from June 1967 until April 1968. Progressing through the lower enlisted ranks, he received promotion to sergeant in April, less than two years after beginning active duty, while undergoing training with the 3rd Replacement Company, Staging Battalion, at Camp Pendleton in preparation for his departure for Vietnam.

Payne served in Vietnam with Headquarters Battalion, 1st Marine Division, from April 1968 until May 1969, first with Headquarters Company; then with the 3rd Interrogation and Translation Team, Sub-unit #1, Service Company; and finally again with Headquarters Company. For his service in Vietnam, Payne was awarded the Navy Achievement Medal with Combat V. The citation reads, in part:

> [Sergeant Payne] displayed outstanding professionalism and initiative despite extremely adverse conditions and the difficulties of a combat environment. Distinguishing himself by his consistently high level of efficiency, he materially enhanced the operational effectiveness of his unit. Participating in numerous major combat operations, including Operations Houston, Scotland I, and Napoleon/Saline II, he skillfully conducted numerous interrogations which yielded a large amount of intelligence for the command and resulted in the seizure of several enemy supply caches. As a result of his diligence and seemingly unlimited resourcefulness, he gained the respect and admiration of all who observed him and contributed significantly to the accomplishment of his unit's mission.

From June 1969 until his release from active duty in June 1970, Payne served at Camp Pendleton, California, first with Headquarters Company, Headquarters Battalion, 5th Marine Division, then with various units of the 5th Marine Expeditionary Brigade.

In addition to his Navy Achievement Medal, Payne received the Combat Action Ribbon, and the Good Conduct, National Defense Service, Vietnam Service, and Vietnam Campaign Medals. Though he failed to qualify on the rifle range at Parris Island, he later qualified as both a Rifle Marksman and a Pistol Sharpshooter.

Military records indicate that a Lynne Payne received a dependent's identification card, suggesting that Payne got married while still on active duty. In May 1971, while he was an inactive reservist, he was promoted to staff sergeant.

Gaetan L. Pelletier

No one with this name showed up on the Myers list, and a letter forwarded to the last address the VA had for him got no reply, but in March 1996 I received records from NPRC that said Pelletier had enlisted from Madawaska, Maine. I had my own access to computerized telephone records by then, and though no Gaetan Pelletiers turned up anywhere, sixty-nine other Pelletiers were listed in northern Maine. Figuring that one of them must be related to Gaetan, I wrote to all of them. On March 18, 1996, Pelletier called me. His sister had gotten one of my letters and had forwarded it to him.

From our conversation and the NPRC records, I learned that Pelletier was born in Canada on August 25, 1946. A Canadian citizen and a high school graduate bilingual in French and English, he was living in Madawaska, Maine, at the time of his enlistment. He joined the Marines on the Buddy Plan with Gerard Sirois.

After boot camp and basic infantry training, he was sent to the Schools Battalion at Camp Pendleton, California, where he received training as a bulk fuel man (1391). He was then assigned to various units of the 1st and 5th Force Service Regiments at Pendleton from November 1966 until April 1967, when he received a medical discharge because of severe stomach ulcers. During his ten months of service, he received promotion to private first class and the National Defense Service Medal.

After his discharge, Pelletier returned to northern Maine, but the only employment he could find was shift work at a paper mill, which was hard on his ulcers, so he went to Connecticut with some friends. He tried to get a job at the Pratt & Whitney aircraft engine company, but says they wouldn't hire him because he was not a U.S. citizen.

He did find work, however, making pistols for the Colt Company, but was not permitted to make the M-16 rifle, again because he was not an American. After three years with Colt, he returned to Maine briefly, then went back to Connecticut, but a friend told him there was work to be had in Florida, so he went and has been in south Florida ever since. He worked on transmissions for Lincoln Mercury for eleven years, but now works for Ford.

Pelletier has been married since 1971, and has two grown sons. His wife and children are all U.S. citizens by birth, he says, but Pelletier is still Canadian. "The only restrictions," he says of not being a U.S. citizen, "are that I can't vote and I can't work for Pratt & Whitney. Oh, and I can't make M-16 rifles either."

Roger D. Pentecost

None of the three Roger Pentecosts on the Myers list ever answered my initial search letter, but on January 5, 1995, I decided to call all three of them because I was learning by then that at least some of the men who received my letters just never got around to responding to them. On the second call, I reached Pentecost's father. Whether he'd gotten one of my letters sixteen months earlier, and if so whether he'd forwarded it to his son, he didn't say. But when I explained who I was, he did give me his son's telephone number.

When I reached Pentecost later that day, he said he didn't remember me but considered us brothers nevertheless because we had gone through Parris Island together. From our conversation, and records received from NPRC in February 1996, I learned that Pentecost was born on August 23, 1946. A high school graduate, he enlisted in the Marines from Nashville, Tennessee. After boot camp and basic infantry training, he received on-the-job training as a general warehouseman (3051) with Headquarters & Support Company, Base Materials Battalion, Camp Lejeune, North Carolina, from September to November 1966.

Pentecost next received orders to Vietnam, but first spent two months with the 4th Replacement Company, Staging Battalion, Camp Pendleton, California, rather than the usual four weeks, because the first month he was assigned to mess duty. Though his orders were originally for the 3rd Marine Division, he says, when he arrived in Vietnam in February 1967 he was assigned to Headquarters & Maintenance Squadron 17, Marine Wing Support Group 17, 1st Marine Air Wing.

"I lucked out," he says of his reassignment from ground forces to the air wing. Near the end of his initial thirteen-month overseas tour of duty, Pentecost voluntarily extended for an additional six months and was assigned to temporary duty with Headquarters & Headquarters Squadron, Marine Corps Air Station, Iwakuni, Japan, from January until May 1968. He then went back briefly to his original unit, H&MS-17, MWSG-17, before returning to the United States. He was separated from active duty in June 1968 with the rank of lance corporal. His decorations and awards include the National Defense Service, Vietnam Service, and Vietnam Campaign Medals and a Certificate of Commendation.

After his release, Pentecost worked for a number of years in transportation as an operations manager, but since 1978 he has been employed by the Tennessee Valley Authority as a security specialist. He also served in the Army Reserves from 1974 to 1980, then transferred to the National Guard, where he currently holds the rank of staff sergeant. His first marriage of nineteen years ended in divorce in 1990, but he has since remarried. He has three grown children from his first marriage and a youngster from his second. He lives in Alabama.

Audie G. Peppers

Ben Myers found no one with this name during his August 1993 phone search. In early 1994, the VA notified me that Peppers had filed a claim for veterans' benefits, but he had done so before the VA began using social security numbers as claim numbers. The VA did forward a letter to the last address they had for him, but a year later I was informed that it had come back undeliverable.

Then in October 1995 I received records from NPRC indicating that Peppers had been living in Lake City, Florida, at the time he enlisted, so I checked my own computerized phone directory and found an Audie G. Peppers in Lake City. I called the number on November 6, 1995, and found another Platoon 1005er.

From our conversation and the NPRC records, I learned that Peppers was born on September 29, 1946, and grew up in Decatur, Alabama. He graduated from high school and completed a year and a half of college before joining the Marines. After boot camp and basic infantry training, he received additional training at Camp Pendleton, California, as an artillery fire direction controller (0844).

In December 1966, Peppers was assigned to Battery F, 2nd Battalion, 13th Marines, also at Pendleton. In March 1967 he was transferred to Battery D of the same battalion, and in April the battery was sent to Hawaii as part of the 1st Marine Brigade.

In January 1968 the battery received orders to Vietnam, but by then Peppers had less than six months to serve in the Marines—too little time to be sent to Vietnam—so he remained in Hawaii, first with the brigade's Headquarters & Support Company, then with Service Company of the Headquarters & Support Battalion until his release from active duty in June 1968. A lance corporal, Peppers was awarded the National Defense Service Medal.

Peppers began working for the Veterans Administration, now the Department of Veterans Affairs, a few years after his release, and has been with the VA ever since. He currently works in the maintenance and air conditioning section of a VA hospital in northern Florida. Married since 1968, he has a grown daughter and a grown son.

Peppers says that, after its arrival in Vietnam, his old artillery battery got overrun during a battle, and a lot of the men were killed or wounded. "You wonder if you could have done anything if you'd been there," he says. "But working in a VA hospital, I see what really happens." In spite of what happened to Battery D—or maybe because of it—he doesn't regret not going to Vietnam. "I'm still here in all my pieces," he says.

Clarence B. Potts, Jr.

The land on which Clarence Potts's farm perches, like most of West Virginia, looks as if God had crumpled it up in His fist like a sheet of paper, then left it where it lay. It is all irregular tucks and folds, all up and down, steep little hills separated by narrow valleys called hollows carved between the hills by small rivulets that periodically transform themselves into raging torrents.

Though the Potts farm is only five miles outside of Buckhannon, it takes a good fifteen to twenty minutes to drive there because Tallmansville Road lurches from one sharp turn to the next, at times almost doubling back on itself as it switchbacks its way up one side of a ridgeline and back down the other.

As you drive along, you notice at the mouth of each little rural lane a small structure that looks like a cinderblock telephone booth. These are called bus sheds, and families build them for their children to stand out of the weather while waiting for the school bus each morning.

The land all around you is breathtakingly beautiful, but as those ubiquitous bus sheds mutely suggest, it can also be harsh and cold and unforgiving. Even if you have spent your whole life on it, and know it as you know the rhythm of your own heartbeat, it can turn on you without a moment's warning. Potts knows about this. From the big picture window of his house, he can see up the hill to his mother's house, the house in which he himself grew up, so he knows the land as well as he knows

Corporal Clarence B. Potts, Jr., 1st Shore Party Battalion, Vietnam, 1967.

the rhythm of his own heartbeat. And it has turned on him not once but twice; each time, it has cost him dearly.

The first accident came in 1989 when he and his son Andy were cutting timber. A tree they felled tore a limb from another tree on its way down, and before Potts could react, the limb had struck him in the head. He didn't regain consciousness for four days, and after four operations— two on his brain, one on his left eye, and one on his jaw—he still has double vision in his left eye, though the terrible headaches that used to plague him are pretty much gone.

After a year and a half, he had recovered enough to go back to work, but in 1991 he had a second accident. This time he was mowing hay on a steep hillside when the tractor rolled over on him. This time he did not lose consciousness, but he ended up pinned beneath the tractor with engine oil and gasoline dripping down on him.

Though he was fortunate in that there was no fire, and doubly fortunate in that a passing motorist who stopped to investigate the upturned

The Potts family, 1996. Left to right: *son Andy, daughter Darlene, wife Eva, and Clarence.*

tractor heard his cries for help, he came away with five broken ribs, three broken vertebrae, and a ruptured spleen. "That was nobody else's fault but mine," he says about rolling the tractor. The accident has changed his life permanently, and not for the better.

In both cases, Potts was taken from the scene of the accident to the hospital by helicopter—medevacked, we would have said in Vietnam—an irony not lost on Potts, whose job in Vietnam as a shore party man (1381) had been to call in medevac choppers for wounded fellow Marines.

Though Potts was born in Swickley, Pennsylvania, he is West Virginian through and through. His maternal grandparents used to live in a house now owned by a neighbor—you can't see it from the picture window, but you can from the front porch—and the house Potts lives in now used to belong to his paternal grandparents. His father bought their eighty-three-acre farm in 1944, renting it out for the first five years while working a factory job in Swickley, but he returned to West Virginia in 1949, when Potts was three, and worked the farm until his death in 1988.

Potts had first written to me on February 10, 1995, in response to the second of two letters the VA forwarded to him. I came to see him on September 20, 1996, during a swing through West Virginia that included visits with Tom Erickson and Tim Jenkins. Soon after I arrived, his wife and son said their good-byes and headed off to upstate Pennsylvania to attend a relative's wedding, but Potts graciously gave up a weekend of celebrations to visit with me.

An only child, Potts grew up working the farm with his father. They grew wheat, corn, and potatoes; raised milk cows and beef cows, hogs, and chickens; and tended orchards that yielded apples, peaches, pears, plums, and persimmons. Potts's father never did own a tractor, working the land with a team of horses instead. The farmhouse itself consisted of three rooms and a pantry. There was electricity, but no telephone or plumbing.

"We took sponge baths," says Potts, remembering when water had to be pumped by hand from an external well and carried into the house. Later an inside pump was installed, but the house still had no bathroom until about the time Potts joined the Marines. "When I was a kid," Potts jokes, "people used to crap outside and eat inside. Now it's all different; you crap inside and go out to eat."

When he wasn't working the farm, Potts and his friends would go to the movies or ride homemade motor scooters, swim in the summer, and go sledding in the winter, and there always seemed to be a community fair or a county fair to look forward to. As for school, Potts says, "I wasn't much of a student," though he did manage to graduate from Buckhannon-Upshur High School in June 1966.

By that time, he'd already joined the Marine Corps on a 120-day delayed enlistment program. "It was either get drafted or join the Marines," he explains. "It was a job, wasn't it? And it was national security, too, serving your country. What kind of choices did we have back then? I wasn't no draft dodger like the President of the United States."

Of his first night at Parris Island, Potts recalls thinking, "'What the hell did I do? What am I doing here?' It was a shock to me." Nevertheless, he managed to thrive in boot camp. Standing six feet five inches tall, he arrived weighing 150 pounds; eight weeks later, he left weighing 175—and none of the extra weight was fat. "I never did feel like I wasn't going to make it," Potts says of boot camp.

"Now Vietnam," he adds. "That was a different story. That was for your life." He got his first hint that the stakes had risen when the chartered airliner carrying him to Vietnam suddenly began a precipitous descent to the runway at Da Nang. "It was so steep," he says of the approach, "you could have rolled a cardboard box down the aisle of the plane."

After deplaning, the arrivals loaded into "cattle cars" (tractor trailer trucks used for transporting troops) for the ride to the transit facility, but not before being warned to check under the seats for grenades that might have been placed there by Viet Cong infiltrators. Potts could see Vietnamese civilians doing laundry on the base and living right beside the airfield, something he found deeply disturbing, given the warning he'd just received about grenades. "There shouldn't have been no Vietnamese anywhere near that airfield," he says. "They should have killed them all."

Arriving in December 1966, Potts was assigned to 1st Shore Party Battalion along with fellow Platoon 1005ers Francis Langley, Tim Jenkins, and Wayne Kelly. The following month, he got an even more forceful reminder of how high the stakes were when Langley and five other 1st Shore Party men died along with four crewmen in a helicopter crash. Potts attended the memorial service the battalion chaplain held for his dead comrades.

Over the course of his tour, Potts worked out of Chu Lai, then Da Nang and Phu Bai. The shore party's main job was to get supplies into the field and casualties out. Helicopter support teams usually consisted of three men equipped with a PRC-25 radio. Potts spent much of his time on HSTs, but during the course of his tour he was also assigned to temporary additional duty on three occasions, spending a month as a military policeman with the 1st MP Company, and attending movie projector school in Japan and armorers' school in Okinawa. He also spent four months as a general warehouseman in Da Nang, storing rifles and gear for men going on R&R.

When he was in the field, Potts says, "I always saved one bullet, just in case." One time, the column he was in came under sniper fire. The tanks in the column turned their guns in the direction from which the fire had come and returned fire, so Potts opened up with his automatic M-14. "I didn't see anybody or nothing," he says, "and that's the only time I ever fired at anybody."

Another time, during a Viet Cong night mortar attack, a huge chunk of shrapnel landed where Potts had been lying only seconds before. "It didn't make any difference if you were good or bad or black or white or an asshole or what," he says. "If you got hit, you got hit. That's all. I had guys shot out from behind me and in front of me, but I was never hit."

Not that he didn't expect to be hit. In fact, though in high school he'd begun dating Eva Margaret Kimble, who lived just over the hill from the Potts farm, he broke off the relationship when he joined the Marines for fear that he wouldn't be coming back from Vietnam. By the time his thirteen-month tour of duty was almost over, however, he was feeling confident enough to extend it by another six months, and while he was home on the thirty-day free leave given to anyone willing to extend, the relationship was rekindled.

Meanwhile, because of a bureaucratic screwup, it took the Marine Corps six months to tell him he'd made lance corporal. He only found out when he tried to return what he thought was an overpayment one payday, thinking that if he didn't report the overpayment then, he'd only have to pay it back down the road. Four days later, he was promoted to corporal. "I went from private first class to corporal in less than a week," he says, still marveling at his meteoric rise nearly three decades later. He made sergeant midway through his six-month extension.

Potts finally left Vietnam for good in August 1968. Returning to the States, he never encountered any of the difficulties many veterans recount so bitterly. "Them hippies didn't bother me," he says. "Long hair, earrings, whatever. You treat me right, I'll treat you right." Indeed, he remembers an elderly couple in the Chicago airport who gave a waitress twenty dollars to buy drinks for Potts and his traveling companions, all of whom were in uniform.

Assigned to 2nd Shore Party Battalion at Camp Lejeune, North Carolina, Potts almost immediately went on a four-month Caribbean cruise aboard the USS *Plymouth Rock*. When the cruise ended in February 1969, he and Eva were married. "We didn't have this, and we didn't have that," he says of their life together in North Carolina, "but we got by, you know." He spent his last eleven months at Lejeune as 2nd SP Battalion armorer, receiving a four-month early out on his four-year enlistment.

Back home in West Virginia, Potts took a job running a cutoff saw in a lumber mill making planks for railroad boxcar floors, but found his workmates so lazy that they made his own job both dangerous and difficult, so he quit after two months and found a better-paying job tending wells for a land and mineral company. After a year and a half at that job, however, in December 1971 he was hired by Corhart Refactories, a company owned by Corning Glass Works that makes bricks for the linings of steel mill furnaces.

Over the next twenty years, he would progress from the glue line to brick loading, then to the mold shop, and on to finishing, finally earning a position in the maintenance department along with a journeyman's card. He would also get laid off five times for periods ranging from three and a half months to twenty-one months, but each time he would eventually be called back.

At the same time, he continued to help his father with the farm, though the operation became ever simpler with the passing years. They kept less and less livestock, didn't replace aging fruit trees, and planted fewer crops. The barn and other outbuildings were torn down. To make the hay easier to mow, fences were removed and rocks pulled out. By the time Potts's father died, the farm's main crop was (and still is) hay, which was used for sale or barter.

From 1970 on, Potts also served as a volunteer firefighter with the Washington District Fire Department in Tallmansville, just down the road from the farm. And all of his adult life, Potts has been an avid hunter. On one wall of the living room is a poster-sized color photograph of a bear caught up in a tree, the tree's branches covered with snow. On the facing wall is a second poster-sized color photo, this one of Potts posing with the carcass of that same bear. On yet another wall are four mounted sets of deer antlers, one with several hats hanging from it.

Then came the accidents, especially the second one, and everything changed. Potts could not return to work at Corhart and has had to go on permanent disability. His ability to work around the farm, even just to mow the hay once a year, has been severely curtailed. After the second accident, the fire department made him a life member, but he can't do firefighting anymore. He can't do much hunting either. The long rides in the pickup truck to bear country over in Randolph County are too hard on his back, and even hunting around the farm he's afraid he'll trip over a snow-covered stump and roll down a hill. "I can't take that anymore," he says.

"Not a lot," he replies, when asked what he does these days. "Watch television. Tend the garden. Raise rabbits. [He has about fifty rabbits at the moment, which he keeps in pens out behind the house and sells to a commercial wholesaler.] I'd like to be to where I can just tear up the world again, but I can't. That's just the way it is. It ain't a happy thing to be on disability. I'd rather be working. People see you do any work at all, they think you're faking."

One thing that has given Potts a great deal of joy, however, is the arrival in September 1995 of Levi Winston White, his first grandchild, the son of Potts's daughter, Darlene, and her husband, Bruce. (Darlene was born in 1970, Potts's son, Andy, in 1972). A framed portrait of Levi graces the living room, where no guest can possibly miss seeing it.

There is also a framed portrait of Potts in a dress blue uniform hanging on the living room wall. "Eva did that," he says. While he's not by any means ashamed or bitter about his time in the Marines, he's also not shy about saying that if he had it to do over again, he'd join the Air Force. He was never too fond of the "do stuff better" attitude he found in the Corps, the deeply ingrained notion that the Marines always have to be and always are better than everybody else, nor was he happy about having to make do with inferior gear and less of it while trying to make a virtue of the deficiencies. He still remembers dropping in on the Seabees (the U.S. Navy Construction Battalion) at Phu Bai, where the mess hall regularly served ice cream, steaks, and cold drinks.

As for the war itself, he thinks the United States could have won it if we had been willing to be more ruthless. "Start in the south and sweep north," he says. "Kill everything. Could you pick out a Democrat from a Republican around here, just by looking at them? How could you tell VC over there? Just kill everything. Whenever the firing stops, then we stop. Don't fool around.

"Should we have been there?" he asks, then answers his own question. "No, I don't think so, but we did our duty. We served our country. You were there fighting a useless war, but if you don't try to help these little countries, then the Communists were gonna take over. Look who's running Vietnam now: the Communists." Still, he adds, if he knew then what he knows now, he wouldn't have been willing to go to Vietnam. "We lost that war, didn't we?" he says. Then he raises his arms from his sides, palms up, and shrugs his shoulders.

Howard A. Purcell, Jr.

None of the four Howard A. Purcells on the Myers list responded to my initial search letter. Purcell did file a claim for veterans' benefits, but he did not respond to the letter forwarded to him by the VA. According to records received from NPRC in February 1996, he was born in Valley Township, Pennsylvania, on March 3, 1948, and was living in Coatesville, Pennsylvania, at the time of his enlistment. A high school graduate, he joined the Marines on the Buddy Plan with Lonnie Milligan. After boot camp and basic infantry training, Purcell received four weeks of training as an administrative clerk at the Personnel Administration School back at Parris Island, receiving promotion to private first class upon completion of his course of study.

Purcell's first duty assignment was with the Marine Barracks, U.S. Naval Base, Long Beach, California, but before he arrived in late November 1966, he spent three weeks as a patient at the U.S. Army Hospital, Valley Forge, Pennsylvania. He then spent the next nine months at Long Beach, including one month on mess duty, before receiving orders to Vietnam. He reported to Staging Battalion at Camp Pendleton in September 1967, but was then absent without leave for nearly a month and subsequently confined briefly before being sent overseas.

Purcell served in Vietnam with 2nd Battalion, 12th Marines, an artillery regiment, from November 1967 until June 1968, first with Headquarters Battery, then with Battery F, and finally again with Headquarters Battery. Promoted to lance corporal in May 1968, Purcell was released from active duty upon his return from Vietnam a month later. His decorations include the National Defense Service, Vietnam Service, and Vietnam Campaign medals.

Richard Quashne, Jr.

Because he is a retired state trooper, Rick Quashne can legally carry a concealed weapon. The application for a permit has been lying on his desk since he retired from the Delaware State Police in August 1995, but he hasn't filled it out yet. "I suppose I'll submit the paperwork eventually," he says, "but I don't want to carry a gun anymore. I've been taking a gun to work ever since I got out of high school. Think about that."

Not yet fifty, Quashne is already on his third career. His first consisted of four years in the Marines. His second spanned twenty-five years with the Delaware State Police, the first five as a civilian, the last twenty as a uniformed officer. Then just weeks after he hung up his trooper's uniform, he became the security and surveillance manager for Dover Downs Slots, Delaware's new gaming casino.

You might think he'd want a weapon in this new line of work, but if somebody wants to rob the casino, he says, they're likely to show up with Mac and Uzi assault rifles, so what's he supposed to do with a .38

Sergeant Richard Quashne, Jr., cleaning the canopy of an A-6 Intruder, Marine All Weather Attack Squadron 553, Chu Lai, Vietnam, 1969.

revolver? Besides, he explains, it would be foolish and dangerous to shoot it out in a crowded casino when there are safer and smarter ways to prevent robberies.

When he retired from the state police as a master corporal, Quashne intended only to find something to do for five years until son Rich (Richard Quashne III, a senior at Salesianum High School) graduates from college and wife Brenda (the former Brenda Maples of Asheville, North Carolina) retires from teaching kindergarten in New Castle County's Colonial School District. He and Brenda own property in Southport, North Carolina, a small fishing town on the Intercoastal Waterway, and they've always planned to retire there.

But the more one learns about Quashne, the harder it is to imagine him sitting in a rocker on the front porch watching the world go by. In Vietnam, while working night shift on the Chu Lai flight line, he volunteered to attend Vietnamese language school during the day because, he figured, "I might as well go to school as drink beer." In Japan the following year, he studied Japanese through a University of Maryland extension program. After the Marines, he spent five years earning a bachelor of science degree in criminal justice from Brandywine College and the University of Delaware while working full time rotating shifts in a

Delaware State Police regional communications center. As a uniformed trooper, he received a Superintendent's Citation for his off-duty charity work.

From all appearances, taking it easy is not a concept Quashne readily embraces. Moreover, while it's not impossible, it also isn't easy to imagine Quashne living anywhere other than his native state. Except for his stint in the Corps, he has spent his entire life in Delaware.

So have all his relatives, apparently. Quashne had not appeared on the Myers list, but seven other Quashnes did—all of them living in Delaware. I wrote to them all and got a letter back from Quashne's cousin, who gave me his telephone number. When I reached Quashne on September 10, 1993, he told me he'd already heard from his father and two other relatives that I was looking for him. We got together in his Middletown home on February 10, 1996.

Sergeant Quashne helping an A-6 Intruder pilot from VMA (AW)-553 *get ready to take off, Chu Lai, Vietnam, 1969.*

The Quashne family, 1995. Left to right: son Rich, Rick, family pet Tory, and wife Brenda.

The son of a painter in a General Motors assembly plant, Quashne was born in Wilmington, the oldest of two sons and a daughter (his mother died when he was just two, but his father remarried a few years later). He grew up playing ice hockey, which has remained a lifelong passion, and he also played baseball for Henry C. Conrad High School.

After graduating in 1966, he says, "I didn't want to go to college right away, and I knew I would be drafted. I was in a kind of rebellious stage. My dad was in the Navy in World War II, but I didn't want to join the Navy because I couldn't swim that well. I figured if I'm gonna die, I'm gonna die with the best, and the Marines are the best. Besides, I always do things the hard way; that's why I joined the Marines—and the state police, too."

Boot camp was "eight weeks of hell," he says, but the physical aspects weren't as hard as he'd expected. His high school baseball coach, who had been an Army drill instructor, had made the baseball team do a lot of running. Consequently, he says, "When I got to Parris Island, I was in great shape."

What he remembers most is the heat. "It was so hot all the time," he says. "All you wanted to do was drink." He also remembers watching recruits in Motivation Platoon, a special disciplinary unit, aimlessly moving piles of sand from one side of a field to the other, and thinking to himself, "Whatever I do I'll die doing it, but I'm not getting sent to this.

"I took the DIS seriously," he continues, "but I wasn't afraid of them. 'If I do what they tell me,' I figured, 'they'll leave me alone.' I gave them no reason to mess with me. I kept my act together and my mouth shut. I don't want to sound crazy, but I enjoyed boot camp. It's probably just the way I am. I'm a very structured person."

After boot camp and basic infantry training, Quashne was sent to Memphis, Tennessee, and later to Whidbey Island, Washington, and Yuma, Arizona, where he underwent extensive training to become a jet aircraft mechanic (6031). Finally, nearly a year after he'd enlisted, he was assigned to Marine Attack Squadron 224 based at Marine Corps Air Station, Cherry Point, North Carolina.

Quashne didn't like Cherry Point, which he describes as being "in the middle of nowhere. You go off base and people hate you. All they want is your money." Largely for something to do, he began taking courses through an extension program run by East Carolina University, and became friends with several ECU students, who invited him to visit the main campus. He began to spend a lot of time at ECU, which offered a much friendlier atmosphere than what he found around Cherry Point. "It was easy to meet girls," he explains succinctly.

Indeed, he met Brenda at ECU on a blind date arranged by another Marine. The other Marine wanted to borrow Quashne's car to take his girlfriend to the university's Homecoming Weekend, but Quashne wouldn't hand it over, and reluctantly agreed to double-date only if the other Marine's girlfriend could get him a date with "the girl who doesn't like Marines," as Brenda had been described to him. To Quashne's surprised dismay, Brenda agreed, though as she explains long after the fact, "I only did it to help out a friend."

The reluctant couple watched ECU's football team get beaten that day by Louisiana Tech, quarterbacked by future Pittsburgh Steeler Terry Bradshaw. To top it off, by chance they ended up sitting only a few rows in front of another ECU student Quashne had been dating, which quickly put an end to *that* relationship.

It came out right in the end, of course, and the Quashnes will celebrate their twenty-fifth wedding anniversary in June. "We've never been separated," Quashne says, "We've never had a major fight." Nevertheless, it wasn't exactly love at first sight. Quashne still wanted out of Cherry Point, and just two months later, in the summer of 1968, he finally managed to finagle orders to Vietnam. "I didn't know if I was even going to see her when I got back, but she was someone to write to."

Of his arrival in Vietnam, he says, "It was just like Parris Island all over again. Just like getting off the bus that first night." The airfield at Da Nang had just been hit by rockets moments before Quashne's airplane landed. There were no lights on anywhere, so everyone had to scramble hurriedly off the plane in complete darkness and near-pandemonium. It took Quashne twenty-four hours just to figure out where to go.

He ended up at Chu Lai, assigned to VMA (AW)-553—the AW stands for "all-weather"—a squadron of A-6 Intruders. Starting out as a mechanic, he rapidly advanced to plane captain, and then to assistant noncommissioned officer in charge of the flight line, responsible for seeing that the squadron's planes were fueled, loaded with the proper ordnance, and ready to go.

Quashne, by now a sergeant, usually worked night shift on the flight line, and after completing Vietnamese language school, he would often spend his days on S-5 civil affairs patrols, escorting doctors, nurses, and Kit Carson scouts to nearby hamlets, part of the American attempt to "win the hearts and minds" of the Vietnamese. Quashne himself had no sense of winning or losing anything, however. "It's just survival," he explains. "You just try to make it back. I was just doing my year. I knew nothing I did was going to make any difference."

It was not an easy time to be in Vietnam. In the wake of the assassination of Martin Luther King, Jr., relations between black and white Marines were sometimes "really ugly," Quashne says. Marijuana was readily available in the nearby hamlets, and many Marines, black and white, availed themselves of it. Quashne spent what should have been his rest and recreation leave escorting a squadron member, busted for illegal drugs, to the Da Nang brig.

In the spring of 1969, Quashne's squadron was withdrawn from Vietnam and sent to MCAS Iwakuni, Japan, where he served out the remainder of his overseas tour. Returning to the U.S. was hard, he says, because the world had gone on without him; many people didn't even know where he'd been. "But I never heard any of that 'baby killer' stuff," he adds. "I never got any of that."

While he was home on leave, he went to see Brenda, and the relationship quickly became serious. Assigned to Headquarters & Maintenance Squadron 32, MCAS Beaufort, South Carolina, he drove up to ECU every chance he got, and on the day he got out of the Corps in June 1970, he presented her with a diamond engagement ring he'd bought at the Beaufort post exchange.

While Brenda finished her last year of college, Quashne started his first year. He also began working in the state police communications center, a forerunner of what has become the 911 police emergency system. In 1971, Brenda graduated from ECU and found a kindergarten teaching position in Delaware, and the two of them tied the knot and bought a house. It wasn't easy getting through college while working full time, Quashne says, especially working rotating shifts. He often worked weekends for others so that they would work for him while he went to class during the week. Sometimes he took vacation to get to class. Sometimes he missed class altogether. "It was hard," he says. "I didn't come out with straight A's, but I made it."

When he finished his degree in 1975, he intended to take the tests for the Federal Bureau of Investigation and the Secret Service. A friend wanted to take the test for the Delaware State Police, so Quashne went along because he figured it would be good practice. At each successive level of testing—written, oral, polygraph, mental—he was told to return again for another test. When he finally completed the whole sequence, he was asked why he wanted to be a Delaware trooper.

"You never gave me a chance not to be here," Quashne replied. "You just kept telling me to come back."

Quashne says the state police training academy was as tough and demanding as boot camp. It lasted for six months, recruits could only go home on weekends, and restrictions—such as no food except what was provided at meals—were much like those on Parris Island. Quashne's class, incidentally, was the first in Delaware State Police history to include women.

Quashne spent his first five years in uniform as a patrol officer before becoming a detective. He has been involved in just about every kind of case you can think of: high speed auto chases, missing persons, burglaries, kidnappings, prostitution, fraud. He helped solve the murder of the niece of Milwaukee Braves pitching great Warren Spahn. "Twenty years of this," he says, "you end up with a lot of cases."

Of all his cases, however, the one he is most proud of is an obscene telephone harassment case he solved about eight years ago. Over a period of six months, he received periodic complaints from women and girls about a male caller who would intimidate them into disrobing and fondling themselves. The caller used many different ploys, but a typical one might work like this:

The caller reaches a fourteen-year-old girl at home alone. He asks for her father, explaining that the father is in a lot of trouble because he owes the caller ten thousand dollars. After a series of questions designed to elicit one "yes" answer after another—"It's harder to say 'no' once you've said 'yes' a whole lot of times," says Quashne—the caller says he'll forgive the debt if the girl will do what he asks.

"I really wanted to get this guy," Quashne says. "He was verbally raping these girls." Finally he realized that many of the women and girls were getting calls the day after they had appeared in the local newspaper, so he set up a "sting." He got a young woman from the communications center to pose as a tennis player, and had the photograph run in the newspaper with a fake name that would send the caller to a telephone number where Quashne had a female trooper waiting. As Quashne had surmised, the man called the next day, the call was traced, and the man was apprehended. He served seven years in prison, Quashne says with satisfaction, and as a direct result of this case, the law was changed from a misdemeanor to a felony.

Quashne has always found time for charity work as well, and he has been able to put his lifelong love of ice hockey to good use in several different ways. Organizing hockey games variously involving the Washington Capitals, the Philadelphia Flyers, the Flyers farm system, and the Flyers "alumni," he has helped raise thousands of dollars for the Special Olympics and the Sunshine Foundation. In addition, the "Silver Bullet Tournament" (officially known as the East Coast State Police Hockey Tournament)—which grew out of a Delaware State Police hockey team started by Quashne and a few other troopers and annually involves police ice hockey teams from all over the northeastern U.S. and eastern Canada—raises money for various local charities.

Quashne also served as editor of *The Delaware Trooper,* the official magazine of the Delaware State Troopers Association, from 1992 until his retirement. But, says Quashne, "you gotta know when it's time to go," and by the summer of 1995, he felt it was time to go.

"I've got a whole new life now," he says of his job at Dover Downs Slots, a job he enjoys and from which he may not be too eager to retire.

Hired three months before the new casino opened, Quashne was responsible for developing and implementing security and surveillance systems and procedures. Now that the casino is operating, he manages a staff of four supervisors, seven surveillance officers, and twenty-five full-time and part-time security guards.

The casino itself has 571 slot machines, a restaurant and bar, and a stage with live entertainment nightly. Built on the grounds of Dover Downs race track, it offers horse racing in season, as well as simulcast horse racing, televised NASCAR racing, pay-per-view events like boxing, and special events such as last January's Super Bowl party. The casino is owned by Dover Downs and run by Caesar's World Gaming, while the slot machines are owned by the Delaware Lottery Commission.

His new job can be very demanding, he says, often requiring fourteen-hour days. He works every day, adds Brenda, calling in to check on things even on days he's supposed to be off. Because of the demands on his time, he has largely had to give up or curtail a number of his favorite recreational pursuits, including ice hockey, hunting, and fishing.

One thing he hasn't given up, however, is golf, a love for which he and his son share. "Last summer I could still beat Rich," says Quashne, "but he's getting to the point where he can beat me now. This summer might be a little tough."

Reflecting on his life, Quashne says, "If I had it to do again, I'd do it the same way." And what does he think now of the war in Vietnam? "It was just a phase in my life," he says. "I had no control over it, but I'm not going to say I got screwed or anything like that. I chose to go in. I chose the Marine Corps. I chose to go to Vietnam. And I came back in one piece. I have no regrets. Whether the war was right or not, I can't say."

John R. Ramsell

"There's gonna be times when you'll wish you were back in your mother's womb," Jack Ramsell remembers Senior Drill Instructor Oliver telling the men of Platoon 1005. Most of the platoon, Staff Sergeant Oliver knew, would find themselves in Vietnam within months.

Oliver's prediction, says Ramsell, turned out to be chillingly accurate. One long and terrifying night at Cua Viet less than a year later, Ramsell found himself and his unit under intense artillery fire from North Vietnamese guns on the far side of the Demilitarized Zone, and all he could do was hunker down in a sandbagged bunker, wishing he was anywhere but here, and praying.

Ramsell had always taken religion seriously. He'd taken his Bible to Parris Island with him, one of the few items that was not confiscated on the night of his arrival. He believed in God and Judgement Day. But prayer had always been, he says, "an academic exercise, a ritual." This night was different. This night he prayed, as the Bible says, "with real intent."

Private John R. Ramsell, August 1966. (PB)

Moreover, as the incoming rounds kept falling, and the roar of the explosions and the shrieking shrapnel filled the air around him, he began for the first time to think about what it must be like to be caught in the midst of a B-52 bombing raid, to be drowned in napalm, or shelled by 175mm "Long Tom" cannons.

And he found himself praying not just for himself, not just for his comrades, but for the Viet Cong and North Vietnamese as well, feeling for the first time empathy for his enemies. And for the first time in his life, he believes, his prayers were answered. No one in his unit was killed or even wounded that night, and for no reason Ramsell can explain except divine intervention, there was no U.S. retaliation for the NVA bombardment. Not "Long Toms," nor naval gunfire, nor F-4 Phantoms.

"People used to say I was lucky in Vietnam," Ramsell says, but he doesn't think it was luck. "There is a relationship between people and God. Heavenly Father allows things to happen. They are always good things if we let them be good."

The Ramsell family, 1994. Clockwise from center: *John, daughter Elissa Joyeaux, wife Melissa Anne, daughter Raquel Lynne, daughter Yvonne Anne, and daughter Gwendolyn Jane.*

Ramsell joined the Marines because he needed time. He'd graduated from North Tonawanda High School, between Niagara Falls and Buffalo, in 1964, but had gone back for post-graduate math and science courses he needed to get into forestry school. When it became apparent that he was going to be drafted before his courses were finished, he enlisted in the Marines because the Corps was the only service at the time that offered delayed enlistment.

"My father was a strong disciplinarian," Ramsell says of boot camp, "so I understood discipline, but it was harsher than I thought it would be. I kept thinking, 'Human beings don't treat each other like this.'" At Parris Island, he encountered black Americans for the first time. He often had a lot of trouble understanding them, he says, and didn't feel as though he managed to integrate very successfully. He was therefore both surprised and touched when Roosevelt Tharrington, Jr., a black Marine who had been his bunkie, came up to Ramsell's parents on graduation day and told them, "You've got a nice son."

After boot camp and infantry training, Ramsell went to welding school, then to staging at Camp Pendleton, arriving in Vietnam in January 1967, where he was assigned to the 1st Amtrac Battalion. He did not return to the United States until his three-year enlistment expired in June 1969. In spite of that hellish night at Cua Viet, Ramsell extended his overseas tour not once, not twice, but three times.

"I was under the impression," he explains, "that the government couldn't send two family members to Vietnam at the same time." By early 1968, when Ramsell would have been due to rotate home, one of his three younger brothers (he also has a sister) was in the Army. Aware that a disproportionate number of casualties occurred in the first few months of a tour of duty, Ramsell felt he had a better chance of surviving, given his experience, then his brother did. "I thought it was best for our family if I were the only one to be in Vietnam."

One of the tricks Ramsell's experience had taught him was always to walk the flank when on patrol. "We had so many patrol leaders who insisted on using the trails and roads—places where mines and booby traps were most likely to be planted. I didn't want to walk on the trails. That was nuts."

During his two and a half years overseas, he was twice detached to Okinawa for periods of several months, where he repaired amphibious tractors too badly damaged to be worked on in Vietnam. Each time he returned to Vietnam, the deteriorating conditions of both the war and the Vietnamese civilian population were ever more apparent.

"You can't force people to be democratic," he says. He recalls a Vietnamese farmer saying, "Whether the Communists are here or the Americans are here, I will do the same thing every day." On another occasion, he heard a Vietnamese politician say, "Americans have made our women whores and our children beggars." By the time he left Vietnam, he says, "I was ashamed of what the Americans were doing."

Ramsell came home depressed and withdrawn. Two weeks after he returned, he says, "My father sat me down and said, 'You're not making any progress. You need to get back into the community. Get a job. Do something. It's behind you.' At the time, I thought he was being pretty unsympathetic, but it was the best advice I ever got. I appreciate it now."

Though he had wanted a career in forestry, his deepest aspiration was to raise a family, and he discovered that forestry didn't pay enough to do that. "Even a laborer at Lawless Container Corporation earned three thousand dollars a year more than a forester with a four-year degree," he says, so he went to work for Lawless. Now he was in a position to begin a family—if only he could find the right woman to marry.

Once again he turned to God. "I'm a high school graduate," he prayed. "I'm a fairly decent person. I have a job. I'm responsible. I need a wife and family." A few days later, at a church picnic he was chaperoning as a youth counselor, he met the woman he'd been hoping to find. The only problem was that Melissa Anne Welch was then just fifteen years old.

Neither set of parents was happy about the relationship, but Ramsell and Welch persisted. They were married two years later, in 1972, before Melissa graduated from high school—though graduate she did, and with excellent grades. Their first child, Yvonne Anne, was born a year later, but that didn't stop Melissa from earning an associate of arts degree from Bryant Stratton College in 1978.

Meanwhile, after two years at Lawless Container and a brief stint with Modu-craft, a manufacturer of gaming boards and tables, Ramsell spent seven years as a baker for Thiele's Bakery. In 1980, however, the Ramsells left their native state, and he took a job as a laborer with Checkers Moving and Storage in Oshkosh, Wisconsin. Ramsell explains the decision to move thus:

One of his neighbors happened to be at home when someone tried to break into the neighbor's house. When the neighbor called the police, he was told that if he harmed the burglar, they would arrest him. "Not the burglar," Ramsell says. "The police were threatening to arrest my neighbor. That's when I decided New York state was no longer the place for me."

Ramsell worked in Oshkosh less than a year before he and Melissa discovered Friendship, Wisconsin, a small town that had been settled by people from Friendship, New York, not far from North Tonawanda. "Even the place names were the same," says Melissa, "the streets, and the creek. It just felt like home." They bought a house outside of town, and have lived there ever since.

Actually, the house is well out of town, as I discovered when I came to visit on April 2, 1995. It was a Sunday afternoon, and the Ramsells had just returned from church. Their oldest daughter wasn't with them, but the three younger girls were all in matching dresses, bubbling with energetic sweetness, all smiles and giggles for the stranger who had come to see their father.

I had written to the only John R. Ramsell on the Myers list, and on September 4, 1993, I'd found a terse and tense message on my answering machine: "This is John Ramsell." Just that and a phone number. When I called back, he sounded guarded and hesitant, as if he wasn't really sure he wanted to be talking to me. He told me he'd been to the Vietnam Veterans Memorial while in Washington, D.C., on union business, and had found Billy Blades's name. He asked me who else from the platoon had been killed. When I mentioned the others, he said that Roosevelt Tharrington had been his bunkie.

Finally he said, "May I ask how you got my address?" I told him about Ben Myers and the computerized printout he'd sent me. After that, Ramsell seemed to relax somewhat. At the end of our conversation, he wished my family well with a sincerity that startled me. It seemed to come from the heart.

A year and a half later, when I came to visit, he greeted me with dignified formality, but the more he talked and the more I listened, the more at ease with me he seemed to feel. No doubt it didn't hurt that his daughters seemed to think I was an okay guy. By the end of the day he had accorded me the privilege of calling him "Jack," a liberty, I understood by then, he did not extend to everyone. It was a gesture I found deeply touching and still value to this day.

Ramsell told me that he worked two years at a sawmill after the family moved to Friendship, then three years for a commercial floor-cleaning service, before taking his current job in 1985 with Castle Rock Container Corporation, where he manufactures ink for the presses that print corrugated boxes and serves as chief steward for Local 131 of the Union of International Paperworkers.

Along with the house the Ramsells bought came forty acres of land, most of it pine forest. They had long dreamed of being self-sufficient, living off the land, and had already studied beekeeping, raising goats, and quilting. They bought seven milk cows and the equipment needed to milk them. "I had this idealistic notion of farmers sharing information and helping each other," Ramsell says, "but we discovered that farmers don't share information until they see if you'll make it."

"Then they'll tell you what you did wrong," adds Melissa, laughing. "It was a disaster." She is much quicker to laugh than is her husband, who measures his thoughts and speaks with deliberation. But he can't help responding to his wife's merriment, and soon he is telling the story of a night when Melissa had to milk all seven cows without his help.

"When the cows aren't milked," he explains, "they hurt, and they let you know they hurt by bellowing. By the time she got to the last cow, the cow was down on her knees praying for Melissa to milk her."

They lasted a year as dairy farmers. Then they switched to sheep, building a herd of about a hundred. But they didn't know enough about sheep farming either; their American-bred sheep varied in size and grade, reducing their value, and were neither good breeders nor good mothers. So the Ramsells finally sold the whole herd, along with the geese and ducks they'd been raising. "You think about those idyllic scenes with geese and ducks wandering in the yard," says Melissa, "but you don't think about the mess they make. Droppings everywhere!"

With each attempt, however, they were gaining valuable experience. And their accountant, of all people, gave them some good advice. "Don't take advice from any farmer in the red," he told them. "There's a reason why he's in the red. Don't buy any product that hasn't been on the market for at least three years. And get rid of all your equipment."

"We had a tractor big enough to plow 250 acres a day," Melissa explains almost gleefully, as if still amused by how little they knew.

They tried sheep again, but this time started with North Country Cheviots and Clun Forest sheep, two English breeds that reached North America via Canada. They now have ten adult ewes, an adult ram, a juvenile ram, and eight lambs. They milk the sheep, selling the milk at sixty-five dollars a hundredweight (versus twelve dollars a hundredweight for cows' milk) to be made into blue and Roquefort cheese. The lambs are fattened for six to eight months, then sold for slaughter. They also sheer the sheep, make batts from the wool, and sell the batts for quilting.

Their goal is to build a herd of forty to fifty sheep, plus lambs, and to provide adequate grazing on their own land for a herd that size. To that end, they hired a local logger to clear the trees, leaving enough to protect the land. Thirty of their forty acres are planted in corn by a nearby farmer with whom the Ramsells evenly split both the cost and the harvest. Over the next seven years or so, most of the land will go to grazing, so the corn is helping to break down the stumps and roots of the logged-out trees and prepare the soil for pasturage.

"The farmer who helps us is a chemical farmer," Ramsell explains, meaning that he puts chemical fertilizers on his own crops, "but he tolerates us using sheep manure on our corn instead of chemicals. We want our farm to reflect our ecological, ethical, and theological values."

Theology—religion—remains central to Ramsell's life, more so now than ever before. Though raised Presbyterian, soon after coming to the Adams-Friendship area (the two towns are contiguous) the Ramsells were introduced to the Church of Jesus Christ of the Latter Day Saints—the Mormon Church—by an electrician who was doing some work on their house, and they eventually converted.

For more than a decade after Yvonne was born, the Ramsells had tried without success to have another child, but almost immediately after their conversion, Melissa became pregnant with Gwendolyn Jane, now 8. The next year, she became pregnant with Raquel Lynne, 7. "Let me tell you," Ramsell jokes, "breastfeeding is *not* an effective method of birth control." The youngest member of the family, Elissa Joyeaux, is three.

Ramsell doesn't think it a coincidence that the three youngest girls arrived on the heels of the family's conversion to the Mormon Church. And he is extremely active in the church. He has served as president of the Men's Organization, counselor to the president of the Adams-Friendship Branch, and primary teacher and is currently both young adult Sunday school teacher and seminary teacher.

He especially enjoys working with young adults. "It's an important time in people's lives," he explains. "What should they do after high school? Should they join the military? Should they get married? Are they going to stay in the Church? All these questions come up within a few short years, plus their hormones are going nuts. It's very challenging, but rewarding, to teach them. 'I'm dying,' I tell them. 'I'm on the down side of my life, but you are the strength of the nation. You must have a moral anchor.'"

Ramsell believes that the Book of Mormon and the Mormon Church provide that anchor. "Morals and ethics should be taught in the home and the church," he says. "Schools should reflect the highest morals and ethics, but schools should not teach morals and ethics. Schools should teach the basics: reading, writing, math."

Schools are a sore subject with Ramsell. Yvonne, now 22 and a student at the University of Wisconsin in Madison, was diagnosed with a brain tumor during her junior year of high school, and operated on in the middle of her senior year. "Most of her teachers required her to take midterm exams ten days after the operation," Ramsell says. As if that were not enough, one teacher said Yvonne had missed so much work that she could not make it up, and gave her an F for the course.

Three things resulted from that experience, Ramsell says: Yvonne lost a college scholarship because of the failed course; Melissa went to work making pizzas for Kwik Trip, a minimarket and gas station chain, to help make up for the lost scholarship; and the Ramsells started investigating home-schooling. Today, all three of the younger girls are getting home-schooling, following a curriculum developed by the Mennonites. Melissa, who still works one day a week at Kwik Trip, recently turned down the company's offer of a full-time job as advertising director in order to stay at home with the children.

"We complement each other," Ramsell says of himself and his wife. "We have different interests and different approaches. It takes a lot of talk and a lot of love. I know of my relationship with Heavenly Father from Vietnam, and I keep calling on that relationship for strength. Mormons don't believe that marriage lasts only until one partner dies. We believe marriage is for eternity.

"Most Americans don't think in terms of eternity," he adds, "but when you do, it helps to put things in perspective." Things like a daughter's cancer. Things like a fifteen-year-old schoolgirl who became a life's companion. Things like a nightmare night at Cua Viet when Jack Ramsell discovered the power of prayer.

Henry J. Ray III

None of the four Henry J. Rays on the Myers list responded to my initial search letter. Ray did file a claim for veterans' benefits, but he did not respond to the letter forwarded to him by the VA. I received records from NPRC in November 1995 that indicate Ray was born on October 5, 1947, and was living in Calvert City, Kentucky, at the time of his enlistment. He had worked as a busboy in a restaurant prior to enlisting, and did not finish high school (though he did receive a General Equivalency Diploma in 1968 while still on active duty). After boot camp and basic infantry training, he received additional training as a machine gunner (0331).

Ray served from November 1966 until December 1967 with Company M, 3rd Battalion, 4th Marines, first as an ammunition carrier, then as a machine gunner, and finally as a machine-gun team leader and squad leader. Most of this service, including eleven major combat operations, was in Vietnam, but in April 1967 Ray's battalion boarded the USS *Princeton* at the mouth of the Cua Viet River east of Dong Ha and sailed for Okinawa, returning to Dong Ha by air in May. On September 26, he sustained a fragmentation wound of the lower right arm, though it was not serious enough to require evacuation.

From January 1968 until the following June, Ray served with various companies of the 2nd Battalion, 8th Marines, 2nd Marine Division. Though nominally based at Camp Lejeune, North Carolina, he sailed for the U.S. Naval Base at Guantanamo Bay, Cuba, aboard the USS *Sandoval* in mid-January, returning to Camp Lejeune by air just prior to his release from active duty in June 1968.

Ray was a corporal at the time of his release. His decorations include a Presidential Unit Citation, and the National Defense Service, Vietnam Service, and Vietnam Campaign Medals. Because his records indicate that he was wounded in combat, presumably he was awarded the Purple Heart Medal as well.

Kenneth J. Reavis

In the summer of 1995, Ken Reavis and his wife took a trip to Wyoming. From their home in Yadkinville, North Carolina, they traveled seven thousand miles in nineteen days, stopping to enjoy the sights in Saint Louis and Kansas City, Missouri; Pueblo and Mesa Verde, Colorado; Jackson Hole, Wyoming; Yellowstone and Glacier National Parks; and Deadwood, South Dakota.

That works out to an average of 368 miles a day, every day for almost three weeks. At sixty miles an hour, that's six hours of driving each day. ("We didn't stop much after Deadwood," Reavis says. "Once you've seen the wheat fields and cornfields, you've seen 'em.") That's a pretty ambitious schedule for a couple of middle-aged soon-to-be-grandparents, but here's the good part: they did the whole trip, Wolf Creek and Monarch Passes included, on a 1380cc Harley-Davidson FLH motorcycle.

Since 1968, the year Reavis married Carolyn Goodwin, "there hasn't been a time that we haven't had some sort of motorcycle," he says. He bought his first bike, a 1955 Harley-Davidson, for two hundred dollars while he was stationed at Camp Pendleton, California. "I bought it from an old gunnery sergeant," he says. "I say old. He probably wasn't as old as I am now. He seemed old then." Reavis was just 20 and newly mar-

Sergeant Kenneth J. Reavis (right) *the day before this discharge from the Marine Corps, June 1970. Reavis no longer remembers who the officer in the photo is.*

ried. He seldom rode without Carolyn back then, and twenty-eight years later, that's still the way it is. "She loves to ride as much as I do," he says.

Reavis first met Carolyn in church when he was 14 and she was 13. It was pretty much love at first sight, and they began dating—as soon as their parents would allow it—two years later. By the time Reavis graduated from Yadkinville High School in 1966, they'd been an item for four years already, but marriage was out of the question while Carolyn was still in high school.

Meanwhile, "there was nothing much around here to do," he says. "Factory work, construction work, the tobacco fields. I'd done all that part time and summers. The job options seemed like dead ends. And also I had two uncles who'd been in the Marines in World War II. [His own father was a World War II Navy veteran.] I guess that sort of impressed me. You know how that sort of thing is." So he enlisted for four years in the Marine Corps. "I figured I'd go right through training and go straight to Vietnam," he says. "The war in Vietnam didn't scare me a bit, though I guess it should have."

Boot camp was a different matter, however, at least initially. "I was scared to death when I got there," he says, "but when you see all those other people there—some bigger and some smaller, all kinds of people— and they're all making it, you figure you can hack it too."

One of his most vivid memories from Parris Island is of a time when he dropped his rifle on the floor. Drill Instructor Evans picked it up and gave him a vertical butt stroke to the stomach with it. "It knocked the wind out of me," Reavis recalls. "I'm still surprised it didn't break a couple of ribs." Fortunately, he had better luck on the rifle range than in the barracks, qualifying as a Rifle Expert.

Given a military occupational specialty of 1391, bulk fuel man, Reavis spent four weeks after boot camp and basic infantry training learning how to handle bulk fuel—which, he explains, was not stored in rigid tanks, but rather in huge rubber bladders—before being assigned to Supply Battalion, 5th Force Service Regiment at Pendleton.

A year later, he was still there, along with most of the rest of his bulk fuel company, when the Corps came looking for volunteers for Vietnam. "After being at Pendleton for a year, we'd volunteer for just about anything," he says, adding that almost all two hundred men in his company

Ken and Carolyn Reavis at the Badlands of South Dakota during a seven-thousand-mile motorcycle trip, July 1995. Guess what kind of motorcycle they were riding.

volunteered. Reavis was not among the eighty men chosen. Only then did the volunteers learn that they were going to Vietnam not as bulk fuel men, but as infantry riflemen. "After that," he says, "nobody volunteered anymore."

In November 1967, because he could type sixty words per minute, Reavis was reassigned to the Supply Battalion's Headquarters & Support Company, first as an administrative clerk (0141), then as a legal clerk (0121). In April 1968 he attended Naval Justice School to learn court reporting, and legal technicalities and proceedings. While his MOS was not officially changed to court reporter (4422) until January 1970, that was his primary duty for his last two years in the Corps.

Court reporting required intense concentration. Rather than typing on a specially designed stenographic machine the way a civilian court stenographer does, Reavis had to talk into a face mask attached to a recording device, trying to repeat verbatim every word spoken in the courtroom. The recording machine actually produced something like a 45rpm single record, but smaller and very flimsy. Recording quality was poor, and it was hard to understand on playback. "It wasn't a very good system," he says.

The battalion-level court to which Reavis was assigned could, if defendants were found guilty, hand out reductions in rank, fines, brig time, and bad conduct discharges. Once a trial concluded, Reavis had to write up a summary of the proceeding—unless the court handed down a BCD. In that case, the entire trial had to be transcribed and typed out, a tedious undertaking that could take two to three weeks of concentrated work.

In addition to court reporting, Reavis did legal administrative work, helping to schedule court-martials, advising officers of appearance times, transporting documents between battalion and regimental levels. "There were countless documents we had to type up," he says. "I can't even recall now what they were, but we were always busy."

Initially willing and even eager to go to Vietnam, Reavis says he stopped trying to get sent there after he and Carolyn married. And after he became legal chief for the battalion, he realized that he was not going to be sent because he was simply too good at his job and the people he worked for didn't want to train a replacement. Besides, he says, "If anybody came into my office and saw those stacks and stacks of paper, nobody else would want the job. I guess it all worked out pretty well. I was so at east with my job that I never really thought about going to Vietnam.

"It was a really good job," he continues. "I could have re-upped and stayed in another two years, but this antiquated system of typing seven copies of everything just really got to me. And the recording device was antique. It was really hard to pick up your own words. If word processors and photocopy machines would have been available to me then, my life might have turned out very differently."

But his decision to get out after four years also had to do with his discomfort at the fact that so many people could seriously and detrimentally affect one's career. "If you veered a little to the left or the right, there was always somebody waiting to step on you. Not that I ever had any trouble," he adds, but he wasn't going to press his luck. Instead, he took his sergeant's stripes, his Good Conduct Medal, his wife, and his daughter Kimberly (Jennifer would be born two years later), and went home to Yadkinville.

Reavis's father had made a good living doing construction work, so that's what Reavis decided to do. He worked several different jobs between June 1970 and March 1971 before hiring on with Daniel Construction. "They paid better than anyone else," he says. He spent two years with Daniel, helping to build a new plant for a textile company, then spent the next five years with Gilbert Engineering building wastewater treatment plants and installing underground piping.

Reavis returned to Daniel Construction in 1978 (subsequently acquired by the Fluor Corporation and renamed Fluor Daniel), initially helping to build a nuclear power plant, later working at a tire cord plant owned by Hoechst Celanese. Eighteen years later, he's still there, though Fluor Daniel is not.

As Reavis explains it, the tire cord plant is so constantly in need of expansion, new equipment, and other major construction work that Hoechst Celanese simply hires a construction company on an ongoing basis for what is called contract maintenance. Fluor Daniel had the contract for many years, but lost it in 1992 to the Bechtel Corporation. Except for two or three senior executives, however, Bechtel immediately hired all of the Fluor Daniel people who had been working at the tire cord plant.

Along the way to his current position as a construction engineer, Reavis has worked as an equipment operator, operator foreman, crane operator, civil foreman, ironworker, millwright foreman, and general foreman. He is unusual in that most construction engineers are college-educated while he is not, but "after so much experience," he says, "you know what to do." Occasionally a college-trained engineer will treat Reavis condescendingly or resentfully, he says, "but the biggest majority of them appreciate what you do for them."

One of the major problems that comes up is with blueprints prepared by off-site mechanical engineers. "These guys are five hundred miles away," he says. "They're working from blueprints that are thirty years old. They have no idea what on-site changes have been made since the plant was first built. I've seldom seen a set of blueprints that doesn't have a mistake." And because of his vast on-site experience, Reavis can spot errors that others miss.

Just such a situation has recently been developing. Old equipment that has been in place at the Hoechst Celanese plant since 1965 must be removed and replaced with more modern equipment. When the conversion begins, Reavis will be in charge of a construction coordinator, two crew supervisors, and two construction crews that will work around the clock in twelve-hour shifts. "I don't know how I'm going to manage it," he says, but as the saying goes, time is money, and Hoechst Celanese wants the conversion done rapidly so that the plant will be shut down for the shortest time possible.

Back in 1970, Reavis never imagined he'd end up as a construction engineer. "I really enjoyed operating equipment, and still do it when I get the opportunity. I keep brushed up on it," he says, taking the operator's seat when someone is out sick or extra help is needed. "If this job ever goes," he says, "I can always get another job as an operator."

Both Fluor Daniel and Bechtel are international corporations with job sites all over the world, and Reavis could easily have become a construction globe-trotter, but he has always preferred to stay at home. His roots are in Yadkinville, where I spent an afternoon with him on August 18, 1995, and family and friends are clearly what matter most.

Every October, Reavis and several dozen friends and neighbors from Yadkinville troop off to the Outer Banks of North Carolina where they fish for bluefish and red drum with rods and reels, and spearfish for flounder. From the time he was nine, Reavis was also an avid hunter, especially of rabbits, though he's all but given up hunting in recent years. "You just stand in one place," he says, "and good dogs'll bring the rabbits right to you, but there's been so much development that it's hard to find a good place to hunt anymore."

The ski boat in the garage doesn't get much use these days either, now that the kids are grown. (Kimberly, a post office letter carrier like her mother, is married and expecting a child; Jennifer is a greeter at a Chevrolet dealership in nearby Winston-Salem.) But Reavis's true love—at least after Carolyn and the girls—is motorcycling.

Every summer, he and Carolyn take a ten-day to twelve-day trip, and this past summer it was nineteen days. Next summer they hope to go to Nova Scotia. They've been known to camp along the way, but that requires carrying a lot of extra equipment, so usually they stay in motels, planning as they go, and calling ahead for reservations a day at a time. Every March, they also go to Daytona Race Week, and every May they go to Myrtle Beach for the Carolina Harley-Davidson Dealers Rally. "It's all just an excuse to get on a bike and ride," he says.

And biking has always been both a sociable and a family activity. The Reavises made the trip to Wyoming and back in the company of four other people on three other bikes. When the kids were younger, they went on all of the biking trips, too, riding along in cars and vans with other relatives and friends too numerous to be carried on the bikes. "It's always been a family deal," he explains. "I've never worried about taking the kids to rallies and other bike events. Motorcycle people as a whole are pretty good people. I don't care if they're Hell's Angels or whatever. Most of them leave you alone."

Since he got that first Harley-Davidson back at Camp Pendleton, Reavis has owned just about every kind of motorcycle ever made—Triumphs, Nortons, Indians—but over the years he's gravitated toward Harley-Davidsons, and he's ridden only Harley-Davidsons since 1993. "They've got better suspension," he says. "You don't take as much of a beating." For a similar reason, he doesn't use his sidecar much anymore either. "Without the sidecar," he explains, "the bike steers itself. With the sidecar attached, you have to steer all the time. At forty-seven, your muscles kind of tighten up on you."

For safety reasons, Reavis doesn't ride at night. "Too much chance of hitting a deer," he says. For the same reason, because he leaves for work at 5:30 in the morning when it's often still dark, he usually doesn't ride to work; when he does, he leaves plenty of time so he can drive slowly. And while he can ride in the rain comfortably if he wears a rain suit, he tries to avoid riding in thunderstorms because of the danger.

He has had only one serious accident in all his years of riding. No bones got broken, he says, but he got scraped up pretty severely, and the damage might have been worse if he had not been wearing a helmet. That experience notwithstanding, Reavis opposes mandatory helmet laws, believing that it ought not to be the government's place to tell riders what they must wear.

He was surprised this past summer at the number of western states that have already repealed their mandatory helmet laws, and thinks North Carolina's law will not be on the books much longer. Reavis won't ride on interstate highways without wearing his helmet, laws or no laws, but he admits that he wouldn't wear it on shorter trips if it were not required by law, "though I guess there's just as much danger of getting hit on a short trip as on a long one," he admits a little sheepishly.

Kimberly's husband Stephen has a Harley-Davidson. Kimberly herself used to have a 650cc Yamaha, but she gave it up because, as Reavis explains, "she's pretty small and the bike was pretty big," so now she rides with husband Stephen. Only Jennifer did not catch the biking bug, says Reavis, though she'll ride with her father once in a while. Carolyn, for her part, is still as enthusiastic as she ever was. "The bike hardly ever leaves home without Carolyn on it," he says. As for the people who dress up in leather with the vests and the chains and all the other motorcycle trappings, says Reavis, "They're bikers. We're just people who ride bikes."

Albert L. Remsburg, Jr.

Remsburg did not turn up on the Myers list, but his VA claim number was also his social security number, so MIE, Inc., was able to give me three addresses for him, all in Maryland. I wrote to all three in the winter of 1994. Two came back undeliverable; the third, to Middletown, went unanswered. I wrote again to the third address six months later; this time the letter came back marked "Forwarding Order Expired," but the postal label containing this information also included a new address in Brunswick, Maryland. Why the post office couldn't just have sent my letter on, rather than sending it back, is a mystery to me, but life's full of mysteries. I readdressed the letter and sent it to Brunswick, but it and a second letter a few months later went unanswered.

Then in early 1995, after I acquired my own national telephone directory, I found an Albert C. Remsburg back in Middletown, so I called on February 24, 1995, and got Remsburg's mother, who told me he was living in Florida. She said she didn't have his address or telephone number, but that he called every weekend and she would give him my message. Two days later, Remsburg called me.

Based on our conversation, and records received from NPRC in February 1995, I learned that Remsburg was born in Libertytown, Frederick, Maryland, on March 25, 1947. He worked for two years as a bricklayer while still in high school, and graduated from high school in 1966. After boot camp and basic infantry training, he was sent to the 2nd Air-Naval Gunfire Liaison Company, Force Troops, Fleet Marine Force Atlantic, Camp Lejeune, North Carolina, where he received training as a shore fire control party man (0849). He remained with 2nd ANGLICO from September 1966 until February 1967, except for a month of temporary duty with the Marine Barracks, U.S. Naval Base, Guantanamo, Cuba.

Remsburg arrived in Vietnam in April 1967. He served briefly with Headquarters Battery, 2nd Battalion, 11th Marines, before being transferred in May to Communications Company, Headquarters Battalion, 1st Marine Division. In January 1968 he was transferred to Sub-unit #1 of the battalion's Service Company, where he remained until shortly before his release from active duty in May 1968.

While in Vietnam, Remsburg participated in five major combat operations including the battle for Hue City during the 1968 Tet Offensive. He also spent a total of five weeks on mess duty, a common assignment for junior enlisted personnel. He was awarded the National Defense Service, Vietnam Service, and Vietnam Campaign Medals.

After his release, he returned to Maryland, but eventually moved to Florida, where he works as a house builder. He has been twice married and twice divorced, and was living with his 32-year-old girlfriend in the Jacksonville area when we spoke. A letter I sent in July 1997 came back marked by the post office: "Moved Left No Address."

Paul E. Robison, Jr.

I had no luck tracking Robison until I received his records from NPRC in February 1996. These indicated that he had come from Maryland, so I checked my national telephone directory and found three Paul Robisons in Maryland. I called all three; the first two were dead ends, but the third call got me Robison's mother, who told me he was living in Mount Savage near Cumberland, Maryland. She didn't feel comfortable giving me his telephone number, but said she would give him my message.

I waited four days, then called directory assistance for Mount Savage and got his number myself. I reached Robison on the first try. He said his mother told him I'd called. He also said he was married with two grown children, a daughter and a son, and that he had lived in West Virginia after he got married but then returned to Maryland, where he manages a uniform rental company for Omni Services, for whom he has worked since the late 1970s.

In late May 1996, I wrote to request an interview with him, and during a follow-up phone call on June 2, we arranged to get together on the 23rd, the day after I was to visit Gary Davis, but when I called to confirm the meeting on June 17, he told me that he'd changed his mind and didn't want to be interviewed. When I told him I'd already rented a car and made hotel reservations, he said that it wouldn't be hard for me to cancel them. To my several attempts to find out what had caused him to change his mind, he would only say, "I just don't feel comfortable." He would not explain further.

The records I received from NPRC indicate that Robison was born on March 17, 1948. A high school graduate, he was sworn into the Marine Corps at Baltimore, Maryland. After boot camp and basic infantry training, he received additional training as a machine gunner (0331). He arrived in Vietnam in December 1966 and was assigned to Company H, 2nd Battalion, 3rd Marines, first as an ammunition carrier, then as a machine gunner.

In March the battalion traveled by ship to Okinawa, spending six weeks reequipping and retraining before being redesignated Battalion Landing Team 2/3 and returning to Vietnam by ship. In April, during Operation Beacon Star II in Quang Tri Province, Robison earned the Navy Commendation Medal with Combat "V" during an engagement in which another platoon from his company was pinned down by enemy fire. His citation reads, in part:

> Realizing the seriousness of the situation, Lance Corporal Robison immediately maneuvered to a position from which he could deliver effective M-60 machinegun covering fire in support of the beleaguered unit. Disregarding his own safety, he repeatedly exposed himself to the heavy enemy fire to reposition his weapon and deliver accurate fire against the enemy, which enabled casualties to be expeditiously evacuated to areas of relative safety.

On June 18, during Operation Beacon Torch in Quang Nam Province, Robison sustained a shrapnel wound to the left leg. On July 6, while on Operation Beaver Track/Cimarron in Quang Tri Province, he received a shrapnel wound in the left arm. Two days later, during the same operation, he received another shrapnel wound, this one to the left hand.

Though none of the wounds required evacuation, it was standard policy to transfer a man out of Vietnam after he received a third Purple Heart. Robison was therefore sent to the Service Battalion at Camp Smedley D. Butler on Okinawa, where he served as a brig guard (8151) from July until November 1967.

From December 1967 until July 1968, Robison served as a machine gunner with Company K, 3rd Battalion, 6th Marines, at Camp Lejeune, North Carolina, including a three-month cruise aboard the USS *Boxer*. In July he was assigned to the Marine Barracks, U.S. Naval Station, Patuxent River, Maryland, first as a guard, then as a guard noncommissioned officer.

Robison was released from active duty in June 1969 with the rank of sergeant. In addition to his Navy Commendation Medal and three Purple Hearts, he was awarded a Presidential Unit Citation, the Combat Action Ribbon, and the National Defense Service, Vietnam Service, and Vietnam Campaign Medals.

Alexander J. Salisbury, Jr.

A year out of Eddystone High School in southeastern Pennsylvania, Alex Salisbury was working at Honeysuckle Farms, a local ice cream stand. It was the spring of 1966, and the war in Vietnam was taking ever larger numbers of young American men. Salisbury and two coworkers "knew we were going to get drafted, and we didn't want to go in the Army, so we decided to enlist in the Marines.

"I can still see us like it was yesterday," he says. "We're down there running around in Memorial Park getting in shape. Like we were going to try out for some sports team. We weren't thinking about going to war. We had no idea what it really meant."

The three young friends intended to enlist on the Buddy Plan, but before they actually signed up, Salisbury got a letter from Selective Service ordering him to report for induction into the Army, so he decided not to wait for his two friends, enlisting on his own.

"That first night at Parris Island," he recalls, "when they didn't let us sleep, I thought, 'Okay, well, tomorrow night they've gotta let us sleep.' But we were up all the next night too, making and remaking our beds. We didn't sleep for days. I kept thinking, 'There's gotta be some kind of law or something.' I can't even remember when they finally let us sleep. It's all just a blur.

"I didn't find boot camp all that difficult, though," he continues. "At home I did things like wash the dishes, make beds. I had the discipline already. And I was in good shape. I was fairly strong. It was like playing a sport, playing a game. Like hanging from that rope and sliding down [one of the obstacles on the Confidence Course, a super obstacle course every recruit must complete before graduating]—that was fun. I enjoyed the challenge of boot camp."

The only thing he worried about was getting sick. He recalls doing

Corporal Alexander J. Salisbury, Jr., in the backyard of future wife Lois Nickerson's house in Chester, Pennsylvania, 1968.

The Salisbury family, 1994. Clockwise from lower left: *Alex, Jr., daughter Tracy, son Alex III, son Brent, and wife Lois.*

calisthenics, what we called physical training or PT, inside the barracks with all the windows and doors shut until the squad bay deck was literally awash in sweat. "We'd go to bed all sweaty and then the temperature would drop during the night," he says. "If I got sick, I knew I wouldn't be able to keep up.

"And the other thing I didn't like was getting up in the morning and having to rush around, hurry, hurry. I would rather have gotten up a half-hour earlier every day and taken my time getting ready. But you know, they wanted you to feel rushed. They wouldn't let you get up before they told you to. They wanted you to have to hurry.

"I remember the day of the drill competition [when the four platoons of D Company competed to see which was best at close order drill]. We came in second. I thought for sure we'd be up all night doing PT because we lost, but when we got back to the barracks [Drill Instructor] Evans said, 'You men were cheated today. You were the best.' It was the first time any of the DIs called us men. That meant something because Evans was the toughest [of our three DIs]."

Just before graduation, when each recruit received his basic military occupational specialty, Salisbury found out he'd been made a clerk-typist and would be sent straight back to the administrative school on Parris Island after basic infantry training. "All I could think of was not coming back to Parris Island," he says. "I wanted out of there, so I asked Sergeant Evans if anything could be done about my orders.

"Evans kind of grabbed me around the throat, grabbed my collar, and said, 'This is the Marines! We tell you where to go, and that's where you go!' I only enlisted for two years. I always figured I'd end up in the infantry in Vietnam. I never dreamed I'd end up in admin school. Everybody was getting orders to FMFWesPac [Fleet Marine Force, Western Pacific]."

After eight more weeks on Parris Island, which turned out to be considerably less rigorous than his first eight weeks had been, Salisbury was assigned to Marine Medium Helicopter Squadron 262 based at MCAF New River, North Carolina. At the time, he was dating Lois Nickerson, whom he'd met while working at Honeysuckle Farms and whom he would marry in 1969, and he came home to Eddystone every chance he could, often sharing rides with two other members of Platoon 1005 from the Philadelphia area, Rey Waters and Stephen Sofian.

"We used to swoop all the time," he says of those long car rides home, a ritual known as "swooping." "A lot of times, whoever I was riding with would be going to New York or Philadelphia or Atlantic City, so I'd get dropped off at Exit Two of the New Jersey Turnpike and I'd walk from there to Eddystone. I'd cross the [Delaware] River on the Chester-Bridgeport Ferry.

"One night I walked all the way to the ferry dock and discovered it wasn't running because of a strike, so I had to walk all the way back to the main highway. I didn't have any gloves with me, and it was really cold, so I had to pull a pair of socks out of my ditty bag and put them over my hands."

Salisbury is sitting at the kitchen table of his split-level home in Marcus Hook, Pennsylvania, not far from Chester, where he was born, and Eddystone, where his family moved when he was a kid. Only one Alexander J. Salisbury had appeared on the Myers list, and when I didn't receive a reply to my initial search letter after three weeks, I decided to call. Salisbury was at work, but his son told me I had the right man, so I called again the next day, September 23, 1993, and reached him. He told me he'd gotten my letter and was meaning to reply. He remembered my name well, he said, but couldn't place my face, so he'd gotten out the platoon's group photograph and had been looking at it. "It brings back a lot of memories," he said.

A year later, on September 22, 1994, I made the short drive from my home in Philadelphia to his in Marcus Hook to get him to tell me some of those memories. Just as he begins to talk about a mid-air collision of two helicopters that took the lives of thirty-eight Marines at New River, Lois enters the room.

"We heard about that on the news," she says. "It was terrible. We didn't know if Alex was on one of those choppers or not."

"I was supposed to be," Salisbury says. "They were going to some jungle survival school or something like that. I was supposed to go too, but my boss, a gunny sergeant, said the admin people were too busy and couldn't be spared. So instead of being on that flight, I ended up preparing letters to the families of the dead." By the time the job was completed, it was Friday night and too late to find anyone to swoop with. "It was the only time I ever took a bus home," he says. "But I just had to get out of there."

With half his enlistment still ahead of him, Salisbury continued to assume that sooner or later he'd get orders for Vietnam. Then in late spring 1967, his squadron received orders to embark on a six-month Caribbean cruise. "I still couldn't believe it," he says. "It wasn't until I actually got on the ship that I knew I wouldn't be going to Vietnam. By the time we got back, I'd be way too short to get sent to Vietnam. I wouldn't have enough time left in the Marines."

Meanwhile, Salisbury's brother (he also has two sisters) was drafted into the Army and sent to Vietnam, where he eventually received a Purple Heart for shrapnel wounds from a grenade. "I was disappointed that I didn't get sent to Vietnam," he says. "We're the Marines, we're the tough guys, but I'm in an office and my brother's in Vietnam."

Assigned to the USS *Guadalcanal*, Salisbury found himself and his squadron frequently moving from ship to shore (usually Guantanamo, Cuba) and back again. "The main purpose of the cruise seemed to be to train pilots for Vietnam. They'd fly us off the ship, then fly us back on again, then fly us all back off again."

Still, he says, "The office people, we really had it good. We had our office up in the bow, and the [officers and staff NCOs] didn't bother us too much. They wanted [the service record books and unit diaries] squared away. They didn't mess with us."

The grunts on board didn't fare so well. "Their quarters were down in the belly of the ship," he explains. "It was hot and miserable down there. They didn't do anything except play cards and wait in the chow line. Most of them were Vietnam veterans just serving out the rest of their enlistments. They were a wild bunch. We'd hit port and they'd head straight for the bars and get drunk. There'd be fights on the dock. Fights in the club at Guantanamo. The MPs had their hands full. The choppers were always running medevacs."

The cruise ended in November 1967, and the squadron returned to New River, where Salisbury, a corporal, finished out his enlistment. "I enjoyed what I was doing," he says. "I did good work. They gave me a job to do, and I did it. One time they sent me to unit diary school and I graduated tops in my class, even though a lot of the men in the course had already worked on unit diaries and I hadn't. I'm proud of that."

He wore his uniform home his last day on active duty, June 14, 1968, "but I didn't feel comfortable. People seemed to resent it. It's a shame because it was something to be proud of, even if I didn't go to Vietnam." As he talks, a framed portrait of him in Marine dress blues is visible in the living room, quietly placed among other family photographs, including several of their three children: Tracy, 23, a graduate of West Chester University who works for Sears; Alex III, 19, a warehouseman for a plumbing supplier; and Brent, 13, an eighth grader.

"It's tough for young people today," Salisbury says. "Even a college degree isn't a guarantee for them. When I was getting out of the Marines, jobs were easy to get. The question was: What job do you want? My father was a finisher at Scott Paper Company, so I got a job there, but I was working a rotating shift schedule and I didn't like that, so I took a job at Westinghouse as a sweeper." The pay was less than at Scott, but he only had to work days, and there was more opportunity for advancement.

"Actually," he says, "I turned the job down at first. I didn't want to be a sweeper. But the man who was doing the hiring was an ex-Marine helicopter pilot, and I think he took a liking to me. He called my mother up and told her, 'Please tell him to come back. He won't be a sweeper for long.'"

And he wasn't. This particular Westinghouse facility built gas and steam turbines, and the manufacturing process required huge cranes. Soon after he was hired, Salisbury became a crane repairman. "I'll tell you," he says, "I had sixteen good years there. We had cranes up to 350 tons mounted on railroad tracks thirty feet up in the air. Every day we worked on the cranes and the elevators. It was very interesting. I always thought, 'This is too good, it can't last.' I knew I'd never retire from there."

And he didn't. In 1983, Westinghouse closed the plant, moving part of the work to Canada and the rest to Japan. Salisbury feels the unions were largely to blame for the closing. "[The workers] were too protected," he says. "Most of them wouldn't work. If they didn't like the job they were assigned to, they'd refuse to do it. Or they'd spend all day on one job instead of finishing it and going on to another job. Some of us worked hard, but we couldn't do it all."

He next found work as an electrician at the Philadelphia Navy Yard, and ended up working on his old ship, the *Guadalcanal,* which came in for a twenty-year overhaul. "That was really exciting," he says. "I went all over the ship. It really brought back memories." But the job itself wasn't permanent and offered no benefits, so after nine months he took a more secure job as a packager in the British Petroleum lubrication oil plant in Marcus Hook, which paid less but offered good benefits.

Six months later, he was offered a supervisor's position. "When I went to work at BP," he says, "I never thought about being a supervisor. I just did my job, and I tried to do it well. I've always worked hard." When the lube oil plant closed, he was shifted to the warehouse of the Marcus Hook BP refinery.

Currently, Salisbury supervises six workers and oversees an inventory of $20 million. "Every piece of inventory that comes in and goes out gets counted," he says. "Bolts, pumps, gaskets, you name it, everything you need to keep the refinery working. It's all computerized. There's nothing like a computer. That typing I had [in the Marines] really comes in handy."

Already drawing a small pension from Westinghouse, Salisbury could retire from BP in six years at age 55, but probably won't. "Maybe when my youngest is out of college," he says, "I don't know. I've worked ever since I was fourteen years old. I enjoy work. I enjoy going down there [to the warehouse], and I thank the Lord that I *can* work."

When he's not working, Salisbury takes an active part in the Chichester Wesleyan Church, where he's a member of the board of administration, a post his wife has previously held. He goes fishing with his sons, he's helped to coach Tracy's softball team, and a few years ago he coached Brent's baseball team to the championship of the Sun Oil Youth League in nearby Chester.

And then there's deer hunting, something he's avidly pursued since his father first took him hunting as a child. He always goes to the same place, English Center, near Williamsport in north central Pennsylvania. "I won't go to Ridley Park," he says of a local state park where deer are both plentiful and docile. "That's too easy. That's not what I go hunting for. I enjoy going back into the woods and blending in. I enjoy nature and the solitude.

"I'm a disciplined person," he continues. "I can go into the woods and sit there all day. I got a buck the first seven times I went out. I've seen at least one buck twenty of the last twenty-five years. When I see one, I don't raise my rifle right away. I let him get used to the smell in the air. Sometimes they'll come right up under my tree. They won't know I'm up there. I could get a deer every time if I wanted to, but often I don't shoot. I just watch. The laurel's so thick, it's hard to get a deer out once you shoot it. Hey, I'm not twenty-eight anymore. It's hard work just to walk in there, let alone drag a deer out."

Salisbury tells how he used to go hunting with his brother, and when he'd get a deer, he would sing the Marine Corps Hymn as he dragged it out of the woods. "It was a friendly competition," he says, chuckling softly. "I was just needling him a little."

Does he ever wish that he, like his brother, had gone to Vietnam? "Yes!" he replies emphatically. "I expected to go when I joined. I was ready to go. Was it luck that I didn't? I don't think so. God has a plan for each of us. It wasn't part of God's plan for me."

In front of him on the table is his red, oversized hardback platoon book. It's lying open to the pages that contain small portraits of the eighty men in the platoon, five to a row, five rows to a page. "Sure, I wish I'd gone. Even if the war was screwed up, you have to be proud of the guys that served. Even if you didn't like the war. I don't think that anybody who wasn't in Vietnam should say anything about it."

He points to the photograph of John L. Harris, Jr., and then to William C. Blades III. "They're heroes," he says. "Those boys are heroes. They thought they were doing the right thing. You can't tell them what they did was wrong. They're dead. They're heroes."

Ronald L. Schirmer

When you think of retirement, what do you think of? Sarasota, Florida? Tucson, Arizona? Golf? Recreational vehicles in Yellowstone National Park? Spending time with the grandchildren? How about a full-time job as a maintenance chief at a restaurant with another part-time job as a small business consultant while your wife works as a waitress? And while you're at it, why not reroof your house with your own two hands, detach the back porch, and rebuild it as a storage shed?

Corporal Ronald L. Schirmer with his bride, the former Rena Ann Toomer, December 1968.

That's how retired master sergeant Ron Schirmer is spending his time these days, and it's not exactly by choice. On the day he retired—November 10, 1993, the 218th birthday of the Marine Corps—his income dropped by 50 percent. At the same time, he had to buy a house of his own for the first time, plus a second car, while making advance payments for various utility hookups. He needed a lot of cash up front.

"We had a tough time getting settled," he says. "We'd spent six of the last seven years overseas, so we couldn't get a head start on anything. We had to start from scratch." They found a modest ranch-style house on a quiet street that ends on Bogue Sound near Swansboro, North Carolina, wife Rena's hometown, and they borrowed heavily, loading up all their credit cards and taking out a mortgage.

Only now, four years later, are they beginning to get on top of things. Until recently, both their grown sons and their daughter-in-law and grandson were crammed into the house with them. But Schirmer doesn't waste time complaining, and he doesn't regret his decision to spend a quarter of a century in the Marine Corps.

Spending much of that time in the administrative field allowed him to

Master Sergeant Ron Schirmer, U.S. Marine Corps (Retired), 1997.

master the ropes of bureaucracy. "I learned to use the system for what I wanted. I wanted to see things and travel. I wanted my family to travel. Everywhere we went, I used the system to allow my family to do things we wanted." Moreover, five of Schirmer's postings were for two years or more (at one point, the family didn't move for seven years), so Rena and the boys—Paul, Rena's son from a previous relationship, whom Schirmer adopted in 1969, and Ron II, born in 1970—were required to move far less often than many military families.

Schirmer hadn't intended to make a career of it when he enlisted. Indeed, he even got out after finishing his initial three-year enlistment and went back to his native Delaware. But after three years as a civilian, he enlisted again. "I just had to get back into it," he says. "I don't really know what it was. The pull of the travel and everything."

He enlisted the first time, a year after graduating from Georgetown High School in 1965, to avoid the draft. "The only way to stay out of getting drafted was to enlist, get married, or go to college," he explains. "I didn't have anyone I wanted to marry, and I couldn't afford to go to college."

After graduation, he spent the following year completing a program in mechanical and architectural drafting at Sussex Vocational Technical Center, but the military draft loomed over him. In high school, Schirmer had played football, wrestled, and run track. Unbeknownst to him, his coaches were working on getting him a college athletic scholarship. Unbeknownst to them, he joined the Marines in February 1966 on a delayed enlistment. By the time he learned that they'd gotten him a scholarship, he was a week away from leaving for Parris Island.

As for choosing the Marines, Schirmer says, "I figured if I was going to go, I wanted to be trained by the best. I was expecting it to be hard," he says of boot camp. "That's why I joined."

After boot camp, Schirmer was trained as a machine gunner (0331) and arrived in Vietnam in November 1966. He was assigned to Company E, 2nd Battalion, 3rd Marines. In March 1967, the battalion went by ship to Okinawa, traded in their M-14 rifles for the newer M-16s, and spent six weeks training and refitting. Redesignated Battalion Landing Team 2/3, the battalion then returned to Vietnam, living aboard ship off the coast and deploying by helicopter to wherever they were needed, going ashore from a few days to a few weeks at a time, almost always in hot spots.

During one such deployment at the western end of the Demilitarized Zone in the vicinity of Khe Sanh, Schirmer's company was advancing up Hill 881 North when they came under sniper fire, so the company withdrew and dug in for the night on nearby Hill 861. In the early morning hours before dawn of the next day, elements of the North Vietnamese Army attacked in strength. Schirmer says the NVA advance teams responded in English when challenged by the Marines on the company perimeter, causing confusion and hesitation and allowing the attackers to get in close before opening their assault.

During the ensuing battle, Schirmer sustained shrapnel wounds and a bullet wound to the arm. He was evacuated to the hospital ship USS *Repose,* where he recuperated for several weeks, but he was back in action by May 20. "The stitches weren't even out yet," he says. Altogether, he participated in twenty-one combat operations before returning to the States in December 1967.

His next assignment, the last of his first hitch, was with the 8th Motor Transport Battalion at Camp Lejeune, North Carolina. To earn some extra money, he took a second job as a bartender at Cushing Corners in Jacksonville. There he met and began dating another employee; through her, he met Rena Ann Toomer, a friend from nearby Swansboro. Soon Schirmer was dating Rena instead, and in December 1968 they were married.

The following June, by then a sergeant, Schirmer got out and moved his family to Bridgeville, Delaware, where he took a job driving a snack truck route selling Mrs. Ihre's Potato Chips. After three years as a civilian, however, he decided to go back into the Corps. Because he'd been out for so long, he could only return as a private first class, three grades below the rank he'd achieved during his first hitch, so he started back up the ladder from there.

But he didn't return as a machine gunner. "I didn't feel like getting shot at like I was the first time," he says. "I'd already been shot up enough. I asked for military police or the administrative field, but they couldn't make up their minds, I guess, so they sent me to the MPs as an admin man."

He spent a year with base MPS at Camp Lejeune, where he received meritorious promotions to lance corporal and corporal; then a year with Marine Fighter Attack Squadron 232 in Japan, Thailand, the Philippines, and Okinawa, where he picked up sergeant again; another year at Lejeune with base personnel; then two years with the Inspector & Instructor Staff training reserves in Buffalo, New York, where he was promoted to staff sergeant.

After two more years at Marine Corps Air Station, Cherry Point, North Carolina, Schirmer applied to be a drill instructor. "I was looking for a way out of there," he says of the assignment he was in at the time, explaining that too many of his coworkers, especially those who'd never served in Vietnam, routinely complained about nothing and made a habit of avoiding the unpleasant jobs that needed to be done. Here's where learning the ropes came in handy:

Schirmer's commanding officer and executive officer refused to re-lease him for drill instructor duty, saying that he was too valuable as an admin chief. But he was due to renew his reenlistment contract, and he knew that in the process of doing that, he could apply for new orders di-rectly to Headquarters Marine Corps. He did, and HQMC gave him orders to Drill Instructor School. "Oh, they were mad about that," Schirmer says of his CO and XO, "but there wasn't a thing they could do about it."

Drill Instructor School, he says, turned out to be tougher than boot camp itself, both mentally and physically. "You didn't have the extreme verbal harassment," he explains, "but you were challenged to keep up. Everything we learned in boot camp was just the tip of the iceberg. DIS have to learn all that and more because they have to teach it. And all the PT we did in boot camp? Remember, our DIS had to run out in front of us. They had to be in better shape than we were."

But Schirmer got through the training and was assigned to the 1st Re-cruit Training Battalion at Parris Island, the same battalion he'd been in as a recruit with Platoon 1005. The old War War I–era two-story wooden bar-racks were gone, however, replaced by three-story brick barracks like the ones only 3rd Battalion had had back in 1966. Instead of three DIS with 80 recruits, there were now four DIS and 100 to 110 recruits per platoon.

Before his first platoon had finished it's training cycle, Schirmer was appointed senior drill instructor. He tried to model himself on Platoon 1005's senior drill instructor, J. J. Oliver. "He was firm but always in con-trol," Schirmer says of Oliver. "He was a kind of father figure. I wanted to do it like that. I would talk to a recruit like he was my son."

Unfortunately, sometimes he also talked to his wife and sons like they were recruits. Once you master the booming voice needed by Marine DIs, it's hard not to use it. "They still get on me about that sometimes," he says with chagrin. But he tried very hard not to let a bad day on the drill field affect his family life. "It all depended on what you made of it," he says of duty as a drill instructor, explaining that he would often share stories of the day's goings-on with his family in order to bring them into his life on the drill field rather than excluding them or taking things out on them.

He spent three years at Parris Island, picking up gunnery sergeant along the way, then went to Marine Corps Air Station, Iwakuni, Japan. But less than a year later, he was given a choice between recruiting duty or returning to the drill field. "I saw what recruiting duty was like when I was with I&I in Buffalo," he says. "I didn't want anything to do with it." So back to South Carolina he went.

Immediately upon arrival, he was invited to become a depot inspector, "better known as a spy," he says. Depot inspectors would review the DIs' training syllabi and lesson plans and generally make sure DIs were properly adhering to regulations and procedures. "Hey, I just got here," Schirmer replied. "Why don't you let me get my feet wet?" He was allowed to take one platoon through its training cycle, then he became an inspector.

DIs were not supposed to subject recruits to excessive physical or mental abuse. They were also not supposed to "PT" recruits beyond certain fixed time limits or immediately after meals. Inspectors carried stopwatches and would actually time DIs to see that these regulations were followed. "Every day we'd pick different events and activities to check out," Schirmer says. "The DIs never knew when we were coming." One thing especially Schirmer would not tolerate: "If we caught DIs telling recruits that 'spies' were coming, we would nail them for disrespect. It was insulting, and it set a bad example for the recruits."

Not only the barracks had changed since 1966. One change that is almost incomprehensible to Marines of my generation and earlier is that DIs aren't supposed to swear at recruits anymore, or subject them to unwarranted and degrading insults. It's hard to imagine Marine Corps boot camp without bellowing drill instructors constantly reaching for new standards in colorful language.

Of course, Schirmer admits, rules do get bent, especially in the later stages of training after the troublemakers, the dead wood, and those who can't hack it have been weeded out. "By the third phase [of the training cycle]," he says, "[the recruits] know what to do and how to do it. These boys aren't gonna say anything. They want to finish. These are the guys who are gonna finish. If they mess up now, you can get right up in their faces and they're gonna eat it right up. And they did."

The DIs pushed the rules and limits all the time, he says, but most of them were good at what they did. "I'd always give 'em a fair chance," he says. During his three years as an inspector, he only had to relieve a few of them.

The recruits of the 1980s, he adds, were as good as the recruits of the 1960s, but there were some differences. "They have to have more brain power," he says of the newer recruits, "because of the technical side of things. When we joined, if you could shoot a gun, that was all they needed at the time." But most of the differences, he thinks, are reflections of changes in society. He says racial tensions were more pronounced in the eighties, both blacks and whites seeming more resistant to integration. "We didn't seem to have all that much of a problem," Schirmer says of Platoon 1005.

After his second three years at the recruit depot, where he also did competitive shooting with the Parris Island Rifle & Pistol Team, Schirmer packed up his family and went to Iwakuni, where he ran the joint reception center. "Anybody and everybody that came there," he says, "I greeted." After three years in Japan, during which he was promoted to master sergeant, he spent another three years with the adjutant's office at Kaneohe, Hawaii, again accompanied by his family, before spending a final year back at Cherry Point. On the day he retired, with the birth of Ronald Lee Schirmer III, he and Rena became grandparents.

During his long career—twenty-four years, seven months, and sixteen days on active duty—Schirmer amassed a pile of decorations and awards that include the Purple Heart Medal, the Vietnamese Cross of Gallantry, the Navy Commendation and Navy Achievement Medals, the Armed Forces Expeditionary Medal, seven Good Conduct Medals, two Meritorious Masts, and three Letters of Appreciation.

Only 46 when he retired, however, Schirmer couldn't afford—quite literally—to rest on his achievements. He soon went to work as the maintenance chief at the Cherry Point McDonald's restaurant, where he maintains the building and keeps all the equipment in working order. Operating as Schirmer Enterprises, he also helps people set up Amway distributorships. It's a busy life, but a good one. After twenty-nine years of marriage, Rena still calls "I love you" before going out the door on a routine errand, and Schirmer calls back, "Love you, too." Paul works at the same McDonald's his father does, and Rons II and III live only a few miles away.

Also only a few miles away, across the sound on Bogue Bank, is where my family happened to spend a week's vacation in the summer of 1997. I'd already located Schirmer through records provided by NPRC and my national telephone directory, so I drove over to visit on August 11. It was the second of two vacation days I gave up that week for Platoon 1005, having spent the day before with Cogie Godfrey up in Kinston, but I don't regret either day.

One of the few regrets Schirmer has concerns the war in Vietnam. "Every time we went out," he says of his time in the war zone, "we were always on the winning side. We lost some people, but we always took whatever we were supposed to take. We lost the war because there was too much politics. We couldn't fire back until we were fired upon. We weren't supposed to keep a round in the chamber. If they had lifted the restrictions and said, 'Finish it off,' I know we could have won."

George T. Schrenker

Only one George T. Schrenker appeared on the Myers list, so I thought I might get lucky, as I had with Albon, Denfip, Haas, Mahone, McBirney, and Salisbury, but the man who answered the phone when I called turned out to be from the World War II generation and knew no one with his name who'd been in the Marines. A few months later, I learned that the man I was looking for had applied for veterans' benefits, but had initially done so prior to July 1972, so his claim number was not his social security number, and he never answered the letter forwarded to him by the VA.

From NPRC records I received in October 1995, I learned that Schrenker was born in Baltimore, Maryland, on September 3, 1946. Prior to his enlistment, he worked as a stock boy in a grocery store. He graduated from high school in 1966. After boot camp, where he failed to qualify on the rifle range, and basic infantry training, he received additional training as a communications wireman (2511) at Camp Pendleton, California, before being assigned to the Communications Company of Headquarters Battalion, 5th Marine Division, also at Pendleton, from December 1966 to July 1967.

Schrenker was reassigned to Vietnam in August 1967, serving there until September 1968, first with the Communications Company of Headquarters Battalion, 3rd Marine Division, then with Headquarters & Support Company, 3rd Battalion, 4th Marines. On May 16, 1968, in the vicinity of Khe Sanh, he sustained shrapnel wounds to the head, right arm, and back. Upon completion of his tour in Vietnam, he was assigned to Marine Air Base Squadron 31, Marine Air Group 31, Marine Corps Air Station, Beaufort, South Carolina, where he served from October 1968 until his release from active duty in February 1970.

Schrenker received promotion to private first class in October 1966, to lance corporal in January 1968, to corporal in June 1968, and finally to sergeant in June 1969. In addition to the Purple Heart Medal for wounds received in action, his decorations include the Combat Action Ribbon, a Presidential Unit Citation, and the Good Conduct, National Defense Service, Vietnam Service, and Vietnam Campaign Medals.

Since I now knew that Schrenker had come from Baltimore, and by then had a directory of my own, I checked and found a listing in Baltimore for George T. Schrenker. I wrote to that address, but got no reply, so I called on February 9, 1996. I got an answering machine, but later that day I received a call from Schrenker's son, George T., Jr., who provided the following information:

Schrenker still lives in Baltimore, but is presently 100 percent disabled, having been diagnosed by VA doctors as paranoid schizophrenic. He was married for a number of years, but is now divorced. In addition to his son, he also has a daughter. He used to live with his brother, but since his brother died, he has been living alone. His affairs are handled mostly by others, including his son.

According to George, Jr., Schrenker's daughter has a learning disability, which her brother believes may be Agent Orange–related, but her father has never done any of the paperwork to get possible compensation for her, saying only, "It's in the Bible."

"I have to warn you," said George, Jr., "he talks like that." The younger Schrenker says his father has never talked to him about Vietnam or the Marines, but does worry that his son, who is in the National Guard, might be called up and sent away.

George, Jr., gave me his father's telephone number, but cautioned me that I was not likely to have much luck talking to his father. I then called George, Sr., but before I'd gotten two sentences into explaining who I was and why I was calling, Schrenker said, "I have to go now. God bless you," and hung up.

James Schroeder

I had no luck finding Schroeder by any of the methods available to me. His name did not appear on the Myers list, and though he filed a claim for veterans' benefits, the letter the VA forwarded to him came back undeliverable. Records received from NPRC in September 1995 indicate that he was born on February 19, 1948, and was living in Philadelphia, Pennsylvania, at the time of his enlistment. After boot camp and basic infantry training, he received additional training as an admin man (0141) at the Basic Personnel Administration School back at Parris Island.

From November 1966 until September 1967, he served with Headquarters & Headquarters Squadron, Marine Air Training Center, Naval Air Station, Glenview, Illinois. From November 1967 until November 1968, he served in Vietnam with Headquarters & Support Company, Headquarters & Support Battalion, 1st Force Service Regiment, Force Logistics Command. From December 1968 until his release from active duty in June 1970, he served with Company A, Headquarters Battalion, Headquarters Marine Corps, Arlington, Virginia.

Schroeder achieved the rank of sergeant in June 1969. His decorations include the Good Conduct, National Defense Service, Vietnam Service and Vietnam Campaign Medals.

Michael V. Shepherd

Fifteen Michael Shepherds showed up on the Myers list. In response to my initial search letter, two replied that they were not the man for whom I was looking; none of the others responded. The VA could find no record that Shepherd ever filed a claim for veterans' benefits. Records I received from NPRC in September 1995 gave neither a place of birth nor a place of enlistment, though I did learn from those records that Shepherd dropped out of high school in 1966 during his senior year. After boot camp and basic infantry training, he received additional training as a combat engineer (1371) at the Marine Corps Engineering School, Camp Lejeune, North Carolina.

From November 1966 until December 1967, he served with Company D, 13th Engineering Battalion, 5th Marine Division, Camp Pendleton, California. In May 1967 he underwent additional training at the Naval Air Station in San Diego, after which his military occupational specialty was changed to atomic demolitions technician (1372). In December 1967 he was transferred from Company D to Company A of the 13th Engineering Battalion, where he remained until his release from active duty in June 1968. He received promotion to private first class in October 1966, to lance corporal in April 1967, and finally to corporal in March 1968, and was awarded the National Defense Service Medal.

Gerard G. Sirois

Aroostook County, Maine, is about as far north as you can go in the United States without leaving the contiguous Lower Forty-eight. Large portions of the Canadian provinces of New Brunswick, Quebec, and Ontario actually lie south of Aroostook County. But the county is not a howling wilderness; though forests and wildlife abound, small towns and villages dot the landscape, and much of the land itself has long since been cleared and is actively farmed. The geography consists of broad, flat, rolling hills, and the horizons are vast and expansive.

Most of the people in Aroostook County came originally not from the British colonies to the south but rather from the north, the descendants of French explorers and settlers who entered the heart of North America three hundred years ago by way of the Saint Lawrence and Saint John Rivers. Even today, the French language is nearly as prevalent as English, and many people don't even begin to speak English until they start school. Northern Maine is a bilingual culture, comfortable with it, and proud of it.

If you're driving on U.S. Route 1, only a two-lane road in Aroostook County, you must constantly be on the lookout for moose. If you hit a moose at fifty or sixty miles an hour, the collision will destroy your car and probably kill you. Moose are big animals. The danger is greatest in the early morning and early evening, when the light plays tricks, but if you are both lucky and sharp-eyed, these are also the times you just might spot a moose feeding in a beaver pond beside the highway.

Standing up to its belly in water, the moose will drop its whole head beneath the surface and graze on what grows on the bottom, coming up

Lance Corporal Gerard G. Sirois getting ready to chow down on a meal of C-rations, Vietnam, 1967.

for air every once in a while, water dripping from its long droopy snout, cascading from its antlers. If you have parked on the shoulder of the road to watch, it will turn its head and stare at you as it chews, but, deciding you pose no threat, it will soon turn away again and plunge its head under the water for another mouthful of food.

Only a few hundred yards north of just such a beaver pond between Caribou and Madawaska, the last town on Route 1 before you cross the Saint John River into Edmunston, New Brunswick, along the highway but up on a hill, stands a beautiful new wooden house with both the Stars 'n' Stripes and a black-and-white POW/MIA flag flying from the balcony. The whole first floor is a garage; the second floor a living area. There are multiple windows on all four sides, with only one stairway leading up to the living quarters, and that reachable only after first entering the garage.

"It's a guard tower," says Gerard Sirois. "Nobody's going to sneak up on me." The house took Sirois two years to build. He designed it himself, did most of the work himself, and is proud of his achievement. "I'm

Gerard Sirois riding in the back seat of a convertible through Madawaska, Maine, during the Sirois-DuPlessis family reunion in 1991. The reunion, of which Sirois was the chairman, brought together 1,100 people from fifteen states and five Canadian provinces. (Because of a shoulder injury, Sirois's left arm is in a sling.)

a jack-of-all-trades," he says. "I'll try anything. Nothing is impossible to me." He's now in the process of landscaping the hillside and yard.

The property is just down Route 1 from the family farm near Saint David on which Sirois grew up. His father was a second-generation farmer who grew potatoes and oats on ninety acres, along with a few cows, pigs, and chickens. And of course the whole family pitched in because that's what you do on a family farm. Still, Sirois found time to run on the cross-country team his last two years at Madawaska High School and to take joy rides across the river into Canada to buy beer with his cousin, who had a car. On graduating in 1966, Sirois joined the Marines with seven other Madawaska buddies, only one of whom, Gaetan Pelletier, also ended up in Platoon 1005.

It was through Pelletier that I located Sirois. Pelletier hadn't seen Sirois for many years, but said he still knew people in northern Maine who might be able to locate him. A week and a half later, on March 29, 1996, Pelletier called with Sirois's phone number. When I reached Sirois that day, he told me he'd gotten several letters from me (I'd been sending letters to various people named Sirois through the Myers list, the VA, and my own phone list for several years), but hadn't responded because he figured I'd either find him on my own or I wouldn't. "I learned my lesson," he said. "I don't volunteer anymore."

And like a number of the other men, Sirois volunteered little in that first telephone conversation, so I was more than a little apprehensive when I went to visit him on June 16, 1997, but he turned out to be a kind and thoughtful host. During the two days and two nights I spent with him, he took me moose watching in the mornings and evenings, cooked me mooseburgers for lunch, and gave me a tour of northern Maine and southern New Brunswick that included the spectacular Grand Falls of the Saint John River, the eerie emptiness of the now-abandoned Loring Air Force Base, the family farm where he grew up (no longer in the family), and the Saint John Valley Vietnam Veterans Memorial in Madawaska.

The monument is a statue of a grunt—an infantryman—carrying an M-60 machine gun, the weapon Sirois carried in Vietnam. The base of the statue holds the names of the dead from the Saint John Valley, while the bricks of the walkway around it bear the names of those who helped to pay for the memorial. One brick reads, "G. G. Sirois 1/7 Mar. 12.66–8.68." A plaque on the monument reads, "This memorial is dedicated to the loved ones of Vietnam conflict veterans who have been directly affected by psychiatric impairment and chemical agents used by the U.S. government in Vietnam."

Sirois himself is highly critical of the Vietnam War and the government that sent him to fight it, but his greatest wrath is reserved for Marine boot camp, and for Drill Instructor Evans in particular. The moment the bus that brought Sirois and the other recruits to Parris Island pulled up to the receiving barracks, he says, "all hell broke loose. That's when I realized I'd made a big mistake. And it didn't get any better."

Like many people in northern Maine, Sirois grew up speaking French. The only times he ever spoke English were in school, and even then, though teachers were supposed to require students to speak English, the rule was only loosely followed. By the time he graduated from high school, though he could understand English well enough, he could speak it only slowly and with difficulty.

This had never presented any problem in Aroostook County. "I was under the impression, heck, there'd be no need to be able to speak English. That's why when I hit boot camp, it was a rude awakening. The physical part wasn't so bad because of the farm work and cross country," says Sirois, who was and is a strapping six feet plus, "but the harassment was a nightmare." Sergeant T. W. Evans rode Sirois especially hard, "dumb Canuck" being the kindest thing Evans ever called Sirois. "He had something out for me from the first day," says Sirois. "Oliver was a fair individual. He had a job to do and he did it. Evans, that motherfucker, was on my ass from Day One. I looked for him the whole time I was in Vietnam. I had a bullet for him. You know how it was over there. You could take care of someone and make it look okay."

Still, he concedes, "boot camp was a good life experience for me. I'm not a quitter. You can kick me in the teeth, but I'll come back at you. That's one thing the Marines instilled in me. I'm not a quitter."

Sirois enlisted in the Marines, he says, because his recruiter promised him training as a heavy equipment operator, but instead he was trained as a machine gunner (0331) and found himself in Vietnam before the end of 1966 with A Company, 1st Battalion, 7th Marines. At first he didn't question U.S. policy in Vietnam, but after five or six months, he began to have second thoughts.

"The thing that sticks in my mind," he explains, "is the bullshit you had to go through. If you saw the enemy, you had to call it in to company, they called it in to battalion, and so on. By the time they figured out what to do, the VC were long gone." It also disturbed him that "when civilians got killed, no problem, just stick a chicom [Chinese communist] grenade on 'em, or an AK [AK-47 assault rifle], they became VC. The only time we got in trouble was when we killed a water buffalo—and we only killed it because it was charging us. Those buffalo didn't like our smell. When we went into villages," he says, "we would grab the village head and make him drink the well water before we would drink it. He drank whether he was thirsty or not."

Sirois discovered to his surprise that many older Vietnamese spoke French, and because of this he learned something even more astonishing. "We thought we were big, bad, and mean when we got there, but we were ill prepared. They'd been fighting the French for years before we got there. When we'd get one [kill a VC], we'd celebrate like crazy—cut their ears off, drop the ace of spades on 'em—but they always knew where we were. They were incredible people. I admired them. They were smart. What's garbage to us was a gold mine to them. They could make a single-shot rifle from a trip flare. If the Vietnamese had had the resources we had, they'd have licked us twice over. I shouldn't even be here. There's so many times I nearly stepped on a Bouncing Betty. Or the guy in front of me gets it. The guy behind me."

Still, when his thirteen-month tour was up, he extended for another six months, even though he had to extend his two-year enlistment by two months, because he didn't want to go to Camp Lejeune, North Carolina. "I knew with my attitude I'd wind up in jail," he explains. "If I'm gonna play games, I might as well stay here and play games. I knew if I extended, I'd get put in the rear with the gear and the beer."

By this time a corporal, Sirois was transferred to Headquarters & Support Company, where his duties included keeping the club stocked with beer and soda, and supplying both the battalion's commanding officer and sergeant major with hard alcohol. "They didn't ask me how I got stuff," he says. "The wheeling and dealing was up to me. I got pretty good at it. You scratch my back, I'll scratch yours."

Released from active duty in August 1968, Sirois returned to Maine and got a job with Fraser Paper Company in Madawaska. "I did anything and everything," he says. "Cleaning foils in the paper mill—that was a dirty job. Then I was sixth man on the paper machine, lowest man on the crew, lots of grunt work."

But things did not go well. He was busted for underage drinking. He got hassled in bars when his hair was short, and hassled by a different crowd when he let his hair grow long. He recalls one night when he decked a father and son, each with one punch, because they were taunting him about his long hair. He was drinking heavily, on and off the job, and taking whatever other drugs came his way. He knew his days at the paper mill were numbered. "I was not a team player," he says. "There was no way I was going to work there for a lifetime. That's when I started thinking about going back in the service. Whichever branch gave me the best deal, that's the one I'd go in."

In July 1971, Sirois enlisted in the Air Force, which took him back at his old grade of E4 and trained him as an asphalt technician. Over the next eighteen years, he was stationed successively at Loring Air Force Base, Maine; Ie Shima, Okinawa; Norton AFB, California; Sembach, Germany; Barksdale AFB, Louisiana; and finally back at Loring. There were also temporary assignments to Guam and Saudi Arabia. In 1982, he was retrained for aircraft maintenance on KC-10 aerial refuelers, and during his last three years at Loring, he was given charge of a fleet of stepvans, de-icers, jeeps, and other vehicles worth over $1.5 million.

All through these years, however, Sirois's fortunes were mixed. He continued to drink heavily, becoming notorious for the number of cars he totaled while driving drunk. He was never reduced in rank, and even earned twenty-two decorations (some from the Marines, but most from the Air Force), including three Air Force Commendation Medals for exemplary performance of duty, one of which was awarded on the day of his retirement in 1989, but he received only two promotions in those eighteen years, achieving the rank of technical sergeant (E6). His first marriage in 1980, which produced a son, ended in acrimonious divorce seven years later, and a second marriage in 1989 also ended in divorce, though not so bitterly.

Six months after his retirement from the Air Force, Sirois returned to Loring, this time as a civilian doing seasonal snow removal, at least until Loring was permanently closed in 1994, taking whatever jobs he could find in the summers: golf course grounds crew, truck driver, grader operator, farm worker, gas pump jockey—"Wherever I could make a buck," he says. Most of these jobs he ended up quitting. "I never went looking for trouble," he says, "but I don't like people getting in my face."

Meanwhile, what began in 1989 as a disability claim with the Veterans Administration for lower-back problems grew to include disk deterioration in the neck, arthritis in the knees, and finally post-traumatic stress disorder. In January 1996, Sirois was awarded 100 percent disability. "I battled the VA for six and a half years," he says, "but I finally won." He can tell you horror story after horror story about the VA, and does so with a mixture of contempt and relish. He has spent time in in-patient programs for both PTSD and alcohol rehabilitation, but quit each in disgust before completing them. He says one psychiatrist told him everybody in Maine was stupid because they all got drafted or enlisted, bragging that in his whole medical school class of 380, no one ever served in the military. He says another counselor fell asleep while Sirois was talking to him, but when Sirois reported the incident, the only consequence was that Sirois got labeled a troublemaker.

"There are some good people at the VA," he says, "but there's a lot of dead wood." One of the better VA counselors introduced Sirois to a book called *PTSD: A Handbook for Clinicians,* edited by Tom Williams and published by Disabled American Veterans. "It was like reading my autobiography," he says. For the first time, how he'd been feeling and behaving for the past twenty-five years began to make sense to him. "It helped to explain a lot of things. The multiple car accidents, the drinking and driving, that's survivor's guilt. I realize today that my ill fortunes from Vietnam were playing against me all along." These days, he takes medication for PTSD and depression.

But if Sirois has had his difficulties over the years, he's certainly not a "trip-wire vet." He may own forty acres of Maine woods, but he's built his house right alongside the busiest highway in northern Maine, and his nearest neighbors are only a quarter of a mile away. "I do what I want to do when I want to do it," he says. He gets up early and goes to bed early. He watches TV, mostly movies, tinkers with various projects, and in the winter rides his snowmobile. Last winter, he put thirty-four hundred miles on it between December and March. His father is no longer living, but his mother and all three siblings live within thirty or forty miles of him—almost right next door by Aroostook County standards—and he sees them and his four nephews and three nieces regularly.

Indeed, the morning we stopped in for breakfast at the Lakeview Restaurant overlooking Long Lake near Saint Agatha we found his older sister Theresa and her daughter Tracy having breakfast with Theresa's sister-in-law. Sirois says he has only gotten to know his younger brother and sister since 1987 when he returned to northern Maine for good—they used to be afraid of him, he says; they were 10 and 12 when he came back from Vietnam, and he was not a friendly or approachable guy back then—but he and Theresa have always been close. "She's seen the worst of me," he says, "but she's always been there for me."

"He's a good man," Theresa says of her brother. "He's always been there for me. He's always been there for my kids. When we were growing up, we used to go at it like cats and dogs, but he's always been there for me. You didn't talk about what we used to do when we were kids, did you?" she says in mock horror, then laughs.

Later, back home, Sirois reflects again on the Vietnam War. He had at least three confirmed kills, he says, and he's always felt bad about it. When he was younger, Theresa got him to go talk to the nuns who had taught him in school, but he didn't buy their arguments. "'Thou shalt not kill,'" he says. "It doesn't say you can kill for your country. What were we doing in Vietnam? Nothing. It was all for nothing. Pointless. You learn in school, 'We the People,' but that's all bullshit. The politicians did what they wanted; they didn't care about the people.

"Just like this Desert Storm thing," he continues. "Now they admit there was chemicals over there. Well, no shit. We've known that for five years. What were we doing in Somalia? What are we doing in Bosnia? The U.S. just wants to be the tough guy." He flexes both biceps like a circus strongman.

And would he join the Marines again if he had it to do over? "Fuck, no," he says without a moment's hesitation. "I'd have crossed over the bridge at Edmunston and kept going north. Hell, the guys who did that got more of a welcome home than I did. If I'd have done that, I'd still have my mind intact. I wouldn't wake up at night in a cold sweat, hearing voices."

Kenneth E. Smith

I would love to have found Smith because the records I received from NPRC are by far the most intriguing—indeed, they are baffling—but trying to find Kenneth Smith is like trying to find John Green or Robert Johnson. Even after I learned in August 1996 that he'd come from somewhere around Baltimore, Maryland, there were still far too many Kenneth Smiths to try contacting them all, and although he had filed a claim for veterans' benefits, the letter forwarded by the VA came back undeliverable.

The NPRC records indicate that he was born on June 27, 1948, graduated from high school in 1966, and was sworn into the Marine Corps at Baltimore. After boot camp, where he earned a Rifle Marksman's Badge, and basic infantry training, Smith received additional training at the Marine Corps Engineering School, Camp Lejeune, North Carolina, before being assigned in November 1966 to Company C, 13th Engineering Battalion, 5th Marine Division, Camp Pendleton, California.

Here's where it gets puzzling. This period of his service ends on January 26, 1967. The record then resumes two years and two months later on April 8, 1969, with Smith undergoing the same basic infantry training he had completed two and a half years earlier, and with the same unit—2nd Infantry Training Battalion, 1st Infantry Training Regiment, Camp Lejeune, North Carolina—after which he was assigned to the Military Police & Guard Company, Headquarters & Support Battalion, also at Camp Lejeune, where he served until his release from active duty in April 1971.

There is no explanation for the long break in service between January 1967 and April 1969, but Smith did not receive his final discharge upon completion of the mandatory six-year total obligation every enlistment contact requires until August 1974, indicating that he received no credit for reserve service, either active or inactive, during his hiatus from active duty.

The record does indicate that Smith earned the rank of corporal, and received the National Defense Service Medal and a Meritorious Mast. As of 1971, he was living in Clear Spring, Maryland, and was married, with one daughter.

Stephen E. Sofian

One of the most difficult things about doing this book was having to let go of someone I'd worked so hard to find, having to recognize that I couldn't always get a man's story, even after I'd found him. Jerome Carter was one of those. So were Steven E. Dudley, Milligan, Robison, Schrenker and some others. Sofian was one of the hardest to let go of.

He hadn't shown up on the Myers list, but Rey Waters remembered that he came from Atlantic City, New Jersey, and Ben Myers had found another Sofian in Atlantic City, so I called on September 23, 1993. The man who answered started out suspicious and ended up hostile. When I explained who I was, he said Sofian wasn't there. When I asked when I might reach him, he said Sofian lived in Maine. When I asked how I might reach him, he said, "What do you want him for after all these years?" His tone of voice was belligerent. I explained for a second time, but he would give me no further information. When I asked if he would give Sofian my name and address, he said, "I'm not interested in that." Then he hung up.

But he'd said Sofian lived in Maine, so I called directory assistance, got a number in Brunswick, and reached Sofian on the first try. He said he'd moved to Maine only two months earlier, after spending many years in the Atlantic City area, and that I'd probably been talking to his brother. He'd told his family not to give out his phone number, but seemed irritated that they'd refused to pass my message on to him.

Sofian said he'd spent three years in the Marines, most of that time at the Marine helicopter base at New River, North Carolina, and used to come home on weekends with Alex Salisbury. After he got out, he worked with computers for twenty years with the Federal Aviation Administration, but had recently been "put out on the street," he said, as a result of what he called "reduction of force." He'd had a difficult time finding other work, but, needing twenty-five years for a government pension, he'd finally taken a pay cut and relocated to Maine to work for the Department of Defense at Naval Air Station Brunswick. "I don't know how I'm going to get used to the weather up here," he said. He mentioned also that he'd been married for sixteen years and had three grown stepchildren.

In March 1995 I wrote to Sofian hoping to arrange an interview in June when I came up to see Haas, Don Bowles, and the Blades family, but Sofian wrote back on April 4 that June would be a bad time for him, adding that it looked like the time would be awkward for quite a while. He explained that there'd been another round of reductions, and while he'd survived the cut, he was now on permanent graveyard shift with only Sundays off. He did say, however, that he would try to keep in contact with me so that maybe we could get together in the future.

Nine months later, on December 10, 1995, Sofian called to tell me he'd moved but was still in Brunswick. He began by saying only, "This is Steve," and it took me some few moments to realize who it was. He mentioned that his job situation was still not good, but didn't elaborate. Then he told me that he didn't remember much about boot camp. He'd joined on the Buddy Plan with another kid from New Jersey, and his parents and he had thought, "Oh, how nice, he'll have a buddy," but it turned out that he hardly saw the guy, never talked to him, and couldn't now even remember his name.

Sofian then told me about a staff noncommissioned officer he used to work for at New River who promised to promote him to corporal if he shaved off his moustache. Sofian shaved, got his promotion, then immediately grew his moustache back, but the staff NCO didn't get mad at him because the staff NCO believed in alien space ships—claiming to have seen them—and Sofian was the only one who would listen to his stories without making fun of him. "I never made fun of anyone in my whole life," Sofian said.

A few weeks later, I received a Christmas card signed, "Steve & Dolores Sofian," and a few weeks after that, Sofian called to ask for the address and phone number of his old Parris Island and New River buddy Salisbury. He said he was eager to talk to me and asked how soon I could get to Maine.

In October 1996 I received Sofian's records from NPRC, which indicated that Sofian was born on November 25, 1947. He graduated from high school and was living in Atlantic City, New Jersey, at the time of his enlistment. After boot camp and basic infantry training, he received additional training as an admin man (0141) at the Basic Administration School at Parris Island.

From October 1966 until June 1968, Sofian served with Marine Heavy Helicopter Squadron 461, Marine Aircraft Group 26, at Marine Corps Air Facility, New River, North Carolina. During this time, he returned to the admin school at Parris Island for additional training between January and March 1968.

In June 1968, he was transferred to Marine Medium Helicopter Squadron 264, MAG-26, also at New River, with whom he served until April 1969. During part of this time, the squadron was deployed aboard ship in the Caribbean Sea. He spent his last two months with Marine Observation Group 1, MAG-26, still at New River, before being released from active duty with the rank of corporal in June 1969. His decorations include the Good Conduct and National Defense Service Medals.

Four months after his records arrived and eleven months after we'd last talked, I wrote, asking if I could visit in June on my way up to northern Maine to see Gerard Sirois. I followed up the letter with a telephone call on March 16, 1997, reaching his wife, who said rather brusquely that Sofian wasn't there.

When I explained who I was and why I was calling, she said they were going to be in New Jersey for the month of June. I said maybe I could come over to New Jersey to see him, since I lived in nearby Philadelphia. She said she wouldn't want to impose on the relatives with whom they'd be staying. I said we could go out to a coffee shop or something. She then said that her husband had nothing to say to me and I should take him off my list. When I said that the last time he'd called me, he seemed willing and even eager to talk, she said she wasn't going to explain the circumstances of that.

Uncannily, her demeanor almost identically paralleled that of Sofian's brother, with whom I had first spoken three and half years earlier: none too friendly to begin with, downright hostile by the end. It seemed to me time, and perhaps way past time, to let this one go.

Stephen T. Summerscales

Stephen Summerscales didn't have to join the Marines. Had he wanted to, he could have avoided the military altogether. Though living in Media, Pennsylvania, at the time of his enlistment, he was born in Toronto, where his father, William, British-born and Canadian-reared, was a Presbyterian minister. The family, which also included an older sister, subsequently moved to Vancouver, then to California, before coming to the Philadelphia area in 1960.

"Steven had dual citizenship," says William Summerscales, now a professor emeritus at Teachers College, Columbia University. "He could have chosen to become a Canadian at age eighteen, and legally avoided military service. I don't know why, but for some reason he wanted to join

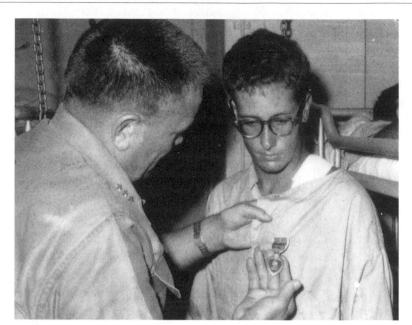

Lance Corporal Stephen Summerscales receiving his second Purple Heart Medal from the commanding general of the 3rd Marine Amphibious Force on board the hospital ship Repose, *May 1967.*

the Marines." He left for Parris Island on June 17, 1966, one day after graduating from Penncrest High School. "Boot camp was a real challenge for him," says Professor Summerscales.

A challenge he thrived on. In his first letter home, he wrote, "I really love the food down here. It has 5000 calories a day, and I eat them all. We have 20 minutes to eat and every one of those minutes I'm eating! The Drill Instructors are real strict, [but] they are very intelligent, and you can learn a lot from them."

One month later, he wrote, "We have been seeing movies on Communism and Viet Nam lately—I guess they are trying to make us want to go over there, even though they tell us how bad it is. I think all of us will go over sooner or later—I hope sooner for me. You get more pay and also advancement is better."

Still later he wrote, "I am getting to love the Marine Corps very much. . . . I will really miss my D.I.'s when I get out [of Parris Island]. . . . They can be mean, but they are just trying to teach us to watch out for ourselves once we leave here."

"He came home a rootin', tootin' Marine," says his father. "He thought the Marine Corps was the greatest." With an MOS of 0331, machine gunner, he reported to Camp Pendleton for staging, and found himself in Vietnam with the 4th Marines, 3rd Marine Division, less than six months after he'd enlisted. Excerpts from his letters home tell their own story:

December 3, 1966: "These guys [in my unit] tell you how they treat the V.C. and it makes you sick. Some of these Marines are really sick in the head. They enjoy telling about what they do in the battlefield. I can really understand why so many Far Easterners despise the Americans."

February 26, 1967: "We received sniper fire occasionally. Usually if we were fired upon by a village, we would burn it down since all the people were classified as 'unfriendly' or V.C. sympathizers. . . . But I still don't like the idea of some Marines killing every creature that moves after dark.

Corporal Stephen T. Summerscales (prone) *with his M-60 machine gun and assistant gunner, Vietnam, 1967.*

Stephen Summerscales, circa 1972.

I know when the U.S. bombs certain targets, they kill many innocent people, young and old alike."

March 2: "They bombed [our area] with jets. Afterwards, we went into the villages to see what was left . . . and burned everything in sight. In my opinion, we are wasting men and material on this war. These people don't want our help and we don't want to be here."

April 14: "Last night I was told I owe the government $158. . . . We are here risking our lives, living under conditions barely fit for an animal at times and then they tell you that *you owe* Uncle Sam money—Bull! I'm fed up with these Government people!"

April 22: "Today we went on a sweep and got hit. Two tanks were put out of action. I shot my gun, but it had many malfunctions. I don't think I've ever been more scared. . . . I was hit by a small piece of shrapnel. It barely cut the skin, but they still are putting me in for a Purple Heart. I really feel bad about it because some get wounded so badly and they get the same thing; others die for it."

April 30: "This place is really getting on my nerves. There's nobody to tell your problems to and so you always think about them. I think for the first time I regret joining."

May 8 [from a hospital in Da Nang]: "At quarter to three last night [the North Vietnamese] started mortaring and dropping artillery onto Con Thien. [Then] they started attacking. I was hit by a dart from a beehive round from one of our own tanks. . . . About 8 a.m. it was over and I went over to get medical aid. The squad my gun was attached to were either all dead or wounded. . . . I walked over to where the dead were and found, shocking, that some of my best friends were dead. . . . I never want to go back to the DMZ, but I know I will. I want to live so much."

May 10 [from the hospital ship *Repose,* where Summerscales spent a month recuperating]: "Today I really had a shock. One of my good friends was in the same ward as me, and I couldn't even recognize him! His whole face is just one big red sore with most of his hair gone. Also, he has a lot of shrapnel in both legs. . . . Both hands were burned too. There are more of my friends on this ship, but after seeing Sanders like that and knowing he isn't the worst, I don't want to see them. . . . A three-star general awarded [a second Purple Heart] to me. He said we killed 200 Commies at Con Thien that night and did a good job, but that still doesn't bring back my dead friends."

May 27: "Those people that really get under my skin are the protest marchers, but I'll probably be the biggest protester when I come home, so why complain?"

July 23 [back in the field]: "The only thing that stands out in my mind is making it back to the World."

July 29: "I don't care where we go [in Vietnam] as long as I can see the sun rise every morning and go down in the evening."

October 17: "We just finished an operation yesterday . . . We were on the way back a couple of times and we got fired on. They said to keep going and not fire back. Hell, you spend 13 months looking for the gooks and then you run away! . . . This war . . . is so backwards it's pitiful. I wonder if they blundered so much in World War II."

October 20: "If I possessed the ability to write, I could make a novel out of my experiences over here."

November 10: "I never did get my [in-country] R&R because of the operation. It was an 'abortion' and was run all wrong. A lot of Marines were killed and wounded senselessly."

November 22: "It's going to be odd coming home with probably a whole new outlook on life. I know you won't approve of everything I do and say, but I'm still your son."

What that new outlook would be did not become apparent for several more years. Summerscales, with nearly eighteen months still to serve on his enlistment, was sent to Camp Lejeune. There he managed to get assigned as a clerk because, as he'd written back in July, "I don't feel like being in Camp Lejeune as a 'grunt.' I think I would go crazy playing 'war games' with other Marines."

When Summerscales was separated from active duty in April 1969, he immediately went to Florida, where he got a job as a lifeguard at Deerfield Beach. "Do you want to be a lifeguard all your life?" Professor Summerscales recalls asking him as the summer advanced. Finally, in September, Summerscales returned to his mother's home in Media (his parents, separated since 1962, divorced in 1969); he enrolled at Delaware County Community College and got a part-time job at the local post office.

"He made the Dean's List and seemed to be doing okay," says Professor Summerscales. But he wanted time off work at Christmas, and the post office wouldn't give it to him, so he quit. "There was also some sort of incident involving LSD," says Professor Summerscales, though he does not know the details.

Summerscales continued to live with his mother until August 1970 when she found marijuana in the basement. "Steve was one of those who thought pot should be legalized," says Professor Summerscales. Soon afterwards, Summerscales moved to New York City, where his father, now remarried and an administrator at Teachers College, was living. He secured a room in Reldnas Hall, a student apartment building owned by Teachers College, and enrolled in Columbia's General Studies program.

Among the courses he took was creative writing. "He was determined to write about Vietnam," says Professor Summerscales, "but he was not succeeding in his efforts. It was a frustrating experience for him."

Meanwhile, in early winter 1971, Summerscales "got into some kind of trouble at Reldnas," says his father. "He was doing pot or whatever, I don't know." He left Reldnas and returned to Media, but soon quarreled with his mother again about marijuana, and once more returned to New York. He wanted to buy a motor launch from a family friend, and live on it with his father and stepmother Elpida, and when Professor Summerscales would not co-sign for a loan to buy the boat, he became very angry. Eventually he took a small room at John Jay College.

About this time, in early April 1971, Summerscales told his father about a Filipina woman he had met, announcing that he was going to become a father. Soon afterwards he disappeared for a few days, then Professor Summerscales got a call from a doctor who said that his son was in the hospital recovering from some bad LSD. "He's lucky to be alive," the doctor told the professor.

"From there on it got worse," says Professor Summerscales. "There were times when he was perfectly reasonable and a delight to be with and times when he seemed to be off the deep end."

In late May 1971, Summerscales was detained by the New Jersey State Police in East New Brunswick for hitchhiking and suspicion of auto theft. Just as things were almost cleared up and he was about to be released, he complained about having his rights violated, and according to a friend who was with him, the police first knocked him down, then arrested him, charging him with disorderly conduct. "The charges were dropped ten months later," says Professor Summerscales, but "the incident added to the resentment Stephen was already feeling about authority."

That June, Summerscales went back to the Philadelphia area, then hitchhiked to California. He was gone most of the summer, but in September reappeared in New York and, with help from his father, found an apartment on 122nd Street and once again enrolled in the General Studies program. "As the year ended," says Professor Summerscales, "I was increasingly concerned about the fluctuations and unpredictability of his behavior."

Summerscales's daughter was born in November 1971, but he did not mention this to his father until well into the spring of 1972. Then in June, without his father's knowledge, he took a part-time job in the office of Institutional Development at Teachers College, where his father was the director. Within days his immediate supervisor found his work unsatisfactory—no work was getting done at all—and fired him.

When confronted by his father, Summerscales explained that the first set of alumni records he was sent to retrieve bore the same name as the first friend of his who had died in Vietnam. "I suggested that such psychic pain might indicate a need for some counseling and offered to get him help," says Professor Summerscales, "but he made no decision at that time.

"One of the great things we had together was playing squash," he continues. "We tried to play several times a week, but one day he called to cancel our squash appointment. 'I need to see you,' he said." They talked about Vietnam all that afternoon, then resumed the conversation that evening.

According to Professor Summerscales, his son told him of seeing Viet Cong prisoners taken up in helicopters and tossed out at one hundred feet to induce other prisoners to talk; of checking villages after air strikes and finding dead elderly women and children; of how when he'd come home and tried to explain to his high school friends about the horrors he'd seen, they wouldn't believe him, accusing him of exaggeration.

Professor Summerscales persuaded his son to spend the night on the couch. "He had terrible nightmares that night," Professor Summerscales says. "He kept calling out to me in a child's voice. I spent most of the night sitting beside him. At one point he asked me, 'Is the war still going on?' I was beside myself. I knew he was in real trouble."

Professor Summerscales persuaded his son to accompany him to Saint Luke's Hospital in the morning, and after consultations with a doctor, Summerscales agreed to remain at the hospital for observation. "It was the most poignant moment of my life," says Professor Summerscales. "Steve was going up the steps, and he turned back to me at the landing and put his arms around me. 'Dad,' he said, 'there is one thing I want you to know, whatever happens, and that is I love you.'"

Summerscales remained at Saint Luke's for six weeks, then was released to an outpatient group therapy program. He also got a job with a radio and television repair service. He was soon fired from the job, however, and was released from the therapy program for being in possession of marijuana.

Summerscales next applied to be a cab driver. "During the licensing process, they questioned his citizenship," says Professor Summerscales. "Image that. He served in 'Nam, spent three years in the Marines, and they questioned his citizenship. It's another example of the troubles he had with authority.

"Things went on like that until the following March," Professor Summerscales continues. "He had good days and bad days. I was trying to help him out financially as well as I could." One Friday night in late March 1973, Summerscales came to his father and stepmother's apartment for dinner, as he often did; he complained of not feeling well, but when Elpida called the next day, he explained the he'd only been sick to his stomach and assured her he felt okay.

That Monday morning, Summerscales did not show up for a scheduled squash game with his father, nor did he answer his telephone, but that wasn't unusual because he often took off unannounced for a few days at a time. It was not until Wednesday that Professor Summerscales learned his son had jumped from the roof of his apartment building three days earlier. An autopsy revealed neither drugs nor alcohol in his system.

A note in his typewriter said, "What are your voices that are calling me? I'm coming, sweet Jesus."

"If the note in the typewriter is his, and I have to assume it is," says Professor Summerscales, "then he decided that death was better than the pain. It's strange comfort, and small comfort, but I'm thankful that his destructive urges didn't get directed at others. You know, some men did that. You know about PTSD, don't you?"

I do know about PTSD, and though I know there's probably nothing I could have done had I known about PTSD back then, it seems to me at least a modest irony that all through the years Summerscales was wrestling with his demons, I was only three miles away from his mother's home in Media, wrestling with my own demons at Swarthmore College, where I often felt—as I wrote in *Passing Time*—like "a freak in a carnival sideshow." I think I can understand in some small measure what he must have been going through.

And because I am a parent now myself, I can only too well imagine how terrible it must be to bury a child, and how very much more so when death is self-inflicted.

When I first went looking for Summerscales, of course, I didn't know he was dead. He died four and a half years after he returned home from Vietnam, and his name does not appear on the Vietnam Veterans Memorial, but the name Stephen Summerscale—with no middle initial and without the last "s"—turned up on the Myers list. Since the listing was for Media, not far from Philadelphia, I called, and the woman who answered turned out to be his mother.

I told her who I was and who I was looking for. She told me briefly what had happened to her son. Talk about an awkward moment. I didn't have the heart to ask her why her son's name was still listed in the phone book after twenty years, and she didn't have the heart to go through an interview, but she passed my name and number on to her former husband, and though it wasn't easy for him either, he and I spent a long afternoon together in his office at Teachers College on November 4, 1994.

Summerscales is survived by his father; his mother, Ruth, a retired elementary school teacher; his sister, Marjorie (one of her four children is named Stephen after his uncle); and his daughter, Jean Marie, who graduated from Marymount College in 1994, and who has no memory of her father. At the interment service, Professor Summerscales read Section III of W. H. Auden's poem "In Memory of W. B. Yeats," altering the words to suit the occasion of his son's death:

Earth, receive another guest:
Stephen now is laid to rest.

The gravestone itself reads:

STEPHEN T SUMMERSCALES
PENNSYLVANIA
CPL U S MARINE CORPS
VIETNAM
JAN 9 1948 MAR 25 1973

Johnny S. Taormina

I got Taormina's social security number through the VA claim system and his address from the subsequent trace done by MIE, Inc., and wrote to him, receiving a brief but cordial reply dated March 15, 1994. Based on this and the records I received from NPRC in April 1996, I learned that Taormina was born on September 6, 1947, in Centreville, Alabama, and is a high school graduate. He qualified as a Marksman on the rifle range at Parris Island. After boot camp and basic infantry training, he was assigned to the Student Company, Schools Battalion, at Camp Pendleton, California, in October and November 1966.

Taormina served in Vietnam from December 1966 to January 1968, first with 3rd 8" Howitzer Battery, 11th Marines, then with 3rd 155mm Gun Battery, also 11th Marines, and finally again with 3rd 8" Howitzers.

Back in the U.S., he spent January and February 1968 assigned to the Marine Aviation Detachment, Naval Air Base Training Command, Pensacola, Florida, then spent the remainder of his time in the Corps serving successively with Company A, 8th Motor Transport Battalion, Force Troops, Fleet Marine Force Atlantic; Headquarters & Support Company, 1st Battalion, 6th Marines; and then again with Company A, 8th Motor T. He was released from active duty in June 1969 with the rank of sergeant. His decorations include a Presidential Unit Citation, and the Good Conduct, National Defense Service, Vietnam Service, and Vietnam Campaign Medals.

Taormina still lives in his hometown of Centreville, Alabama, with his wife and two children. He wrote that it was a pleasant surprise to hear from me, signing his letter "Sam Taormina" with "Johnny S. Taormina" written in parentheses below that.

Joseph B. Taylor

"When I enlisted in the Marines," says Joe Taylor, "Vietnam didn't mean a thing to me. It might as well have been Lower Slabovia. Everybody else wanted to be John Wayne. I wanted to be my grandfather."

Taylor's grandfather was Sergeant Major Clarence Boyd Smith, a veteran of thirty-seven years in the Corps. Taylor grew up with a photograph of his grandfather, taken in China, in which Sergeant Major Smith is sitting in a chair with his arms and legs crossed, a Marine private standing on either side of him. "He looked like somebody," Taylor says. "My other relatives treated him like the black sheep because he joined the Marines, but I always thought he was the only family member who ever did anything with his life."

Taylor's parents separated before he was born, and soon divorced, so he never knew his father. Growing up in Pittsburgh, Taylor's life revolved around sports. He played football and volleyball for South Side High School, and as sports editor for the school newspaper, he covered

Lance Corporal Joseph B. Taylor of Company D, 1st Battalion, 7th Marines, Vietnam, 1968. The weapon he is holding is a .45 caliber pistol.

Left to right: *Joe Taylor, son Joe, Jr., and wife Becky at Joe, Jr.'s graduation from high school, 1993.*

all the other teams the school fielded. But the day after he graduated in 1966, he left for Parris Island to become a Marine like his grandfather.

To his chagrin, he was relegated to the "Fat Body Platoon" on his arrival. "Fat Bodies" were allowed to eat nothing but skim milk, dry cereal, salad, and meat. "No salt, not even ketchup or mustard," he says. "I got so used to that diet that even after [Staff Sergeant] Oliver let me off it, I still didn't eat a normal meal until the night before graduation."

During an interview to help determine his military occupational specialty, Taylor recalls, "I told this WM [woman Marine] that I'd written for the school newspaper. She asked me the chemical composition of ink, and other questions I couldn't answer, so they made me a grunt. I was happy about being an 0311 [rifleman]. I was going to be a real Marine."

Taylor's first assignment after training was with 2nd Battalion, 8th Marines, based at Camp Lejeune. Not until July 1967 did he receive orders to Vietnam, ending up with Company D, 1st Battalion, 7th Marines. "Our regimental CO greeted the new arrivals with a copy of the

Landing Party Manual," says Taylor. "First he tore out all the pages; then he held up the two covers and said, 'This is what applies to Vietnam.'"

One-Seven was located around Hill 55, west of Da Nang and just north of what the Americans called "Dodge City," a particularly hostile area. When Taylor first arrived, his platoon had only eleven men. As a lance corporal he served as a squad leader; as a corporal he served as a platoon sergeant. After a night ambush during which Taylor's patrol killed five women who worked at the battalion's laundry and barbershop—and captured two SKS carbines, an AK-47, and two 9mm pistols—Taylor's company commander ordered him to take rest-and-recreation leave. "'You're getting sick, Taylor,' he told me. 'You're enjoying this too much.' He gave me five hundred dollars in greenbacks and ordered me to leave immediately."

Taylor earned his first Purple Heart when he got shot in the chest during a firefight. He thought he'd crashed into a tree while diving for cover, he says, until a corpsman put a casualty tag on him after the shooting stopped. "You've been hit, stupid," he remembers the corpsman saying. At a hospital in the rear, doctors told him he'd have to wait two weeks to have the bullet removed from his armpit, but he didn't feel like waiting, so he checked himself out of the hospital and returned to the field. (He finally had the bullet removed at a Veterans Administration hospital in 1970.)

One week later, on July 2, 1968, Taylor collected his second Purple Heart, along with a ticket back to the World, when an enemy mortar round dropped into his fighting hole. It blew off everything he was wearing except his shorts, boots, and glasses, and left shrapnel in his head, arms, legs, and torso. Within days, he ended up at Bethesda Naval Hospital in suburban Washington, D.C.

Soon after his arrival, he was awakened one morning by a "good-looking redheaded WM corporal," he says. "I thought I'd died and gone to heaven," but she explained that she was the liaison between Marine patients and the Navy staff. "She asked me if I needed anything," he says. "I looked her over slowly from toe to head and back—twice—then I said, 'That about does it.' She told me maybe I needed to talk to the first sergeant. I told her I didn't need any first sergeant; I was looking at what I needed."

Six weeks into his hospitalization, his medical officer ordered him to take ten days' special liberty to try to get adjusted. When Taylor asked him what he was supposed to get adjusted to, the doctor replied, "Go get laid so you'll stop bothering my nurses!" Shortly thereafter, he was released from the hospital and returned to light duty at Henderson Hall, Headquarters Marine Corps.

In December 1968, Taylor joined Company L, 3rd Battalion, 6th Marines, at Camp Lejeune, but in February 1969 he was transferred to Company F, 2nd Battalion, 8th Marines at Guantanamo Bay, Cuba, where he served as a sector noncommissioned officer. Guantanamo was experiencing severe moral, discipline, and race problems, and Taylor became part of a special group of Marines handpicked to help restore order.

Taylor was shocked by the situation he found. "I'd never run into Marines with a 'screw you' attitude," he says. "I was taught that a Marine did what a Marine was supposed to do. I could understand morale problems with the war and all. (My own feeling was, 'If we're not going to win it, we shouldn't be in it; this is wrong.' The really bad part was that I started agreeing with the protesters at home.) But not the race stuff; I couldn't understand that. How could you be in Vietnam together, both of you depending on each other, color doesn't mean anything, then you come home and suddenly color means something? I couldn't understand it."

(Taylor still can't understand it. He used to belong to the American Legion until the day a few years ago when he invited a black former Marine to his local post for a few drinks. Afterwards, other post members accused Taylor's friend of stealing some missing pool cues. "Where was he supposed to put them?" Taylor asks derisively. "In his pocket? They wouldn't have made those accusations if the man had been white." Taylor has never gone back.)

Taylor had enlisted for four years, but because of force reductions, he was released from active duty almost a year early. He returned home to Pittsburgh and took a job with the Pittsburgh & Erie Railroad. Laid off after just two months, he took another job with American Bridge Company, but was again laid off, this time after eighteen months. He took a third job with Dravo Shipbuilding, but was fired for punching out a supervisor. ("He kept poking me in the chest," Taylor explains. "I asked him to stop, but he said he was a supervisor and he could do whatever he wanted, so I punched him.")

Taylor looked for other work, but because he was a member of the steelworkers' union, nonunion employers wouldn't hire him, assuming he would quit as soon as a higher-paying union job became available. Meanwhile, Taylor had married Rebekah Blackman in 1970. Now he found himself unable to support the two of them, let alone start the family they both wanted, so in January 1972 he reenlisted in the Marines as a private first class.

Within months, because of Taylor's metalworking experience, his CO suggested that he transfer from the infantry to the engineers. He became a 1316, metalworker and welder, and was promoted to lance corporal, then to corporal, but at the end of his first two-year reenlistment his career officer suggested he transfer yet again, this time to the air wing, where promotions and advancement would be more rapid.

"I always thought 'wingies' weren't real Marines," Taylor says, "but he took me to [Marine Corps Air Facility] New River, and here were men with high-and-tight haircuts, squared away uniforms. They looked like real Marines. Then my company CO said, 'Find a better field,' and I thought, 'If the CO says so, that's what I'm going to do.' Of course," Taylor adds, laughing, "the career officer and my CO didn't tell me about twelve hours on and twelve off, eighteen hours on the flight line, stuff like that."

After six months' training at Millington, Tennessee (Naval Air Station Memphis), Taylor graduated first in his class as a 6042, aviation structural mechanic (later changed to 6142, helicopter structural mechanic), then spent the next five years in a succession of fixed wing and helicopter squadrons in California and Japan. Because so many of the men who worked for Taylor reenlisted, the CO of Marine Air Group 36 made Taylor the group career planner, and because Taylor was so effective in that capacity (Taylor's secret, he says: "Don't bullshit the men; tell them the truth"), he was sent to recruiters' school in San Diego.

After eight weeks of training, Taylor went home to Pittsburgh as a recruiter, and his first year went well. Then disaster struck. As Taylor tells it, he recruited a single man with a dependent daughter, which was approved by HQMC. Once at Parris Island, however, the new recruit told his drill instructors that he also had an illegitimate son, that he'd told Taylor about his son, and that Taylor had told him to tell no one else.

"I never knew about his son," Taylor insists. "He never told me. I had no motivation to recruit the kid fraudulently. I'd already made my quota for the month. He and his buddy were my sixth and seventh enlistments." But Taylor was charged with fraudulent enlistment, found guilty in an Article 15 proceeding, fined, and relieved of duty. A staff sergeant at the time, Taylor knew he would never receive another promotion (and he never did). "It was the only time in my entire time in the Corps that I felt the Marine Corps broke faith with me."

Taylor returned to duty with Marine Medium Helicopter Squadron

261, based at New River, North Carolina, first in the metal shop, later in maintenance control. The following year, 1981, the squadron embarked aboard the USS *Guam* for a routine Mediterranean cruise, but when the ship pulled in at Rota, Spain, they immediately began loading live ordnance and other war materials. The next morning, news broke that Israel had invaded Lebanon. The *Guam* headed straight to the eastern Mediterranean, spending four of the next six months off the coast of Beirut. The squadron was based aboard ship, but two helicopters remained ashore at all times, for medical evacuation and other duties, with crews rotating every four days.

The squadron returned to New River in late 1981, but in October 1983 embarked again for what the men thought was going to be another Mediterranean cruise. When he awoke on the first morning at sea, however, Taylor noticed the sun rising off the port side of the ship, indicating that the fleet was headed south, not east. Told they were just going to "show the flag" in the Caribbean, they did not learn their real mission until five hours before it began: Operation Urgent Fury, the invasion of Grenada.

The squadron itself was assigned to help evacuate American medical students from the island. "What we were told," Taylor says, "was: 'Go in and get them out; if you meet resistance, get rid of it.'" But resistance to the invasion force—mostly from Cuban engineers and Soviet advisors—was largely ineffectual, and though the squadron did lose two Cobras to hostile fire and a CH-46 to mechanical failure, evacuation of the medical school went smoothly. "The hard part for the grunts," says Taylor, "was that everybody rushed out and wanted to hug and kiss them."

From Grenada, the squadron sailed directly for the eastern Mediterranean again. Only after they were underway did they learn about the disaster that had occurred a week earlier in Beirut when a suicide bomber blew up a U.S. barracks, killing over 250 Marines. "Hell," Taylor says, "I think I knew half the staff NCOs in that barracks." He holds the secretaries of state and defense responsible for the bombing because, he says, "they tried to make the Marines ambassadors for the U.S. They didn't want us to look like a permanent occupation force, so we weren't allowed to dig in or carry live ammo."

He also faults then-Commandant P. X. Kelley. "He was a yes-man," Taylor says. "He should have put his career on the line for his Marines." But Taylor has only praise for Kelley's successor, Al Gray, a former enlisted man Taylor describes as "an old-fashioned kick-ass Marine." During that second cruise, Taylor says, Commandant Gray asked him what the men needed in Beirut. "I told him LAAWs [light anti-armor weapons], heavy weapons, sandbagged bunkers, things like that. The next day, we had all that stuff."

Taylor says the main difference between his first and second trips to Lebanon was that the men around him weren't young kids anymore, but rather seasoned young Marines. "Come showtime," he says, "those young Marines were good. They can call it the New Corps, but the New Corps is just as good as the Old Corps."

When the squadron returned to New River in 1984, Taylor was transferred from HMM-261 to Headquarters & Maintenance Squadron 26, where he became the MAG-26 aircraft material condition inspector. "I could ground an entire squadron for up to thirty days just like that," he says. "I was known as the prick headhunter by all the squadron COs."

He also became the hazardous materials disposal officer. "All those federal and state inspectors [from the Environmental Protection Agency and the Department of Environmental Resources] would come in hoping to nail your ass," he says. "They were harder on the military because they knew they had a captive audience. Civilian businesses could just move or close down. To be honest, though, the regulations were good. We worked with some dangerous materials. They really needed to be handled properly."

On December 31, 1988, Taylor retired from active duty, having served a total of twenty years and fifteen days. He and Becky and their two sons (Joe, Jr, born in 1973, and James Corbett, born in 1975) went home to Pittsburgh. Taylor took a job as a driver with Owens Transportation [subsequently bought by National School Bus Service, Inc.], eventually working his way up to his present position as safety supervisor responsible for on-the-road safety, accident investigation, Occupational Safety and Health Administration compliance, and liaison with the general public ("mostly parents," he says) and the school districts served by National.

In addition to these duties, Taylor is a state-certified school bus instructor, and for the past six years he's served as a judge for the vehicle pretrip safety inspection event at the Pittsburgh School Bus Road-e-o. He is also earning an associate's degree from International Correspondence Schools, upon completion of which he hopes to transfer to Robert Morris College, where his younger son is currently a sophomore marketing major (Joe, Jr. is the dairy manager for a local supermarket.)

I met Joe, Jr., and Becky during a long day I spent with Taylor on July 22, 1995. Taylor started me off that morning with the biggest omelet I've ever attempted to eat, at Jo Jo's, a local Pittsburgh family-run diner where he's clearly a regular. I managed to finish most of it before we went up to his row house in a working-class neighborhood of the city and talked for the rest of the morning and right on through the afternoon into the evening, when Becky finally insisted we stop and eat the dinner she'd made. Then we talked some more.

Looking back on his career, Taylor says, "There's a few things I'd do differently. I'd start working on my degree sooner. I'd have taken my family on an overseas tour of duty. Especially in Asia. It would have been a great opportunity to live in a foreign culture. But mostly I'd leave most things in place.

"Even Vietnam wasn't that bad some of the time. It was a beautiful place to be. Like we used to say, the only thing wrong with Vietnam was the war. Could we have won it? Damn straight we could have. Take out all the [North Vietnamese] heavy industry, shut down their ports so they couldn't get shipping in, blockade the entire coastline. But the will to win was not in the Congress, not in the Senate. What the U.S. lacked wasn't the tactics or the strategy, but the will to win."

Roosevelt Tharrington, Jr.

Roosevelt Tharrington was one of the last members of Platoon 1005 to receive orders to Vietnam, and he did not arrive there until March 25, 1968, more than twenty-one months after he'd joined the Marines. The next day he was assigned to Company B, 3rd Amphibious Tractor Battalion, 1st Marine Division. Eight days later, on April 3, Corporal Tharrington was dead, killed when the wrecker he was driving detonated a land mine while towing a disabled amphibious tractor in the vicinity of Da Nang. Not yet 21 years of age, he left behind a widow, the former Joyce Thompson; a three-year-old son, Baron Lee; a widowed mother; and a sister.

In a letter Tharrington's sister sent to me, she said that she keeps a picture of her brother on top of her television set, adding that he was so young when he died. She said that sometimes she goes to the cemetery where he's buried just to talk to him. She asked me if I could understand that.

The Vietnam Veterans Memorial Directory listed Tharrington's hometown as Durham, North Carolina, and though Ben Myers found no Tharringtons in Durham, he did find eleven of them elsewhere in North Carolina. None of them responded to my initial search letter in September 1993, but once I had my own directory, I found twenty more Tharringtons listed in Durham alone, and wrote to all of them, too. On March 16, 1995, I received the letter from Tharrington's sister, Annie Tharrington Harrington, whose mother had received one of my letters. A month later, on April 15, I got a telephone call from Tharrington's son, who said an aunt had received another of my letters and passed it on to his mother, who had given it to him. I had already received Tharrington's records from NPRC in February 1995.

Tharrington was born on December 3, 1947, in Brassfield, Granville County, North Carolina. His father, Roosevelt, Sr., was a Navy veteran of World War II and a sharecropper who grew tobacco. He died in February 1954, leaving his widow, Annie L., to raise the two children, Roosevelt, Jr., and Annie.

Tharrington graduated from Durham's Menick-Moore High School in 1966 and immediately joined the Marines. He was apparently the only member of Platoon 1005 who was already a father when he arrived at Parris Island. After boot camp and basic infantry training, Tharrington spent three months at Camp Pendleton, California, receiving training as a tracked vehicle repairman (2142) before being assigned in December 1966 to Headquarters & Support Company, 2nd Amphibious Tractor Battalion, at Camp Lejeune, North Carolina, where he remained until receiving his orders for Vietnam.

Corporal Tharrington was posthumously awarded the Purple Heart Medal for the wounds that killed him. By order of the Commandant of the Marine Corps, the medal was presented to his widow along with his National Defense Service, Vietnam Service, and Vietnam Campaign Medals. His widow and his mother were each also presented with Gold Star lapel buttons in his memory.

Tharrington's sister thanked me for caring enough to remember her brother and the other members of Platoon 1005, adding that she believes they deserve to be remembered also.

Tharrington is buried in Glennview Memorial Park in Durham. His widow (who never remarried), mother, and sister all still live in the Durham area, as do his two nephews. His son, married and with a child of his own, Baron Lee Tharrington, Jr., is a computer consultant living in Charlotte, North Carolina.

"I never really knew my father," Baron Tharrington said when we spoke. "I was only three when he was killed."

It's different, of course, for Tharrington's sister, whose memories are still vivid these many years later. It took her ten years to return to his grave, she wrote. She wanted to go, but each time she would attempt to do so, something held her back. When she finally did go, she said, it was as though they had just buried him. She couldn't believe the emotions that overwhelmed her that day, but now she goes to his grave frequently. She told me she still misses him.

Thomas N. Tucci

"I didn't know anything about anything when I enlisted," says Tom Tucci. "I didn't go in for any cause. I just went in to get my time done. Just get my two years done and get out. Two years was the minimum I could do. If there hadn't been a two-year enlistment in the Marines, I wouldn't have joined the Marines; I'd have joined the Army."

As he talks, however, it becomes clear that Tucci did know at least one thing when he enlisted: he knew he wanted to marry Linda Bennard, the girl who lived across the street from his uncle on the other side of the Delaware River from the working-class neighborhood of South Philadelphia where Tucci grew up. When he wasn't playing baseball, he says, "I mostly hung on street corners. If it hadn't been for Linda, I'd have probably ended up as some stumblebum somewhere."

They had already been dating for several years when Tucci graduated from Bishop Neumann High School in 1965, but Linda was two years younger and marriage was out of the question while she was still in school, so Tucci had some time to pass. He took a job with a small business restoring furniture, and enrolled in the evening program at La Salle College.

"I wasn't very serious about being a student," he admits, and in the winter of 1966, when a friend suggested that they join the Marines, the two young men went down to the recruiting office immediately—though Tucci joined on a delayed enlistment so that he could take Linda to her Haddon Heights High School prom that spring before he left for active duty.

"I had no idea what the Marines would be like," he says. "I couldn't tell you what the Marines were. Parris Island was a shock. I was scared to death the whole time." He vividly remembers seeing Motivation Platoon, the disciplinary unit where errant recruits moved huge piles of sand from one arbitrary spot to another with buckets and shovels in swelter-

Corporal Thomas N. Tucci with his M-60 machine gun, 2nd Battalion, 9th Marines, Vietnam, 1967.

ing southern heat while drill instructors sat in beach chairs vocally supervising them.

"My biggest fear was getting shit-canned and sent to Motivation Platoon," he says. "One time the DIs found a rusty razor blade in my shaving kit. 'If you cut yourself shaving,' they said, 'you'll get lockjaw.' I didn't know what lockjaw was. I thought I was headed for Motivation Platoon." He wasn't, but, he recalls, "I did a lot of push-ups that day."

"I never slept under the covers at Parris Island," he says. "I never made a bed in my whole life." It was so hard to make the bed to the DIs' satisfaction, he explains, that once he'd gotten it right, he didn't want to mess it up again. "Summerscales did the same thing," he adds, referring to Stephen Summerscales, Tucci's bunkie.

"I didn't qualify on the rifle range," he continues. "That's always bothered me because I never got another chance to try. I'd been shooting good all week, but qualification day was real windy." He missed qualify-

Five generations of Tom Tucci's family, 1995. Clockwise from top center: *Tom, daughter Daniele Stewart, grandmother Carmella Angelozzi, grandson Matthew Stewart, mother Elizabeth Tucci.*

ing by a mere five points. "I thought the DIs would really get on me, but they never said anything about it."

Assigned an 0300 basic infantry military occupational specialty out of boot camp, Tucci was made an 0331, machine gunner, when he got to the infantry training regiment at Camp Geiger, North Carolina. "They just went down the list and assigned MOSs alphabetically," he says. "That's why Summerscales and I were both made machine gunners. We were at that end of the alphabet—Bobby Worrell too."

After ITR and home leave, Tucci went through staging battalion at Camp Pendleton, California, and arrived in Vietnam in late November 1966, where he was assigned to 2nd Battalion, 9th Marines. Though nominally part of the weapons platoon, the machine gun teams were spread among the rifle companies, and Tucci went to 1st Platoon, F Company, then located at Cam Lo.

For the next nine months, he would be frequently engaged in combat in northern I Corps, participating in fourteen major operations and numerous small-unit actions. "When you're in a firefight, it's mass con-fusion," he says. "You don't know what's going on. Somebody shouts, 'Guns up!' and you just go. Nobody ever told [the infantrymen, or grunts] anything. I never looked at a map over there. People just said, 'Go over there,' or 'Follow him.' I didn't have a real shower from the time I got there until March. We used to wash in the rain, or in a stream, one squad washing while the others covered you."

All the operations, the various contacts and incidents, blur together after so many years, and Tucci can't recall which operation was which, but vivid memories remain nevertheless. "There was one big operation in the DMZ in the summer of 1967," he says. "It involved the whole 3rd Marine Division. We had four of those dive-bombers out in front of us, prop planes [A-1 Skyraiders], going around and around like a ferris wheel. Then some B-52s came over real low. We were pushing [a large group of North Viet-namese soldiers] in front of us, and [the planes] were having a field day."

That same day, Tucci's unit was ordered to dig up four fresh graves that had been discovered. "Somebody wanted to know what killed them," he says, "and if any of them were Chinese. There were rumors that the Chinese were getting into the fighting. I wouldn't help dig up the graves. I told them it was against my religion. Digging up the dead, I didn't want any part of that. I told them I had to stay with my gun. One of the bodies—it was wrapped in a poncho or some kind of plastic sheet—it looked pretty tall to be Vietnamese." But Tucci was never told what the exhumations revealed.

"We got ambushed later that same day," he adds. "My assistant gunner got killed. He got shot in the chest." Tucci puts a finger in the middle of his own chest to indicate where the bullet struck. "He was a black guy from Chester [Pennsylvania]. Lance Corporal Benny Price. I never did go see his parents when I got back. We lost five Marines that day."

Tucci recalls a time his unit went into a village in a free fire zone. They were ordered to kill every living thing, but not to fire their weapons. He doesn't know why they couldn't shoot, but it was the first time he'd ever seen anybody wring a chicken's neck. There was one water buffalo, and they tried to kill it with bayonets, but it was too big, its hide too tough, so finally their lieutenant said to shoot it. Then they burned the whole village.

In another free fire zone, Tucci's unit came upon two very old peo-ple, a man and a woman. "She couldn't stand up straight," he says. "She was all bent over. And he couldn't even walk. They looked like they were ninety years old." Leaflets had already been dropped warning everyone to get out of the area, so some of the men wanted to kill the couple, but other Marines said no, and finally the two people were flown out on a helicopter. Then the Marines burned the village down. "That was their home," Tucci says of the old couple.

"One time we walked right into an NVA camp," he recalls. "It was right at dusk. The camp wasn't very big, but there was a hut, and several beds." A lone NVA soldier rose to greet the Marines. "The gook thought we were his unit coming in," Tucci explains. The Marines fired on the NVA, but he somehow managed to get away.

Late in the summer of 1967, Tucci began having problems with what amounted to sleepwalking; he would appear to be awake when he took his turn on perimeter watch, but in fact would be sound asleep. After several occurrences, his squad leader, Corporal Carmen Ianacone, sent him to the battalion aid station, and from there he was sent to the hospital ship *Sanctuary*, where he spent exactly one day undergoing psychiatric evaluation.

"There were guys who were really in bad shape, bouncing off the walls," he says. "They really had a rubber room. I told the shrink, 'I'm not crazy. I want to go back to my unit.'" The doctor diagnosed Tucci's problem as "battle fatigue." He sent Tucci back, but told him he would arrange a transfer. Tucci didn't want the transfer, but a few weeks later, he was reassigned to the General's Platoon of the 3rd Marine Division.

"It was a bullshit job," he says of the General's Platoon. "All we did was hang around the rear and patrol the perimeter at Phu Bai. Like Phu Bai was going to get overrun or something [Phu Bai was one of the largest Marine bases in Vietnam]. I feel bad that I had to leave [2/9] because I thought I was good at what I did."

Wearing combat boots because supply didn't have any dress shoes to give him, Tucci came back to the U.S. just in time for Christmas 1967. In early 1968, he reported in to E Company, 2nd Battalion, 8th Marines, at Camp Lejeune, North Carolina. He spent about a month and a half at Lejeune, where 2/8 had a rear element, then joined the main body of the battalion at Guantanamo Bay, Cuba, where the Marines stood perimeter guard.

"It was kind of whacky there," he says of Guantanamo. "Everybody was an E4 or above. We'd all been to Vietnam already. Everybody was short time, and nobody gave a damn. Discipline was bad. We lived in these flimsy barracks, built by the Cubans, I think. There were no windows, and it was really hot. Guys would bash holes in the walls with their bayonets to let some air in. But there were lots of activities: the beach and water sports, baseball, softball."

Tucci spent three months in Cuba before being released from active duty in June 1968. He returned to his job restoring furniture, but though the pay was good, the job provided no health benefits, so when Tucci married Linda in September, he took a job as a laborer for General Electric Aerospace. At the same time, however, he also applied through the Veterans Administration for an apprenticeship program at the Philadelphia Navy Yard, and in January 1969 an opening became available for an apprentice machinist.

He spent four years as an apprentice, for which he received GI Bill benefits to supplement his wages, spending one week each month in the classroom and three weeks on the job. Next came four years as a journeyman machinist, followed by eight years as a machinist foreman. Then in 1985, though still at the Navy Yard, he transferred to a totally different field, becoming an industrial specialist for shipbuilding, which involved doing feasibility studies for the Navy.

Finally, in 1992, he left the Navy Yard after twenty-three years to become one of the original members of the Defense Logistics Agency's Industrial Analysis Support Office. "I still do pretty much what I did before," he says, "but now I do it for the whole Department of Defense, not just the Navy Department.

"What effect will cutting this or that program have on the DOD?" he asks, by way of explaining what his job actually involves. "What is the likely effect of canceling this weapon system? Can the company that provides it survive if we cancel it? Can we offer the company a service life extension contract for an existing weapon system rather than building a new one? Will it be cheaper to give a company a small order to keep it going, rather than letting the company go under and finding that we have to start again from scratch somewhere down the road? Is this company unique, or can another company provide the same service or system?

"We're not in this to save companies," he says. "We're in it to help decide what the Department of Defense needs and what it can get rid of." He points out, however, that he and his office only provide an assessment of any given program. The actual decisions are made by the Office of the Secretary of Defense in conjunction with Congress. "When it comes down to it," he says, "the decisions are mostly political."

Though Tucci has lived in suburban New Jersey ever since he and

Linda got married—as the family has expanded, so have the living quarters: first an apartment, then a bungalow, and finally a two-story colonial—he grew up in a row house in South Philadelphia, the same house in which his parents still live, and has worked most of his life in South Philly.

It was through his parents that I found him. George Osada remembered that Tucci was from South Philly. On December 28, 1994, I checked my Philadelphia phone book, and though I found no Thomas Tuccis, a bunch of other Tuccis were listed, some with South Philly addresses, so I started calling. I got Tucci's parents on the first try, his father's name being Albert, and they passed my name and number on to their son, who called me two days later. On February 5, 1995, I paid Tucci a visit, driving across South Philly on my way to the Walt Whitman Bridge and Tucci's home in South Jersey.

Two of the Tuccis' three children still live at home: Michele, 25, a graduate of Rutgers University–New Brunswick and an electrical engineer, is named for the Beatles song of the same name, which was the first song Tucci heard when he got back to the U.S. from Vietnam; Tom, Jr., 18, is a senior at Gloucester Catholic High School, where he is active in soccer, swimming, baseball, and drama. The middle child, Daniele, 22, is married, the mother of Tucci's grandson, Matthew, and a student at Rutgers–Camden.

"When we first got married, I was whacky," Tucci says.

"Tommy was shaky," Linda adds, elaborating. She describes a flashback Tucci had when he fell asleep on her mother's sofa just after returning from Vietnam. She explains that when the children were little, she had to be careful that they didn't disturb their father when he was sleeping for fear that he might reflexively strike out if startled awake.

"He was totally different when he came back from Vietnam," she says. "He's really nervous, and he sometimes lacks confidence in himself. Not with his job, but in other ways. He can be pretty hard on our son sometimes; he gets angry about little things. He doesn't like to go to parties. And he won't eat outside. Even when we're having a barbecue, everyone will be out in the yard, and he'll bring his food in here and eat it."

"I hate bugs," Tucci says. He tells of killing a centipede in Vietnam that was easily a foot long with legs as thick and long as toothpicks. Then he recalls a leech that attached itself to his thigh and gorged until it burst, drenching his leg with his own blood.

"He never talks about Vietnam except when he's with other men he was in the Marines with," Linda says.

"If we'd wanted to win that war," he says, "we could have won it in two weeks. We never lost a firefight when we wanted to win it. We had overwhelming firepower. We could have gone straight to Hanoi. I don't understand it. The politicians screwed up Vietnam. I supported Desert Storm. I think that was the best Army we ever put into the field. But there were a lot of good soldiers in Vietnam too. I served with a lot of heroes, but the politicians screwed it up."

Asked if he would enlist again, knowing what he knows now, he readily replies that he would not. Still, he has never considered removing the "U.S.M.C." tattooed on his left forearm, even though a new laser process has been developed that allows inexpensive and relatively pain-free tattoo removal without scarring. "Summerscales and I got tattooed together," he says. "We were out drinking in San Diego just before we left for Vietnam. We were joking about the short life expectancy of machine gunners, and we just went and got tattoos that night.

"I always knew I would come back alive," he says, in spite of the fact that so many of the men around him didn't. "That was the plan. Do my two, come home, and get married. That was the plan. I wrote that to my father when I was in Vietnam. I always knew I'd come back alive."

Jessie F. Waters

Jessie Waters has a sense of humor. When I asked him what he does these days, he replied that he lives on the beach, eats oat grass and whatever scraps of food people give him, and hangs around the phone booth looking for spare change. I couldn't see his face, since we were talking on the telephone, but his voice was absolutely deadpan. Only after a prolonged silence—in truth, I wasn't sure how to respond—did he admit that, well, actually he co-owns and runs the Kitty Hawk Iron & Steel Works, Inc., a prefabricating company in Harbinger, North Carolina. "I was married once," he added, "but that was a long time ago. Now I live with an eleven-year-old cat."

Waters called me on March 16, 1994, after receiving the letter I'd sent by way of the VA. From our conversation and records I received from NPRC in April 1996, I learned that he was born on October 27, 1946, and grew up in Windsor, North Carolina. He joined the Marines on the Buddy

Plan with Kelly Dilday. Along with Warren Hills, Jr., he was designated by Platoon 1005's drill instructors as platoon "house mouse" because of his diminutive size. The house mice served as "gofers" for the DIS, running errands, getting coffee, taking care of the duty room, and performing other tasks as required. Upon graduation from boot camp, he received a meritorious promotion to private first class.

After boot camp and basic infantry training, he received additional training as an aircraft mechanic at the Naval Air Technical Training Center, Naval Air Station, Memphis, Tennessee, before being sent to Chu Lai, Vietnam. He was in Vietnam for the Tet Offensive of 1968. "I spent my last forty-eight days in a bunker," he says. "When I found out they wanted to kill me, I canceled my extension and went home."

From Vietnam, he went to Marine Corps Air Station, Yuma, Arizona. He was released from active duty in June 1970 with the rank of lance corporal. His decorations include the National Defense Service, Vietnam Service, and Vietnam Campaign Medals.

Milton R. Waters, Jr.

If Rey Waters's school guidance counselor back at Sterling High in Stratford, New Jersey, is still on the facility, someone ought to fire him. Thirty years ago, he advised Waters to forget college, telling him he'd never amount to anything and steering him away from academics and into the general studies curriculum. Today, Waters is senior manager for finance with the Vanstar Corporation, the world's largest computer networking company.

Then again, no one back then—not even Waters himself—could have imagined the path his life would follow, though hindsight clearly reveals that Waters always had more on the ball than his guidance counselor ever suspected. After all, how many people have their own business by the age of twelve? Or hold down three jobs simultaneously at age sixteen? That kind of driving determination has brought Waters a lifetime of successes, and there are almost surely more still to come.

The only son and third of four children born to an auto mechanic and a homemaker, Waters grew up embarrassed by the family's house, which he describes as "by far the oldest in the neighborhood," and by the hand-me-down clothes he wore. He determined very early in his life that he wasn't going to "live poor," and by age nine he was earning money by working for his uncle, who had a business cleaning barbershops and restaurants.

Three years later, he started his own cleaning service, which he operated continuously right up until the day before he left for Parris Island. During his last two years of high school, he had two other jobs as well: clerking in a drive-through milk store, and playing two or three paying engagements per month as rhythm guitarist in a rock-and-roll band called The Extras.

Private First Class Milton R. Waters, Jr., 1967.

Then one day in February of Waters's senior year in high school, his uncle told him that he'd almost certainly be drafted when he graduated. Waters replied that he'd join the Marines if that happened, and when his uncle said he'd never make it in the Marines, Waters didn't wait to be drafted, but instead went out and immediately signed a delayed enlistment contract. "I joined the Marines to prove to Uncle Bob that I could hack it," he says. He left for active duty in June 1966.

Waters almost didn't hack it, he says. One day not long after boot camp began, one of the drill instructors asked. "Who can drive a truck?" When Waters replied that he could, he found himself pushing a lawn mower. That night, probably due to his exposure to the freshly cut grass, he had a severe asthma attack. Afraid he would be sent home for medical reasons, he begged Senior DI J. J. Oliver not to report the incident. Oliver didn't, and Waters has never had another asthma attack since that day.

Nor has he ever managed to unseal an envelope with a kiss. During mail call one day, Waters received a letter from his then-girlfriend with "S.W.A.K." written on the back of the envelope. When Drill Instructor Evans asked him what that meant, Waters replied, "Sealed with a kiss."

Rey Waters (right) *with wife Linda and son Ken during Ken's first leave after his graduation from boot camp at Parris Island, 1993.*

Since it was sealed with a kiss, Evans said, Waters ought to open it with a kiss, and when Waters failed to accomplish that task, even after prolonged and diligent effort, Evans ordered him to run through all four D Company squad bays shouting, "Sealed with a kiss, but couldn't open with a kiss."

Years later, Waters clearly relishes the humor of that incident. He is less sanguine about what he perceives to be his one great failure during boot camp: he did not qualify on the rifle range. "I couldn't see fifty feet," he says. "I told the DIS, and they had my eyes checked, but the doctor said I was fine and wouldn't give me glasses." He missed qualifying by four points, and even his subsequent qualification in 1968 with both rifle and pistol has never quite removed the sting of that initial "UNQ"(unqualified).

After boot camp and basic infantry training, Waters spent seven months at aviation school in Memphis, Tennessee, learning to be an aircraft safety mechanic (6361), then joined Headquarters & Maintenance Squadron 24 at Marine Corps Air Station, Cherry Point, North Carolina, where he worked on air conditioning, pressurization, oxygen, and ejection seats on F-4s, A-6s, T-1As, and occasionally C-130s.

In September 1967, however, Waters was pulled out of the hangar and temporarily assigned to be the squadron's Secret & Confidential clerk. H&MS-24 had orders for Vietnam, and because the planes would be doing highly classified photographic reconnaissance over North Vietnam, anyone who worked on or around the aircraft needed top-secret clearance, so the S&C office had a lot of work to do before the squadron embarked.

Waters adapted to his new assignment so quickly and effectively that by December his commanding officer awarded him a Meritorious Mast. At the same time, in the fall of 1967, his new boss, Captain Robert Walden, encouraged Waters to join him in a business course the captain was taking through an Eastern Carolina University extension program. Waters did very well in the class. These successes, Waters says, began to work a positive change in his own self-image.

Then in the winter of 1968, Waters was offered a special job with the Marine Barracks at Charleston Naval Base, South Carolina. The Marine Corps was just in the process of converting from a single-entry accounting system to a double-entry system, a program called Project Prime, and Waters was invited to participate in the conversion. He initially turned the assignment down because it would have required extending his four-year enlistment by another two years, but says, "The Marines got so mad at me for turning it down that they sent me to South Carolina anyway."

So when H&MS-24 embarked for Vietnam, Waters headed for Charleston to help implement Project Prime. At the time, he didn't mind not going to Vietnam. He'd volunteered for Vietnam in 1967, but had been turned down because he did not yet have enough experience as a mechanic. Then in February 1968, he got married. "I wasn't so eager to go to Vietnam after that," he says.

Waters's last two years in the Corps gave him the knowledge, confidence, and experience that would direct his professional career thereafter. Up until 1968, he explains, the Marine Corps had no real accounting system (nor did the Navy). Each year, the Corps got an appropriation from Congress. "If you wanted more money," he says, "you spent everything, then asked for more the next year. You didn't need to explain where the money went." Project Prime, also known as the Resources Management System, introduced accountability for the first time. "You had to justify what was spent," he says, "explain what was done with the money. That's what business does."

Again Waters mastered his new job rapidly and thoroughly, becoming a self-trained allotment accounting man (3471) competent enough to be sent to Marine Barracks up and down the east coast to teach other Marines how to implement the new system. In January 1969, he received a meritorious promotion to corporal, his officer-in-charge writing, "L/Cpl Waters is not a 3471 by MOS, but he has through his own initiative and study developed to a point of being far superior in his abilities and his performance than that expected of his rank."

Up until 1969, Waters had been assuming that after his release from active duty, he would look for work as a mechanic with a civilian airline, but well before his release in June 1970, he began to consider possibilities in the business world. His first civilian job turned out to be as a cost accountant with John Donnelly & Sons, a company specializing in billboard advertising.

Waters spent two years with Donnelly in Miami, Florida, before receiving a transfer to Boston. Immediately on arrival, he realized that he couldn't live in Boston on the salary Donnelly was paying him. Within two weeks, he took a job as a national account billing administrator with Honeywell Information Systems, Inc.

In this capacity, he handled the merger of General Electric's computer subsidiary into Honeywell, and did it so well that other Honeywell divisions began trying to recruit him. "'You are one of the fair-haired boys of Honeywell,' my boss told me," Waters says. "'You just tell us where you want to go.'" In 1974, he chose Dallas, Texas, where he became an associate branch administrator.

He was now the youngest controller in the company. "I had money, a car, a house," he says. "I had everything, but I still wasn't happy." That April, he says, "my boss called me in one day and asked, 'Who sits on the throne of your life? Right now, you do, but you're not happy. If Christ is sitting up there, your life won't be perfect, but you'll have someone to lean on, and you'll have a happy life.'"

Waters was not convinced, but the following month, while staying in a hotel during a business trip, he stayed up most of a night reading and rereading a pamphlet his boss had given him called *The Four Spiritual Laws*. "I looked in the mirror at six o'clock in the morning and thought, 'You're ugly,'" he says. "And I got down on my knees and prayed, 'God, I need you.' I stopped drinking, smoking, and carousing all in the same day: May 10th, 1974. It was the turning point of my life."

His marriage, however, turned out to be harder to save than his soul, and in 1976, three months after Waters accepted a promotion to branch administrator in Atlanta, Georgia, the marriage ended in divorce. The following year, on a blind date arranged by a friend, Waters met Linda Wisdom DeVore, a widow whose first husband (a "blue water Navy" Vietnam veteran) had died of cancer in 1974. "I looked at her," says Waters, "and God said to me, 'That's your new wife.'" He proposed after one date, and they were married three months later.

Meanwhile, feeling that Honeywell no longer fully appreciated his contributions to the company, he took a new position in Atlanta with the Datapoint Corporation as finance and administration manager for the southeast U.S. region. He spent three years with Datapoint, then three more years as a regional controller for Wang Laboratories, before he and Linda started their own company, Lael Corporation, in 1983.

Lael is Hebrew for "devotion to God," and the corporation specialized in computer hardware and software for churches. During this same period, he and Linda also bought an employment agency in Kingsport, Tennessee, and transformed it into a business that, working in conjunction with the state and federal governments, found jobs for badly battered women. "I felt like we really made a difference in those women's lives," says Waters.

In 1986, however, Wang decided it wanted Waters back, and began aggressively trying to recruit him. After Wang's third offer, Waters talked it over with his pastor and decided it was God's will that he return to Wang. He remained at Wang for five additional years, first as area controller, then as an account executive, before turning to what he does now, which he describes in the following way.

"I'm a turn-around artist. I go into companies that are about to go belly-up and turn them around. I can tell you what's wrong with a company just by looking at a three-page financial statement. I can go into a company and within a couple of hours tell you everything that's wrong with it and how to fix it. It's a gift from God. It's a kind of gift the Lord has given me."

In 1991 he was hired as a consultant by an Arlington, Virginia, software company, CKI Inc., to help prepare them for bankruptcy. Instead, he became vice president for operations, effectively taking over day-to-day management, and by 1993 the company was sound enough to go public. He then moved on to North Carolina to become chief financial officer of the Blethen Group, where he boosted total sales nearly 50 percent in less than two years before accepting his current position with Vanstar in suburban Atlanta.

I met with Waters there on May 11, 1995. Only one Milton Waters had appeared on the Myers list—the man I was looking for, as it turns out—but the letter I received from him on September 7, 1993, was signed Rey, not Milton. When we finally got together—during a trip that included visits with Lessie Langley, Charles Mahone, and Gary Williamson—he explained that he'd dropped his first name somewhere along the way in favor of his middle name. We spent the morning at Vanstar and the rest of the day at his home in nearby Woodstock (Georgia, not New York). In the evening, we joined Linda for dinner at a Mexican restaurant.

"I'm not interested in job hopping," he insists. "I'm just interested in taking negative situations and turning them into positive situations. Once I've got a positive, it's not so much fun anymore." Though he sometimes has to fire people who won't change their attitude or approach, as he did the then-president of the Blethen Group, usually he succeeds with less draconian measures. "It's mostly finding out what motivates people and then offering that to them. I don't have to be heavy-handed. They know I'm their boss. I try to work through positive reinforcement and encouragement."

As if to underscore that point, sitting on the desk in his office at Vanstar is a small plaque that reads, "Whatever is true, noble, right, pure, lovely, admirable, if anything is excellent or praiseworthy, think about such things. Philippians 4:8."

Waters doesn't expect to remain at Vanstar much longer. Once again, he has turned a negative into a positive, having already increased his department's productivity by 37 percent with no additional personnel, and he and Linda would like to return to North Carolina, where they still own a home. "I'd like to find opportunities to work with Linda again," he says. "She has abilities I don't have—like patience. I'd like to bring her into what I do."

Meanwhile, even in the midst of a booming career, he manages to find time for a myriad of other activities, among them:

- Independent consulting, which he does out of his home, usually charging no fee. Currently, he is assisting in the start-up of a Native American magazine from Two Bears Publications, profits from which will benefit tribal scholarship funds.
- Christian ministry, which he does both at home and abroad. A non-denominational full gospel Christian with a certificate from the Institute of Ministry in Bradenton, Florida (all of which is also true

for Linda), Waters teaches courses on prayer and on hearing God's voice and the different ways in which God speaks. He recently taught at a weekend men's conference in Georgia, and he and Linda frequently travel to Germany to teach in full gospel communities in Plauen, Wiesbaden, and Augsburg. They are hoping to travel soon to Albania to help teach Albanian Christians how to set up small businesses.

· Writing Christian novels. Waters has nearly completed one manuscript, titled *We Look for Light,* which he describes as a story about modern-day healing. "I'm trying to show that God heals today, but to do it without boring people with a lot of religion and scripture." He has also begun work on a novel about a family of Christian politicians in Camden, New Jersey, "who through generations," he says, "tackle the political scene with honesty and morality from the mid-1800s to the present."

· Keeping track of the sprawling Waters family. Waters has three grown children from his first marriage: Rey III, 26, a security-alarm designer and installer in Florida; Lynn 25, an administrative assistant in Atlanta; and Dawn, 23, a Florida photographer and model who is also the mother of Waters's grandson, Johnny. He also adopted Linda's two children from her first marriage: Kathy, 25, who works for a computer graphics company in North Carolina; and Ken, 21, a Marine corporal currently stationed at MCAS El Toro, California. Their youngest child, Daniel, 16 and a high school junior, is still at home.

All in all, it's already been a pretty full life for a man whose high school guidance counselor told him he'd never amount to anything. As he looks back over the years, Waters has few regrets, but one of them is that he never went to Vietnam. "I often wonder what it would be like if I had gone," he says. "I thought we should have been in Vietnam. My only complaint was that we didn't annihilate them. I still feel we should have blown North Vietnam off the map. I feel we abandoned South Vietnam. I don't have a fondness for Jane Fonda or Bill Clinton. I don't have a lot of respect for those who evaded their responsibilities."

Gary L. Williamson

Williamson called me on September 27, 1993, having received one of the twenty-nine letters I'd sent to Gary L. Williamsons on the Myers list. I subsequently interviewed him for two hours at his home in Alpharetta, Georgia, on May 13, 1995. On August 3, 1996, I received records from the National Personnel Records Center that did not square with what Williamson had told me about his military service. I wrote to Williamson that same day, explaining the discrepancy and asking if he could offer any explanation for it, but I never received a reply.

According to his Service Record Book, Williamson was born May 10, 1947. He was assigned successively to 1st Recruit Training Battalion, Recruit Training Regiment, Marine Corps Recruit Depot, Parris Island, South Carolina, June 19 to August 13, 1966; 2nd Infantry Training Battalion, 1st Infantry Training Regiment, Marine Corps Base, Camp Lejeune, North Carolina, August 25 to September 12, 1966; Student Company, Schools Battalion, Marine Corps Base, Camp Pendleton, California, October 7, 1966 to August 4, 1967. He held the rank of private and was awarded the National Defense Service Medal.

Bobby R. Worrell

None of the six Bobby Worrells on the Myers list responded to my initial search letter, but Larry Maxey remembered that Worrell had come from Centreville, Alabama, so in February 1995 I checked my national phone directory and found only one Bobby Worrell in Alabama. I also noticed that it was the same address and telephone number as one that had appeared on the Myers list in September 1993. When I got no reply to my second letter either, I called on March 28, 1995. Bingo.

Worrell told me he'd gotten my letters and had meant to respond, but hadn't gotten around to it. From our conversation and records received from NPRC in February 1996, I learned that he was born in Six Mile, Alabama, on September 17, 1948, and graduated from Bibb County High School in 1966. After boot camp and basic infantry training, he received additional training as a machine gunner (0331). He arrived in Vietnam in

November 1966, and was assigned to Company L, 3rd Battalion, 4th Marines, operating in Quang Tri Province.

On February 28, 1967, while participating in Operation Prairie II, he sustained a concussion wound and was evacuated to the 3rd Medical Battalion in Dong Ha, where he was treated and released. On March 27, he sustained a fragmentation wound to the right hand during Operation Prairie III, and on May 18, during Operation Hickory, he received another concussion wound.

Neither of the last two wounds required evacuation, but on receiving a third Purple Heart, he was automatically transferred out of Vietnam, which was standard policy. He spent the remainder of his overseas tour of duty as a processing clerk at Camp Smedley D. Butler Transient Facility on Okinawa, returning to the U.S. in November 1967.

Worrell was next assigned as an admin man (0141) to Headquarters Company, Headquarters Battalion, 2nd Marine Division, at Camp Lejeune, North Carolina from December 1967 until early May 1968 when he was sent for two months to Personnel Administration School at Parris Island, South Carolina, returning to Camp Lejeune in late June.

In August 1968, Worrell returned to Vietnam, this time with 3rd Shore Party Battalion, 3rd Marine Division, first as an admin man with Headquarters & Support Company, then as admin chief with Company C. In January 1969 he was transferred to Company E, 2nd Battalion, 9th Marines, where he served as admin chief until just prior to his release from active duty in May.

Worrell achieved the rank of sergeant. In addition to his three Purple Hearts, he was also awarded a Presidential Unit Citation, and the Good Conduct, National Defense Service, Vietnam Service, and Vietnam Campaign Medals.

After his release from active duty, Worrell completed college in three years, receiving a degree in accounting in 1972. He has worked for the U.S. General Accounting Office ever since. For many years he lived and worked in the Atlanta area, but is once again back in his native Alabama. He is married and has two sons, born in 1977 and 1980.

After-Action
Report

I

Through Mike West of the United States Marine Corps Drill Instructors Association, I eventually learned that Senior Drill Instructor Jesse J. Oliver retired with the rank of gunnery sergeant and lives in North Carolina, Assistant Drill Instructor Timothy W. Evans retired as a master sergeant and lives in Pennsylvania, and Drill Instructor Daniel S. Bosch retired as a gunnery sergeant and lives in Ohio. I considered trying to interview each of these men as well, but finally decided against it. Grateful as I am to our DIs for their professionalism and dedication to duty, it is my fellow recruits—my peers—about whom I wanted to know, and there is little our DIs could have added to their stories.

A tour of duty for a drill instructor would have varied according to a number of circumstances, but let's take two years as a ballpark figure. In the mid-1960s, the training cycle was eight weeks. Allowing for annual leave ("vacation" in civilian terms), a DI would train twelve platoons in two years on the drill field. At 80 men to a platoon, that works out to 960 bald-headed, green-clad, nearly identical recruits in the course of a DI's drill tour. I cannot imagine that our DIs have any memory of any of us.

To us, our DIS were the center of the universe; to them we were undoubtedly just another platoon in a long succession of platoons, just part of the job—and, at that, a job they did more than thirty years ago.

II

As I said at the beginning of this book, when I first set out in search of Platoon 1005 back in June 1993, I had no idea how many of the men I'd be able to find after so many years or whether such an undertaking was even possible. My first real break came through a casual suggestion from Jack Shulimson at the Marine Corps Historical Center in Washington, D.C., who included the CAP Unit Veterans Association newsletter among a handful of places I ought to try publishing locator notices. Tom Harvey, the newsletter's editor, ran my notice in the July 1993 issue. With only 508 members, the odds that one of them might also have been a member of Platoon 1005 were slim—and turned out to be zero.

But Master Sergeant Ben Myers, U.S. Army (Ret.), saw my notice, and if you've read this far, you know by the number of times you've encountered "the Myers list" what a help he turned out to be. Not only a help, but for any Marine a lesson in humility as well: since this is, from start to finish, a book about Marines, I can't help noting the wry little irony that the man who took my pipe dream of tracking down the men I'd gone through boot camp with and turned it into a real possibility was a soldier, not a Marine. By the end of 1993, I had found twenty-seven members of Platoon 1005 directly or indirectly as a result of the information he provided.

But the euphoria that swept over me in September and October, as I found one man after another, rapidly cooled when I began to consider: what next? The men were scattered from Arizona to Maine, from Wisconsin to Florida. To go around and meet them all, we'd be talking airplanes and hotels and rental cars—a lot of time and a lot of money. I couldn't justify pouring large amounts of either into a project like this in the hope that someday somewhere down the years I might earn it back in book sales. Truth be told, sales of my previous books did not support such thinking.

The Quakers have an expression I've always liked and have often found useful: waiting for the way to open. If you're facing a dilemma or a decision of some sort, and you don't know how to proceed or which choice to make, don't do anything; just wait. Sooner or later, the situation will clarify itself and the right course will become more apparent—the way will open. By late 1993 and into the new year, I found myself waiting for the way to open. I hadn't abandoned my search—indeed, by this time I'd learned how to tap into the VA claim system and was still finding platoon members, though at a much slower pace—but I had no idea how to proceed. Mostly I didn't think about it much because the only option then available—to proceed at my own expense—was not an option.

Meanwhile, beginning in late 1993, Mokie Pratt Porter and Gayle Garmise, the editors of *The Veteran,* the magazine of Vietnam Veterans of America, invited me to do some writing for them. I did three articles in the first half of 1994. The third was a sort of recap of what I'd found out so far about the members of Platoon 1005. By this time, the summer of 1994, I was beginning to think that unless I wanted to take out a second mortgage, I'd gone about as far as I could go with Platoon 1005. In doing the article, I was only trying to recover some portion of the money I'd already spent in postage and telephone calls, but Porter and Garmise liked my article and asked me to do profiles of the men I was finding, one per issue of the magazine.

I had been thinking all along in terms of a book, not a series of articles, but, in essence, this arrangement would amount to VVA paying for my research in return for the articles. The way had opened.

That's when I actually began traveling around visiting people. Each visit was always preceded by a good deal of anxiety. In most cases, I had little inkling of what sort of person I would find or how comfortable I would feel. As I said before, the world is full of strange people. Who knows how weird things might get? And what do I mean by weird? Use your imagination. I certainly did in the weeks prior to a visit. But as you already know, I got out alive and unscathed every time, and have a lot of good memories for my trouble.

The first profile appeared in the November 1994 issue of *The Veteran,* and even as I proceeded with the interviews, I renewed my efforts to find other platoon members I had not yet located. I knew from the beginning that I would never be able to locate everyone, but the more men I found, the more I felt driven to find as many of them as it was humanly possible to find.

It became a competition, a game, even a matter of honor. I kept a running count, like roll call: who's present, who's accounted for, who's still missing. I began to think of it in terms of the Marine Corps tradition of never abandoning anyone on the field of battle. No one gets left behind. If you think this is just hype, ask any Marine about the withdrawal from the Chosin Reservoir in Korea (the Korean name is actually Changjin) in November 1950, when a single division of Marines fought its way through ten Chinese divisions from Yudam-ni to Hungnam in bitter Manchurian cold and came out with all of their wounded, most of their dead, and most of their equipment. No one gets left behind. Not if there's any way on God's Marine Corps Green Earth to prevent it. Everyone comes out together.

(This is worth a digression: Just as I learned in Vietnam that a good deal of the apparent nonsense of boot camp turned out to have a useful purpose after all, this tradition of never abandoning anyone has a functional purpose, too. If you find yourself in a hopeless situation on the battlefield from which extrication seems impossible, you are likely to surrender, or to stop fighting and just die, in one way or another simply to give up. But if you believe that sooner or later, an hour from now or a week from now, whether you are dead or not, other Marines *will come* to get you, then you are much more likely to keep fighting because you might as well be alive when they get there. This turns out to be good for you because you have a better chance of surviving. And it turns out to be good for the Marine Corps because the Corps doesn't want you to die; it wants you to fight.)

So I kept searching for the missing members of Platoon 1005 while interviewing the men I'd already found. I could only do eleven interviews a year, because that's how often the magazine was published. This was slower than I would like to have worked, but it wasn't as if I had any particular deadline to meet—not for completing a book—so I resigned myself to slow but steady progress, grateful to be making any progress at all.

But in November 1996, apparently due to financial constraints, *The Veteran* reduced publication to only six issues a year. At a stroke, the length of time it would take me to finish the interviews was doubled. Again, there was nothing I could do but accept what couldn't be changed and hope I could get to everyone willing to be interviewed before we were all too senile to remember anything.

Then in July 1997, Porter (Garmise had moved on by then) told me that my series, "Platoon 1005," would not be continued beyond the December issue. Swell, I thought, what do I do now? I felt certain I could still locate more of the men for whom I'd yet found only military records if I just kept digging. And I knew there were still ten or twelve or more of the men I'd already found who were willing to be interviewed. I had visits already scheduled with Kelly Dilday and Jessie Waters. I wanted to meet Larry Maxey, who had called three times to give me new leads on where to find other platoon members; Jeffery Brown, who had seen a copy of *The Veteran* in a barbershop and remembered that he'd moved without sending me his new address; Langston Branch, who like the Tin Man of Oz wanted a heart; Roger Pentecost; Audie Peppers; Sam Taormina and all of the others.

Without even realizing I'd done it, I'd gradually allowed myself to imagine that I might just find them all, that I might at least account for every one of them and actually visit with fifty or even sixty of them. I had allowed this to become a matter of the heart, and it was hard to let go.

But I had to. My situation was now exactly as it had been in 1993: I did not have the resources to continue on my own time and at my own expense. That was reality.

The more I thought about it, however, the more I began to realize that it wasn't the whole reality. I wasn't where I had been in 1993. I now had military records for seventy-seven platoon members, had heard from or could account for three-fourths of them, and had met and interviewed thirty-two of them. I'd known virtually nothing about Platoon 1005 when I'd begun. I knew a hell of a lot about them now.

And I also had to recognize that no matter how long I stuck with this project, none of these men's stories would ever be finished until each of us was dead. People's lives go on. Already Rey Waters has taken a new job and moved back to North Carolina, as he said he was hoping to do back in May 1995. David McBirney has moved from Virginia to Utah. Joe Taylor has joined a more inclusive American Legion post. Tim Jenkins has completed the nursing course he had not yet begun when we visited in September 1996. I could go on researching and updating the stories of all of these men for the rest of our lives and still never be done.

I would have liked to ask Ken Smith what that twenty-six-month break in his military service was all about, or Dan Hawryschuk how he'd come to be born in Germany, or Greg Hawryschuk what it was like to go through boot camp with his older brother, or Gaetan Pelletier why a Canadian citizen would join the U.S. Marines.

But I had to remember that in the beginning I had not known if I would be able to learn anything at all about any of these men. I had to remember that I had set out to put lives to the names and faces that appeared on the one-dimensional pages of my old red platoon book, and I had succeeded in doing that. And I'd already spent four years on it with at least another year ahead of me to turn what I'd found into a book (more like twenty months, it would turn out to be). Just as the way had opened in August 1994, the way was opening again in July 1997: time now to let the search go; time now to write the book you've just read.

III

There are just a few things I would like to add, however, before I close. In the course of my search for a publisher—always an interesting experience (as in the ancient Chinese curse, "May you live in interesting times")—one editor wanted me to discard my alphabetical presentation and reorganize the book into chapters: growing up, boot camp, the war, the postwar years, that sort of thematic structure. It's a reasonable way to organize a book like this, but it was important to me to give each man his own place. Whatever boot camp did for us, what it did to us was to strip away our individuality, reducing us to interchangeable parts in what we used to call the Green Machine (having no idea, of course, just how apt that image was). To whatever degree it might be possible, I wanted to restore each man's individual self, to give him a permanent place in my memory and on the printed page.

Another editor wanted me to focus exclusively on the tragic lives and exciting lives and strange lives, those men whose stories the editor thought out of the ordinary in some way and therefore compelling. "Basically the problem is encapsulated in the title," he said. "The stories are indeed—and merely—ordinary. . . . Most readers are not going to remain interested in average Joes' lives." Like I said, this is America, and he's entitled to his opinion, but if I have learned anything in the course of this undertaking, it is that no life is ordinary. Every life is fascinating if you take the time to notice. Everyone has a story to tell if you take the trouble to listen. Every life is its own little drama. If you have read this far and not yet understood the irony of my title, then one of us has missed the mark.

IV

When I first met the small-press publisher Merritt Clifton, after corresponding with him for more than three years, he was completely taken aback to discover that I was a slightly built 140-pounder only five feet seven inches tall. He'd been expecting to find a six-foot-two-inch brawler, broad-shouldered and powerfully muscled. Why? Because he knew I'd been a Marine sergeant. It had not occurred to him that a Marine sergeant could be a scrawny little guy incapable of bench-pressing his own weight. Talk about generalizations.

Or stereotypes, which are only generalizations in bodily form. Bob Fink would have satisfied his expectations, but imagine Clifton's surprise if he'd met our platoon "house mice," Jessie Waters and Warren Hills. They made me look big. We came in all shapes and sizes from tall and skinny Harry Nelson to broad and stubby Tom Erickson.

And that was just the superficial stuff. You will surely have noticed, in the course of your reading, just how remarkably diverse a group we were—especially when you consider how self-selecting we were, all of us enlisting in the Marine Corps in the summer of 1966. Look at where these men came from, why they joined, how they feel about boot camp and the war and the Marine Corps, what they think of the government and the nation, the antiwar movement, how they were treated when they came home, what they've done with their lives. Choose any point of comparison and you find, even among this small group of men, different opinions, different experiences, different circumstances, different attitudes.

Indeed, the diversity of these men's lives and thoughts and feelings has been one of the most fascinating and instructive rewards of my labor. One would do well to apply the lesson as broadly as possible: if a group so seemingly homogeneous can be so various in so many ways, so can a group of young black men standing on Upsal Street in Philadelphia, so can gay people or Muslims or New Yorkers or hockey players or police officers or Serbians or substitute any and all groups about whom you think you've got their measure. Most men who fought in Vietnam weren't baby killers, and most antiwar protesters never said they were.

V

My friend Peter Rollins, once a Marine captain who fought in Vietnam, corrects me whenever I describe myself as an ex-Marine. He says, "No, Bill, you're a former Marine." And I say, "No, Peter, *you're* a former Marine. I'm an *ex*-Marine. As in ex-con. As in ex-spouse. Like that." I do this because it's fun to tweak him, though he's long since gotten wise to me and the almost ritualized exchange has become a good-natured acknowledgment that however much we may disagree about the Vietnam

War, the U.S. government, or the state of the world, we have that bond between us, that we were both once United States Marines.

I was impressed time and again with how much that bond seemed to mean to so many of the men in Platoon 1005. It was my entry—in most cases, my only entry—into the lives of men who were often initially distrustful or at least skeptical of this stranger who suddenly materialized out of a past three decades distant. And in many cases, that bond immediately or quickly removed from me the stigma of stranger, making me instead a brother, a comrade, a friend.

How deeply those feelings ran I didn't press very hard to discover. No doubt at least some of these men (though certainly not all of them) would have felt far less comradely if I'd spent any time expounding upon my attitudes about the war. But I had come to listen, not to talk, and their perceived bond with me was clearly genuinely felt. As was and is mine to them. Several people who know me pretty well and who also kept up with "Platoon 1005" in the VVA *Veteran* have remarked to me that they were surprised at my ability to write so respectfully and even affectionately about men who hold beliefs so different from mine, who frame the world so differently from me. That I was able to meet these men on their own terms without being judgmental has something to do with what I wanted to accomplish when I undertook this project and something to do with my own growth over the years. But it also has something to do with that bond between us.

Of course, that bond didn't do me much good with Paul Robison or Steven E. Dudley or Lonnie Milligan or Leonard Hibbler or any of the other men who never responded to my calls and letters or who declined to be interviewed. God only knows what reasons they had—I surely don't—but our having been in the Marines, even having been in Platoon 1005 together, wasn't enough to overcome those reasons. There's an old expression maybe you've heard: once a Marine, always a Marine. Maybe it's true. Maybe it isn't. Maybe it's true for some men, but not for others.

VI

You will recall that this whole project began when I encountered that group of young black men on Upsal Street one afternoon in June 1993, and how that got me to thinking about my boot camp buddy John Harris, the first black friend I ever had.

I'm sorry John never got to live the rest of his life. I'm sorry he never got to hold his son in his arms even once, let alone know the joy of watching him grow into the man John III has become. A lieutenant of Marines. Imagine that. I'm sorry I had to meet his widow instead of his wife. And I'm sorry he never got to meet my wife and daughter. But Anne and Leela know who John Lee Harris, Jr., was, and why he matters still.

In a poem called "Mostly Nothing Happens," I wrote this about him:

> Harris's girlfriend was pregnant
> when we were young, and every night
> the two of us would read her letters,
> flashlights pressed against the floor.
> God help us if our drill instructors
> caught us, but gentleness was rare
> and we were very much in need
> of gentleness on Parris Island,
> so together we would read
> those gentle letters.

* * *

> . . . I was scared to death
> of drill instructors huge as houses,
> mean as pit bulls, psychopathic maniacs
> out to keep the Viet Cong from killing me
> by killing me themselves, or so I thought.
> Who at seventeen could understand
> how terrifying war would be,
> how much more obscene? This place
> was worse than any place I'd ever been.
> I thought I'd never leave alive.

> To my surprise, so did Harris.
> Urban, street-smart, soon-to-be-a-father
> Harris, just as scared as I was.
> And his voice so soft, his hand
> upon my wrist when we were reading
> softer still, a heart so big
> I thought that mine would burst.
> Through all those lonely southern nights,
> through all that frightened Carolina summer,
> those two boys from Perkasie and Baltimore
> stuck together and survived.

Parris Island. What a trip. It's nice to have a friend when you're lonely and scared. I hope John Harris died quickly and with buddies close at hand. I'm grateful to have known him.

And I'm grateful so many of the other men of Platoon 1005 were willing to share so much of themselves with me. I wish them well, the ones who spoke with me and the ones who did not, the ones who leveled and the ones who did not, the ones who've succeeded and the ones who have not, the dead and the wounded, the good and the bad, the ones I found and the ones I didn't, all seventy-nine of them. Whatever came before or after, didn't we travel a long way together in the eight weeks from the night the bus pulled up in front of that receiving barracks so far from anything familiar. Weren't we grand stepping across the parade deck in perfect close-order formation, precise and confident, passing in review on graduation day, August 12, 1966. Weren't we handsome and proud and strong. Wasn't that as fine a moment as any of us would ever live. Platoon 1005, Company D, 1st Recruit Training Battalion, Recruit Training Regiment, Marine Corps Recruit Depot, Parris Island, South Carolina. Didn't we think we bestrode the world. Didn't we have a lot to learn.

Notes on Basic Training, Staging, and Travel

Upon completion of boot camp, every male Marine was given several weeks of basic infantry training with the Infantry Training Regiment. For Marines coming out of MCRD San Diego, ITR was at Camp Pendleton. For those of us coming out of MCRD Parris Island, ITR was at Camp Lejeune. Only after this two-tiered basic training—boot camp and ITR—did Marines go off to whatever specialty training they were to receive.

Once a Marine received orders to Vietnam, he automatically reported first to Staging Battalion at Camp Pendleton, where he received three to four weeks of additional infantry training, regardless of his MOS, before being sent to Vietnam. I have not mentioned staging in most of the men's profiles except when there was some special reason to do so, but you can assume that if a man went to Vietnam, he did so only after completing his training with one of the replacement companies of Staging Battalion.

Most Marines traveled to and from Vietnam either by military aircraft or, more often, by chartered civilian airliner. Some Marines, however, did travel by ship.

A Note on the
Enlistment Contract

Back in 1966, when the men of Platoon 1005 joined the Marines, every military enlistment contract was for a total of six years, which was to be fulfilled by some combination of active duty, active reserve, and inactive reserve. The options were

1. six months of active duty followed by five and a half years of active reserve duty (active reserves served one weekend a month and two weeks each summer); these men were called "six-month reservists";
2. two years of active duty, followed by three years of active reserve and one year of inactive reserve;
3. three years of active duty, followed by two years of active and one year of inactive reserve;
4. four years of active duty, followed by one year of active and one year of inactive reserve.

I signed a three-year enlistment, for instance, so I was supposed to serve two years of active reserve duty followed by a year of inactive reserve (inactive reserves don't go to weekend meetings or summer camp, but are still legally members of the armed forces and can be called up for active duty in an emergency).

In practice, however, the active reserve ranks were so flush during the Vietnam War (I suspect filled with men who wished to avoid both service in Vietnam and the stigma and/or difficulty of avoiding service in Vietnam in less conventional ways) that active reserve duty was waived for anyone who had served in Vietnam. If one can generalize from the records of the men in Platoon 1005, it seems that no one who served on active duty for at least two years was required to perform active reserve duty.

In any case, one did not actually receive one's discharge from the military until the completion of the six-year enlistment contract, except under exceptional circumstances (such as Gaetan Pelletier's medical discharge under honorable conditions because of severe stomach ulcers, for instance). That is why, in most of these profiles, you will repeatedly find the term "released from active duty" rather than "discharged," the discharge itself coming two to four years after the release from active duty.

Enlisted Rank Structure
of the Marine Corps

E1 Private (Pvt.)

E2 Private First Class (PFC)

E3 Lance Corporal (LCpl.)

E4 Corporal (Cpl.)

E5 Sergeant (Sgt.)

E6 Staff Sergeant (SSgt.)

E7 Gunnery Sergeant (GySgt.)

E8 1st Sergeant (1st Sgt.) or Master Sergeant (MSgt.)

E9 Sergeant Major (SgtMaj.) or Master Gunnery Sergeant
(MGySgt.)

Major Marine Corps Bases
(and Navy bases with
large Marine detachments)

Beaufort: Marine Corps Air Station, Beaufort, South Carolina

Cherry Point: Marine Corps Air Station, Cherry Point, North Carolina

El Toro: Marine Corps Air Station, El Toro, California

Futema: Marine Corps Air Facility, Futema, Okinawa

Guantanamo Bay. U.S. Naval Base, Guantanamo, Cuba

Iwakuni: Marine Corps Air Station, Iwakuni, Japan

Lejeune: Marine Corps Base, Camp Lejeune, North Carolina

Little Creek: Naval Amphibious Base, Little Creek, Norfolk, Virginia

Memphis: Naval Air Technical Training Center, Naval Air Station, Memphis, Tennessee (also known as NAS Millington)

Millington (see Memphis)

New River: Marine Corps Air Facility, New River, North Carolina

Parris Island: Marine Corps Recruit Depot, Parris Island, South Carolina

Pendleton: Marine Corps Base, Camp Pendleton, California

Quantico: Marine Corps Base, Quantico, Virginia

San Diego: Marine Corps Recruit Depot, San Diego, California

Santa Ana: Marine Corps Air Station (Helicopter), Santa Ana, California

Yuma: Marine Corps Air Station, Yuma, Arizona

There were and are many other bases where Marines might be assigned, but these are the ones most frequently referred to in this book.

Glossary

AFB: Air Force Base

Amtrac: amphibious tractor

ANGLICO: Air-Naval Gunfire Liaison Company

Article 15: nonjudicial disciplinary proceeding under the Uniform Code of Military Justice

ARVN: Army of the Republic of Vietnam (the South Vietnamese Army)

AWOL: absent without leave

BCD: bad conduct discharge

BLT: Battalion Landing Team

Boot Camp: initial recruit training, either at Parris Island or at San Diego

Buddy Plan: a program that guaranteed two men enlisting together would be assigned to the same training platoon in boot camp

CAG: Combined Action Group (parent organization of the CAPs)

CAP: Combined Action Platoon (made up of Marines and Vietnamese PFs)

CO: commanding officer

DI: drill instructor

DMZ: Demilitarized Zone (in Vietnam, at the 17th parallel)

FLC: Force Logistics Command

FLSG: Force Logistics Support Group

FMF: Fleet Marine Force

FO: forward observer

FOIA: Freedom of Information Act

FSR: Force Service Regiment

H&HS: Headquarters & Headquarters Squadron

H&MS: Headquarters & Maintenance Squadron

H&S: Headquarters & Support (either Company or Battalion)

HMH: Marine Heavy Helicopter Squadron

HMM: Marine Medium Helicopter Squadron

HMMT: Marine Medium Helicopter Training Squadron

HQ: headquarters

HQMC: Headquarters Marine Corps

HST: helicopter support team

I&I: Inspector & Instructor Staff

ITR: Infantry Training Regiment

ITT: interrogation & translation team

JROTC: Junior Reserve Officers' Training Corps

LAAM: light anti-aircraft missile

LAAW: light anti-armor weapon

LZ: landing zone

MABS: Marine Air Base Squadron

MACG: Marine Air Control Group

MACS: Marine Air Control Squadron

MAG: Marine Aircraft Group

MB: Marine Barracks

MCAF: Marine Corps Air Facility

MCAS: Marine Corps Air Station

MCAS(H): Marine Corps Air Station (Helicopter)

MCB: Marine Corps Base

MCRD: Marine Corps Recruit Depot

MHTG: Marine Helicopter Training Group

MIE, Inc.: Military Information Enterprises, Inc., a locator service founded by Lieutenant Colonel Richard S. Johnson, U.S. Army (Ret.)

MOS: military occupational specialty (indicated by a four-digit number)

MP: military police

MWSG: Marine Wing Support Group

NAS: Naval Air Station

NATTC: Naval Air Technical Training Center

NB: Naval Base

NCO: noncommissioned officer (corporals and sergeants)

NCOIC: noncommissioned officer in charge

NLF: see VC

NPRC: National Personnel Records Center (located in Saint Louis, Missouri)

NVA: North Vietnamese Army (more properly called the People's Army of Vietnam or PAVN)

OCS: Officer Candidate School

PAVN: see NVA

PB: Platoon 1005 graduation book, similar to a high school yearbook

PF: Popular Forces (South Vietnamese militia)

PMAG: Provisional Marine Aircraft Group

POW/MIA: prisoner of war/missing in action

PT: physical training

PTSD: post-traumatic stress disorder

R&R: rest & recreation

ROTC: Reserve Officers' Training Corps

SEAL: sea, air, land (an elite Navy unit, or a member thereof)

SFCP: Shore Fire Control Party

SP: Shore Party (almost always with Battalion)

SRB: service record book

TNANG: Tennessee Air National Guard

UA: unauthorized absence

USO: United Service Organizations

VA: Department of Veterans Affairs (formerly the Veterans Administration)

VC: Viet Cong (southern Vietnamese guerrillas, more properly called the National Front for the Liberation of South Vietnam, or NLF)

VMA: Marine Attack Squadron

VMCJ: Marine Composite Reconnaissance Squadron

VMFA: Marine Fighter Attack Squadron

VMGR: Marine Aerial Refueler Transport Squadron

VMO: Marine Observation Squadron

WM: female Marine (literally: woman Marine)

XO: executive officer